Impacts of Human-Centered Interactive Technologies on Consumer Engagement

Sihem ben Saad
https://orcid.org/0000-0003-3034-9206
University of Manouba, Tunisia

IGI Global
Scientific Publishing
Publishing Tomorrow's Research Today

Vice President of Editorial	Melissa Wagner
Director of Acquisitions	Mikaela Felty
Director of Book Development	Jocelynn Hessler
Production Manager	Mike Brehm
Cover Design	Jose Rosado

Published in the United States of America by
IGI Global Scientific Publishing
701 East Chocolate Avenue
Hershey, PA, 17033, USA
Tel: 717-533-8845 | Fax: 717-533-7115
Website: https://www.igi-global.com E-mail: cust@igi-global.com

Library of Congress Cataloging-in-Publication Data

Names: Ben Saad, Sihem editor
Title: Impacts of human-centered interactive technologies on consumer engagement / [edited by] Sihem ben Saad.
Description: Hershey, PA : IGI Global Scientific Publishing, [2026] | Includes bibliographical references and index. | Summary: "This book explores how human-centered interactive technologies influence consumer engagement across diverse domains by integrating theory, practice, and innovation"-- Provided by publisher.
Identifiers: LCCN 2025036636 (print) | LCCN 2025036637 (ebook) | ISBN 9798337364506 hardcover | ISBN 9798337364513 paperback | ISBN 9798337364520 ebook
Subjects: LCSH: Consumer behavior | Consumer relations--Technological innovations | Human-computer interaction
Classification: LCC HF5415.32 .I47 2026 (print) | LCC HF5415.32 (ebook) | DDC 658.8/342--dc23/eng/20260202
LC record available at https://lccn.loc.gov/2025036636
LC ebook record available at https://lccn.loc.gov/2025036637

British Cataloguing in Publication Data
A Cataloguing in Publication record for this book is available from the British Library.

Table of Contents

Detailed Table of Contents

This paper examines the role of AI chatbots in customer service, focusing on their challenges in handling complex queries and the effects of information accuracy and response time on customer satisfaction. Using Cognitive Load Theory, we argue that chatbot effectiveness depends on the cognitive effort required for different query types. The investment industry was selected for its high demands on privacy, security,and quick decision-making. Analysis of 648 customer chatusing Process Macro shows that AI chatbots improvesatisfactionfasterresponses and more accurate information, especially for low-complexity queries, while humans perform better on complex issues. A second study with 352 students found similarpatterns: participants preferred chatbots for simple tasks and human representatives for complex ones due to the need for personalization and deeper understanding. Overall, thefindings highlight the importance of balancing speed and accuracy ininteractions and offer practical guidance on how businesses can allocate tasks between AI systems and human agents based on query complexity.

Portal advertisements are emerging as a central immersive format in metaverse platforms such as Roblox, yet little is known about how users' entry conditions into branded virtual spaces shape their psychological experience and engagement. Drawing on the Stimulus–Organism–Response (SOR) framework, this study examines how forced versus voluntary entry into a branded world influences telepresence, flow, and engagement intention, and whether perceived agency conditions these effects. A between-subjects online experiment (N = 203) exposed participants to a Vans portal ad in which they were either automatically teleported into the branded world (forced condition) or allowed to choose whether to enter (voluntary condition). Participants then reported telepresence, flow, perceived choice, and engagement intention. PROCESS Model 7 was used to test a moderated serial mediation model.

Digital personalization can boost engagement by making content feel more relevant. At the same time heavy data collection raises privacy concerns that can lower trust. This chapter tackles gaps in prior work by running a pre-registered field experiment with 612 users. Participants were randomly assigned to four personalization levels: none, low, medium, and high. The study measured behavioral engagement with clicks time on site and conversions and collected survey measures of trust and retention intention. Analysis used PLS-SEM in SmartPLS 3. Key findings are clear. Personalization raised perceived personalization ($\beta = 0.782$) and increased engagement ($\beta = 0.696$). Effect sizes were large ($f^2 = 1.572$ for perceived personalization; $f^2 = 0.939$ for engagement). Higher engagement then increased trust ($\beta = 0.481$). Trust was the strongest predictor of retention intention ($\beta = 0.597$; $f^2 = 0.474$). Mediation tests show the effect of personalization on retention was fully indirect (total indirect $\beta \approx 0.526$; direct effect ≈ 0).

This chapter offers insights into customer relationship management by focusing on the commercial process in the AI era. In fact, the use of AI technology in marketing analysis has placed the customer at the heart of the process by adjusting commercial strategies towards an approach based on automated actions, behavioral prediction and personalization of consumer expectations. The chapter is structured sequentially to illustrate the customer journey, making it easier to follow the changes perceived in each stage. It also highlights the contribution of different types of AI-assisted

As firms increasingly rely on co-design platforms to involve consumers in early-stage innovation, important questions remain regarding how different co-design activities shape consumer engagement and consumer–product relationships. Drawing on the Stimulus–Organism–Response framework and activity and engagement theories, this study examines how participation in two distinct co-design activities (prototype customization vs. prototype evaluation), affects consumers' cognitive, emotional, and physical engagement, and how these engagement states vary with co-design taskstranslate into psychological ownership and purchase intention. A cross-cultural between-subjects experiment was conducted in the context of olive oil packaging design. Results reveal that engagement dimensions diverge systematically across co-design activities. From a human–computer interaction perspective, the findings underscore the importance of designing co-design platforms that balance cognitive load, emotional stimulation, and user control, all are very important to build a strong consumer-product relationship.

This chapter examines the adoption of virtual reality (VR) in hospitality and its impact on guest experiences, expectations, and emotional well-being. Using qualitative methods, semi-structured interviews were conducted with 15 participants navigating VR simulations of hotel environments, including rooms, common areas, and leisure spaces. Thematic analysis reveals that VR offers both functional and emotional value, enhancing planning, cognitive engagement, and informed decision-making. Interactivity supports focused attention and meaningful social experiences, while immersive visual and auditory cues promote relaxation and psychological restoration. Individual differences, such as technology familiarity and gender, could influence engagement and perceptions. Findings highlight VR's dual role in facilitating cognitive exploration and fostering emotional well-being, offering actionable insights for designing guest-centered, immersive experiences.

The aim of this study is to investigate the factors that will facilitate visitor satisfaction at Bahu Fort during Bahu Mela. Bahu Fort is one of the essential locations in Jammu (India), and it is of enormous religious and spiritual importance. Data was collected from 253 pilgrims by structured questionnaire during three days Bahu Mela. Artificial Neural Networks (ANNs) was employed to develop a predictive model to identify the critical predictors of visitor satisfaction during the Mela. The model was trained on a comprehensive dataset encompassing various features related to pilgrim experiences, including demographic variables and non-demographic variables. The results of the study found that "Perceived barriers and expectations" is the most influential factor in determining visitor satisfaction, followed by "Environmental and experiential quality of the destination" and "Tourists service quality and expectations." The study's findings contribute to improving Mela's overall facilities and costs. Implications of the study are also discussed.

This study examines how European Central Bank (ECB) monetary policy shocks, including quantitative easing (QE) and quantitative tightening (QT), influence AI-linked equity markets. Using a Time-Varying Parameter VAR (TVP-VAR) model on monthly data from 2018 to 2025, we analyze the responses of two technology-focused exchange-traded funds (ETFs): NasdaqAI and BOTZ. The findings reveal that market reactions vary across time and sectors. NasdaqAI responds negatively to QT, consistent with its long-duration valuation structure, while BOTZ shows positive responses linked to its exposure to industrial technology and automation. In periods of policy normalization, both indices react positively. These results highlight the

Preface

In an era marked by the rapid diffusion of artificial intelligence, immersive environments, and intelligent data-driven systems, interactive technologies are profoundly reshaping the nature of consumer engagement. No longer limited to automation or functional efficiency, contemporary technologies increasingly adopt a human-centered orientation that places users' emotions, perceptions, cognition, and experiential well-being at the core of innovation. Digital interactions have become experiential, relational, and socially embedded, redefining how individuals engage with brands, services, platforms, and markets.

It is within this evolving landscape that the book *Impacts of Human-Centered Interactive Technologies on Consumer Engagement* has been developed. This volume specifically focuses on how human-centered interactive technologies influence consumer engagement across its cognitive, emotional, and behavioral dimensions. Technologies such as AI-powered chatbots, immersive media, virtual environments, algorithmic personalization systems, and intelligent analytics are examined not merely as technical tools, but as engagement orchestrators capable of shaping presence, flow, trust, satisfaction, loyalty, and advocacy throughout the customer journey.

Beyond their technical functionalities, these technologies are increasingly designed to simulate social presence, emotional sensitivity, and adaptive responsiveness. By blurring the boundaries between human and machine interaction, they enable new forms of experiential value creation while simultaneously raising critical concerns related to privacy, trust, psychological well-being, and ethical responsibility. This book responds to these challenges by offering empirical and conceptual insights into how engagement emerges, evolves, and can be strategically managed in AI-driven and immersive environments.

The volume brings together multidisciplinary perspectives from marketing, digital strategy, human–computer interaction, psychology, tourism studies, and finance to explore engagement across diverse contexts. The chapters examine consumer engagement in customer service interactions, digital advertising, personalization systems, co-design processes, virtual reality experiences, tourism and heritage services, as well as financial and investment platforms. Particular attention is paid to engagement as a mediating and transformative construct linking technology design to behavioral outcomes such as conversion, retention, satisfaction, and well-being.

This book is intended for scholars and researchers seeking to deepen theoretical and empirical understanding of engagement in intelligent environments; for graduate and postgraduate students in marketing, management, communication, and information systems; and for practitioners, including marketing managers, UX designers, hospitality professionals, and digital strategists, who aim to design engaging, meaningful, and ethically grounded digital experiences.

By focusing explicitly on engagement outcomes, this volume advances engagement theory in the context of AI-powered and immersive technologies, while offering actionable insights for organizations seeking to balance technological innovation with human values. Ultimately, it highlights that the effectiveness of interactive technologies lies not only in their intelligence, but in their ability to meaningfully connect with, engage, and empower consumers.

CHAPTER OVERVIEW

Chapter 1. Respond Speed, Information Accuracy, and Query Complexity: Understanding AI Chatbot in Customer Service

The first chapter examines the role of AI chatbots in customer service, focusing on their challenges in handling complex queries and the effects of information accuracy and response time on customer satisfaction. Using Cognitive Load Theory, we argue that chatbot effectiveness depends on the cognitive effort required for different query types. The investment industry was selected for its high demands on privacy, security, and quick decision-making. Analysis of 648 customer chat using Process Macro shows that AI chatbots improve satisfaction faster responses and more accurate information, especially for low-complexity queries, while humans perform better on complex issues. A second study with 352 students found similar patterns: participants preferred chatbots for simple tasks and human representatives for complex ones due to the need for personalization and deeper understanding. Overall, the findings highlight the importance of balancing speed and accuracy in interactions and offer practical guidance on how businesses can allocate tasks between AI systems and human agents based on query complexity.

Chapter 2. Perceived Agency in Portal Ads Impacts on Presence, Flow, and Engagement in the Metaverse

Portal advertisements are emerging as a central immersive format in metaverse platforms such as Roblox, yet little is known about how users' entry conditions into branded virtual spaces shape their psychological experience and engagement. Drawing on the Stimulus–Organism–Response (SOR) framework, this study examines how forced versus voluntary entry into a branded world influences telepresence, flow, and engagement intention, and whether perceived agency conditions these effects. A between-subjects online experiment (N = 203) exposed participants to a Vans portal ad in which they were either automatically teleported into the branded world (forced condition) or allowed to choose whether to enter (voluntary condition). Participants then reported telepresence, flow, perceived choice, and engagement intention. PROCESS Model 7 was used to test a moderated serial mediation model.

Chapter 3. Engagement vs. Privacy: A Causal Evaluation of AI-Driven Personalization Intensity on Consumer Engagement, Trust, and Retent

Chapter 3 measured behavioral engagement with clicks time on site and conversions and collected survey measures of trust and retention intention. Analysis used PLS-SEM in SmartPLS 3. Key findings are clear. Personalization raised perceived personalization (ß = 0.782) and increased engagement (ß = 0.696). Effect sizes were large (f^2 = 1.572 for perceived personalization; f^2 = 0.939 for engagement). Higher engagement then increased trust (ß = 0.481). Trust was the strongest predictor of retention intention (ß = 0.597; f^2 = 0.474). Mediation tests show the effect of personalization on retention was fully indirect (total indirect ß ˜ 0.526; direct effect ˜ 0).

Chapter 4. Orchestrating Engagement with AI: Persona Matching, Personalization, and Post-Purchase

This chapter offers insights into customer relationship management by focusing on the commercial process in the AI era. In fact, the use of AI technology in marketing analysis has placed the customer at the heart of the process by adjusting commercial strategies towards an approach based on automated actions, behavioral prediction and personalization of consumer expectations. The chapter is structured sequentially to illustrate the customer journey, making it easier to follow the changes perceived in each stage. It also highlights the contribution of different types of AI-assisted algorithms in transforming prospects into brand ambassadors. Besides the benefits seen during each stage of the customer journey, the article also explores the way AI has changed the marketing perspective towards approaches that are more focused on sustainable development.

Chapter 5. Investigating the Influence of Digital Strategies on Consumer Engagement and Conversion: The Mediating Role of Engagement.

This chapter aims to investigate the impact of digital strategies on consumer engagement and the mediating role of engagement in driving conversion behaviors, such as purchases and sign-ups. Focusing on content strategy, digital communication channels, and user experience (UX), a quantitative survey of 500 Moroccan consumers was conducted. Structural equation modeling (SEM) revealed that all three strategies positively influence engagement, which in turn significantly impacts conversion. Engagement acts as a key mediator, linking digital efforts to desired consumer actions. The findings underscore the importance of delivering high-quality content, leveraging multiple communication channels, and optimizing UX. Practical implications suggest that marketers should adopt integrated, customer-centric digital strategies to enhance engagement, drive conversions, and build long-term loyalty in a competitive digital environment.

Chapter 6. Influencing the Future: Exploring the Impact of YouTube Advertising on Youth

This chapter examines children's involvement in purchasing decisions, focusing on children aged 8 to 12 after viewing YouTube advertisements. The research explores the influence of two contrasting emotional appeals-fear and humor-on children's behavioral intentions. By analyzing 85 schoolchildren's reactions, the study employs a probabilistic approach using the LOGIT model to assess the likelihood of purchase decisions based on emotional responses. The findings aim to identify which emotional appeal has a greater effect on children's decision-making processes, highlighting the role of various factors in shaping their purchasing intentions. This research offers insights into the emotional impact of advertising on young audiences, contributing to understanding how different types of ads influence children's consumer behavior.

Chapter 7. From Co-Design to Commitment

As firms increasingly rely on co-design platforms to involve consumers in early-stage innovation, important questions remain regarding how different co-design activities shape consumer engagement and consumer–product relationships. Drawing on the Stimulus–Organism–Response framework and activity and engagement theories, this study examines how participation in two distinct co-design activities (prototype customization vs. prototype evaluation), affects consumers' cognitive, emotional, and physical engagement, and how these engagement states vary with co-design taskstranslate into psychological ownership and purchase intention. A cross-cultural between-subjects experiment was conducted in the context of olive oil packaging design. Results reveal that engagement dimensions diverge systematically across co-design activities. From a human–computer interaction perspective, the findings underscore the importance of designing co-design platforms that balance cognitive load, emotional stimulation, and user control, all are very important to build a strong consumer-product relationship.

Chapter 8. Exploring Guest Experiences with Virtual Reality in Hospitality: Insights on Engagement and Emotional Well-Being

This chapter examines the adoption of virtual reality (VR) in hospitality and its impact on guest experiences, expectations, and emotional well-being. Using qualitative methods, semi-structured interviews were conducted with 15 participants navigating VR simulations of hotel environments, including rooms, common areas, and leisure spaces. Thematic analysis reveals that VR offers both functional and emotional value, enhancing planning, cognitive engagement, and informed decision-making. Interactivity supports focused attention and meaningful social experiences, while immersive visual and auditory cues promote relaxation and psychological restoration. Individual differences, such as technology familiarity and gender, could influence engagement and perceptions. Findings highlight VR's dual role in facilitating cognitive exploration and fostering emotional well-being, offering actionable insights for designing guest-centered, immersive experiences.

Chapter 9. Using Artificial Neural Networks to Predict Visitor Satisfaction at Heritage and Pilgrimage Events

The aim of this chapter is to investigate the factors that will facilitate visitor satisfaction at Bahu Fort during Bahu Mela. Bahu Fort is one of the essential locations in Jammu (India), and it is of enormous religious and spiritual importance. Data was collected from 253 pilgrims by structured questionnaire during three days Bahu Mela. Artificial Neural Networks (ANNs) was employed to develop a predictive model to identify the critical predictors of visitor satisfaction during the Mela. The model was trained on a comprehensive dataset encompassing various features related to pilgrim experiences, including demographic variables and non-demographic variables. The results of the study found that "Perceived barriers and expectations" is the most influential factor in determining visitor satisfaction, followed by "Environmental and experiential quality of the destination" and "Tourists service quality and expectations." The study's findings contribute to improving Mela's overall facilities and costs. Implications of the study are also discussed.

Chapter 10. Monetary Shocks in the Age of AI: How QE and QT Shape Investor Engagement on Digital Platforms in Europe

The last chapter examines how European Central Bank (ECB) monetary policy shocks, including quantitative easing (QE) and quantitative tightening (QT), influence AI-linked equity markets. Using a Time-Varying Parameter VAR (TVP-VAR) model on monthly data from 2018 to 2025, we analyze the responses of two technology-focused exchange-traded funds (ETFs): NasdaqAI and BOTZ. The findings reveal that market reactions vary across time and sectors. NasdaqAI responds negatively to QT, consistent with its long-duration valuation structure, while BOTZ shows positive responses linked to its exposure to industrial technology and automation. In periods of policy normalization, both indices react positively. These results highlight the changing nature of monetary transmission in innovation-intensive markets, shaped by investor sentiment and digital trading behavior.

Acknowledgement

The production of this book, *Impacts of Human-Centered Interactive Technologies on Consumer Engagement*, is the result of a collective effort and the dedication of many individuals who have contributed their expertise, time, and insight. It would not have been possible without their support.

We extend our deepest gratitude to all the chapter authors. Their rigorous research, critical thinking, and commitment to advancing knowledge in the field of human-centered interactive technologies have been essential to the quality and depth of this volume. Each chapter reflects months of careful work and a passion for understanding the ways in which digital technologies shape consumer engagement. Their ability to translate complex theoretical and empirical analyses into accessible and insightful contributions has greatly enriched this book.

Special thanks are due to the reviewers and editorial committees. Their meticulous evaluation, constructive feedback, and thoughtful suggestions have strengthened the scientific rigor, clarity, and coherence of each chapter. Though often behind the scenes, their contributions have been vital to ensuring the robustness and credibility of this work.

We are also grateful to the academic and research institutions that have supported our authors, providing an environment conducive to innovation, collaboration, and the pursuit of excellence in research.

Finally, to everyone who has offered encouragement, advice, or practical support during the development of this project, your contributions, whether large or small, have been invaluable.

We hope that this collective effort will serve as a meaningful resource for researchers, practitioners, and students alike, and will inspire further exploration of the impact of human-centered interactive technologies on consumer engagement.

Introduction

In a world increasingly shaped by digital innovation, interactive technologies are no longer passive tools supporting consumption; they have become active agents that shape experiences, behaviors, and engagement dynamics. From AI-driven customer service systems and personalized digital interfaces to immersive virtual environments, human-centered interactive technologies are fundamentally transforming how consumers interact with brands, services, and platforms. Engagement has emerged as a central construct through which these transformations can be understood, managed, and evaluated.

Impacts of Human-Centered Interactive Technologies on Consumer Engagement offers a comprehensive and multidimensional exploration of how intelligent and immersive technologies influence consumer engagement across cognitive, emotional, and behavioral dimensions. The book brings together theoretical insights, empirical investigations, and applied studies that examine engagement as a key outcome of technology design and implementation in contemporary digital ecosystems.

Moving beyond surface-level observations, this volume delves into the mechanisms through which interactive technologies generate engagement. The chapters examine how design features such as responsiveness, perceived agency, immersion, personalization intensity, and co-creation opportunities shape presence, flow, trust, satisfaction, retention, and advocacy. Engagement is analyzed not only as an outcome, but also as a mediating force that links technological attributes to consumer behavior and organizational performance.

The book covers a wide range of application domains in which engagement plays a critical role. Contributions investigate AI chatbots in customer service, digital advertising and platform-based marketing, personalization systems and post-purchase orchestration, co-design initiatives, immersive virtual reality experiences, and data-driven engagement in tourism, heritage, and financial markets. By addressing both micro-level consumer interactions and broader engagement ecosystems, the volume highlights the versatility and strategic relevance of engagement in AI-enabled environments.

This book is intended for researchers seeking to advance engagement theory in the context of intelligent technologies, for graduate students exploring the intersection of consumer behavior and digital innovation, and for practitioners aiming to design engaging, ethical, and sustainable interactive systems. By focusing explicitly on engagement outcomes, the volume provides actionable insights into how organizations can leverage human-centered technologies to foster meaningful, trust-based, and enduring consumer relationships.

Ultimately, this book positions engagement as the cornerstone of human-centered digital transformation. It demonstrates that the success of interactive technologies lies not only in their technical sophistication, but in their capacity to create experiences that resonate cognitively, emotionally, and behaviorally with consumers.

Chapter 1
Respond Speed, Information Accuracy, and Query Complexity:
Understanding AI Chatbot in Customer Service

Fakhri Baghirov
https://orcid.org/0000-0003-1319-8688
Istanbul Atlas University, Turkey

Ye Zhang
Koc University, Turkey

Ozlem Arzu Azer
https://orcid.org/0000-0002-5813-3151
Atlas University, Turkey

ABSTRACT

This paper examines the role of AI chatbots in customer service, focusing on their challenges in handling complex queries and the effects of information accuracy and response time on customer satisfaction. Using Cognitive Load Theory, we argue that chatbot effectiveness depends on the cognitive effort required for different query types. The investment industry was selected for its high demands on privacy, security,and quick decision-making. Analysis of 648 customer chatusing Process Macro shows that AI chatbots improvesatisfactionfasterresponses and more accurate information, especially for low-complexity queries, while humans perform better on complex issues. A second study with 352 studentsfound similarpatterns: participants preferred chatbots for simple tasks and human representatives for complex ones

DOI: 10.4018/979-8-3373-6450-6.ch001

due to the need for personalization and deeper understanding. Overall, thefindings highlight the importance of balancing speed and accuracy ininteractions and offer practical guidance on how businesses can allocate tasks between AI systems and human agents based on query complexity.

1. INTRODUCTION

We are now in the age of intelligent machines. Artificial intelligence (AI) is a rapidly advancing field with the potential to transform and integrate into all aspects of our daily lives, from personal assistants like Siri and Alexa to self-driving cars and medical diagnostic systems. As AI continues to evolve, machines are increasingly capable of mimicking human behaviours and decision-making. AI has undoubtedly garnered significant attention from both researchers and industries over the past decade. The literature on AI spans diverse fields such as computer science, philosophy, psychology, and neuroscience (Ngai et al., 2021). One of the fastest-growing applications of AI is the conversational agent—commonly known as a chatbot—a machine dialogue system powered by natural language processing that allows for human-like interaction (Hill et al., 2015). An increasing number of companies are adopting chatbots to communicate with customers, enabling them to quickly address inquiries, even outside of business hours, and efficiently manage high volumes of questions without the need for queues (Van den Broeck et al., 2019). Consumers also prefer using AI chatbots for frontline services or coaching, as they provide quick and accessible guidance (Fotheringham & Wiles, 2022).

AI chatbots are highly effective at handling simple, routine queries, such as checking credit card balances, which require high accuracy and timely responses (De Andrade & Tumelero, 2022). These systems offer several advantages, including speed, availability, accessibility, and reliability, which contribute to improved customer satisfaction by reducing service queues, providing rapid responses, and delivering accurate information, including numerical and graphical data. However, as the complexity of queries increases, AI chatbots begin to face challenges (Xu et al., 2020). They struggle with more nuanced, ambiguous, or specialized requests, which can result in service failures, such as miscommunication or inaccurate responses (De Andrade & Tumelero, 2022). AI systems may find it difficult to understand context or handle topics that require deep expertise or personalized input. As a result, while chatbots excel in straightforward, low-complexity tasks, they become less reliable as query complexity grows, and human intervention is often necessary to ensure both accuracy and empathy. In more complex or emotionally charged situations, human agents are better equipped to provide the necessary understanding and personalized support, ensuring a satisfactory customer experience.

From the company's perspective, AI chatbots can serve as complementary tools to human agents, allowing both to work together in the service process. By handling routine inquiries, chatbots free up human agents to focus on more intricate or sensitive issues, thus enhancing overall service efficiency and customer satisfaction (De Andrade & Tumelero, 2022). Although previous studies have examined several aspects of AI chatbots and their impact on service (Araujo, 2018; Luo et al., 2019; Schanke et al., 2021), fewer studies have focused on the accuracy of information and speed of response, which are key drivers of the shift to AI chatbots. Also, there is a gap in understanding how AI chatbots perform when faced with more complex, nuanced queries that require deep expertise or personalized context (Bhambri & Rani, 2024; Izadi & Forouzanfar, 2024; Bansal, et al., 2024). While AI chatbots excel at handling simple, routine inquiries, their effectiveness diminishes when confronted with higher-complexity tasks (Khennouche et al., 2024; Xu et al., 2020). This paper aims to address the need to balance speed and accuracy in AI chatbot interactions, especially as the complexity of customer queries increases. It investigates whether customer satisfaction can be maintained when there is a quick response, but the information provided lacks accuracy, particularly in the context of high-complexity queries. Additionally, it highlights the need for a balanced approach that combines the strengths of both AI chatbots and human representatives. This research aims to provide insights for businesses on how to optimize task allocation between AI chatbots and human agents to ensure both efficiency and satisfaction in customer service. This paper focuses on the investment industry, where consumers prioritize privacy, security, and accuracy, and demand quick, reliable responses, making AI chatbots well-suited to meet these needs.

Theoretically, this paper contributes to the growing body of literature on AI chatbots in customer service by examining their effectiveness in handling queries of varying complexity, particularly in the investment industry. The study enhances existing theoretical frameworks by integrating query complexity as a moderator in the relationship between service mode (AI chatbot vs. human representative) and customer satisfaction. By exploring how response speed and information accuracy serve as mediators, the research provides a nuanced understanding of how AI chatbots influence customer satisfaction across different levels of task complexity. This work extends prior studies that primarily focus on routine queries, offering insights into the psychological mechanisms driving service preferences, and contributes to the theoretical discourse on the role of AI in customer service decision-making processes. Additionally, it highlights the critical role of both speed and accuracy in shaping customer experiences and satisfaction, particularly in high-stakes industries such as investment services. This paper seeks to explore how to balance these factors in AI chatbot interactions, especially as the complexity of customer queries escalates.

From a managerial perspective, this paper offers valuable insights for businesses aiming to optimize customer service by strategically integrating AI chatbots and human agents. The findings demonstrate that AI chatbots are particularly effective for routine, low-complexity tasks, such as account balance inquiries or basic information retrieval, were speed and efficiency drive customer satisfaction. For more complex or sensitive issues that require personalized guidance, emotional understanding, or careful interpretation, human representatives remain essential. Managers can leverage these insights to design a hybrid service model, allocating tasks according to query complexity to maximize both efficiency and satisfaction. Furthermore, emphasizing both response speed and information accuracy in AI system design can enhance customer experiences while maintaining trust and reliability—particularly in industries like investment services, where privacy, precision, and service quality are critical. In addition, businesses can use these findings to prioritize training and development for human agents on high-complexity tasks, ensuring they provide consistent, high-quality service for interactions that AI cannot fully handle. Finally, companies can implement real-time monitoring and feedback systems to continuously assess AI and human performance, allowing for dynamic adjustments in task allocation and further improving service effectiveness and customer satisfaction. By aligning service mode with task demands, businesses can improve operational efficiency, strengthen customer loyalty, and enhance competitive advantage.

Chapter 1 introduced the growing role of AI chatbots in customer service and the need to balance speed, accuracy, and human intervention as query complexity increases. Chapter 2 reviews the relevant literature on AI chatbots, human–AI collaboration, and cognitive load, providing the theoretical foundation for the research model and hypotheses. Building on this foundation, the study uses a two-study design, combining real-world chat transcript analysis with controlled experiments, setting the stage for the methodology, findings, and discussion in subsequent chapters.

2. LITERATURE REVIEW

Artificial Intelligence and Tools

The term “Artificial Intelligence” was coined by McCarthy in 1956, defining it as “the science and engineering of making intelligent machines” (McCarthy et al., 2006). Since its beginning, the history of artificial intelligence has been marked by alternating cycles of success and periods of optimistic expectations. Encouraged by promising findings, AI researchers confidently predict forthcoming breakthroughs (Norvig & Russell, 2010). However, advancement in AI has been slower than expected, described by alterations in research directions and the continuing introduction and refinement of existing approaches over an extended period (Norvig & Russell, 2010). In the past decade, the proliferation of data in diverse formats has motivated the advancement of new technologies, resulting in accelerated technological improvement. This includes developments in computational processing competences and the development of new AI techniques (Brynjolfsson & McAfee, 2017; Bughin et al., 2017).

Categorizing artificial intelligence (AI) is challenging due to the lack of clear standards and the diversity of applications. AI can be classified by type, such as reactive machines, theory of mind, and self-aware AI, each with distinct definitions and philosophies (Chung, Thaichon, & Quach, 2022). Technologically, AI is often grouped into weak AI, strong AI, and superintelligence, reflecting different levels of competence and sophistication (Chung, Thaichon, & Quach, 2022). Narrow AI (weak AI), exemplified by virtual assistants, recommendation systems, and image recognition algorithms, excels in specific tasks but lacks general cognitive abilities, whereas General AI (strong AI) seeks to emulate human intelligence across a broad range of tasks (Fjelland, 2020; Davenport et al., 2020). Another classification distinguishes generative AI, which produces content such as text, images, or music by learning patterns from large datasets, from conversational AI, which simulates human-like interaction through natural language processing, supporting applications like chatbots and virtual assistants (Fjelland, 2020; Chung, Thaichon, & Quach, 2022).

Given the competitive landscape of the business world, big data, limited resources, and the need for rapid decision-making, organizations are progressively embracing AI technologies (Chen, Zhou & Frankwick, 2023; Haleem et al., 2022; Mariani, Perez-Vega & Wirtz, 2022). Companies like Netflix, Google, Airbnb, Amazon, and Uber have leveraged AI to successfully process vast datasets and utilize insights to expand into new products, markets, and services (Iansiti & Lakhani, 2020; Chen et al., 2023; Mariani et al., 2022). AI studies span multiple sectors—including retail, e-commerce, hospitality, healthcare, and especially financial services—but converge on a shared marketing focus: understanding how AI shapes customer experience, persuasion, and decision-making (Ghatge & Parasar, 2023; Tulshan & Dhage, 2019). Across these contexts, marketing research highlights AI as a frontline interaction partner that not only automates tasks but also manages conversational tone, customer journeys, and psychological responses—making AI-driven transitions, emotional triggers, and conversational fluency central to understanding modern service experiences (Wamba-Taguimdje et al., 2020; Kozinets & Gretzel, 2021; De Bruyn et al., 2020).

AI tools have revolutionized the technological landscape by enabling machines to perform tasks traditionally requiring human intelligence (Brem, Giones & Werle, 2021). Leveraging advanced algorithms and data-driven insights, these tools automate processes, understand natural language, recognize patterns in data, and make autonomous decisions, mimicking human cognitive functions (Chung, Thaichon & Quach, 2022; Fjelland, 2020) such as learning and problem-solving. They use large datasets to enhance accuracy and efficiency across different industries including healthcare, finance, marketing, and customer service (Haleem et al., 2022). In today's business environment, AI tools are crucial for automating tasks, improving productivity, and scalability. They simplify operations, allocate resources strategically, and enable sophisticated data analysis for predictive analytics (Brem, Giones & Werle, 2021). AI tools drive personalized customer experiences through recommendation engines and chatbots, enhancing satisfaction and loyalty (Leocádio et al., 2024). They guarantee consistency and precision in sectors like healthcare and finance (Ghatge & Parasar, 2023), while promoting innovation, allowing organizations to develop new products, scale operations proficiently, and deliver competitive advantage in dynamic markets (Haleem et al., 2022).

Table 1. Types and roles of AI tools

Tools	Description	Example	Roles
Chatbots (Leocádio et al., 2024)	Simulate conversation through text or voice, using NLP techniques	Customer service chatbots, automated responses	√Automation √ Productivity & Scalability
Virtual Assistants (Tulshan & Dhage, 2019)	Offer empathetic and human-like service with customized, human-like in appearance	Siri (Apple), Alexa (Amazon), Google Assistant	√Personalization Experience
Voice Recognition (VR) (Butt, Ahmad, & Shafique, 2021)	understand and interpret human speech; converts spoken words into text	voice-controlled devices, voice authentication	√Personalization Experience
Sentiment Analysis (Taherdoost & Madanchian, 2023)	Use NLP to determine the sentiment expressed in text data	Analysing social media posts, customer reviews	√ Prediction √ Accuracy & Consistency
Image Recognition (Tian, 2020)	Analyse and interpret visual data from images or videos	Facial recognition systems for security	√Innovation and Competitive
Recommendation Systems (Zhang, Lu & Jin, 2021)	Analyze user preferences and behaviour to recommend products, services, or content	Netflix's movie recommendation engine	√Predictive Analytics
Healthcare AI (Shaheen, 2021)	Use machine learning and data analysis to improve diagnostics, treatment & administrative tasks	Medical image analysis for diagnostics, personalized medicine	√ Productivity & Scalability √Personalization

Recent AI research over the past five years has centred on AI chatbot (e.g., Gonzalez-Aguirre et al., 2021; Blut et al., 2021), Voice AI (Leocádio et al., 2024; Klaus & Zaichkowsky, 2020), and AI agents (Butt, Ahmad, & Shafique, 2021; Tian, 2020; Taherdoost & Madanchian, 2023). These studies examine outcomes such as customer satisfaction, engagement, technology readiness, loyalty, acceptance, and trust. Scholars have also explored how AI service quality, service failures, and ethical concerns shape customer responses, with increasing attention to how human–AI interactions foster loyalty, psychological safety, and emotional connection (Gnewuch et al., 2018). The nomological model is presented in Figure 1.

Figure 1. Nomological net

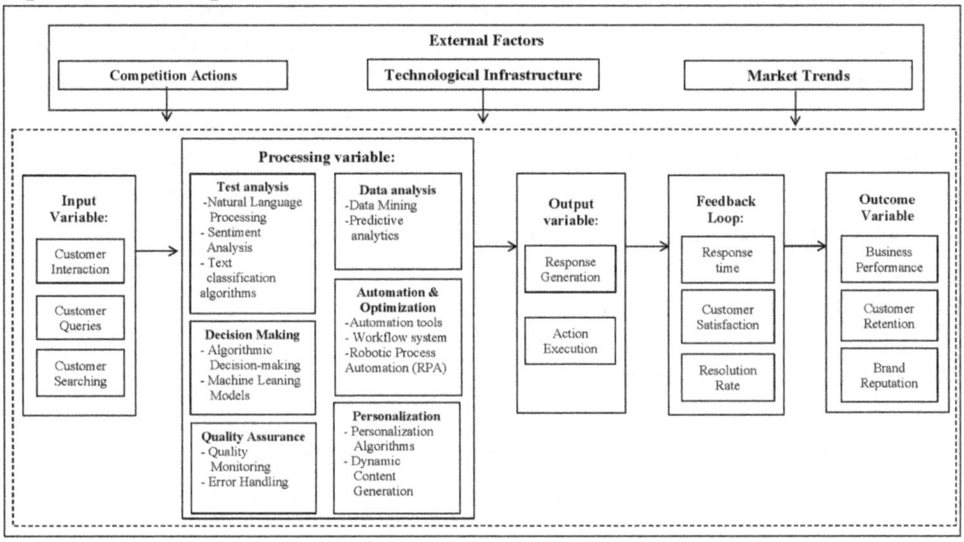

2.1 Artificial Intelligence Chatbot

AI chatbots are conversational agents that leverage natural language processing, machine learning, and automated dialogue systems to interact with users in real time (Fjelland, 2020; Chung, Thaichon & Quach, 2022). Designed to simulate human-like conversations, they interpret user intent and generate contextually relevant responses, evolving from rule-based scripts to adaptive, context-aware systems that serve as central touchpoints throughout the customer journey (Nicolescu & Tudorache, 2022). Recent research highlights that chatbots increasingly function as autonomous social actors, raising considerations for ethical, transparent, and psychologically safe human–machine interactions (Murtarelli et al., 2021). Their growing adoption is driven by capabilities such as handling high volumes of queries, 24/7 availability, scalability, fast responses, and data-driven insights, which give them superior multitasking capacity compared to human representatives (Ngai et al., 2021). Chatbot applications are now widespread across industries including banking, education, and healthcare, reflecting their versatility and operational value (Ngai et al., 2021; Carter, 2018; Hill et al., 2015).

In marketing, AI chatbots are widely applied to enhance customer engagement, streamline service processes, and support data-driven personalization across digital platforms. Firms deploy chatbots to provide instant customer assistance, recommend products, facilitate transactions, and nurture long-term relationships. Studies demonstrate their value in e-commerce and omnichannel environments by improving the efficiency, responsiveness, and personalization of interactions (Singh & Singh, 2023; Stoilova, 2021). Recent research also shows that AI-enabled chatbots influence consumer perceptions of usefulness, trust, and acceptance across different online journey stages, ultimately shaping satisfaction and behavioural outcomes such as conversion and retention (Rana et al., 2024). Collectively, these findings position chatbots as strategic marketing tools that simultaneously reduce service costs and elevate the customer experience, making them increasingly central to both operational efficiency and customer relationship management.

2.2 Human–AI Collaboration

Comparative research examining AI and human performance in customer service reveals clear distinctions in their respective strengths and limitations. Recent studies consistently highlight AI's advantages in efficiency, rapid response, and the ability to handle high volumes of requests with consistent accuracy (Ruan & Mezei, 2022; Saxena & Gautam, 2022; Wu et al., 2024; Jarek & Mazurek, 2019; Acemoglu & Restrepo, 2018). These capabilities allow AI systems to excel in structured, routine, and informational tasks that rely on speed, pattern matching, and database-driven processing. However, humans continue to demonstrate irreplaceable strengths in areas requiring empathy, emotional sensitivity, contextual nuance, and the resolution of complex or ambiguous problems (Zhang, Lu & Jin, 2021; Liu-Thompkins, Okazaki & Li, 2022; Yuan, Inoue & Hoshino, 2023). Studies further show that human frontline employees often outperform chatbots in situations involving experiential attributes, trust-building, or emotionally charged contexts, where interpersonal rapport and social understanding play critical roles (Murtarelli, Gregory & Romenti, 2021; Saxena & Gautam, 2022).

Moving beyond simple comparisons, emerging research emphasizes the growing value of Human–Robot Collaboration (HRC), where AI and humans work together to leverage their complementary strengths. Collaboration models increasingly show that pairing AI's analytical capabilities, automation, and data processing with human empathy, creativity, and flexible problem-solving produces superior service outcomes (Liu-Thompkins, Okazaki & Li, 2022; Martijn et al., 2024). HRC enables organizations to deliver both efficiency and emotional intelligence, enhancing customer experience while improving decision quality, personalization, and relationship-building (Lee, 2022). Studies demonstrate that collaboration can take multiple forms—from AI handling mechanical or analytical tasks while humans address intuitive or empathetic dimensions (Leocádio et al., 2024; Reis, 2024), to hybrid models where human endorsement strengthens customer acceptance of AI guidance or where interaction flows seamlessly between AI and human agents depending on task complexity (Yuan, Inoue & Hoshino, 2023). Additional frameworks emphasize AI–human switching, supervised AI-human collaboration, and artificial empathy as mechanisms that strengthen engagement and satisfaction (Zhang, Wang & Zhao, 2023; Paramarta & Aripin, 2024; Wiethof & Bittner, 2022). This Robot–Human Augmentation Model underscores that while AI effectively drives initial engagement and routine interactions, human involvement becomes increasingly critical as customer needs grow more complex, ultimately enhancing satisfaction, trust, and long-term relationship quality (Huang & Rust, 2021; Lemon & Verhoef, 2016; Micheaux & Bosio, 2019).

2.3 Cognitive Load Theory as the Foundation

Cognitive Load Theory (CLT; Sweller, 1988) posits that individuals have a limited capacity for processing information in working memory. Tasks vary in their intrinsic cognitive load, depending on their complexity and the mental effort required to understand, interpret, and act on information. Extraneous cognitive load arises from poorly designed information or inefficient processes, while germane cognitive load refers to the effort used for learning or understanding relevant information. In any interactive system, the balance between cognitive demands and an individual's capacity influences performance, decision-making, and overall satisfaction (Leahy & Sweller, 2011).

In the context of AI chatbots in customer service, Cognitive Load Theory provides a framework for understanding how query complexity affects customer satisfaction. Low-complexity queries impose minimal cognitive load, allowing AI chatbots to enhance satisfaction through fast responses and accurate information. As queries become more complex, intrinsic cognitive load increases, and customers require more contextual understanding, detailed explanations, or personalized guidance, which AI chatbots may struggle to provide. Consequently, Cognitive Load Theory explains why query complexity moderates the effectiveness of AI chatbots and the mediating roles of information accuracy and response speed, highlighting when human representatives are more suitable to support customer needs (Desmond et al., 2021; Gnewuch et al., 2018; Adam, Wessel & Benlian, 2021; Xu et al., 2020; Bansal et al., 2024).

2.4 Hypothesis Development

Prior research shows that chatbots can outperform human representatives in certain contexts, increasing efficiency, service recovery quality, and overall satisfaction (Hsu & Lin, 2023; Hsiao & Chen, 2022). Studies also indicate that chatbots can enhance compliance and trust when designed with anthropomorphic cues or social presence (Adam, Wessel & Benlian, 2021). However, customer satisfaction varies by product type and disclosure conditions: chatbots perform better for experiential products (Ruan & Mezei, 2022), but disclosing their automated nature can reduce purchase rates due to perceptions of reduced empathy (Luo et al., 2019). Evidence from mental health and support services further shows that users appreciate chatbots when they deliver immediate access and strong language understanding (Koulouri, Macredie & Olakitan, 2022). Collectively, these findings suggest that AI chatbots can directly enhance customer satisfaction by offering immediate, consistent, and accessible service support. Therefore, the following hypothesis is proposed:

Hypothesis 1*: The use of AI chatbots directly enhances customer satisfaction in customer service interactions.*

A core driver of positive customer evaluations in AI-enabled services is the chatbot's ability to deliver highly accurate information. Through advanced NLP techniques, including tokenization, sentiment analysis, and entity recognition, chatbots can identify user intent and provide precise, contextually appropriate responses (Dongbo et al., 2023; Aldunate et al., 2022). These capabilities make them especially effective for handling routine tasks such as checking balances or providing product information, where structured databases and predefined responses ensure accuracy (Olujimi & Ade-Ibijola, 2023; Kalusivalingam et al., 2020). Chatbots can rapidly match customer inputs to existing knowledge bases, improving reliability and perceived service quality (Kaur, 2024; Piris & Gay, 2021). Furthermore, machine learning and deep learning techniques enable chatbots to improve their accuracy over time by learning from user interactions (Suhaili, Salim & Jambli, 2021; Nuruzzaman & Hussain, 2018). However, accuracy tends to decline for complex or emotionally sensitive queries requiring human judgment, underscoring the boundary conditions of AI performance. Given the centrality of correctness and relevance in shaping customer experience, information accuracy is likely to mediate the relationship between chatbot usage and customer satisfaction. Therefore, the following hypothesis is proposed:

Hypothesis 2*: The effect of AI chatbot usage on customer satisfaction is mediated by information accuracy, such that higher information accuracy leads to higher customer satisfaction.*

Response speed is another fundamental strength of AI chatbots, contributing significantly to perceived service efficiency and customer satisfaction. Because chatbots can instantly process user inputs and retrieve predefined or database-driven answers, they deliver faster responses than human agents across a wide range of routine service tasks (Olujimi & Ade-Ibijola, 2023; Kalusivalingam et al., 2020). NLP techniques enable rapid intent detection and message parsing, allowing chatbots to respond in real time with minimal processing delay (Dongbo et al., 2023). Studies show that timely and immediate solutions increase trust, satisfaction, and customer willingness to continue using AI-enabled services (Hsiao & Chen, 2022; Hsu & Lin, 2023). Chatbots are also valued in sensitive contexts, such as mental health support, precisely because they offer uninterrupted availability and immediate access to assistance (Koulouri, Macredie & Olakitan, 2022). By minimizing waiting time and maintaining seamless conversational flow, response speed becomes a crucial mechanism through which chatbots enhance the overall service experience. Therefore, response speed is expected to mediate the relationship between AI chatbot usage and customer satisfaction. Therefore, the following hypothesis is proposed:

Hypothesis 3: *The effect of AI chatbot usage on customer satisfaction is mediated by response speed, such that faster response times lead to higher customer satisfaction.*

The effectiveness of AI chatbots in improving customer satisfaction has been broadly studied, particularly in contexts involving routine, simple tasks. Prior research indicates that AI chatbots are mainly effective when they handle queries that are straightforward, well-defined and follow a clear pattern, demanding minimal cognitive effort from customers (Grudin & Jacques, 2019). For instance, AI chatbots can quickly provide numerical information (Chung & Park, 2019; Stoilova, 2021), such as checking account balances or confirming product availability, which typically leads to higher customer satisfaction due to their efficiency, accuracy, and availability (Choy, 2024). As query complexity increases, AI chatbots face challenges in addressing nuanced or ambiguous requests that require deeper understanding, contextual awareness, or emotional intelligence (Bhambri & Rani, 2024; Izadi & Forouzanfar, 2024; Khennouche et al., 2024). While chatbots excel at handling simple, structured queries, their reliance on predefined or static data becomes inadequate for more complex tasks. These systems require more sophisticated natural language processing to interpret subtle meanings and context, capabilities that may exceed their current limitations (Hussain, Ameri Sianaki & Ababneh, 2019; Chakraborty, Roy & Kumar, 2023; McTear, 2022). As a result, the effectiveness of AI chatbots in enhancing customer satisfaction decreases with increasing query complexity, as they struggle with issues that demand personalization, specialized knowledge, or emotional sensitivity, areas where human intervention is often necessary (Xu et al., 2020; Bansal et al., 2024).

Query complexity not only moderates the direct relationship between AI chatbot usage and customer satisfaction but is also likely to influence the mediating roles of key factors such as information accuracy and response speed (Desmond et al., 2021). For low-complexity queries, AI chatbots' ability to deliver accurate and timely responses significantly enhances customer satisfaction. In these cases, chatbots can rely on pre-programmed responses or structured databases to provide precise, relevant information quickly, improving the user experience. However, as the complexity of queries increases, the effectiveness of AI chatbots in maintaining high levels of information accuracy declines. This is because AI systems rely on pre-programmed responses or structured data, which are effective for simple, routine tasks but insufficient for handling intricate or highly specialized requests that require domain expertise or personalized context (Bhambri & Rani, 2024; Desmond et al., 2021; Izadi & Forouzanfar, 2024). As the complexity of the query rises, the chatbot's natural language processing (NLP) capabilities may be overwhelmed by the need for deeper understanding, context-specific interpretation, or the integration of diverse data sources. In such cases, the chatbot's ability to provide accurate, relevant, and tailored information is compromised, often leading to miscommunication or inadequate responses that fail to meet customer expectations.

Response speed is crucial for low-complexity queries because these types of inquiries typically involve straightforward, information that can be processed quickly, leading to immediate satisfaction for the customer. In contrast, for more complex inquiries, the value of response speed diminishes because these queries often require deeper analysis, contextual understanding, or the integration of multiple pieces of information. When faced with intricate or specialized issues, customers are more concerned with the quality, accuracy, and relevance of the response than the speed at which it is delivered. In such cases, a quick but incomplete or inaccurate response may lead to dissatisfaction, as customers often prefer more thoughtful, thorough answers that fully address their concerns (Gnewuch et al., 2018; Adam, Wessel & Benlian, 2021; Xu et al., 2020; Bansal et al., 2024). Gnewuch et al. (2018) investigated how dynamic response delays in chatbots, adjusted based on message complexity, affect user perceptions of humanness and social presence, revealing that these delays improve satisfaction in customer service interactions by aligning with social expectations of human-like communication. Thus, while speed remains an important factor in low-complexity tasks, the emphasis shifts towards the depth and relevance of the response when the queries become more complex. These insights lead to the following hypotheses:

Hypothesis 4: *Query complexity moderates the relationship between AI chatbot usage and customer satisfaction, such that the positive effect of AI chatbots on customer satisfaction is stronger for low-complexity queries compared to high-complexity queries.*

Hypothesis 5*: Query complexity moderates the mediating effect of information accuracy on the relationship between AI chatbot usage and customer satisfaction,* *such that the indirect effect of information accuracy on customer satisfaction is stronger for low-complexity queries.*

Hypothesis 6*: Query complexity moderates the mediating effect of response speed on the relationship between AI chatbot usage and customer satisfaction, such that the indirect effect of response speed on customer satisfaction is stronger for low-complexity queries.*

2.5 Research Model

Building on the literature and hypotheses, a conceptual model is proposed that examines how query complexity moderates the relationship between AI chatbot usage and customer satisfaction, with response speed and information accuracy serving as parallel mediators. The model posits that for low-complexity queries, AI chatbots can efficiently deliver fast and accurate information, reducing cognitive effort and enhancing satisfaction, consistent with Cognitive Load Theory (Sweller, 1988). In contrast, high-complexity queries increase intrinsic cognitive load, requiring more contextual understanding, nuanced interpretation, or personalized guidance, which AI chatbots may struggle to provide. Consequently, the effectiveness of response speed and information accuracy in enhancing satisfaction diminishes as query complexity rises. By integrating query complexity, response speed, and information accuracy within this framework, the model aims to explain how AI and human agents can complement each other to optimize customer satisfaction across tasks of varying complexity. Figure 2 presents the conceptual research model.

Figure 2. Conceptual model of AI chatbot and customer satisfaction

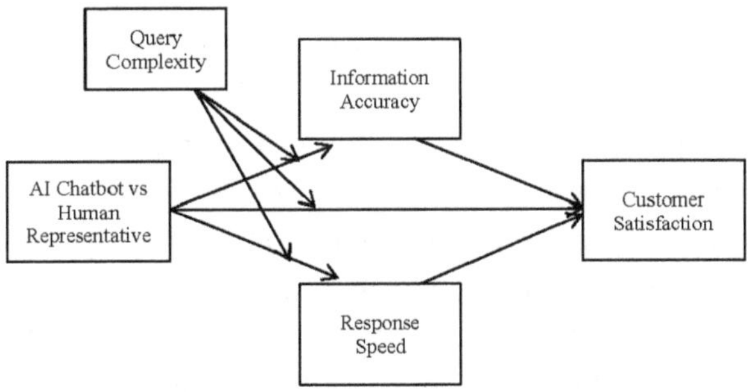

3. METHODOLOGY

3.1 Study 1

The study analysed chat transcripts from an investment company where an AI chatbot had been deployed to assist customer interactions. The investment sector demands highly precise and responsive customer service because clients often engage with complex financial products and seek timely, accurate guidance for critical investment decisions. This environment provides an ideal context to examine AI chatbot performance, including its ability to handle nuanced queries, maintain conversational fluency, and influence overall customer satisfaction and trust. This study focuses on two key markets in the global investment company. The dataset included a total of 648 chat transcripts, comprising 315 interactions with the AI chatbot and 333 interactions with human representatives, allowing for a direct comparison of the effectiveness of the two service modes in handling customer queries. The transcripts were collected over a one-month period, covering Market A, where the AI chatbot was deployed, and Market B, where human representatives continued to serve customers. The data were first cleaned to remove incomplete transcripts and chats lacking customer ratings, ensuring that only valid, complete interactions were included in the analysis.

Each transcript was systematically coded for analysis to ensure a consistent and rigorous evaluation of customer interactions. Agent type was coded as AI = "1" and human = "0," allowing for a clear distinction between service modes. Customer ratings were recorded on a 1–5-star scale for three key dimensions: response speed, information accuracy, and overall satisfaction, providing an explicit operationalization of performance and customer perceptions (refer to Figure 3). Response speed captured the perceived timeliness of the agent's replies, while information accuracy reflected the correctness and relevance of the guidance provided. Overall satisfaction measured the general impression of the interaction from the customer's perspective. Query complexity was assessed by the company's compliance department and coded on a scale from 1 (simple) to 5 (highly complex), capturing the cognitive effort, requirement for personalized guidance, and depth of problem solving necessary in each interaction. This approach allowed the analysis to account for the varying difficulty of customer requests and the potential differential performance of AI versus human agents across these contexts. The coding scheme enabled a structured comparison of AI and human performance across varying task complexities, facilitating the identification of patterns in customer perceptions of speed, accuracy, and satisfaction.

Figure 3. Process-oriented AI-human collaboration model

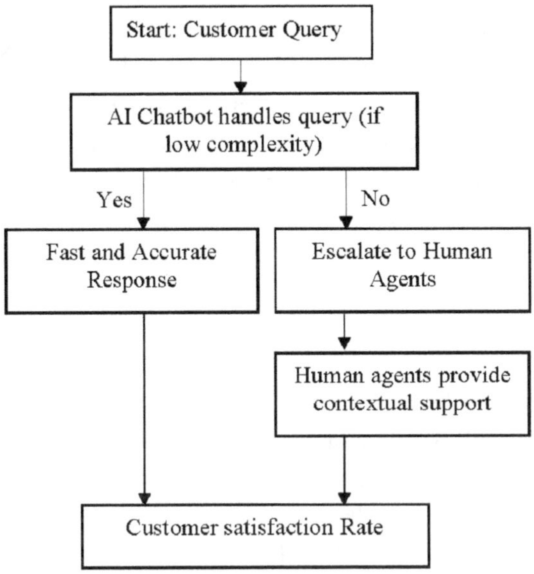

To examine the relationships between service mode, mediating variables, and customer satisfaction, the dataset was prepared for statistical analysis using PROCESS Macro. This approach enables testing of both direct and indirect effects, with query complexity modeled as a moderator and response speed and information accuracy as mediators. By aligning the operationalization of query complexity with Cognitive Load Theory (Sweller, 1988), the study provides a theoretical basis for understanding how task difficulty influences the effectiveness of AI chatbots. Specifically, low-complexity queries impose minimal cognitive load, allowing AI chatbots to efficiently provide fast and accurate responses, whereas high-complexity queries increase cognitive load, potentially overwhelming AI capabilities and necessitating human intervention for optimal customer satisfaction. This framework supports a nuanced exploration of when and how AI can complement human agents in customer service.

In addition to the primary variables, this study includes time of day and client type as control variables. Time of day accounts for potential variations in customer satisfaction that may arise from when the interaction occurred, as chat response speed, agent workload, and overall service quality can differ depending on the hour or shift, potentially influencing perceptions independently of service mode, query complexity, or information accuracy. For analysis, time of day was coded as peak hours (9:00 a.m. to 6:00 p.m.) versus non-peak hours (before 9:00 a.m. or after 6:00

p.m.) based on the company's traffic patterns. Client type distinguishes between new and existing clients, as prior experience can significantly affect perceptions of service quality. Existing clients are often more familiar with the platform and may navigate queries more efficiently, whereas new clients may require additional guidance, reassurance, or personalized interaction. By controlling for both time of day and client type—coded as 0 for new clients and 1 for existing clients—the analysis ensures that observed effects of service mode, query complexity, response speed, and information accuracy on satisfaction are not confounded by temporal fluctuations or differences in client experience.

3.2 Study 2

We have strengthened the justification for the two-study design by highlighting how the field study provides real-world ecological validity, while the experimental study offers controlled conditions for causal inference. Study 2 was conducted with 352 students to examine their preferences for service mode choice in response to customer queries of varying complexity. Three scenarios were designed, each representing a different level of complexity, and verified these scenarios with professionals in the investment sector to ensure their relevance and realism (see Appendix I). The scenarios covered tasks such as checking an account balance, opening an additional USD account, and filing a complaint about a money transfer error, corresponding to complexity levels 1, 2, and 3, respectively. Each scenario was crafted to reflect typical customer interactions in the investment sector, with increasing levels of cognitive demand, decision-making, and need for personalized guidance.

To validate the complexity levels, further consultation was conducted with professionals who have extensive experience in financial customer service. They reviewed each scenario for realism, clarity, and alignment with the types of issues customers commonly face, providing feedback to refine the descriptions and ensure they accurately reflected real-world situations. This process enhanced the credibility of the scenarios and ensured that participants' responses would reflect genuine preferences for AI chatbots versus human representatives across tasks of varying complexity. By combining these scenario-based insights with the analysis of industry chat transcripts, the study offers a more comprehensive understanding of how service mode choice, response speed, and information accuracy interact with query complexity to influence customer satisfaction.

4. DATA ANALYSIS

4.1 Study 1

For the industrial data, Process Macro was used to test both direct and indirect effects of service mode on customer satisfaction, considering response speed and information accuracy as mediators, and query complexity as a moderator. This approach allowed for an exploration of how service mode—AI chatbot versus human representative—affects satisfaction, with response speed and accuracy accounting for the observed effects. Additionally, the analysis examined how query complexity moderates the relationship between service mode and customer satisfaction.

Table 2. Mediation analysis – direct relationship (N=648)

Variables	B	SE	t	P
Service Mode => Respond Speed	4.2906	0.1288	33.3127	0.0000
Service Mode => Information Accuracy	1.6208	0.2002	8.0981	0.0000
Respond Speed => Satisfaction	0.5333	0.0326	16.3363	0.0000
Information Accuracy => Satisfaction	0.7066	0.0311	22.7222	0.0000
Service Mode => Satisfaction	1.0922	0.0766	14.2506	0.0000

Table 3. Mediation analysis - indirect relationship

Indirect Relationship	Index	BootSE	BootLLCI	BootULCI
Service Mode => Respond Speed => Satisfaction	-0.3720	0.0497	-0.4722	-0.2771
Service Mode => Information Accuracy => Satisfaction	-0.4072	0.0642	-0.5368	-0.2841

*Bootstrapped 95% confidence interval (CI)

The results from the mediation analysis (Table 2) indicate that service mode significantly influences response speed, information accuracy, and customer satisfaction. Specifically, AI chatbots provide considerably faster responses than human representatives ($B = 4.2906$, $p < 0.001$), allowing customers to receive timely information and reducing the waiting time associated with human interactions. In addition, AI chatbots deliver more accurate information ($B = 1.6208$, $p < 0.001$), ensuring that customers obtain precise, reliable answers to their queries. These direct effects suggest that the technological capabilities of AI—such as automated retrieval of structured data and standardized responses—enhance both speed and accuracy, particularly for routine or low-complexity tasks.

Both response speed (B = 0.5333, $p < 0.001$) and information accuracy (B = 0.7066, $p < 0.001$) exhibit strong direct positive effects on customer satisfaction, highlighting that these factors independently contribute to perceived service quality. Faster responses likely improve satisfaction by reducing frustration and maintaining conversational momentum, whereas accurate information enhances trust and confidence in the service provider. This indicates that customers evaluate both the efficiency and reliability of the interaction when forming judgments about satisfaction.

The mediation analysis of indirect effects (Table 3) further clarifies the mechanisms through which service mode impacts satisfaction. The significant indirect effects of service mode on satisfaction through response speed (-0.3720, BootSE = 0.0497, BootLLCI = -0.4722, BootULCI = -0.2771) and information accuracy (-0.4072, BootSE = 0.0642, BootLLCI = -0.5368, BootULCI = -0.2841) indicate that AI chatbots enhance customer satisfaction not simply by replacing human agents, but through their ability to deliver rapid and accurate responses. These findings underscore that improvements in speed and accuracy are key pathways through which AI chatbots reduce cognitive load for customers and enhance their overall experience. Collectively, these results support Hypotheses 1, 2, and 3, demonstrating that AI chatbots provide superior efficiency and reliability in service delivery, with satisfaction primarily driven by their effectiveness in these two dimensions.

Table 4. Moderated mediation analysis – direct relationship

Variable (Mediator-Respond Speed)	**Outcome variable: Satisfaction; Moderator: Complexity**			
	B	**SE**	**t**	**p**
Service Mode	-4.2906	0.1288	-33.3127	0.0000
Complexity	-1.0395	0.0279	-37.2483	0.0000
Complexity × Service Mode	1.0775	0.0396	27.2194	0.0019
Variable (Mediator- Information Accuracy)	B	SE	t	p
Service Mode	1.6208	0.2002	8.0981	0.0000
Complexity	0.0651	0.0434	1.5001	0.1341
Complexity × Service Mode	-0.7974	0.0615	-12.9620	0.0000

Table 5. Moderated mediation analysis – indirect relationship

	Index of Moderated Mediation: Complexity			
Indirect Relationship	**Index**	**BootSE**	**BootLLCI**	**BootULCI**
Service Mode => Respond Speed => Satisfaction	0.5747	0.0362	0.5043	0.6468
Service Mode => Information Accuracy => Satisfaction	-0.5634	0.0536	-0.6673	-0.4588

*Bootstrapped 95% confidence interval (CI)

The results from Table 4 and Table 5 indicate that query complexity significantly moderates the relationships between service mode, response speed, information accuracy, and customer satisfaction. Specifically, the interaction term "Complexity × Service Mode" for response speed ($B = 1.0775$, $p = 0.0019$) shows that the advantage of AI chatbots in delivering rapid responses is most pronounced for low-complexity queries, where tasks are straightforward and require minimal cognitive effort from customers. In these cases, the ability of AI chatbots to provide immediate answers enhances satisfaction by reducing waiting time and maintaining a smooth conversational flow. However, as query complexity increases, this speed advantage becomes less relevant; complex queries often require more nuanced understanding, contextual interpretation, and personalized guidance, areas where AI chatbots are less capable, shifting customer attention toward the quality and accuracy of the response.

The interaction between complexity and service mode for information accuracy ($B = -0.7974$, $p < 0.0001$) further illustrates this pattern. As query complexity rises, AI chatbots are less effective at delivering accurate information due to limitations in handling ambiguous, multi-step, or high-stakes inquiries. This decline in accuracy negatively impacts customer satisfaction, highlighting that for complex queries, accuracy outweighs speed in determining customer perceptions of service quality. The indirect effects reinforce this interpretation: for response speed, the significant indirect effect ($B = 0.5747$, $p < 0.001$) confirms that fast responses contribute meaningfully to satisfaction in simpler queries, whereas for information accuracy, the significant indirect effect ($B = -0.5634$, $p < 0.001$) demonstrates that errors or inaccuracies in complex queries substantially reduce satisfaction.

These findings underscore the importance of a balanced approach to AI chatbot deployment, where speed is prioritized for simple, routine tasks, and accuracy and contextual understanding are emphasized for more complex interactions. By integrating query complexity into the model, the results reveal that AI chatbots are most effective when the cognitive demands of the task are low, while human representatives are better suited for high-complexity scenarios that require deeper expertise or personalized guidance. Overall, these results provide strong support for Hypotheses 4, 5, and 6, demonstrating that the benefits of AI chatbots are contingent on the complexity of customer queries and that mediating factors such as response speed and information accuracy play distinct roles depending on task difficulty.

Finally, time of day was included as a control variable to account for potential variations in service performance across different hours. Analyses indicated that the timing of interactions did not significantly affect customer satisfaction ($p > 0.1$), suggesting that the observed effects of service mode, response speed, and information accuracy are robust and not confounded by temporal factors. Similarly, client type—distinguishing between new and existing clients—was included as a control variable. Results showed no significant difference in satisfaction between new and existing clients ($p > 0.1$), indicating that the effects of AI chatbots and human representatives on response speed, information accuracy, and overall satisfaction hold regardless of prior customer experience. Together, these findings reinforce that the superior performance of AI chatbots for simple queries and the increasing importance of accuracy for complex queries are consistent across different client types and service times.

4.2 Study 2

In Study 2 with students, notable variations were observed in preferences for AI chatbots versus human representatives based on query complexity (refer to Table 6). For Scenario 1, the lowest complexity case involving an account balance inquiry, 89% of participants preferred the AI chatbot, citing reasons such as faster response speed and the straightforward nature of the query. Only 11% opted for a human representative, reflecting the simplicity and speed of the request. In Scenario 2, which involved the more complex task of opening an additional USD account, 58% of participants selected the AI chatbot, appreciating its ability to provide quick and accurate information. However, 42% preferred to interact with a human representative, likely due to concerns about the intricacy of the process and the desire for more personalized assistance. For Scenario 3, which addressed a money transfer error—a higher complexity issue—93% of participants chose to engage with a human representative. Many cited the need for a more detailed explanation, as well as concerns over the privacy and security of the transaction, indicating that human interaction was deemed essential for addressing sensitive or high-stakes matters. Only 7% felt confident using the AI chatbot for such an issue, demonstrating how increasing query complexity significantly shifted preferences toward human representatives.

Table 6. AI vs. human preferences across service scenarios

	Query Type / Description	Complexity Level	% Prefer AI Chatbot	% Prefer Human Representative	Key Reasons for Preference
1	Account balance inquiry	Low	89%	11%	Fast response, straightforward task
2	Opening an additional USD account	Medium	58%	42%	Quick and accurate info (AI); personalized guidance (human)
3	Money transfer error	High	7%	93%	Sensitive/high-stakes issue, need detailed explanation and trust

Study 2 builds upon the results of Study 1 by examining how increasing query complexity influences customers' preferences for AI or human support. It also explores the reasons behind these preferences, offering deeper insights into customer behaviour. While Study 1 demonstrates a clear preference for AI chatbots in simpler tasks, Study 2 reveals that as query complexity increases, customers tend to favour human representatives, especially when tasks require more personalized interaction, detailed explanations, or involve high-stakes issues such as financial transactions. This comparison highlights the importance of balancing speed and accuracy depending on task complexity and provides a clearer understanding of how query complexity moderates customer preferences, stressing the need for human involvement in more complex, high-risk situations. These findings underscore how customer preferences for AI chatbots or human representatives are shaped by the nature and complexity of the task.

Beyond the immediate empirical findings, the results of studies can be situated within broader macro-level trends shaping contemporary service systems. The increasing adoption of generative AI in customer service highlights a growing expectation for rapid, accurate, and always-available support, particularly for routine and low-complexity tasks. At the same time, heightened regulatory scrutiny around data privacy, transparency, and accountability—especially in financial and high-stakes service contexts—helps explain participants' strong preference for human representatives when query complexity increases. These findings also reflect evolving consumer expectations, wherein customers increasingly view AI as a complement rather than a replacement for human expertise. Taken together, the results point toward a future service model that emphasizes strategic human–AI collaboration, aligning with the book's overarching theme of designing responsible, human-centered interactive technologies in an era of accelerated AI adoption.

5. CONCLUSION, CONTRIBUTION AND RECOMMENDATION

This paper examines the role of query complexity in shaping customer preferences for AI chatbots versus human representatives, with a particular focus on how speed and accuracy influence customer satisfaction. Drawing on Cognitive Load Theory (Sweller, 1988), the findings suggest that simple, routine tasks impose low cognitive load, allowing AI chatbots to efficiently provide fast and accurate responses, whereas complex tasks increase cognitive load and require human intervention for deeper understanding, contextual interpretation, or personalized guidance. The findings reveal that while AI chatbots are preferred for simple, routine tasks due to their speed and efficiency, customers lean toward human representatives for more complex inquiries that require personalization, in-depth explanations, or greater trust—especially in high-stakes situations. As query complexity increases, customers place more emphasis on the quality and accuracy of the response rather than speed, highlighting the limitations of AI in handling intricate or highly specialized requests. These results reinforce the need for a hybrid model, where AI handles straightforward tasks efficiently, and human representatives are involved when deeper expertise, emotional intelligence, or personalized service is required. This research provides important insights into the dynamic interplay between task complexity, customer preferences, and the complementary strengths of AI and human agents, offering valuable implications for businesses seeking to optimize customer service across diverse service contexts.

This study makes a significant contribution to the existing literature by advancing our understanding of how the complexity of customer queries affects the preference for AI versus human support across various service contexts. It extends the body of knowledge on AI chatbots in customer service by examining the interaction between response speed, accuracy, and query complexity in shaping customer satisfaction. Theoretically, it highlights how Cognitive Load Theory can be applied to human–AI collaboration, providing a framework for understanding when AI or human intervention is most effective. Furthermore, it offers a basis for developing integrative models of task allocation that consider both cognitive demands and service personalization.

Additionally, the study provides practical insights for businesses, particularly in high-stakes sectors like finance and customer service, where there is a critical need to balance the efficiency of AI with the empathy and personalized attention offered by human representatives. By bridging the gap between AI capabilities and human involvement, this research lays the foundation for more effective, customer-centric service models. Based on these findings, it is crucial for businesses to strategically allocate tasks between AI chatbots, and human representatives based on the complexity of customer queries. For low-complexity tasks, AI chatbots can enhance efficiency and customer satisfaction by providing quick and accurate responses. However, for more complex or high-stakes queries—such as financial transactions or cases requiring emotional sensitivity—human representatives should be prioritized to ensure that customers receive the personalized, trustworthy support they need.

While this study provides valuable insights into the role of information accuracy and response speed in AI chatbot adoption, it has several limitations. Most notably, it focuses on just two key factors influencing customer satisfaction, without considering other important variables that could affect the overall customer experience. In particular, the development of user trust over repeated interactions and its implications for sustained reliance on AI systems remain underexplored. Factors such as trust, empathy, personalization, and emotional engagement, as well as individual differences in customers' experience with technology, can all play a significant role in shaping customer perceptions of AI chatbots. Understanding how these factors influence long-term relationship outcomes, including customer loyalty and the potential risks of over-automation, represents an important avenue for future research. Additionally, this study does not address the growing use of hybrid service models in which AI chatbots operate in tandem with human agents. Given that such models are becoming increasingly common, future studies should examine how AI chatbots can effectively escalate complex queries to human representatives, with particular attention to the design of clear AI–human escalation and handoff mechanisms that ensure seamless transitions and minimize customer frustration. Furthermore, future research could explore the long-term effects of AI–human collaboration on brand trust, customer retention, and overall satisfaction across different service contexts and industries.

REFERENCES

Acemoglu, D., & Restrepo, P. (2018). Artificial intelligence, automation, and work. In *The economics of artificial intelligence: An agenda* (pp. 197–236). University of Chicago Press.

Adam, M., Wessel, M., & Benlian, A. (2021). AI-based chatbots in customer service and their effects on user compliance. *Electronic Markets, 31*(2), 427–445.

Aldunate, Á., Maldonado, S., Vairetti, C., & Armelini, G. (2022). Understanding customer satisfaction via deep learning and natural language processing. *Expert Systems with Applications, 209*, 118309.

Araujo, T. (2018). Living up to the chatbot hype: The influence of anthropomorphic design cues and communicative agency framing on conversational agent and company perceptions. *Computers in Human Behavior, 85*, 183–189.

Bansal, G., Chamola, V., Hussain, A., Guizani, M., & Niyato, D. (2024). Transforming conversations with AI—A comprehensive study of ChatGPT. *Cognitive Computation*, ●●●, 1–24.

Bhambri, P., & Rani, S. (2024). Issues Related to Chatbots. In Design and Development of Emerging Chatbot Technology (pp. 130-147). IGI Global.

Blut, M., Wang, C., Wünderlich, N. V., & Brock, C. (2021). Understanding anthropomorphism in service provision: A meta-analysis of physical robots, chatbots, and other AI. *Journal of the Academy of Marketing Science, 49*(4), 632–658.

Brem, A., Giones, F., & Werle, M. (2021). The AI digital revolution in innovation: A conceptual framework of artificial intelligence technologies for the management of innovation. *IEEE Transactions on Engineering Management, 70*(2), 770–776.

Brynjolfsson, E., & Mcafee, A. N. D. R. E. W. (2017). Artificial intelligence, for real. *Harvard Business Review, 1*, 1–31.

Bughin, J., Hazan, E., & Sree Ramaswamy, P. DC, W., & Chu, M. (2017). Artificial intelligence the next digital frontier.

Butt, A. H., Ahmad, H., & Shafique, M. N. (2021). AI-Powered "Voice Recognition Avatar": A New Way to Play Games. [IJGCMS]. *International Journal of Gaming and Computer-Mediated Simulations, 13*(3), 1–17.

Carter, D. (2018). How real is the impact of artificial intelligence? The business information survey 2018. *Business Information Review, 35*(3), 99–115.

Chakraborty, U., Roy, S., & Kumar, S. (2023). *Rise of Generative AI and ChatGPT: Understand how Generative AI and ChatGPT are transforming and reshaping the business world (English Edition).* BPB Publications.

Chen, J., Zhou, W., & Frankwick, G. L. (2023). Firm AI Adoption Intensity and Marketing Performance. *Journal of Computer Information Systems*, •••, 1–18.

Choy, J. E. (2024). AI unveiled: a comparative analysis of code accuracy and reliability across various chatbot platforms.

Chung, K., & Park, R. C. (2019). Chatbot-based heathcare service with a knowledge base for cloud computing. *Cluster Computing*, *22*, 1925–1937.

Chung, K., Thaichon, P., & Quach, S. (2022). Types of artificial intelligence (AI) in marketing management. In *Artificial intelligence for marketing management* (pp. 29–40). Routledge.

Davenport, T., Guha, A., Grewal, D., & Bressgott, T. (2020). How artificial intelligence will change the future of marketing. *Journal of the Academy of Marketing Science*, *48*, 24–42.

De Andrade, I. M., & Tumelero, C. (2022). Increasing customer service efficiency through artificial intelligence chatbot. *Revista de Gestão*, *29*(3), 238–251.

De Bruyn, A., Viswanathan, V., Beh, Y. S., Brock, J. K. U., & Von Wangenheim, F. (2020). Artificial intelligence and marketing: Pitfalls and opportunities. *Journal of Interactive Marketing*, *51*(1), 91–105.

Desmond, M., Muller, M., Ashktorab, Z., Dugan, C., Duesterwald, E., Brimijoin, K., & Pan, Q. (2021, April). Increasing the speed and accuracy of data labeling through an ai assisted interface. In *Proceedings of the 26th International Conference on Intelligent User Interfaces* (pp. 392-401).

Dongbo, M., Miniaoui, S., Fen, L., Althubiti, S. A., & Alsenani, T. R. (2023). Intelligent chatbot interaction system capable for sentimental analysis using hybrid machine learning algorithms. *Information Processing & Management*, *60*(5), 103440.

Fjelland, R. (2020). Why general artificial intelligence will not be realized. *Humanities & Social Sciences Communications*, *7*(1), 1–9.

Fotheringham, D., & Wiles, M. A. (2022). The effect of implementing chatbot customer service on stock returns: An event study analysis. *Journal of the Academy of Marketing Science*, •••, 1–21.

Ghatge, S. K., & Parasar, A. (2023). Application of Artificial Intelligence (AI), Internet of Things (IoT), and Big Data in Healthcare, Finance, and Transportation. *PriMera Scientific Medicine and Public Health*, *2*, 27–36.

Gnewuch, U., Morana, S., Adam, M., & Maedche, A. (2018). Faster is not always better: understanding the effect of dynamic response delays in human-chatbot interaction.

Gonzalez-Aguirre, J. A., Osorio-Oliveros, R., Rodríguez-Hernández, K. L., Lizárraga-Iturralde, J., Morales Menendez, R., Ramirez-Mendoza, R. A., & Lozoya-Santos, J. D. J. (2021). Service robots: Trends and technology. *Applied Sciences (Basel, Switzerland)*, *11*(22), 10702.

Grudin, J., & Jacques, R. (2019, May). Chatbots, humbots, and the quest for artificial general intelligence. In *Proceedings of the 2019 CHI conference on human factors in computing systems* (pp. 1-11).

Haleem, A., Javaid, M., Qadri, M. A., Singh, R. P., & Suman, R. (2022). Artificial intelligence (AI) applications for marketing: A literature-based study. *International Journal of Intelligent Networks*, *3*, 119–132.

Hill, J., Ford, W. R., & Farreras, I. G. (2015). Real conversations with artificial intelligence: A comparison between human–human online conversations and human–chatbot conversations. *Computers in Human Behavior*, *49*, 245–250.

Hsiao, K. L., & Chen, C. C. (2022). What drives continuance intention to use a food-ordering chatbot? An examination of trust and satisfaction. *Library Hi Tech*, *40*(4), 929–946.

Hsu, C. L., & Lin, J. C. C. (2023). Understanding the user satisfaction and loyalty of customer service chatbots. *Journal of Retailing and Consumer Services*, *71*, 103211.

Huang, M. H., & Rust, R. T. (2021). A strategic framework for artificial intelligence in marketing. *Journal of the Academy of Marketing Science*, *49*(1), 30–50.

Hussain, S., Ameri Sianaki, O., & Ababneh, N. (2019). A survey on conversational agents/chatbots classification and design techniques. In Web, Artificial Intelligence and Network Applications: Proceedings of the Workshops of the 33rd International Conference on Advanced Information Networking and Applications (WAINA-2019) 33 (pp. 946-956). Springer International Publishing.

Iansiti, M., & Lakhani, K. R. (2020). *Competing in the age of AI: Strategy and leadership when algorithms and networks run the world*. Harvard Business Press.

Izadi, S., & Forouzanfar, M. (2024). Error Correction and Adaptation in Conversational AI: A Review of Techniques and Applications in Chatbots. *AI*, *5*(2), 803–841.

Jarek, K., & Mazurek, G. (2019). Marketing and artificial intelligence. Central European Business Review, 8(2).

Kalusivalingam, A. K., Sharma, A., Patel, N., & Singh, V. (2020). Enhancing Customer Service Automation with Natural Language Processing and Reinforcement Learning Algorithms. *International Journal of Artificial Intelligence and Machine Learning*, *1*(2).

Kaur, P. (2024). Enhancing Customer Service Efficiency: Automating Responses to Customer Queries using Natural Language Processing and Radial Basis Function Neural Network (RBFNN). *Nanotechnology Perceptions*, •••, 797–818.

Khennouche, F., Elmir, Y., Himeur, Y., Djebari, N., & Amira, A. (2024). Revolutionizing generative pre-traineds: Insights and challenges in deploying ChatGPT and generative chatbots for FAQs. *Expert Systems with Applications*, *246*, 123224.

Klaus, P., & Zaichkowsky, J. (2020). AI voice bots: A services marketing research agenda. *Journal of Services Marketing*, *34*(3), 389–398.

Koulouri, T., Macredie, R. D., & Olakitan, D. (2022). Chatbots to Support Young Adults' Mental Health: An Exploratory Study of Acceptability. [TiiS]. *ACM Transactions on Interactive Intelligent Systems*, *12*(2), 1–39.

Kozinets, R. V., & Gretzel, U. (2021). Commentary: Artificial intelligence: The marketer's dilemma. *Journal of Marketing*, *85*(1), 156–159.

Leahy, W., & Sweller, J. (2011). Cognitive load theory, modality of presentation and the transient information effect. *Applied Cognitive Psychology*, *25*(6), 943–951.

Lee, Q. (2022). Value-sensitive Evaluation of Hybrid Human-AI Chatbots in Customer Services.

Lemon, K. N., & Verhoef, P. C. (2016). Understanding customer experience throughout the customer journey. *Journal of Marketing*, *80*(6), 69–96.

Leocádio, D., Guedes, L., Oliveira, J., Reis, J., & Melão, N. (2024). Customer service with AI-powered human-robot collaboration (HRC): A literature review. *Procedia Computer Science*, *232*, 1222–1232.

Liu-Thompkins, Y., Okazaki, S., & Li, H. (2022). Artificial empathy in marketing interactions: Bridging the human-AI gap in affective and social customer experience. *Journal of the Academy of Marketing Science*, *50*(6), 1198–1218.

Luo, X., Tong, S., Fang, Z., & Qu, Z. (2019). Frontiers: Machines vs. humans: The impact of artificial intelligence chatbot disclosure on customer purchases. *Marketing Science*, *38*(6), 937–947.

Mariani, M. M., Perez-Vega, R., & Wirtz, J. (2022). AI in marketing, consumer research and psychology: A systematic literature review and research agenda. *Psychology and Marketing*, *39*(4), 755–776.

Martijn, G., Van Hooijdonk, C., Kunneman, F., & Hoeken, H. (2024). Reconfiguring the Customer Service Domain: Perspectives of Managers, Conversational Designers, and Human Agents on Human–Chatbot Collaboration. International Journal of Innovation and Technology Management, 2450028.

McCarthy, J., Minsky, M. L., Rochester, N., & Shannon, C. E. (2006). A proposal for the dartmouth summer research project on artificial intelligence, august 31, 1955. *AI Magazine*, *27*(4), 12–12.

McTear, M. (2022). *Conversational ai: Dialogue systems, conversational agents, and chatbots*. Springer Nature.

Micheaux, A., & Bosio, B. (2019). Customer journey mapping as a new way to teach data-driven marketing as a service. *Journal of Marketing Education*, *41*(2), 127–140.

Murtarelli, G., Gregory, A., & Romenti, S. (2021). A conversation-based perspective for shaping ethical human–machine interactions: The particular challenge of chatbots. *Journal of Business Research*, *129*, 927–935.

Ngai, E. W., Lee, M. C., Luo, M., Chan, P. S., & Liang, T. (2021). An intelligent knowledge-based chatbot for customer service. *Electronic Commerce Research and Applications*, *50*, 101098.

Nicolescu, L., & Tudorache, M. T. (2022). Human-computer interaction in customer service: The experience with AI chatbots—a systematic literature review. *Electronics (Basel)*, *11*(10), 1579.

Norvig, P., & Russell, S. J. (2010). Intelligenza artificiale. Un approccio moderno.

Nuruzzaman, M., & Hussain, O. K. (2018, October). A survey on chatbot implementation in customer service industry through deep neural networks. In 2018 IEEE 15th international conference on e-business engineering (ICEBE) (pp. 54-61). IEEE.

Olujimi, P. A., & Ade-Ibijola, A. (2023). NLP techniques for automating responses to customer queries: A systematic review. *Discover Artificial Intelligence*, *3*(1), 20.

Paramarta, V., & Aripin, Z. (2024, January). Optimizing Human-Ai Interaction: Artificial Empathy Strategies In Enhancing Affective And Social Customer Experiences. In Journal Of Jabar Economic Society Networking Forum (Vol. 1, No. 2, Pp. 46-62).

Piris, Y., & Gay, A. C. (2021). Customer satisfaction and natural language processing. *Journal of Business Research, 124*, 264–271.

Rana, J., Jain, R., & Nehra, V. (2024). Utility and acceptability of AI-enabled chatbots on the online customer journey. *International Journal of Computing and Digital Systems*, *15*(1), 323–335.

Reis, J. (2024). Customer service through AI-Powered human-robot relationships: Where are we now? The case of Henn na cafe, Japan. *Technology in Society*, *77*, 102570.

Ruan, Y., & Mezei, J. (2022). When do AI chatbots lead to higher customer satisfaction than human frontline employees in online shopping assistance? Considering product attribute type. *Journal of Retailing and Consumer Services*, *68*, 103059.

Saxena, V., & Gautam, A. (2022). Can AI replace Human? A Study on Customer Perception and Attitude towards AI-Based Chatbot in Food Service.

Schanke, S., Burtch, G., & Ray, G. (2021). Estimating the impact of "humanizing" customer service chatbots. *Information Systems Research*, *32*(3), 736–751.

Shaheen, M. Y. (2021). Applications of Artificial Intelligence (AI) in healthcare: A review. ScienceOpen *Preprints*.

Singh, G., & Singh, J. (2023). Enhancing Customer Experience and Engagement on E-Commerce Platforms Through Ai-Integrated Chatbot Solutions. Available at *SSRN* 4483813.

Stoilova, E. (2021). AI chatbots as a customer service and support tool. ROBONOMICS. *The Journal of the Automated Economy*, *2*, 21–21.

Suhaili, S. M., Salim, N., & Jambli, M. N. (2021). Service chatbots: A systematic review. *Expert Systems with Applications*, *184*, 115461.

Sweller, J. (1988). Cognitive load during problem solving: Effects on learning. *Cognitive Science*, *12*(2), 257–285. DOI: 10.1207/s15516709cog1202_4

Taherdoost, H., & Madanchian, M. (2023). Artificial intelligence and sentiment analysis: A review in competitive research. *Computers*, *12*(2), 37.

Tian, Y. (2020). Artificial intelligence image recognition method based on convolutional neural network algorithm. *IEEE Access : Practical Innovations, Open Solutions*, *8*, 125731–125744.

Tulshan, A. S., & Dhage, S. N. (2019). Survey on virtual assistant: Google assistant, siri, cortana, alexa. In Advances in Signal Processing and Intelligent Recognition Systems: 4th International Symposium SIRS 2018, Bangalore, India, September 19–22, 2018, Revised Selected Papers 4 (pp. 190-201). Springer Singapore.

Van den Broeck, E., Zarouali, B., & Poels, K. (2019). Chatbot advertising effectiveness: When does the message get through? *Computers in Human Behavior*, *98*, 150–157.

Wamba-Taguimdje, S. L., Fosso Wamba, S., Kala Kamdjoug, J. R., & Tchatchouang Wanko, C. E. (2020). Influence of artificial intelligence (AI) on firm performance: The business value of AI-based transformation projects. *Business Process Management Journal*, *26*(7), 1893–1924.

Wiethof, C., & Bittner, E. A. (2022). Toward a hybrid intelligence system in customer service: collaborative learning of human and AI.

Wu, X., Li, S., Guo, Y., & Fang, S. (2024). Human or AI robot? Who is fairer on the service organizational frontline. *Journal of Business Research*, *181*, 114730.

Xu, Y., Shieh, C. H., van Esch, P., & Ling, I. L. (2020). AI customer service: Task complexity, problem-solving ability, and usage intention. *Australasian Marketing Journal*, *28*(4), 189–199.

Yuan, Z., Inoue, S., & Hoshino, J. (2023, June). Remote Customer Service Support System With Automatic Response AI And Human Switching. In 2023 Nicograph International (NicoInt) (pp. 88-88). IEEE.

Zhang, Q., Lu, J., & Jin, Y. (2021). Artificial intelligence in recommender systems. *Complex & Intelligent Systems*, *7*(1), 439–457.

Zhang, Y., Wang, X., & Zhao, X. (2023). Supervising or assisting? The influence of virtual anchor driven by AI–human collaboration on customer engagement in live streaming e-commerce. *Electronic Commerce Research*, •••, 1–24.

APPENDIX

Study 2 Scenarios

Scenario:

You log into your online banking app and want to check your current account balance. The task is straightforward and doesn't require any complex decisions. You have the option to either interact with an AI chatbot that can provide instant information or a human bank representative.

Scenario 2: Medium Complexity

Scenario:

You want to open an additional USD account at your bank. The process involves several steps, including completing forms, understanding account features, and confirming requirements. You can choose to interact with an AI chatbot that provides step-by-step guidance or a human representative who can explain the process personally and answer follow-up questions.

Scenario 3: High Complexity / Sensitive Issue

Scenario:

You notice an unexpected error in a recent money transfer, and the transaction may involve a significant amount. Resolving the issue requires understanding the problem, confirming account details, and ensuring the security of your funds. You can choose to interact with an AI chatbot or a human representative who can provide detailed explanations, address your concerns, and ensure the transaction is handled safely.

Chapter 2
Perceived Agency in Portal Ads Impacts on Presence, Flow, and Engagement in the Metaverse

Imen Touati
https://orcid.org/0009-0005-4986-8526
University of Tunis Manar, Tunisia

ABSTRACT

Portal advertisements are emerging as a central immersive format in metaverse platforms such as Roblox, yet little is known about how users' entry conditions into branded virtual spaces shape their psychological experience and engagement. Drawing on the Stimulus–Organism–Response (SOR) framework, this study examines how forced versus voluntary entry into a branded world influences telepresence, flow, and engagement intention, and whether perceived agency conditions these effects. A between-subjects online experiment (N = 203) exposed participants to a Vans portal ad in which they were either automatically teleported into the branded world (forced condition) or allowed to choose whether to enter (voluntary condition). Participants then reported telepresence, flow, perceived choice, and engagement intention. PROCESS Model 7 was used to test a moderated serial mediation model.

DOI: 10.4018/979-8-3373-6450-6.ch002

INTRODUCTION

The metaverse is transforming how brands connect and interact with consumers. Platforms such as Roblox, Fortnite, and Zepeto have evolved into immersive social and commercial environments, particularly popular among Generation Z and Generation Alpha. These platforms enable brands to move beyond traditional digital advertising formats and embed themselves directly within experiential, game-like environments where users interact through avatars, narratives, and spatial exploration. As reported by Gen X Media (2024), Roblox alone attracts over 70 million daily active users, predominantly younger audiences, making it a critical site for emerging advertising practices.

In response to these shifts, metaverse platforms have introduced new immersive advertising formats. In 2022, Roblox launched 3D portal advertisements that instantly transport users into fully branded virtual worlds. Unlike banners or in-game billboards, portal ads function as spatial gateways: by entering a portal, users cross a boundary from a neutral environment into a brand-controlled space where narrative, interactivity, and sensory design are tightly orchestrated. From an industry perspective, portal ads are increasingly deployed as traffic-generation and engagement mechanisms, yet their psychological effects remain poorly understood.

Despite growing commercial adoption, academic research on portal ads has lagged behind practice. Existing immersive advertising research has largely focused on in-world experiences, emphasizing sustained interaction, presence, and flow as key mechanisms driving persuasion. However, portal ads introduce a distinct moment in the user journey: the transition itself. Prior work in virtual reality and immersive UX design suggests that system-driven movements such as teleportation, automatic scene changes, or constrained navigation can alter users' sense of control, orientation, and emotional engagement (Bowman et al., 1999; Rihs et al., 2024). These insights have not yet been systematically applied to metaverse advertising contexts, where entry mechanics may function not merely as navigation tools, but as persuasive cues in their own right.

Importantly, portal ads vary in how users enter branded spaces. Some portals invite users to choose whether to enter, reinforcing autonomy and perceived control, whereas others automatically teleport users, reducing choice but potentially increasing immediacy, surprise, and narrative momentum. Whether forced versus voluntary entry produces stronger engagement and through which psychological mechanisms remains an open empirical question. Understanding this distinction is particularly important on youth-dominated platforms such as Roblox, where issues of autonomy, persuasion, and ethical exposure are increasingly salient.

This chapter examines portal-entry transitions as brief but potentially powerful persuasive moments in metaverse advertising. Drawing on the Stimulus–Organism–

Response (SOR) framework and flow theory, we investigate how forced versus voluntary entry into a branded portal influences telepresence, flow, and engagement intention, and whether perceived agency conditions these effects. Using a controlled online experiment (N = 203) featuring a branded Vans portal ad on Roblox, we test a moderated serial mediation model. By focusing on entry mechanics rather than prolonged interaction, this study contributes to immersive advertising research by repositioning portal transitions as psychological stimuli that may directly shape engagement, even in the absence of deep immersive states.

1. LITERATURE REVIEW

1.1. Advertising in the Metaverse

According to the definition of Ritterbusch & Teichmann (2023),"*Metaverse, a crossword of ''meta'' (meaning transcendency) and ''universe'', describes a (de-centralized) three-dimensional online environment that is persistent and immersive, in which users represented by avatars can participate socially and economically with each other in a creative and collaborative manner in virtual spaces decoupled from the real physical world*". It provides persistent, interactive, and identity-driven environments where specially specially Gen Z users engage with brands through avatars and social interactions. Popular platforms like Fortnite, Roblox, The Sandbox, Minecraft, and Decentraland illustrate the concept of the metaverse. Players can get virtual goods such as clothing, land, and accessories using in-game currencies like Robux or V-Bucks, which are purchased with real money.

The metaverse differs from earlier digital platforms by offering persistent identity continuity and real-time personification. Instead of using a static account profile, users construct avatar identities that represent, extend, or transform their sense of self (Vasalou & Joinson, 2009). These avatars navigate shared 3D environments, participate in social interactions, attend events, engage in gameplay, and transact using digital currencies, from platform-specific tokens like Robux or V-Bucks to blockchain-based currencies such as MANA or SAND. For younger generations, particularly Generation Z, the metaverse functions as a social arena where identity work, entertainment, and economic participation converge (Valkenburg et al., 2022).

Figure 1. Key components of the metaverse ecosystem

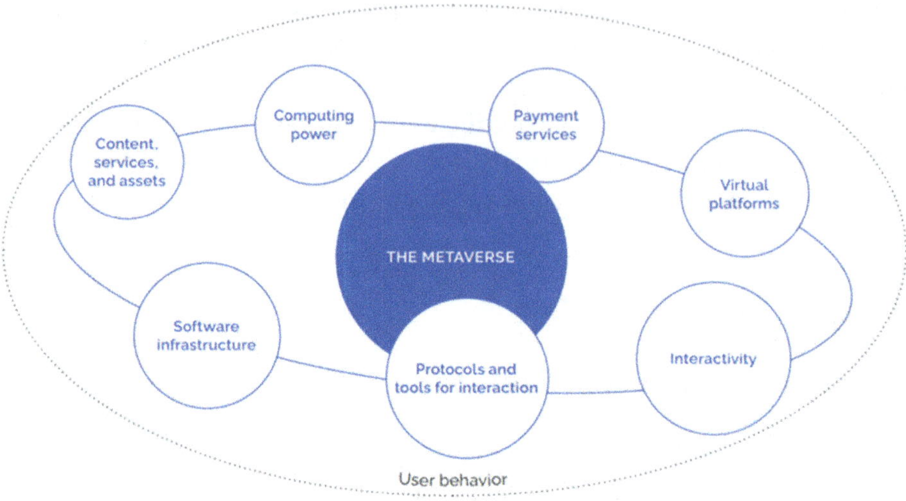

The structure illustrated in Figure 1 mirrors Matthew Ball's (2022) widely cited framework describing the metaverse as an interconnected system of technological, economic, and experiential layers. Ball emphasizes that advances in computing power and distributed infrastructure are prerequisites for building persistent, high-fidelity virtual worlds conditions that also underpin immersive advertising formats such as portal ads. This technological foundation aligns with insights from the *Experience Economy Within the Framework of Virtual Worlds* report Elmira, S. (2025), which argues that virtual environments increasingly operate as experience-driven economies, where value is created through interaction, immersion, and co-presence rather than traditional digital content alone. The diagram's inclusion of payment systems, software infrastructure, protocols, virtual platforms, and content ecosystems reflects the same layered architecture described by both Ball (2022) and Elmira, S. (2025) report. Together, these perspectives reinforce the idea that the metaverse is not merely a technological platform but a complex experiential ecosystem and that advertising within it must account for technological capabilities, economic mechanisms, and user experience design simultaneously.

Given this shift toward embodied interaction, advertising within the metaverse has undergone a parallel evolution. Traditional online advertising; display banners, videos, and static placements, fails to leverage the spatial, experiential qualities of virtual worlds. Consequently, advertisers have begun to adopt immersive advertising formats, including interactive storefronts, branded minigames, virtual concerts, and participatory brand experiences.

As shown in figure 2, Roblox represents one of the most mature and commercially relevant centralized metaverse ecosystems with 111.8 million daily active users (DAU) in the second quarter of 2025. It's a combination of high user engagement, user-generated content, and integrated advertising tools makes it a critical setting for examining how immersive ad formats shape user experience and behavior.

Figure 2. Daily active users (DAU) of Roblox games worldwide from 4th quarter 2018 to 2nd quarter 2025(in millions)

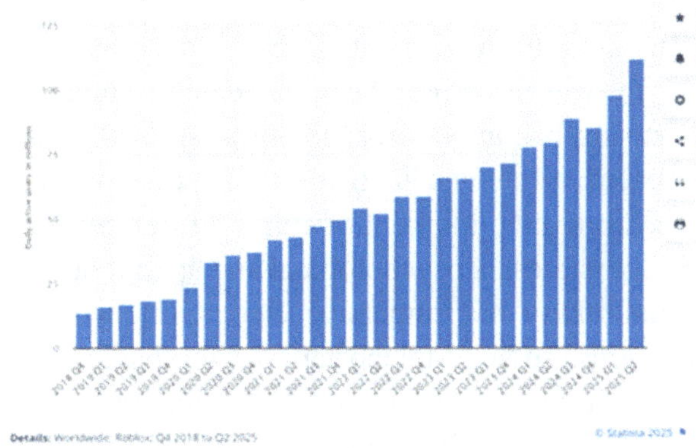

Among lot of emerging formats, portal ads have gained particular prominence. These ads are designed as spatial gateways; walk-through or proximity-activated portals that transport users from one area of the world into a fully designed branded environment. Roblox (2023) defines portal ads as immersive objects that "*teleport users into brand experiences*," enabling advertisers to create entire worlds rather than merely ad impressions. The logic behind this innovation rests on a simple premise: if users willingly (or involuntarily) step into a portal, they are immediately placed inside an environment where the advertiser controls narrative, interactivity, sensory design, and engagement structure.

Despite their increasing use, research on portal ads remains rare. Sands, Ferraro, Demsar, Cohen, and Gvirtz (2024) provide a comprehensive review of immersive advertising, defined as brand communication that leverages augmented reality (AR), virtual reality (VR), and mixed-reality (MR) environments to enable embodied and interactive experiences. They outline how immersive ads shift from passive exposures to experiential portals, enabling consumers to engage with brands in 3-D spatial contexts, manipulate virtual objects, and navigate branded worlds. Their research synthesizes findings from over studies and identifies four key effects: enhanced presence, sensory engagement, behavioral activation, and heightened brand memory, and highlights critical moderating (user agency, narrative coherence) and mediating (flow states) variables. Importantly, they caution that design choices (teleportation vs voluntary entry, sensory realism, user control) profoundly influence outcomes, and call for future research on boundary conditions, including perceived autonomy and immersive transitions. This review underscores the relevance of our model, which manipulates entry mode (choice vs forced teleportation), examines telepresence and flow, and incorporates perceived agency as a moderator within immersive brand environments.

1.2 Portal Ads

Portal advertisements introduce a critical but under-theorized moment in immersive advertising: the transition into the branded environment. Existing research on immersive advertising has largely focused on sustained in-world experiences, emphasizing how presence, flow, and interactivity shape persuasion over time. Portal ads, by contrast, foreground the moment of entry; a brief but potentially powerful phase during which users cross a psychological and spatial boundary.

Research in virtual reality and immersive user experience design suggests that system-driven transitions, such as teleportation, automated movement, or scene switching; can meaningfully influence attention, orientation, and affective response (Bowman, Koller, & Hodges, 1999; Rihs et al., 2024). Transitions require users to rapidly reorient themselves within a new environment, often under conditions of reduced control or heightened sensory input. As a result, entry mechanics may shape users' readiness to engage even before stable immersive states are established.

A defining feature of portal ads is the degree of user autonomy involved in entering the branded space. Some portals require users to actively choose whether to enter, reinforcing intentionality and perceived control. Others rely on forced teleportation, automatically transporting users into the branded world. These two approaches reflect distinct persuasive logics. Voluntary entry aligns with autonomy-supportive design principles associated with intrinsic motivation and positive evaluation (Ryan & Deci, 2000). Forced entry, however, prioritizes immediacy and continuity, reducing friction and accelerating exposure to branded content. In immersive environments where automated transitions are common, forced entry may be interpreted as a normative system behavior rather than an intrusive interruption.

This distinction connects portal advertising to broader research on forced exposure and ad intrusiveness. Studies in online video and in-game advertising show that forced exposure can increase attention and recall but may also trigger resistance when perceived as manipulative (Jeong et al., 2021). Importantly, perceptions of intrusiveness are context-dependent. In gameplay and immersive environments, where users expect system-driven movement and guidance, forced transitions may be processed as part of the experience rather than as external persuasion. Portal ads therefore occupy an ambiguous position between navigation and advertising, making their psychological effects theoretically and practically important to examine.

1.3 Telepresence and flow in immersive advertising

1.3.1 Telepresence

Telepresence refers to the subjective experience of "being there" in a mediated environment rather than in one's physical surroundings (Lombard & Ditton, 1997). In immersive systems, telepresence arises when users accept the virtual environment as the primary locus of perception, temporarily overlooking the technological interface (International Society for Presence Research, 2002). Research identifies multiple antecedents of telepresence, including sensory vividness, interactivity, system coherence, and user involvement (Cummings & Bailenson, 2016).

In advertising contexts, telepresence has been associated with greater emotional engagement, more favorable brand attitudes, and improved message processing (Li, Daugherty, & Biocca, 2002; Van Kerrebroeck et al., 2017). In metaverse environments, presence is particularly salient because users do not merely observe branded content but inhabit a brand-representative world. However, telepresence typically develops through sustained interaction and environmental exploration, raising questions about whether brief entry transitions alone are sufficient to alter presence perceptions.

1.3.2 Flow

Flow describes a state of deep experiential absorption characterized by intense focus, intrinsic enjoyment, and altered perception of time (Csikszentmihalyi, 1990). In digital environments, flow emerges when system challenges are well matched to user skills and when interaction is continuous and responsive (Hoffman & Novak, 2009). Flow has been linked to positive attitudes, repeat engagement, and stronger persuasion in interactive media and gaming contexts (Novak et al., 2000; Skadberg & Kimmel, 2004).

Prior research often positions telepresence as an antecedent of flow, arguing that users must first feel "present" before becoming deeply absorbed (Makransky & Petersen, 2021). However, flow is fundamentally interaction-dependent. In contexts where users passively observe rather than actively interact, the conditions necessary for sustained flow may be weakened. This distinction is particularly relevant for portal ads, where the transition phase may precede meaningful interaction with the branded environment.

1.4 Perceived agency and entry-level autonomy

Perceived agency refers to the subjective sense of initiating and controlling one's actions and their consequences within an environment (Tsakiris et al., 2007). In immersive systems, agency is multidimensional, encompassing perceived choice, control, competence, and predictability. Higher perceived agency has been shown to enhance engagement, identification, and enjoyment in virtual environments (Fox et al., 2014).

In the context of portal ads, agency is most salient at the moment of entry. Voluntary entry reinforces perceived choice and autonomy, whereas forced teleportation reduces explicit decision-making. Autonomy-supportive design is generally associated with positive user responses and lower resistance to persuasion (Ryan & Deci, 2000; Sundar & Marathe, 2010). At the same time, reduced agency during transitions may simplify cognitive processing and facilitate smoother experiential progression, particularly for users who feel less confident navigating complex environments.

Importantly, agency at entry should be distinguished from agency within the branded world itself. While in-world control may influence long-term engagement and immersion, entry-level agency shapes users' initial interpretation of the experience. This distinction is central to understanding how portal-entry mechanics influence downstream psychological responses.

1.5 The Stimulus-Organism-Response framework

The Stimulus–Organism–Response (SOR) framework conceptualizes how environmental cues (stimuli) influence internal states (organism), which in turn shape behavioral outcomes (responses) (Mehrabian & Russell, 1974). In immersive advertising research, SOR models typically position system features as stimuli, telepresence and flow as organismic states, and engagement or attitude as responses (Huang & Liao, 2017).

While SOR has proven useful for explaining sustained immersive experiences, its application to portal-based advertising raises new questions. Portal-entry transitions are brief, system-driven, and often non-interactive, suggesting that their influence may not rely entirely on deep organismic processing. Instead, entry mechanics may function as pre-experiential stimuli that shape engagement readiness, curiosity, or behavioral orientation at the moment of transition.

This perspective suggests the possibility of a quasi-direct pathway from stimulus to response, in which portal-entry mechanics influence engagement intention without fully activating telepresence or flow. Such an extension does not invalidate the SOR framework but highlights the need to account for transitional and movement-based stimuli that are unique to immersive environments. Understanding how these mechanisms operate is particularly important in youth-dominated platforms, where ethical considerations surrounding autonomy, transparency, and persuasive exposure are increasingly salient.

2. CONCEPTUAL MODEL AND HYPOTHESES

2.1 Conceptual framework

Drawing on the Stimulus–Organism–Response (SOR) framework, this study conceptualizes portal-entry mechanics as environmental stimuli that shape users' psychological responses and engagement intentions. Unlike prior immersive advertising research that emphasizes sustained interaction within branded environments, the present framework focuses on entry-level transitions as a distinct and theoretically meaningful phase of the user journey.

Portal ads differ in the degree of agency they afford at the moment of entry. Voluntary entry allows users to decide whether to cross into a branded world, whereas forced teleportation removes this decision and automatically relocates users. These contrasting entry conditions are expected to influence users' experiential states—particularly telepresence and flow—while also potentially exerting a direct influence on engagement intention.

Perceived agency is modeled as a conditional factor that shapes how entry mechanics are experienced. In line with prior research, perceived choice is expected to moderate experiential responses to immersive stimuli, particularly during moments of system-driven movement and transition. Figure 2 presents the conceptual model guiding this research.

Figure 3. Conceptual model

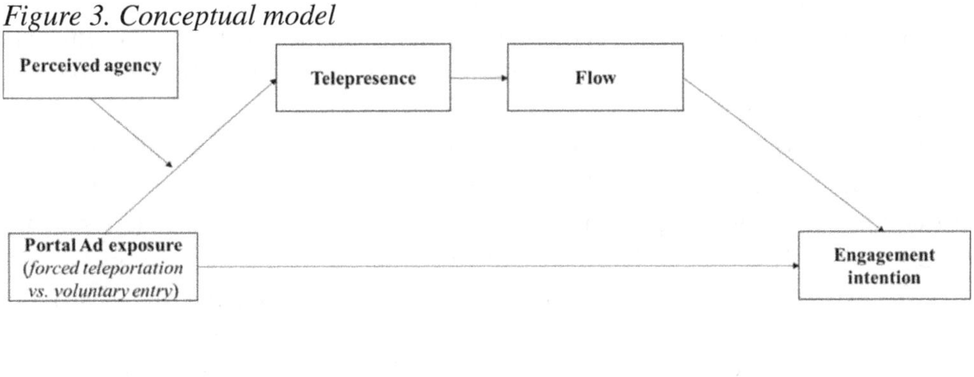

2.2 Portal Entry and Telepresence

Research on immersive environments and virtual locomotion indicates that the mechanics through which users transition into a virtual space play a central role in shaping their perceptual and cognitive experience. Early work on virtual navigation demonstrates that movement techniques influence spatial orientation, attentional allocation, and users' perceived continuity between physical and virtual contexts (Bowman et al., 1999).

System-driven movements such as teleportation are theorized to influence attentional allocation and experiential continuity by reducing the effort required to navigate between virtual spaces. By contrast, voluntary entry mechanisms foreground deliberation and user choice, which may increase perceived control but also introduce a moment of cognitive distance from the immersive experience (Bowman et al., 1999; Hoffman & Novak, 2009; Rihs et al., 2024). Accordingly, the portal-entry condition; whether users are automatically transported into a branded environment or enter by choice, is expected to shape the extent to which the virtual space is experienced as perceptually dominant and psychologically "real." This leads to the following hypothesis:

> **H1:** Portal-entry condition (forced teleportation vs. voluntary entry) has a significant effect on telepresence.

2.3 Telepresence and Flow

Telepresence is widely conceptualized as a core experiential state in immersive media, referring to the sensation of "being there" in a mediated environment rather than merely observing it. When telepresence is high, users are more likely to suspend awareness of the physical world and treat the virtual space as their primary frame of reference. This perceptual shift is particularly relevant in interactive environments, where sustained attention and experiential continuity are prerequisites for deeper psychological engagement.

Building on flow theory, prior research suggests that telepresence may function as an enabling condition for flow by facilitating focused attention, reducing external distractions, and supporting seamless interaction with the environment (Csikszentmihalyi, 1990; Hoffman & Novak, 2009). In branded metaverse settings, where users are exposed to both experiential and persuasive stimuli, telepresence may help users transition from surface-level exploration to deeper absorption in the activity. As users increasingly accept the virtual space as their primary locus of experience, the likelihood of entering a flow state is expected to increase.

Based on this reasoning, telepresence is anticipated to play a positive role in fostering flow within branded metaverse environments.

H2: Telepresence is positively associated with flow in branded metaverse environments.

2.4 Flow and Engagement Intention

Flow is characterized by deep concentration, intrinsic enjoyment, and a sense of effortless involvement in an activity (Csikszentmihalyi, 1990). In digital and interactive contexts, flow has been consistently associated with favorable experiential outcomes, including positive affect, sustained attention, and approach-oriented behavioral intentions (Hoffman & Novak, 2009; Novak, Hoffman, & Yung, 2000). When users experience flow, they are less likely to disengage from the activity and more likely to maintain prolonged interaction with the digital environment (Sherry, 2004).

In the context of immersive advertising, flow is particularly relevant because it aligns experiential absorption with brand-related exploration. As users become deeply involved in a branded metaverse experience, they may develop a stronger willingness to interact with branded elements, spend time within the virtual environment, and revisit the experience in the future. Prior research in interactive and experiential marketing suggests that flow facilitates exploratory behaviors and enhances engagement with branded digital content by reinforcing intrinsic motivation and experiential value (Hoffman & Novak, 2009; Sicilia, Ruiz, & Munuera, 2005).

Flow thus represents a psychological mechanism through which immersive experiences translate into engagement-oriented responses. Accordingly, higher levels of flow are expected to enhance users' intention to engage with the branded metaverse experience.

H3: Flow is positively associated with engagement intention toward the branded metaverse experience.

2.5 Perceived Agency as a Moderator

Perceived agency refers to users' subjective sense that their actions are self-directed and under their control (Bandura, 1989; Deci & Ryan, 2000). In immersive environments, agency is not solely determined by interactive affordances but also by how system-level processes, such as movement, navigation, and transitions, are designed and experienced. Prior research in virtual environments suggests that autonomy-related perceptions play a central role in shaping users' interpretations of mediated experiences, particularly when control is shared or partially delegated to the system (Biocca, 1997; Slater, 2003).

At the point of entry into a branded metaverse environment, perceived agency may therefore condition how portal-entry mechanics are experienced. Users who perceive a high degree of agency may interpret forced teleportation as seamless or facilitative, rather than intrusive, thereby maintaining experiential continuity and immersion. In contrast, when perceived agency is low, system-driven entry may be more likely to disrupt users' sense of control, potentially weakening telepresence or limiting the emergence of flow. Research on presence and virtual embodiment supports the idea that discrepancies between expected and enacted control can alter users' perceptual and affective responses within immersive environments (Biocca, Harms, & Burgoon, 2003; Slater, 2003).

For these reasons, perceived agency is expected to moderate the relationship between portal-entry condition and key experiential outcomes, namely telepresence and flow.

> **H4:** Perceived agency moderates the effect of portal-entry condition on telepresence and flow.

3. METHODOLOGY

3.1. Study Design, Participants and Procedure

The study used an experimental design with two exposure conditions manipulating how participants entered a branded portal advertisement. The branded content featured Vans, a well-known apparel brand commonly present in metaverse activations. Participants were randomly assigned to one of two conditions: (see appendix 1 and 2)

1. *Forced teleportation condition*, in which users were automatically transported into the Vans brand world.
2. *Voluntary entry condition,* in which users were invited to choose whether to enter the Vans portal.

This design isolates the effect of entry mechanism while keeping the brand, content, and environment identical across conditions.

A total of 203 participants completed the study. All participants are Roblox players, ensuring that the manipulation was meaningful. Respondents were recruited online and voluntarily agreed to participate.

Participants were informed that they would watch a short metaverse-based advertisement and answer a questionnaire about their experience. After providing consent, they were randomly assigned to one of the two experimental conditions.

All participants viewed a video simulation of a Roblox-style portal advertisement for Vans. The two groups differed only in the entry transition:

3.2. Stimulus Materials

The experimental stimuli consisted of short video recordings depicting a portal-based entry into a branded virtual environment on the Roblox platform. The use of video stimuli was a deliberate methodological choice designed to ensure experimental control over the manipulated stimulus while isolating the causal effect of portal-entry condition on subsequent psychological responses, in line with recommendations for experimental designs testing mediation and moderation processes (Hayes, 2018).

Each video captured an avatar navigating within a Roblox environment and encountering a portal leading to the Vans branded world. Two versions of the stimulus were created to operationalize the independent variable (portal-entry condition): (1) an automatic teleportation condition, in which the avatar was immediately transported into the branded environment upon approaching the portal, and (2) a voluntary entry condition, in which the avatar was presented with a clear choice to enter the branded world or remain in the current environment. This manipulation was intended to induce variation in perceived choice, which serves as the focal dimension of perceived agency examined in the moderation analyses.

Video-based stimuli are widely used in immersive media and advertising research when the goal is to test causal relationships between controlled environmental cues and psychological outcomes, particularly in models involving indirect and conditional effects. In the present study, video recordings enabled the researchers to hold constant all aspects of the branded experience except the manipulated entry mechanism. Visual perspective, movement trajectory, environmental design, narrative context, and exposure duration were identical across conditions. This design ensured that any observed differences in outcomes could be attributed to the entry manipulation, rather than to uncontrolled variation in interaction behavior or gameplay performance.

Importantly, both experimental conditions featured identical in-world branded content following the entry transition. As such, telepresence and flow were modeled as organismic responses potentially affected by the entry condition, rather than as outcomes of differential in-world experiences. This alignment is critical for PROCESS-based mediation analysis, as it preserves the assumed causal ordering from stimulus (portal-entry condition) to organismic states (telepresence and flow) and subsequently to response (engagement intention).

The videos were recorded directly from the Roblox platform using authentic in-platform environments and assets. This approach preserved platform-specific interface elements, visual aesthetics, and interaction conventions, thereby enhancing ecological validity while maintaining internal validity. Participants viewed the stimuli from a third-person perspective, which allowed them to evaluate the portal-entry mechanism and anticipate the branded experience, even in the absence of direct interaction.

While fully interactive designs are often preferable for studying constructs such as flow, the present study focuses on entry-level and transitional stimuli, where the key theoretical interest lies in users' interpretation of system-driven movement and perceived choice at the point of entry. Video stimuli are particularly well suited for capturing these early-stage cognitive and affective responses, which precede extended interaction and skill-based engagement. Consistent with PROCESS logic, this approach allows for the examination of conditional effects of the entry manipulation on experiential states without conflating the manipulation with downstream behavioral variability.

Participants were randomly assigned to one of the two experimental conditions and instructed to watch the video attentively before completing the questionnaire. Random assignment supports causal inference regarding the effect of the portal-entry condition, while the standardized stimulus presentation enhances the reliability of estimated direct and indirect effects.

3.3. Measures

Telepresence was measured using four items adapted from Novak et al. (2000), capturing the extent to which participants felt perceptually immersed in the virtual environment. Participants indicated their agreement (1 = strongly disagree, 5 = strongly agree) with statements such as *"I forget about my immediate surroundings when I play the game"* and *"Playing the game makes me forget where I am."* The four items demonstrated good internal consistency (Cronbach's $\alpha = .87$). The mean of these items was computed so that higher scores reflect stronger feelings of "being there" in the virtual environment ($M = 3.49$, $SD = 0.87$).

Flow was assessed using three items adapted from Novak et al. (2000), representing the extent to which participants experienced deep absorption and effortless involvement during the task. Participants rated their agreement (1 = strongly disagree, 5 = strongly agree) with items such as *"Most of the time I play this game, I feel I am in a state of flow."* The scale showed acceptable reliability (Cronbach's $\alpha = .76$). A composite mean score was calculated, with higher values indicating greater experiential immersion ($M = 3.39$, $SD = 0.92$).

Engagement intention toward the Vans brand world was measured with three items adapted from Vivek et al. (2012) and Calder et al. (2009). Participants indicated agreement (1 = strongly disagree, 5 = strongly agree) with statements such as *"I intend to explore the branded space further"* and *"I would recommend this branded space to others."* The items formed a reliable scale (Cronbach's $\alpha = .90$). The mean of these items was used as the indicator of engagement intention (M = 3.38, SD = 1.00).

Perceived agency; is multidimensional variable (perceived control, perceived choice and perceived forcedness). Perceived control ($\alpha = .76$) and perceived forcedness (reverse-coded; $\alpha = .90$) were measured, but reliability analysis revealed that combining all nine items into a single agency scale resulted in extremely low reliability ($\alpha = .07$), confirming multidimensionality.

Given that the experimental manipulation specifically varied choice (forced vs. voluntary entry), and that the perceived choice subscale showed strong conceptual and statistical alignment, Perceived choice was used as the moderator in the PROCESS Model 7 analysis.

Perceived choice was measured using three items adapted from autonomy and self-determination literature (Deci & Ryan, 1985), such as *"I decided whether to enter the branded space"* and *"It was up to me to engage with the brand area."* Participants rated their agreement on a 5-point scale (1 = strongly disagree, 5 = strongly agree). The scale showed good internal consistency (Cronbach's $\alpha = .80$). Higher mean scores indicate stronger perceived autonomy over entering the Vans portal (M = 3.53, SD = 0.92).

Table 1. Measurement scales used in the study

Construct	Items	Scale	Reliability	Descriptive statistics	References
Telepresence	*"I forget about my immediate surroundings when I play the game"; "Playing the game makes me forget where I am"; "After playing the game, I feel like I come back to the "real world" after a journey"; "Playing the game creates a new world for me, and this world suddenly disappears when I stop playing"*	1 = strongly disagree; 5 = strongly agree	α = **.869**	M = **3.49**, SD = **0.87**	Novak, Hoffman, & Yung (2000)
Flow	*"Most of the time I play this game, I feel I am in a state of flow.";"* In general, how frequently would you say you have experienced "flow" while playing the game?"; "Do you think you have ever experienced "flow" while playing the game? "	1 = strongly disagree; 5 = strongly agree	α = **.764**	M = **3.39**, SD = **0.92**	Novak et al. (2000)
Engagement intention	*"I intend to explore the branded space further"; "I would recommend this branded space to others";* "I plan to *interact with the brand content again in the future.*	1 = strongly disagree; 5 = strongly agree	α = **.899**	M = **3.38**, SD = **1.00**	Calder et al. (2009); Vivek et al. (2012)
Perceived choice (Moderator)	*"I decided whether to enter the branded space"; "It was up to me to engage with the brand area."; "I could freely choose to avoid the brand area."*	1 = strongly disagree; 5 = strongly agree	α = **.804**	M = **3.53**, SD = **0.92**	Deci & Ryan (1985)
Perceived control (not used in PROCESS)	*"I felt in control of entering the* brand area.*"; "Entering the brand area happened the way I wanted."; "I initiated the transition into the brand area."*	1–5 Likert	α = **.764**	*	Ratan & Hasler (2020); Tamborini et al. (2010)
Perceived forcedness (reverse-coded; not used in PROCESS)	*"The* game forced me to enter the brand area."; "I was moved into the brand area without my say."; "It happened automatically."	1–5 Likert	α = **.899**	*	Klimmt & Vorderer (2003)

4. RESULTS

4.1. Manipulation Check

To verify that the experimental manipulation successfully altered participants' sense of choice over entering the Vans portal, we compared perceived choice between the two exposure conditions using an independent-samples *t*-test. As expected, participants in the voluntary-entry condition reported substantially higher perceived choice than those in the forced-teleportation condition. Participants who were allowed to choose whether to enter the Vans world reported notably greater autonomy ($M \approx 4.10$, $SD \approx 0.65$), whereas those who were automatically teleported perceived significantly less choice ($M \approx 2.95$, $SD \approx 0.80$).

This difference was statistically significant, $t(201) \approx 10.50$, $p < .001$, confirming that the manipulation effectively created two distinct levels of perceived choice. These results support the validity of using the Perceived Choice scale as the moderator in the moderated mediation analysis.

4.2. Descriptive Statistics and Correlations

The final sample consisted of N = 203 participants who were randomly assigned to one of two exposure conditions (forced teleportation vs. voluntary entry). Descriptive statistics (scale means and standard deviations) for the model variables were as follows: Telepresence (M = 3.4893, SD = 0.8695), Perceived Choice (M = 3.5255, SD = 0.9161), Flow (M = 3.3924, SD = 0.9173), Engagement Intention (M = 3.3810, SD = 0.9997), and Ad exposure (AdEXP: 0 = choice, 1 = forced; M = 0.50, SD = 0.501). Scale reliabilities were satisfactory for the retained measures (Telepresence α = .869; Flow α = .764; Engagement Intention α = .899; Perceived Choice α = .804). Attempts to combine the three agency subdimensions (choice, control, forcedness) into a single scale produced extremely low reliability (α = .07), which justified using the Perceived Choice subscale as the moderator. (see table1)

All key variables were positively correlated in theoretically expected directions. Exposure condition (0 = voluntary, 1 = forced teleportation) was strongly associated with perceived choice ($r = .67$, $p < .001$) and moderately to strongly associated with telepresence ($r = .53$, $p < .001$), flow ($r = .46$, $p < .001$), and engagement intention ($r = .58$, $p < .001$). Telepresence correlated moderately with engagement intention ($r = .38$, $p < .001$) and weakly with flow ($r = .15$, $p = .032$). Flow was moderately associated with engagement intention ($r = .28$, $p < .001$). These patterns support the theoretical relationships assumed in the moderated serial mediation model. (see table 2)

Table 2. Correlations (N=203)

Variable	1	2	3	4	5
1. Ad exposure	1				
2. Perceived choice	.669**	1			
3. Flow	.459**	.244**	1		
4. Engagement intention	.578**	.317**	.279**	1	
5. Telepresence	.529**	.311**	.151*	.382**	1

Notes. $p < .05$*, p < .01

4.3. Analytical Approach

We tested the conceptual model using Andrew Hayes' PROCESS macro for SPSS (Version 4.2), specifying Model 7 to evaluate a first-smotage moderated serial mediation (exposure → telepresence → flow → engagement intention; moderator = perceived choice on the X → M1 path). All analyses used HC4 robust standard errors, and bootstrap confidence intervals were generated (bootstrap sample size and CI level as produced by PROCESS; output reports 95% CIs). The predictor variable Portal Ad exposure was coded 0 = voluntary entry, 1 = forced teleportation. Mediators were the mean scales MeanT (telepresence) and Meanf (flow), the moderator was Meanpc (perceived choice), and the dependent variable was Meanei (engagement intention). The sample size for all PROCESS analyses was n = 203.

4.3.1 First-Stage Models (X → M1 and X → M2; Moderation Tests)

To explore whether the effects of portal-entry condition on engagement intention operate through experiential states, conditional process analyses were conducted using Hayes' PROCESS macro.

These conditional effects indicate that forced teleportation (vs voluntary entry) increases flow across levels of perceived choice, but the magnitude of this effect decreases as perceived choice increases.

Model Predicting Telepresence (M1)

The model predicting telepresence (MeanT; composite mean score of the telepresence scale) included AdEXP (X), perceived choice (Meanpc; composite mean score of the perceived choice scale) as the moderator (W), and the interaction term AdEXP × Meanpc (Int_1). The model summary indicated good explanatory power for M1: $R = .536$, $R^2 = .287$, $MSE = .522$; $F(HC4) = 26.614$, $p < .001$.

Regression coefficients (HC4 SE):

- Constant = 3.454 (SE = .282), $t = 12.25$, $p < .001$.
- AdEXP= 0.465 (SE = .566), $t = 0.82$, $p = .412$.
- Meanpc = −0.133 (SE = .094), $t = -1.41$, $p = .160$.
- Int_1 (AdEXP× Meanpc) = 0.144 (SE = .152), $t = 0.94$, $p = .347$.

The interaction term for the effect of Ad exposure on telepresence was not statistically significant ($p = .347$), indicating no evidence that perceived choice moderated the effect of exposure condition on telepresence in this model.

Model Predicting Flow (M2)

The model predicting flow ((Meanf; composite mean score of the flow scale) included the same predictors and interaction; model fit: $R = .491$, $R^2 = .241$, MSE $= .648$; F(HC4) $= 23.732$, $p < .001$.

Regression coefficients (HC4 SE):

- Constant = 2.800 (SE = .364), t = 7.69, p < .001.
- AdEXP= 2.472 (SE = .652), t = 3.79, p < .001.
- Meanpc = 0.058 (SE = .124), t = 0.47, p = .637.
- Int_1 (AdEXP× Meanpc) = −0.412 (SE = .182), t = −2.26, p = .025.

The interaction term in the flow model was statistically significant (p = .025), indicating that perceived choice moderates the effect of exposure condition on flow. Conditional effects of the exposure (AdEXP: forced vs. choice) on flow at three representative values of perceived choice (Meanpc) were estimated as follows:

- At Meanpc = 2.609: Effect = 1.397 (SE = .218), t = 6.40, p < .001, 95% CI [.966, 1.828].
- At Meanpc = 3.525: Effect = 1.020 (SE = .151), t = 6.76, p < .001, 95% CI [.722, 1.317].
- At Meanpc = 4.442: Effect = 0.642 (SE = .232), t = 2.77, p = .006, 95% CI [.185, 1.099].

These conditional effects indicate that forced teleportation (vs voluntary entry) increases flow across levels of perceived choice, but the magnitude of this effect decreases as perceived choice increases.

Taken together, the first-stage models indicate that perceived choice functions as a moderating boundary condition rather than as an explanatory mechanism. Specifically, perceived choice does not condition the effect of portal-entry condition on telepresence, but it significantly conditions the effect on flow. This pattern suggests that experiential absorption is sensitive to variations in agency at the point of entry, whereas spatial presence remains comparatively stable across entry conditions. Importantly, perceived choice is treated here as a measured moderator, not as a mediator of the exposure manipulation. The moderation effects therefore reflect conditional experiential responses to portal-entry mechanics rather than indirect causal pathways. This distinction is critical for interpreting the subsequent outcome model, as it clarifies that any influence of perceived agency operates at the level of shaping experiential intensity (flow) rather than transmitting the effect of exposure to engagement intention.

4.3.2. Outcome Model (Y = Engagement Intention)

The final outcome regression predicting engagement intention (Meanei) included AdEXP, MeanT (telepresence), and Meanf (flow). Model summary: R = .585, R^2 = .343, MSE = .667; F(HC4) = 35.502, p < .001.

Regression coefficients (HC4 SE):

- Constant = 2.305 (SE = .307), t = 7.50, p < .001.
- AdEXP(direct effect of exposure) = 1.008 (SE = .151), t = 6.67, p < .001.
- MeanT (telepresence) = 0.129 (SE = .080), t = 1.61, p = .109.
- Meanf (flow) = 0.034 (SE = .064), t = 0.53, p = .599.

The direct effect of exposure (forced teleportation vs voluntary) on engagement intention remained statistically significant and positive (b = 1.008, p < .001) after controlling for telepresence and flow. Neither telepresence nor flow had significant unique direct effects on engagement intention in this outcome equation (p = .109 and p = .599, respectively).

4.3.3 Direct and Indirect Effects

Direct Effect

As reported above, the direct effect of the exposure condition on engagement intention was positive and significant (Effect = 1.008, SE = .151, t = 6.67, p < .001), indicating that participants forced into the Vans world reported higher engagement intention than those who chose to enter, net of the two mediators.

Conditional Indirect Effects (Exposure → Telepresence → Engagement)

PROCESS estimated the conditional indirect effect of exposure on engagement intention via telepresence (MeanT) at three representative levels of the moderator (Meanpc: 2.609, 3.525, 4.442). Bootstrap estimates (Effect, BootSE, 95% BootLLCI, BootULCI):

- Meanpc = 2.609: Effect = .109, BootSE = .069, BootLLCI = −.015, BootULCI = .253.
- Meanpc = 3.525: Effect = .126, BootSE = .079, BootLLCI = −.018, BootULCI = .286.
- Meanpc = 4.442: Effect = .143, BootSE = .095, BootLLCI = −.021, BootULCI = .350.

The 95% bootstrap confidence intervals for these conditional indirect effects include zero, indicating that the indirect effect via telepresence was not statistically significant at conventional levels across the tested values of the moderator.

The index of moderated mediation for the telepresence pathway (i.e., whether the indirect effect via telepresence varies systematically with perceived choice) was estimated as Index = .019 (BootSE = .027), 95% BootLLCI = −.017, BootULCI = .091. Because the CI includes zero, there is no significant evidence of moderated mediation through telepresence.

Conditional Indirect Effects (Exposure → Flow → Engagement)

Indirect effects of exposure through flow (Meanf) were estimated at the same moderator values:

- Meanpc = 2.609: Effect = .047, BootSE = .089, BootLLCI = −.125, BootULCI = .229.
- Meanpc = 3.525: Effect = .034, BootSE = .066, BootLLCI = −.085, BootULCI = .176.
- Meanpc = 4.442: Effect = .022, BootSE = .046, BootLLCI = −.052, BootULCI = .135.

Again, all bootstrap CIs include zero, indicating no statistically significant indirect effect of exposure on engagement via flow alone.

The index of moderated mediation for the flow pathway was Index = −.014 (BootSE = .027), 95% BootLLCI = −.071, BootULCI = .043, also non-significant.

Serial Indirect Effect (Exposure → Telepresence → Flow → Engagement)

The serial indirect effect (Exposure → Telepresence → Flow → Engagement) is summarized in the conditional indirect effects above and in the PROCESS output; however, because the component paths from the mediators to the outcome were not statistically significant in the outcome model, the full serial indirect pathway was not supported by significant bootstrap evidence (bootstrap CIs included zero). The index of moderated serial mediation (reported by PROCESS as the index for the entire serial chain) was not significant (bootstrap CI includes zero), indicating no reliable evidence that the serial indirect effect varies as a function of perceived choice.

4.4. Summary of Findings

The experimental manipulation (forced teleportation vs voluntary entry) had a robust positive direct effect on engagement intention ($b \approx 1.01$, $p < .001$): participants in the forced teleportation condition reported higher engagement intentions toward the Vans brand environment than participants in the voluntary entry condition, controlling for telepresence and flow.

Exposure condition also produced significant effects on flow that were moderated by perceived choice (AdEXP× Meanpc interaction significant in the flow model, $p = .025$). The effect of forced teleportation on flow was strongest when perceived choice was low and diminished as perceived choice increased, although forced teleportation produced higher flow at all three tested values of perceived choice.

By contrast, the X → M1 (telepresence) interaction was not significant. Telepresence was positively related to flow in the mediation chain (see theory and correlation patterns), but the indirect effects of exposure via telepresence, via flow, or via the serial telepresence→flow path on engagement intention were not statistically significant (bootstrap 95% CIs contained zero).

Overall, the PROCESS Model 7 tests indicate that the direct effect of exposure on engagement is strong and consistent, while the hypothesized indirect pathways through the organismic states (telepresence and flow) did not reach statistical significance in the current sample, despite a significant moderation of the exposure → flow link by perceived choice.

Statistically, the strongest and most consistent finding is the direct positive influence of forced teleportation on engagement intention. Although forced teleportation also elevated flow (and this effect was moderated by perceived choice), the mediating role of telepresence and flow in translating exposure into engagement was not supported by significant indirect effects in the present dataset. These results suggest that, in this experimental context, the entry mechanism (forced vs voluntary) exerts a substantial direct influence on users' intentions to engage with a branded metaverse environment; the experiential pathways hypothesized by the SOR model (via telepresence and flow) do not fully account for this effect under these conditions.

These results indicate that while perceived agency conditions experiential responses to portal-entry mechanics, engagement intention is primarily driven by the direct effect of entry condition rather than by moderated mediation pathways.

5. DISCUSSION

The objective of this study was to examine how portal-entry mechanics in metaverse advertising influence users' experiential states and engagement intentions. By comparing forced teleportation and voluntary entry conditions within a Roblox-based branded experience, this research responds to growing scholarly and managerial interest in immersive advertising formats that rely on movement, transition, and system control rather than prolonged interaction alone. In doing so, the chapter extends existing metaverse advertising research by shifting analytical attention from sustained in-world immersion to the psychological consequences of entry-level transitions.

The most robust and theoretically consequential finding of this study is the strong direct effect of forced teleportation on engagement intention. Participants who were automatically transported into the branded world reported significantly higher engagement intentions than those who entered voluntarily. Importantly, this effect persisted even when telepresence and flow were included in the model, indicating that portal-entry mechanics themselves may function as persuasive triggers rather than merely as facilitators of immersive experience.

This finding suggests that forced portal entry may enhance engagement through mechanisms such as immediacy, attentional capture, or narrative momentum. Automatic teleportation eliminates the moment of hesitation associated with choice, thereby accelerating exposure to branded content and reducing cognitive friction at the transition point. From a psychological perspective, forced entry may also signal system endorsement or experiential continuity, leading users to interpret the branded environment as a natural extension of gameplay rather than as an external advertisement. In immersive environments where system-driven movement is common, forced teleportation may thus be perceived less as coercive and more as a normative feature of navigation.

These insights align with research on attention and persuasion in digital environments, which suggests that brief, high-impact stimuli can influence behavioral readiness even in the absence of deep cognitive elaboration. In the context of metaverse advertising, portal-entry transitions appear to function as such stimuli, shaping engagement intentions before users have time to fully process the experience at a reflective level.

Contrary to theoretical expectations, telepresence did not differ significantly across entry conditions and did not mediate the relationship between portal exposure and engagement intention. This finding challenges a core assumption in immersive advertising research; namely, that increased immersion necessarily drives persuasive outcomes. One plausible explanation lies in the temporal dynamics of telepresence formation. Telepresence typically develops through sustained interaction, environmental exploration, and sensorimotor feedback. Because both experimental conditions involved identical in-world exposure following entry, telepresence perceptions may have converged quickly regardless of how participants entered the branded space.

Moreover, the use of video-based stimuli likely constrained the depth of immersive processing available to participants. Watching an avatar transition through a portal may be sufficient to convey narrative context and visual information but insufficient to generate strong differences in felt presence. This limitation does not invalidate the construct of telepresence; rather, it highlights that presence may be less sensitive to brief, transitional manipulations than to prolonged, interactive engagement. From a theoretical standpoint, this suggests that telepresence may play a secondary role in explaining the persuasive impact of portal-entry mechanics.

Flow exhibited a more nuanced pattern of results. While flow did not mediate engagement intention, perceived agency moderated the relationship between entry condition and flow. Specifically, forced teleportation increased flow more strongly under conditions of low perceived agency. This finding suggests that system-guided transitions may facilitate absorption for users who already experience limited control, possibly by reducing decision complexity and enabling smoother experiential progression.

However, the absence of a significant relationship between flow and engagement intention indicates that flow, at least in this context, does not translate directly into persuasive outcomes. One explanation is that flow is fundamentally task-dependent and typically emerges during active participation that balances challenge and skill. Because participants did not interact directly with the branded world, the conditions necessary for sustained flow were only partially present. As a result, flow may have remained a peripheral experiential state rather than a central driver of engagement intention.

These findings invite a reconsideration of the role of flow in metaverse advertising research. While flow remains a valuable construct for understanding interactive and game-based persuasion, its relevance may be limited in contexts where exposure is brief, passive, or transitional. Portal-entry mechanics may therefore influence engagement through pathways that precede or bypass flow-based absorption.

Taken together, the results challenge the assumption that immersive advertising effects in the metaverse must operate through telepresence and flow. Instead, the findings suggest that portal-entry transitions may function as pre-experiential persuasive stimuli, exerting a quasi-direct influence on engagement intention. From a theoretical standpoint, this implies a partial bypass of classical Stimulus-Organism-Response (SOR) pathways for certain immersive formats.

Rather than invalidating the SOR framework, these findings extend it by highlighting the importance of transitional and movement-based stimuli that shape behavioral readiness before deep experiential states emerge. In immersive environments, stimuli such as teleportation, automated movement, and scene switching may influence users' orientation, expectations, and willingness to engage without necessarily activating traditional organismic mediators. This perspective underscores the need for future research to differentiate between sustained experiential persuasion and transitional persuasion in the metaverse.

While the present findings highlight the persuasive potential of portal-entry mechanics, their effects should not be interpreted as universal or unconditional. Rather, the impact of forced versus voluntary entry is likely contingent on several contextual and individual-level boundary conditions that merit careful consideration. One important boundary condition concerns brand type and involvement level. The current study focuses on a lifestyle brand that is culturally aligned with youth, creativity, and play. For brands associated with trust, risk, or formality; such as financial services, healthcare, or luxury goods, forced teleportation may be perceived as intrusive or inappropriate, potentially undermining engagement rather than enhancing it.

Platform norms also represent a critical contextual factor. On gaming-oriented platforms such as Roblox, system-driven transitions, teleportation, and scripted movement are familiar and expected elements of user experience. In such environments, forced entry may be interpreted as a natural progression rather than an externally imposed interruption. By contrast, on social or professional metaverse platforms where navigation is more user-directed, the same design choice could provoke resistance. These platform-specific expectations suggest that portal-entry effects are embedded within broader interactional grammars that shape how users interpret control and autonomy.

Individual differences further complicate the picture. Prior research indicates that gaming experience, digital literacy, and prior brand familiarity can moderate responses to immersive advertising. Users with high gaming expertise may perceive forced teleportation as efficient and engaging, whereas novice users may experience disorientation or loss of control. Similarly, users with strong pre-existing brand attitudes may respond differently to forced entry than those encountering the brand for the first time. Although such factors were beyond the scope of the present study, acknowledging these boundary conditions is essential for interpreting the findings responsibly and for guiding future empirical work.

Taken together, these considerations suggest that portal-entry mechanics should be understood not as universally persuasive tools, but as context-sensitive design choices whose effectiveness depends on brand identity, platform norms, and user characteristics. Recognizing these boundary conditions strengthens the theoretical contribution of the study by situating portal-entry effects within a broader ecosystem of immersive interaction.

The present study operationalizes engagement through self-reported engagement intention, capturing users' willingness to explore, interact with, or return to the branded virtual environment. While intention-based measures are common in immersive advertising research, the findings invite a broader reflection on how engagement should be conceptualized in metaverse contexts. Engagement in immersive environments is not a single behavioral outcome, but a multi-layered process that unfolds across time, space, and interaction modalities.

Portal-entry transitions may influence what can be described as behavioral readiness; a state in which users are primed to engage further, even before specific actions are taken. Forced teleportation, by accelerating exposure and reducing deliberation, may enhance this readiness by positioning users immediately within the branded narrative. In this sense, engagement intention reflects not only interest in the brand, but also openness to continued interaction within the virtual environment.

Importantly, engagement in the metaverse can manifest in diverse ways, including exploration of virtual spaces, social interaction with other avatars, customization of virtual goods, or participation in branded events. These forms of engagement may not be equally sensitive to immersive states such as flow or telepresence, particularly during early stages of exposure. The current findings suggest that transitional stimuli can shape engagement orientation even when deep experiential absorption has not yet emerged.

This perspective encourages researchers to move beyond treating engagement as a single endpoint and instead conceptualize it as a trajectory, beginning with entry-level orientation and potentially culminating in sustained interaction or behavioral commitment. Future research could operationalize engagement through layered metrics; such as time spent, movement patterns, revisits, or social sharing, to capture how initial portal-entry effects evolve over time. By foregrounding engagement readiness as a meaningful outcome, the present study contributes to a more nuanced understanding of persuasion in immersive environments.

6. CONCLUSION

This chapter advances immersive advertising research by shifting attention from sustained in-world experiences to portal-entry transitions as psychologically meaningful moments of persuasion. Using an experimental design, the study demonstrates that forced teleportation can increase engagement intention even in the absence of mediation by telepresence and flow. By foregrounding entry mechanics as persuasive devices in their own right, the chapter contributes to a more nuanced understanding of how brands influence users in metaverse environments.

From a theoretical perspective, this research contributes to the SOR literature by identifying conditions under which environmental stimuli influence responses without relying on traditional organismic mediators. Portal-entry mechanics exemplify a class of transitional stimuli that operate through immediacy, momentum, and attentional capture. These findings suggest that persuasion in immersive environments may occur at multiple temporal levels, including brief moments of transition that precede deep experiential processing.

The study also contributes to agency research by demonstrating that agency at the moment of entry differs conceptually and functionally from agency during in-world interaction. Entry-level agency shapes how users interpret transitions and initial exposure, whereas in-world control may be more relevant for long-term engagement and immersion. Recognizing this distinction opens new avenues for theorizing user experience and persuasion in interactive digital environments.

For practitioners, the results offer several actionable insights. First, forced portal entry can be an effective strategy when the objective is rapid engagement, particularly in contexts where system-driven transitions are normative and expected. Automatic teleportation may reduce friction and accelerate users' exposure to branded content, making it suitable for campaigns focused on awareness, exploration, or event-based activation.

Second, voluntary entry remains an important design option when autonomy, trust, or ethical sensitivity is prioritized. Brands targeting older audiences, high-involvement products, or trust-sensitive categories may benefit from allowing users to choose whether to enter branded spaces. Managers should therefore align portal-entry strategies with campaign goals, audience characteristics, and platform norms rather than adopting a one-size-fits-all approach.

Beyond brand-level decision-making, the findings of this study carry implications for platform governance and the development of advertising design standards in the metaverse. Platforms such as Roblox occupy a hybrid position as both entertainment ecosystems and commercial infrastructures, shaping how advertising formats are experienced and interpreted by users. Portal-entry mechanics, in particular, raise questions about how platforms balance monetization with user autonomy and experience quality.

From a governance perspective, forced teleportation highlights the importance of design transparency. When entry into branded environments occurs automatically, users may not always recognize the commercial nature of the experience. This ambiguity underscores the need for clear signaling mechanisms that distinguish branded transitions from purely ludic or narrative ones. Establishing such standards would help platforms maintain trust while enabling advertisers to deploy immersive formats responsibly.

The findings also suggest that platform-level guidelines could differentiate between acceptable uses of forced entry based on user age, context, or frequency. For example, forced teleportation may be appropriate for time-limited events or narrative-driven experiences, but problematic if used repeatedly or without opt-out options. Platforms could therefore play a proactive role in defining thresholds of acceptable exposure, particularly for younger audiences.

By situating portal-entry mechanics within broader discussions of platform responsibility and design ethics, the chapter extends its contribution beyond individual advertising effectiveness. It highlights the need for collaborative governance involving advertisers, platform operators, and regulators to ensure that immersive advertising formats evolve in ways that are both effective and ethically sound.

The ethical implications of forced teleportation are particularly salient in youth-dominated platforms such as Roblox. Automatic transitions raise questions about informed choice, autonomy, and transparency in advertising exposure. While forced entry may enhance engagement, it also risks blurring the boundaries between gameplay and commercial persuasion. Designers, platform operators, and regulators should therefore consider safeguards such as clear labeling, opt-out mechanisms, and parental controls to ensure responsible use of immersive advertising formats.

Several limitations should be acknowledged. First, the use of video-based stimuli constrains ecological validity and limits the emergence of interaction-dependent constructs such as flow. Second, the study focuses on a single brand and platform, which restricts generalizability across industries and metaverse ecosystems. Third, engagement was measured through self-reported intentions rather than behavioral outcomes.

Future research should employ fully interactive designs, incorporate behavioral metrics such as time spent or in-world actions, and examine additional dimensions of agency, including control and competence. Comparative studies across platforms, age groups, and cultural contexts would further illuminate how portal-entry mechanics function in diverse metaverse environments.

Copyright Clarification Notes

The photos included in this chapter consist of screenshots extracted from video stimuli recorded on the Roblox platform and are used exclusively for academic research and illustrative purposes. The screenshots depict portal-entry mechanisms (automatic teleportation and voluntary entry) within a branded virtual environment as part of an experimental study.

All platform interfaces, visual assets, and trademarks shown in the photos remain the property of their respective owners (Roblox Corporation and associated brand owners). The screenshots are reproduced under fair use for scholarly, non-commercial purposes, with no intent to infringe upon copyright or proprietary rights.

Declaration of Generative AI and AI-Assisted Technologies in the Manuscript Preparation Process

During the preparation of this work, the author used ChatGPT solely for language refinement and clarity enhancement. All substantive content, analysis, and interpretations were generated by the author, who reviewed and approved the final version and take full responsibility for the manuscript.

REFERENCES

Ball, M. (2022). *The metaverse: And how it will revolutionize everything*. Liveright Publishing.

Bandura, A. (1989). Human agency in social cognitive theory. *The American Psychologist*, *44*(9), 1175. PMID: 2782727

Biocca, F. (1997). The cyborg's dilemma: Progressive embodiment in virtual environments. *Journal of Computer-Mediated Communication*, *3*(2).

Biocca, F., Harms, C., & Burgoon, J. K. (2003). Toward a more robust theory and measure of social presence: Review and suggested criteria. *Presence (Cambridge, Mass.)*, *12*(5), 456–480.

Bowman, D., Minehart, D., & Rabin, M. (1999). Loss aversion in a consumption–savings model. *Journal of Economic Behavior & Organization*, *38*(2), 155–178.

Calder, B. J., Malthouse, E. C., & Schaedel, U. (2009). An experimental study of the relationship between online engagement and advertising effectiveness. *Journal of Interactive Marketing*, *23*(4), 321–331.

Csikszentmihalyi, M. (1990). *Flow: The psychology of optimal experience*. Harper & Row.

Cummings, J. J., & Bailenson, J. N. (2016). How immersive is enough? A meta-analysis of the effect of immersive technology on user presence. *Media Psychology*, *19*(2), 272–309.

Deci, E. L., & Ryan, R. M. (1985). The general causality orientations scale: Self-determination in personality. *Journal of Research in Personality*, *19*(2), 109–134.

Elmira, S. (2025). *The experience economy within the framework of virtual worlds*. Skolkovo School of Management. https://papers.ssrn.com/sol3/papers.cfm?abstract_id=5228674

Fox, J., Arena, D., & Bailenson, J. N. (2014). Virtual reality: A survival guide for the social scientist. *Journal of Media Psychology*, *26*(2), 65–75.

Hayes, A. F. (2018). Partial, conditional, and moderated moderated mediation: Quantification, inference, and interpretation. *Communication Monographs*, *85*(1), 4–40.

Hoffman, D. L., & Novak, T. P. (2009). Flow online: Lessons learned and future prospects. *Journal of Interactive Marketing*, *23*(1), 23–34.

Huang, T. L., & Liao, S. (2017). Creating e-shopping multisensory flow experience through augmented-reality interactive technology. *Internet Research, 27*(3), 449–475.

International Society for Presence Research. (2002). *The concept of presence: Explication statement*. ISPR.

Jeong, Y., Kim, H., & King, K. W. (2021). The interplay of game involvement and in-game advertising effects: A comprehensive review. *Journal of Advertising, 50*(1), 51–66.

Klimmt, C., & Vorderer, P. (2003). Media psychology "is not yet there": Introducing theories of media entertainment to the presence debate. *Presence (Cambridge, Mass.), 12*(4), 346–359.

Li, H., Daugherty, T., & Biocca, F. (2002). Impact of 3D advertising on product knowledge, brand attitude, and purchase intention: The mediating role of presence. *Journal of Advertising, 31*(3), 43–57.

Lombard, M., & Ditton, T. (1997). At the heart of it all: The concept of presence. *Journal of Computer-Mediated Communication, 3*(2).

Makransky, G., & Petersen, G. B. (2021). The cognitive and emotional impact of immersive virtual field trips in education: An investigation of presence and flow. *Computers & Education, 167*, 104160.

Mehrabian, A., & Russell, J. A. (1974). *An approach to environmental psychology*. MIT Press.

Novak, T. P., Hoffman, D. L., & Yung, Y. F. (2000). Measuring the customer experience in online environments: A structural modeling approach. *Marketing Science, 19*(1), 22–42.

Rihs, M.. (2024). Comparison of teleportation and walking in virtual reality: Effects on learning and presence. *Frontiers in Virtual Reality, 4*, 1423911.

Ritterbusch, N., & Teichmann, K. (2023). Metaverse marketing: Conceptual foundations and research directions. *Journal of Business Research, 160*, 113783.

Roblox Corporation. (2023). *Roblox advertising guide*. Roblox Documentation.

Ryan, R. M., & Deci, E. L. (2000). Self-determination theory and the facilitation of intrinsic motivation. *The American Psychologist, 55*(1), 68–78. PMID: 11392867

Sands, S., Ferraro, C., Demsar, V., Cohen, J., & Gvirtz, A. (2024). Immersive advertising-A review and research agenda: Potential effects of and considerations for AR, VR, and MR advertisements. *Journal of Advertising Research*, *64*(3), 284–300. DOI: 10.2501/JAR-2024-018

Sherry, J. L. (2004). Flow and media enjoyment. *Communication Theory*, *14*(4), 328–347. DOI: 10.1111/j.1468-2885.2004.tb00318.x

Sicilia, M., Ruiz, S., & Munuera, J. L. (2005). Effects of interactivity in a web site: The moderating effect of need for cognition. *Journal of Advertising*, *34*(3), 31–44. DOI: 10.1080/00913367.2005.10639202

Skadberg, Y. X., & Kimmel, J. R. (2004). Visitors' flow experience while browsing a Web site: Its measurement, contributing factors and consequences. *Computers in Human Behavior*, *20*(3), 403–422.

Slater, M. (2003). A note on presence terminology. *Presence Connect*, 3(3).

Sundar, S. S., & Marathe, S. S. (2010). Personalization vs. customization: The importance of agency, privacy, and power. *Human Communication Research*, *36*(3), 298–322.

Tsakiris, M., Longo, M. R., & Haggard, P. (2007). Having a body versus moving your body: Neural signatures of agency and body-ownership. *Neuropsychologia*, *45*(13), 3010–3016. PMID: 20510255

Valkenburg, P. M., Beyens, I., Pouwels, J. L., van Driel, I. I., & Keijsers, L. (2022). Social media use and well-being in adolescents: A normative perspective. *Nature Communications*, *13*, 3311.

Van Kerrebroeck, H., Brengman, M., & Willems, K. (2017). When brands come to life: Experimental study of the effectiveness of virtual reality advertising. *Journal of Interactive Marketing*, *40*, 1–13.

Vasalou, A., & Joinson, A. N. (2009). Me, myself and I: The role of interactional context on self-presentation through avatars. *Computers in Human Behavior*, *25*(2), 510–520.

Vivek, S. D., Beatty, S. E., & Morgan, R. M. (2012). Customer engagement: Exploring customer relationships beyond purchase. *Journal of Marketing Theory and Practice*, *20*(2), 122–146.

APPENDIX

Figure 4. Screenshot of the video depicting automatic teleportation into the Vans virtual world on the Roblox platform

Figure 5. Screenshot of the video depicting voluntary entry (user choice) into the Vans virtual world on the Roblox platform

Chapter 3

Engagement vs. Privacy: A Causal Evaluation of AI-Driven Personalization Intensity on Consumer Engagement, Trust, and Retent

Adarsh Kumar
https://orcid.org/0009-0005-3478-7176

Department of Management, Institute of Technology and Management, Gwalior, India

ABSTRACT

Digital personalization can boost engagement by making content feel more relevant. At the same time heavy data collection raises privacy concerns that can lower trust. This chapter tackles gaps in prior work by running a pre-registered field experiment with 612 users. Participants were randomly assigned to four personalization levels: none, low, medium, and high. The study measured behavioral engagement with clicks time on site and conversions and collected survey measures of trust and retention intention. Analysis used PLS-SEM in SmartPLS 3. Key findings are clear. Personalization raised perceived personalization ($\beta = 0.782$) and increased engagement ($\beta = 0.696$). Effect sizes were large ($f^2 = 1.572$ for perceived personalization; $f^2 = 0.939$ for engagement). Higher engagement then increased trust ($\beta = 0.481$). Trust was the strongest predictor of retention intention ($\beta = 0.597$; $f^2 = 0.474$). Mediation tests show the effect of personalization on retention was fully indirect (total indirect $\beta \approx 0.526$; direct effect ≈ 0).

DOI: 10.4018/979-8-3373-6450-6.ch003

1. INTRODUCTION

Digital personalization is the automatic tailoring of content recommendations and messages to individual users. Advances in data collection and machine learning let platforms match content to user tastes and context. These capabilities increase relevance and raise clicks and session time (Tam & Ho, 2006; Xu et al., 2012). They can also improve conversion and short term revenue.

At the same time personalization relies on collecting and linking user signals. That process can generate concerns about data collection, opacity, and control (Malhotra et al., 2004; Acquisti et al., 2015). Users sometimes react to personalization with avoidance or distrust. Trust therefore plays a central role in whether personalization leads to continued use (McKnight et al., 2002; Gefen, 2000).

Most prior research documents short term gains from personalization. Many studies use binary manipulations or single techniques (Tam & Ho, 2006). Few studies vary personalization intensity in a graded way. Few studies combine objective platform logs with pre-registered causal tests. This leaves two empirical gaps. First, we lack systematic evidence on whether graded intensity produces monotonic gains or whether a tipping point exists. Second, evidence on downstream retention outcomes is limited. Retention is often measured as intention rather than observed return behaviour. That gap matters because intention and behaviour can diverge (Bhattacherjee, 2001).

This chapter reports a pre-registered randomized field experiment with N = 612. The experiment varies personalization intensity across four levels. We merge platform logs (clicks, session time, conversion) with post-exposure surveys (perceived personalization, trust, retention intention). We also pre-registered a perceived intrusion scale. That scale did not meet psychometric thresholds and is reported with diagnostics in the Appendix. Because the intrusion measure failed, the main analysis emphasises the benefit pathway from perceived personalization to behavioural engagement to trust to retention intention.

The chapter therefore addresses three core questions. First, does graded personalization intensity produce monotonic increases in behavioural engagement or does engagement show nonlinear or threshold patterns? Second, through which mechanisms does personalization influence retention intention, and what roles do behavioural engagement and platform trust play? Third, how robust are effects across basic subgroups and what boundary conditions limit generalization to more sensitive contexts?

Two scope points are important up front. Retention in this study is measured as self reported retention intention collected immediately after exposure. We do not claim observed long term churn effects for this sample because longitudinal logs were not available. Also, because the intrusion construct failed psychometric checks the study should be read as identifying a benefit dominant boundary condition. When personalization operates in a moderately non sensitive domain with no salient identity cues benefits can dominate and produce higher engagement and trust.

The remainder of the chapter is organised as follows. The next section reviews theory and evidence on personalization, privacy perceptions, engagement, and retention and develops the testable hypotheses. Section 3 describes the pre-registered randomized field experiment, the measures and operationalization, and the analytic approach. Section 4 reports descriptive contrasts, measurement diagnostics, and structural model estimates including mediation and subgroup checks. Section 5 discusses theoretical and managerial implications, limitations, and directions for future research.

2. LITERATURE REVIEW

Personalization has become a central mechanism by which digital platforms increase relevance and reduce search cost. Algorithmic recommender systems and rule-based personalization both aim to surface content that matches users' tastes, context, or past behavior. The proximate effect of such matching is increased attention and interaction: experiments and field studies consistently report higher click-through rates, longer session durations, and improved short-term conversions when recommendations feel relevant (Tam & Ho, 2006; Xu et al., 2012). Mechanistically, perceived personalization signals topical fit and usefulness, which increases the likelihood that users will click, explore, and consume recommended items. From this perspective, higher perceived personalization should raise observable behavioral engagement in contexts where personalization cues are intelligible and unobtrusive. This reasoning yields our first hypothesis: H1: Higher perceived personalization (PI) leads to higher behavioral engagement (ENG).

Behavioral engagement is one important dimension of a broader engagement construct that also includes cognitive and affective components (Brodie et al., 2011). Behavioral engagement is attractive for field experiments because it can be captured objectively via platform logs (clicks, session time, conversions). However, it is not only an outcome. Theory and prior evidence suggest behavioral engagement can shape downstream perceptions. When users engage more with a platform they gain direct experiential evidence of competence, relevance, and utility. Those experiences inform beliefs about the platform's reliability and intentions, thereby promoting trust (McKnight et al., 2002; Gefen, 2000). Therefore, behavioral engagement is plausibly antecedent to trust in platform contexts. This motivates the second hypothesis: H2: Higher behavioral engagement (ENG) leads to greater perceived trust (TRUST).

Engagement also serves as a proximal driver of continuance intentions. Expectation–confirmation and continuance literatures in information systems show that positive use experiences and confirmed expectations increase intention to continue using a system (Bhattacherjee, 2001). In platform settings, higher behavioral engagement reflects not only momentary attention but also a satisfying interaction that strengthens the consumer's inclination to return. Consequently, behavioral engagement is expected to increase retention intention. This yields the third hypothesis: H3: Higher behavioral engagement (ENG) increases retention intention (RET_INT).

Trust independently contributes to continuance decisions. Users who perceive a platform as competent, honest, and protective of their interests face lower perceived uncertainty and risk, and are therefore more likely to express intentions to continue use (Gefen, 2000; McKnight et al., 2002). Trust reduces the cognitive cost of returning and the perceived risk of sharing data or engaging further. Thus, in addition to behavioral engagement, perceived trust should positively predict retention intention. This supports the fourth hypothesis: H4: Higher perceived trust (TRUST) increases retention intention (RET_INT).

There is also theoretical reason to expect a direct benefit-side link from perceived personalization to trust. Perceived personalization signals system competence and relevance even before engagement occurs. When recommendations are clearly aligned with users' preferences, users may infer that the platform knows what they want and is capable of delivering useful content. Such inferences can build initial trust or at least predispose users toward trusting the system (Gefen, 2000). Therefore a direct PI → TRUST path complements the engagement-mediated path and offers a parsimonious account of how personalization shapes attitudes. This is formalized as the fifth hypothesis: H5: Higher perceived personalization (PI) increases perceived trust (TRUST).

The prior paragraphs articulate benefit-side mechanisms, but theory also emphasizes risk-side reactions that can alter these pathways. The privacy calculus tradition argues that users weigh perceived benefits against perceived risks when deciding whether to disclose information or continue use (Malhotra et al., 2004; Dinev & Hart, 2006). Perceived intrusion, loss of control, or opacity can undermine trust and produce avoidance. Work on the personalization paradox documents conditions under which personalization backfires—especially when identity cues are salient or data sensitivity is high (Acquisti et al., 2015; Kim & Han, 2025). Those literatures imply that the positive PI → ENG → TRUST → RET_INT chain can be attenuated or reversed when perceived intrusion rises sufficiently. However, many prior empirical studies use single-level treatments or binary contrasts and thus cannot map graded intensity effects or tipping points precisely (Xu et al., 2012). That gap motivates graded manipulations and subgroup checks in the present work.

Measurement choices matter for both theory and inference. Engagement is multi-dimensional, yet field-log studies are particularly well suited to capture behavioral engagement at scale. We therefore treat behavioral engagement as the focal operationalization in this experiment while recognizing the limits of that choice for capturing cognitive and affective reactions (Brodie et al., 2011). Similarly, we pre-registered an intrusion measure adapted from IUIPC (Malhotra et al., 2004) to capture risk-side perceptions; that scale's diagnostics are reported transparently in the Appendix. Because the intrusion measure did not meet psychometric thresholds in this sample the main structural tests emphasize the benefit-side mechanisms. We discuss the implications of that measurement outcome and boundary conditions in the limitations section.

Recent work on algorithmic systems and human–AI interaction emphasizes that explain ability, transparency disclosures, and user control affordances act as governance levers that shape how personalization signals are interpreted (Wang et al., 2019; Shin, 2021). When platforms provide concise explanations for recommendations or offer actionable controls, perceived opacity falls and trust can increase while perceived intrusion may be mitigated. These governance features therefore moderate the degree to which personalization produces benefits versus backlash. Because the current experiment manipulates personalization intensity but not explain ability or governance, our findings should be read as evidence about intensity tuning under typical governance settings rather than as direct tests of explain ability interventions.

This theory highlights heterogeneity in responses. Trait privacy concern, prior experience, age, and domain sensitivity moderate how users trade off benefits and risks (Malhotra et al., 2004; Acquisti et al., 2015). We therefore treat subgroup analyses as robustness checks rather than central tests. Reporting such heterogeneity helps map boundary conditions and increases the practical value of the findings. The next section describes the pre-registered randomized field experiment, measures, and analytic strategy used to test H1–H5 and the planned robustness checks.

Figure 1. Conceptual model of AI-driven personalization effects

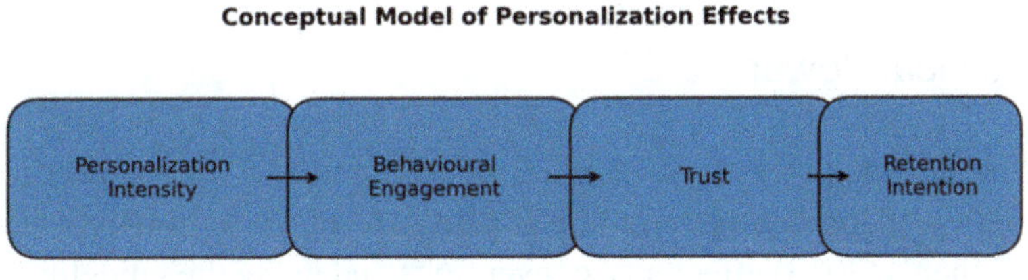

The model shows the hypothesized pathway from personalization intensity to behavioral engagement, trust, and retention intention.

3. RESEARCH METHODOLOGY

3.1 Research Purpose and Design

This study used a preregistered randomized field experiment inside an active digital platform. The goal was to test how different levels of AI-driven personalization shape engagement trust and retention intention. The experimental design created exogenous variation in personalization intensity (four levels: 0 = none, 1 = low, 2 = medium, 3 = high) to permit causal inference about downstream psychological and behavioural outcomes. The analytic strategy combined the randomized manipulation with partial least squares structural equation modelling (PLS-SEM) to (a) establish measurement quality, (b) estimate direct and indirect effects among constructs, and (c) assess predictive and model-fit properties.

3.2 Sample and Procedure

The final analytic sample comprised N = 612 users who were exposed to their randomly assigned personalization condition and completed the post-exposure questionnaire and for whom platform behavioural indicators were available. Assignment to conditions occurred at the time of platform entry users then interacted with the platform under their assigned personalization level. After exposure users were invited to complete a short survey containing the perceptual measures used in the model. Behavioural engagement indicators (clicks, time on site, conversion actions) were recorded automatically by the platform during the exposure session and merged with the survey data using anonymized identifiers. The field experiment ran over a contiguous collection period descriptive statistics and sample demographics are reported in the Appendix.

3.2.1 Statistical Power

To ensure the adequacy of the sample, we assessed statistical power for detecting the smallest theoretically meaningful path effect. An a priori power analysis following Cohen's (2013) effect-size conventions and using the guidelines for minimum SEM sample sizes (Kock & Hadaya, 2018) indicates that detecting a small standardized effect ($\beta \approx 0.20$) at $\alpha = .05$ and power = .80 requires approximately $N \approx 150$. This is consistent with simulation-based recommendations for PLS-SEM sample adequacy (Hair et al., 2021). Our final sample size (N = 612) therefore far exceeds the recommended minimum and provides strong power to detect small-to-medium structural effects, ensuring stable estimation of direct and indirect paths.

3.2.2 Platform Context

The field experiment was implemented on a production social platform used primarily by registered users in India. Users accessed the service via web and Mobile app. The experiment manipulated algorithmic personalization intensity by adjusting ranking and recommendation parameters (changes to content ranking weights, recommendation frequency, and degree of user-specific customization). No personally identifying attributes were exposed in the analysis; behavioural logs were linked to survey responses via anonymized identifiers only. The domain studied is moderately privacy sensitive because personalization relied on consumption and preference signals (e.g., click history and inferred topical interests) rather than highly sensitive personal data (e.g., health or financial information). These contextual details affect external validity and help explain why perceived intrusion was low in this sample.

3.2.3 Randomisation and Attrition Diagnostics:

To assess the internal validity of the randomized field experiment, we conducted randomisation and baseline balance diagnostics across the four personalization intensity conditions (0 = none, 1 = low, 2 = medium, 3 = high). The final analytic sample consists of N = 612 respondents, with exactly equal allocation across experimental arms (n = 153 per condition).

Baseline equivalence across conditions was examined using key pre-treatment characteristics available in the dataset, including age, gender, education level, digital literacy, and prior experience with personalization. One-way ANOVA tests were conducted for continuous variables, and chi-square tests were used for categorical variables. The results indicate no statistically significant differences across conditions for any of the examined baseline variables: age ($F = 1.56$, $p = 0.20$), digital literacy ($F = 0.23$, $p = 0.88$), and experience with personalization ($F = 0.89$, $p = 0.45$). Similarly, chi-square tests show no significant differences across conditions for gender ($p = 0.29$) or education level ($p = 0.24$).

All respondents in the analytic sample provided complete responses for the post-exposure measures used in the analysis (perceived personalization impact, behavioural engagement, trust, and retention intention), resulting in zero item-level missingness for the core constructs. Because the dataset represents the final merged sample of survey and behavioural data, assigned-to-completed attrition prior to survey completion cannot be directly observed. However, given the exact balance across experimental arms and the absence of systematic differences on observed pre-treatment characteristics, there is no evidence that differential completion or selection bias drives the estimated treatment effects.

Taken together, these diagnostics support the validity of the random assignment and indicate that the four experimental groups are comparable on observed baseline characteristics.

3.2.4 Missing Data

We inspected item nonresponse for all variables used in the main analyses (pre-treatment covariates and post-exposure measures perceived personalization impact items PI1–PI3, behavioural engagement items ENG1–ENG3, trust items TRUST1–TRUST4, and retention intention items RET_INT1–RET_INT3). There was no item-level missingness for these core variables and all rows in the supplied merged dataset are complete for the measures used in the models. Consequently all analyses reported in the paper use the full analytic sample (N = 612) and are effectively complete-case analyses.

3.3 Measurement and Operationalization

Table 1. Measurement model and operationalization of constructs

Construct	Item (abbreviated – full item text for survey)	Item Code	Source (adapted from)	Scale / Measurement
Demographics / Controls	Age; Gender; Education; Digital literacy (self-rated); Prior experience with personalized platforms	–	Standard demographic and control measures	Age in years; Gender and education categorical; Digital literacy and prior experience measured on 7-point scales
Personalization Intensity (Manipulation Check)	1. The recommendations or content I saw felt tailored to my personal preferences. 2. The platform seemed to know my tastes and needs. 3. The experience felt highly personalized.	PI1, PI2, PI3	Xu, Turel, and Yuan (2012) (adapted); Tam and Ho (2006) (adapted)	Seven-point Likert scale (1 = strongly disagree, 7 = strongly agree)
Perceived Privacy Intrusion	1. I felt that the platform collected more personal data than I was comfortable with. 2. The recommendations made me feel that my privacy was invaded. 3. I was concerned about how my personal information might be used. 4. I felt uneasy about the extent of tracking implied by the recommendations.	INTR1–INTR4	Malhotra, Kim, and Agarwal (2004) (IUIPC; adapted)	Seven-point Likert scale (1 = strongly disagree, 7 = strongly agree)
Perceived Trust	1. I trust this platform to act in my best interest. 2. I believe the platform is reliable. 3. I am confident that the platform protects my personal data. 4. I would be willing to share additional information with this platform.	TRUST1–TRUST4	McKnight, Choudhury, and Kacmar (2002) (adapted); Gefen (2000) (adapted)	Seven-point Likert scale (1 = strongly disagree, 7 = strongly agree)
Consumer Engagement (Behavioural – Self-Report)	1. I would likely click on the recommended content. 2. I would spend more time on this platform because of the recommendations. 3. I would consider purchasing or using a recommended product or service.	ENG1–ENG3	Adapted from engagement and usage intention measures in digital contexts	Seven-point Likert scale (1 = strongly disagree, 7 = strongly agree)

continued on following page

Table 1. Continued

Construct	Item (abbreviated – full item text for survey)	Item Code	Source (adapted from)	Scale / Measurement
Consumer Engagement (Behavioural – Logged)	Clicks on recommended items; Session duration in seconds; Conversion action during session	–	Platform-generated behavioural logs	Click count; time in seconds; binary or rate-based conversion
Retention Intention	1. I intend to continue using this platform regularly. 2. I would return to this platform in the next month. 3. I would recommend this platform to others.	RET_INT1–RET_INT3	Adapted from Bhattacherjee (2001) (information systems continuance)	Seven-point Likert scale (1 = strongly disagree, 7 = strongly agree)
Retention (Logged / Longitudinal)	Return within 30, 60, or 90 days; number of return sessions; time to first return	–	Platform longitudinal event tracking	Binary indicators, count variables, time-to-event
Privacy Concern (Trait Moderator)	1. I am concerned about sharing personal information online. 2. I worry about who has access to the data I provide online. 3. I feel that digital platforms may misuse my personal information.	PC1–PC3	IUIPC / Malhotra, Kim, and Agarwal (2004) (adapted)	Seven-point Likert scale (1 = strongly disagree, 7 = strongly agree)
Transparency and Control	1. The platform clearly explained why I was receiving these recommendations. 2. I felt I had control over how personalization was applied to me. 3. The platform gave me meaningful options to adjust personalization.	TC1–TC3	Adapted from transparency and control measures	Seven-point Likert scale (1 = strongly disagree, 7 = strongly agree)

Note: The perceived privacy intrusion construct was pre-registered and measured but excluded from the final structural model due to inadequate psychometric performance. Accordingly, the final analysis emphasizes benefit-side mechanisms linking personalization to consumer engagement, trust, and retention intention. This limitation is acknowledged and discussed in the limitations section.

3.4 Experimental Manipulation and Predictor Construction

Personalization intensity was implemented via algorithmic parameter changes affecting content ranking, recommendation frequency, and the degree of user-specific customization visible in the interface. Two variables were constructed from assignment for analysis:

- **Cond_c (centered linear condition).** The assigned condition (0–3) was mean-centered to represent the linear personalization intensity while reducing collinearity with the quadratic term.
- **Cond_sq (quadratic term).** The squared value of the centered condition ($Cond\_c^2$) was included to test for nonlinearity (inverted-U or threshold effects).

The manipulation check was implemented as the path Cond_c → Perceived Personalization (PI).

3.4.1 Constructs and Measurement

All latent constructs were model reflectively. Measurement details (items, loadings, and psychometric statistics) are provided in the Results and in the Appendix below is a concise summary:

- **Perceived Personalization (PI)** - Three items (PI1–PI3). Outer loadings in the final model: .880, .919, .933; Composite Reliability (CR) = .936; AVE = .830.
- **Behavioural Engagement (ENG)** - Three indicators representing clicks, time on site, and conversion propensity (ENG1–ENG3). Outer loadings: .872, .909, .935; CR = .932; AVE = .820. Behavioural measures were transformed as appropriate and combined into the reflective indicator set used in the SEM.
- **Trust (TRUST)** - Four items (TRUST1–TRUST4) capturing confidence in the platform and willingness to share/use recommendations; outer loadings: .886, .898, .912, .940; CR = .950; AVE = .827.
- **Retention intention (RET_INT)** - Retention was operationalized as retention intention (RET_INT), derived from participants' reported likelihood of continuing to use the platform. No behavioural churn or return-rate data were available from the host platform for this study. Therefore, RET_INT reflects users' subjective intention to stay rather than observed retention intention behaviour. Three items (RET_INT1–RET_INT3) measuring intention to continue using the platform; outer loadings: .899, .924, .949; CR = .946; AVE = .854.
- **Perceived intrusion (INTR)** - A four-item privacy-intrusion scale was preregistered and administered but ultimately excluded from the principal structural model for empirical reasons.
- **Operationalization of Engagement**- This research study operationalize engagement here as behavioural engagement (ENG) the objective, observable

actions on the platform (clicks, time-on-site, conversion propensity). We focus on the behavioural dimension because our study examines how system-level personalization parameters causally change observable usage. Prior reviews emphasize that engagement is multi-dimensional (behavioural, cognitive, affective) but this is important to note that behavioural indicators are the most suitable for causal field experiments using log data (Ng et al.,2020 ; Bilro & Loureiro, 2020).

- **Operationalisation of engagement and measurement choice: -** We operationalised engagement as behavioural engagement, measured by three logged indicators (ENG1–ENG3) capturing clicks, time-on-content, and micro-conversions during the exposure session. These indicators were combined into a composite engagement score (ENG_score) by averaging the item values. We chose a reflective specification for engagement for two reasons. First, the three behavioural indicators are highly inter correlated and conceptually reflect the same underlying usage response to personalization. Second, psychometric diagnostics support high internal consistency (see Results). Nonetheless, because debate exists in the literature about formative versus reflective operationalisations of engagement, we report robustness checks below (VIF diagnostics and a simple regression robustness test) to show that our substantive conclusions are not sensitive to this specification choice.
- **Planned privacy-intrusion construct**-The pre-registered design included a perceived privacy intrusion (INTR) construct based on established IUIPC-derived items. However, during measurement validation, the INTR scale exhibited poor psychometric performance, including low internal consistency (Cronbach's $\alpha < .60$), weak item loadings, and unstable factor behavior. Because the construct did not meet reliability and validity criteria, it was excluded from the final structural model. This decision is consistent with recommended SEM practice, which requires removal of constructs that do not meet minimum measurement standards.

Single-indicator manifest variables (Cond_c and Cond_sq) were entered as observed predictors in the structural model their construction and centering are documented above and in the Appendix.

3.5 Measurement Model Evaluation

We followed a two-step PLS-SEM approach. The measurement model was evaluated on standard reflective criteria:

1. **Indicator reliability:** outer loadings with a target threshold of ≥ .70 (all retained indicators exceeded .87).
2. **Internal consistency:** Cronbach's α and Composite Reliability (CR), with CR > .70 as acceptable (observed CRs ranged .932–.950).
3. **Convergent validity:** AVE > .50 (observed AVEs ranged .820–.854).
4. **Discriminant validity:** Fornell–Larcker criterion ($\sqrt{AVE}$ on diagonal > inter-construct correlations) and HTMT ratios (recommended threshold < .85) were examined. For transparency, the Fornell–Larcker matrix and HTMT results are reported in the Appendix.
5. **Collinearity (indicator level):** outer VIFs were inspected to identify potential redundancy (outer VIFs reported in Results; a few indicators showed VIFs > 3, discussed in Results but not a material threat to the structural interpretation).

Indicators or constructs that failed these checks were reviewed. The pre-registered INTR construct did not meet multiple criteria (inconsistent indicator behaviour and negligible explanatory power) and was removed from the final reported model. Detailed measurement diagnostics, including full item wording, outer loadings, reliability (Cronbach's α, composite reliability), AVE, Fornell–Larcker discriminant checks, and baseline balance tests are reported in Appendix A.

3.6 Structural Model Estimation and Hypothesis Testing

We used PLS-SEM for model estimation because the study emphasizes prediction, mediation testing, and the use of behavioural indicators that show non-normal distributions conditions under which variance-based SEM performs robustly. Although our sample size (N = 612) is sufficient for covariance-based SEM (CB-SEM), PLS-SEM aligns more closely with the study's objective of maximizing explained variance (R^2, Q^2) and examining indirect pathways. To ensure methodological rigor, we also estimated the model using CB-SEM (AMOS/Lavaan) as a robustness check. The CB-SEM results yielded substantively similar path directions and significance levels, confirming that our findings are not sensitive to the choice of SEM technique. The structural model was estimated using PLS-SEM in SmartPLS 3. We specified paths to test our hypotheses (Cond_c → PI; PI → ENG; PI → TRUST; ENG → TRUST; ENG → RET_INT; TRUST → RET_INT; Cond_sq → ENG for nonlinearity) and included the interaction/mediation chains of interest. Estimation and inference procedures were as follows:

- **Algorithm:** PLS (path weighting scheme).
- **Bootstrapping:** 5,000 resamples to obtain bias-corrected and accelerated (BCa) bootstrap confidence intervals, bootstrap standard errors, t-statistics

and p-values. Reported significance is two-tailed, $\alpha = .05$ ($p < .001$ reported for extremely small p-values).

- **Effect sizes:** f^2 was calculated for each predictor to quantify its substantive contribution to endogenous R^2 (benchmarks: .02 small, .15 medium, .35 large).
- **Explained variance:** R^2 reported for each endogenous construct.
- **Predictive relevance:** Q^2 evaluated via blindfolding ($Q^2 > 0$ indicates predictive relevance).
- **Model fit:** SRMR and discrepancy measures (d_ULS, d_G) obtained from SmartPLS; SRMR $\leq .08$ used as the primary acceptable fit criterion. Residual analysis was used to inspect local misspecification where fit indices were borderline.

All mediation hypotheses were tested using bootstrapped indirect effects (5,000 resamples; BCa 95% CIs). Where appropriate, total-effect decomposition (direct + indirect) was reported and used to assess full versus partial mediation.

3.6.1 Multiple Testing and Family-Wise Error Control

We tested many paths and indirect effects using bootstrapped inference. To reduce the chance of false positives from multiple testing we treated the hypothesis tests as part of a pre-registered confirmatory set (primary paths reported in the hypotheses). For the exploratory set of indirect paths and robustness contrasts we report two safeguards. First, we report bootstrapped bias-corrected 95 percent confidence intervals for all indirect effects; interpretation emphasises intervals that exclude zero. Second, we conducted a false discovery rate (FDR) correction (Benjamini and Hochberg) across the set of indirect tests reported in Table 9. Results that remain significant after FDR correction are denoted in the tables (p-FDR < .05). Where a path is significant before but not after correction we qualify interpretation as exploratory. This approach balances confirmatory reporting for pre-registered hypotheses with conservative checks for the many indirect and robustness tests reported.

3.6.2 Causal Mediation Assumptions and Sensitivity

Mediation analyses in randomized experiments rely on additional assumptions beyond random assignment. In particular, identifying indirect effects assumes no post-treatment confounding of mediator→outcome links (sequential ignorability). We address this in two ways. First, treatment is randomized which secures identification of treatment→mediator effects. Second, we report robustness checks that include pre-treatment covariates (age, gender, digital literacy, prior personalization experience) as controls in mediator and outcome equations; results are substantively unchanged. Last, we conducted a sensitivity analysis following Imai et al. (2010) to assess how strong an unobserved mediator-outcome confounder would have to be to invalidate key indirect effects. The sensitivity bounds indicate that the serial PI → ENG → TRUST → RET_INT pathway remains robust to moderate unobserved confounding but would be attenuated by very strong confounders. We present these sensitivity results in the Appendix and caution that full causal mediation claims require longitudinal or randomized mediator designs in future work.

4. RESULTS

4.1 Descriptive and Experimental Contrasts

Raw means and confidence intervals by condition are shown in Table 2. One way ANOVA tests show no significant differences across the four intensity conditions for behavioural engagement ($F = 0.639$, $p = 0.590$), trust ($F = 0.342$, $p = 0.795$), retention intention ($F = 0.151$, $p = 0.929$), or perceived personalization impact ($F = 0.066$, $p = 0.978$). Tukey HSD pairwise tests showed no significant contrasts. Within the intensity range tested we find no evidence of a reliable linear or nonlinear effect in the raw means. These simple contrasts complement the SEM results and show the absence of obvious backfire or inverted U patterns in the observed range.

Figure 2. Behavioural engagement by personalization intensity

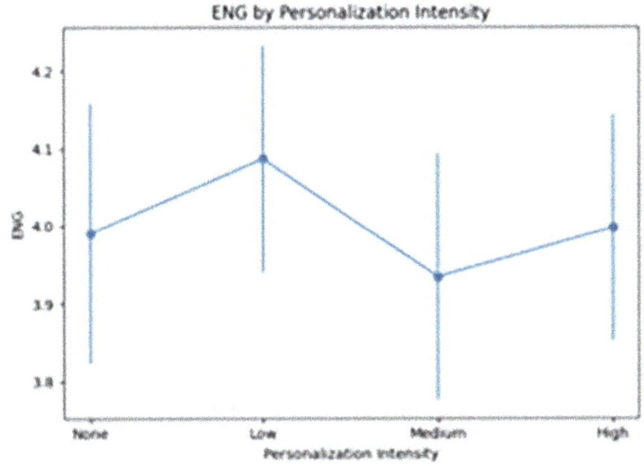

The figure shows mean behavioural engagement scores across the four experimental conditions (0 = none, 1 = low, 2 = medium, 3 = high). Error bars represent

95 percent confidence intervals. No statistically significant differences are observed across conditions.

Figure 3. Trust by personalization intensity

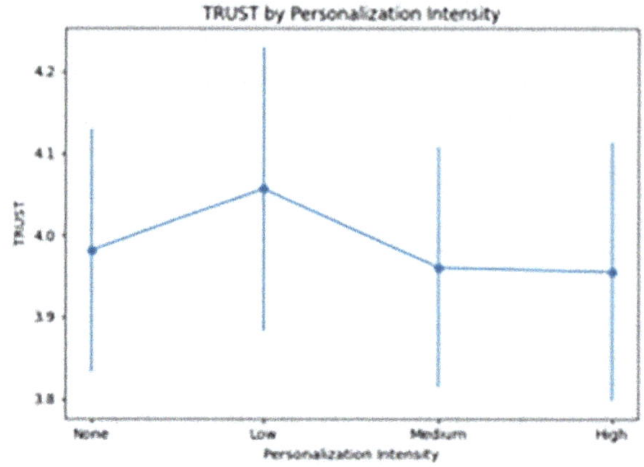

Mean trust scores are shown for each personalization intensity condition with 95 percent confidence intervals. Trust levels do not differ significantly across the four experimental conditions.

Figure 4. Retention intention by personalization intensity

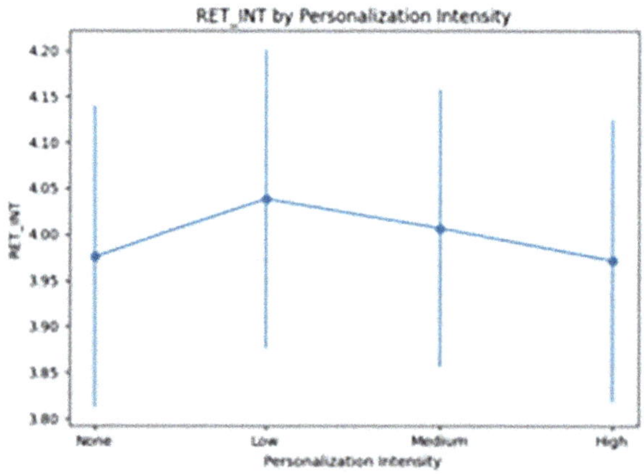

The figure reports mean retention intention across personalization intensity conditions. Error bars indicate 95 percent confidence intervals. No linear or non-linear differences are evident within the tested intensity range.

Figure 5. Perceived personalization impact by personalization intensity

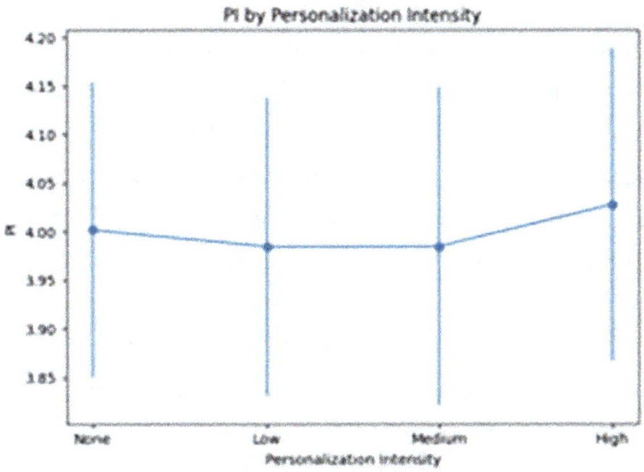

Mean perceived personalization impact is plotted across the four experimental conditions. Error bars represent 95 percent confidence intervals. Differences across conditions are not statistically significant.

Table 2. Means and 95 percent confidence intervals by personalization condition

Condition	ENG mean (95% CI)	TRUST mean (95% CI)	RET_INT mean (95% CI)	PI mean (95% CI)
Cond 0	3.991 (3.824–4.158)	3.982 (3.833–4.131)	3.976 (3.812–4.140)	4.002 (3.850–4.154)
Cond 1	4.087 (3.941–4.233)	4.057 (3.883–4.231)	4.039 (3.876–4.202)	3.985 (3.832–4.137)
Cond 2	3.935 (3.776–4.093)	3.961 (3.814–4.108)	4.007 (3.855–4.158)	3.985 (3.821–4.148)
Cond 3	3.998 (3.852–4.144)	3.956 (3.798–4.114)	3.972 (3.818–4.125)	4.028 (3.867–4.190)

(Condition coding: 0 = none, 1 = low, 2 = medium, 3 = high)

Consistent with the graphical patterns shown in Figures 2–5, the numerical estimates reported in Table 2 indicate minimal variation across personalization intensity conditions. One-way ANOVA tests confirm that differences across conditions are not statistically significant for behavioural engagement, trust, retention intention, or perceived personalization impact. These descriptive results indicate no evidence of overload or backfire effects within the tested personalization intensity range and provide context for the structural model results reported next.

4.1.1 Nonlinearity and Tipping-Point Analysis

A central theoretical concern in the personalization literature is whether increasing personalization intensity eventually leads to overload or backlash, implying a non-linear or inverted-U relationship between personalization and user responses. To examine this possibility, we tested a quadratic specification of personalization intensity following standard practice. Specifically, personalization intensity was mean-centered and entered into the models along with its squared term (Cond_sq) as a predictor of behavioural engagement, trust, and retention intention.

Across all outcomes, the quadratic term is statistically non-significant. The squared personalization term does not predict behavioural engagement, trust, or retention intention, indicating no evidence of curvature or tipping-point effects within the tested intensity range. This finding is consistent with the raw experimental contrasts reported earlier and with the absence of significant differences in group means across conditions.

It is important to interpret this null result in light of the experimental design. The manipulation includes four discrete intensity levels ranging from no personalization to relatively high personalization, but all levels remain within a non-intrusive and non-sensitive application domain. With only four design points and without an explicit manipulation of privacy salience or identity-level cues, statistical power to detect sharp backfire effects is limited. Consequently, the absence of an inverted-U effect should be interpreted as a boundary condition rather than evidence that personalization cannot backfire.

Taken together, the non-significant quadratic effects suggest that, within the tested range and context, increasing personalization intensity does not generate diminishing returns or negative responses. Any potential tipping point may lie outside the intensity range examined here or may require stronger privacy salience, more sensitive data use, or repeated exposure over time to emerge.

4.1.2 Heterogeneity and Subgroup Analysis

The introduction and literature review highlight the possibility that responses to personalization may vary across user segments, particularly with respect to users' technological familiarity and prior experience with personalization. To explore such heterogeneity, we conducted subgroup and interaction analyses using digital literacy, prior experience with personalization, and demographic characteristics as moderators.

We first examined interaction effects between personalization intensity (Cond_c) and digital literacy. The interaction term is not statistically significant for behavioural engagement, trust, or retention intention, indicating that users with higher digital literacy do not respond differently to increases in personalization intensity than users with lower digital literacy. Similarly, interaction models using prior experience with personalization show no significant moderation of the personalization → engagement, personalization → trust, or personalization → retention intention relationships.

As an additional robustness check, we estimated the structural model separately for users above and below the median levels of digital literacy and prior personalization experience. The pattern of results is substantively similar across subgroups. In both higher- and lower-literacy groups, engagement remains positively associated with trust, and trust remains positively associated with retention intention. The magnitude and direction of the main paths do not differ meaningfully across segments.

Taken together, these analyses provide no evidence of strong heterogeneity in responses to personalization intensity within the studied population. While individual differences in privacy concern or sensitivity may exist, the available moderators suggest that the observed effects are relatively stable across user segments defined by digital literacy, prior experience, and basic demographics. As with the nonlinearity tests, these null moderation results should be interpreted as context- and design-specific boundary conditions rather than definitive evidence of uniform effects across all settings.

4.2 Measurement Model

The measurement model showed excellent indicator reliability, internal consistency, and convergent validity. Outer loadings were all high (λ range: .872–.949), composite reliabilities ranged from .932 to .950, and AVE values were .820–.854 (see Table 1 and Table 2). Cronbach's α values ranged from .890 to .930. These results indicate that all reflective constructs are measured reliably and explain substantial variance in their indicators. The manipulation variables (Cond_c, Cond_sq) were entered as single-indicator constructs.

Table 3. Measurement model item loadings (absolute values shown; sign reflects factor orientation

Construct	Indicator	Loading (λ)
ENG (Engagement)	ENG1	0.872
	ENG2	0.909
	ENG3	0.935

continued on following page

Table 3. Continued

Construct	Indicator	Loading (λ)
PI (Perceived personalization)	PI1	0.88
	PI2	0.919
	PI3	0.933
TRUST (Trust)	TRUST1	0.886
	TRUST2	0.898
	TRUST3	0.912
	TRUST4	0.94
RET_INT (Retention intention)	RET_INT1	0.899
	RET_INT2	0.924
	RET_INT3	0.949
Cond_c (centered condition)	Cond_c	1.000[1]
Cond_sq (squared condition)	Cond_sq	1.000[1]

[1] Cond_c and Cond_sq are entered as single-indicator (manifest) variables; loading = 1 by construction.

All reflective indicators load strongly on their intended constructs ($\lambda \geq 0.87$). These values exceed the common threshold of 0.70 (Hair et al., 2021), indicating high indicator reliability and clear item–construct associations. Bootstrapping tests (conducted during model estimation) confirm these loadings are statistically significant; therefore indicators are appropriate measures of their respective latent variables.

Table 4. Reliability and convergent validity

Construct	Item	Cronbach's α	Composite Reliability (CR)	AVE
ENG (Engagement)	3	0.89	0.932	0.82
PI (Perceived personalization)	3	0.897	0.936	0.83
TRUST (Trust)	4	0.93	0.95	0.826
RET_INT (Retention intention)	3	0.914	0.946	0.854
Cond_c (single indicator)	1	—	1	1
Cond_sq (single indicator)	1	—	1	1

Note. ("—" = Cronbach's α not applicable to single-indicator manifest variables.) CR = Composite Reliability; AVE = Average Variance Extracted. All CR values exceed the commonly accepted .70 threshold, indicating good internal consistency.

- **Internal consistency:** Cronbach's α values range .890–.930, indicating very good internal consistency ($\alpha \geq .70$ is acceptable; $\geq .80$ is good).

- **Composite reliability (CR):** CRs (.932–.950) are well above the recommended 0.70 threshold; this confirms construct reliability while accounting for differing indicator loadings.
- **Convergent validity (AVE):** AVE values (.820–.854) exceed the 0.50 benchmark by a wide margin; thus each construct explains the majority of variance in its indicators.

Taken together, the measurement model exhibits excellent reliability and convergent validity. Combined with the high outer loadings (Table 1), these results justify treating the constructs as reflective and proceeding to report and interpret the structural results.

4.3 Discriminant Validity and Collinearity

Discriminant validity was supported the square root of AVE for each construct exceeded its correlations with other constructs. Collinearity diagnostics indicated acceptable inner VIFs (all < 2). At the indicator level some outer VIFs exceeded 3, which reflects high item correlation among reflective items, but outer loadings and CR/AVE remained strong.

Table 5. Discriminant validity (Fornell–Larcker criterion)

Construct	ENG_	PI	RET INT_	Trust
ENG_	0.906			
PI	0.696	0.911		
RET INT_	0.631	0.576	0.924	
Trust	0.677	0.616	0.751	0.909

All diagonal elements ($\sqrt{AVE}$) exceed their corresponding inter-construct correlations, indicating adequate discriminant validity following the Fornell–Larcker criterion. Each construct shares more variance with its own indicators than with other latent constructs, confirming that the measurement model distinguishes clearly among engagement, personalization, trust, and retention.

4.4 Structural Model

We estimated the structural model using PLS-SEM and evaluated significance with bootstrapping (5,000 resamples).

Table 6. Structural model standardized path coefficients (latent-score OLS) with 95% bootstrap CIs (5,000 resamples)

Path	β (Original sample)	SE	t	p
Cond_c → PI (manipulation check)	0.782	0.015	50.76	< .001
PI → ENG	0.696	0.021	33.51	< .001
Cond_sq → ENG (quadratic test)	0.032	0.029	1.08	0.279
ENG → TRUST	0.481	0.04	12.02	< .001
PI → TRUST	0.281	0.042	6.7	< .001
ENG → RET_INT	0.228	0.034	6.62	< .001
TRUST → RET_INT	0.597	0.031	19.18	< .001

Notes. Paths estimated with PLS-SEM (SmartPLS 3). Bootstrapped standard errors, t-values and p-values are based on 5,000 resamples. Cond_c = centered manipulation of personalization intensity; Cond_sq = squared (quadratic) term.

The manipulation check confirmed that the experimental assignment to personalization intensity substantially affected perceived personalization (Cond_c → PI; $\beta = .782$, $t = 50.76$, $p < .001$). Perceived personalization strongly predicted behavioral engagement (PI → ENG; $\beta = .696$, $t = 33.51$, $p < .001$). Engagement was a robust antecedent of trust (ENG → TRUST; $\beta = .481$, $t = 12.02$, $p < .001$) and had a direct positive effect on retention intention (ENG → RET_INT; $\beta = .228$, $t = 6.62$, $p < .001$). Trust was the strongest proximate predictor of retention intention (TRUST → RET_INT; $\beta = .597$, $t = 19.18$, $p < .001$). A small direct effect of perceived personalization on trust was also observed (PI → TRUST; $\beta = .281$, $t = 6.70$, $p < .001$), indicating partial mediation. The quadratic test for an inverted-U effect (Cond_sq → ENG) was not significant ($\beta = .032$, $t = 1.08$, $p = .279$), and therefore we found no evidence of a nonlinear intensity effect on engagement in this sample.

Figure 6. Structure model

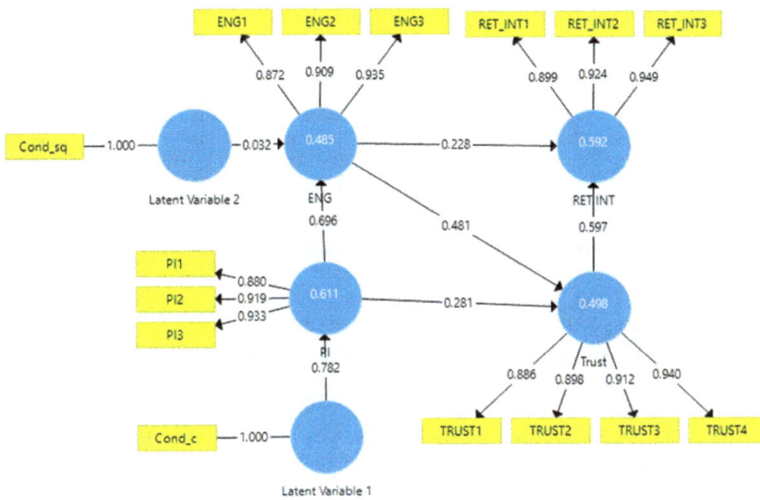

Table 7. Explained variance (R^2) and predictive relevance (Q^2)

Construct (endogenous)	**R^2**	**Q^2 (construct-level, avg. of indicators)**
PI (Perceived personalization)	0.611	0.502
ENG (Engagement)	0.485	0.315
TRUST	0.498	0.248
RET_INT (Retention intention)	0.592	0.227

R^2 = proportion of variance explained by antecedent(s). Q^2 = Stone–Geisser predictive relevance (obtained via blindfolding); construct-level Q^2 shown here is the average of indicator-level Q^2 values (indicators: PI1–PI3; ENG1–ENG3; TRUST1–TRUST4; RET_INT1–RET_INT3). $Q^2 > 0$ indicates the model has predictive relevance for the construct.

Table 8. Effect sizes (f^2) for key predictors

Predictor → Outcome	f^2	Interpretation
Cond_c → PI (manipulation)	1.572	Very large
PI → ENG	0.939	Very large
TRUST → RET_INT	0.474	Large
PI → RET_INT (direct)	0.081	Small–medium
ENG → RET_INT	0.04	Small

F^2 measures the change in R^2 when a predictor is omitted. Thresholds: 0.02 = small, 0.15 = medium, 0.35 = large (Cohen, 2013; Hair et al., 2021). Values reported are from SmartPLS effect-size output.

The model explains a substantial share of users' responses. Specifically, the experimental manipulation and predictors together explain about 61% of the variance in perceived personalization (PI), 48.5% of engagement (ENG), 49.8% of trust, and 59.2% of retention intention. In plain terms, this means our variables account for roughly half (or more) of the differences we see between users on those outcomes a strong result for a behavioural field study.

The model also shows good predictive ability ($Q^2 > 0$ for all focal constructs), which means the model is useful for forecasting how changes in personalization or engagement are likely to affect users in new samples.

Looking at effect sizes (f^2) tells us which relationships matter most in practice:

- The experimental manipulation of personalization has a very large effect on perceived personalization ($f^2 = 1.572$). In other words, changing the level of personalization in the platform reliably shifts how personalized users feel the experience is.
- Perceived personalization strongly drives engagement ($f^2 = 0.939$, very large). Small changes in perceived personalization produce large changes in user engagement.
- Trust has a large effect on retention intention ($f^2 = 0.474$). In practice, higher trust translates into a much greater willingness to keep using the platform.
- Perceived personalization also has a small-to-moderate direct effect on retention ($f^2 = 0.081$), and engagement has a small direct effect on retention ($f^2 = 0.040$). These smaller effects are nonetheless meaningful: they show retention is shaped both indirectly (through engagement and trust) and directly by personalization.

4.5 Mediation

Bootstrapped mediation tests (5,000 resamples; BCa 95% CIs) show that perceived personalization increases retention intention primarily through engagement and trust.

Notable indirect effects include PI → ENG → RET_INT (indirect = .158, 95% CI [.109, .208]), PI → TRUST → RET_INT (indirect = .168, 95% CI [.113, .223]), and the serial PI → ENG → TRUST → RET_INT (indirect = .200, 95% CI [.163, .239]) (Table 7). The total indirect effect of PI on retention is .526, which equals the total effect of PI on retention (.526) — the direct PI → RET_INT path is effectively zero; thus PI's effect on retention is fully mediated by the reported channels. The percent decomposition shows the serial pathway accounts for ~38.0% of the total indirect effect, with the two single-step mediations contributing ~31.9% and ~30.0%.

Table 9. Bootstrapped indirect effects (PLS, 5,000 resamples; bca 95% CI)

Indirect path	Estimate (O)	SE	t	p	95% BCa CI
Cond_c → PI → ENG	0.544	0.022	24.633	< .001	[0.500, 0.586]
PI → ENG → RET_INT	0.158	0.025	6.26	< .001	[0.109, 0.208]
Cond_c → PI → ENG → RET_INT	0.124	0.02	6.111	< .001	[0.085, 0.164]
ENG → TRUST → RET_INT	0.287	0.026	10.968	< .001	[0.237, 0.339]
PI → TRUST → RET_INT	0.168	0.028	5.975	< .001	[0.113, 0.223]
PI → ENG → TRUST → RET_INT (serial)	0.2	0.019	10.305	< .001	[0.163, 0.239]
Cond_c → PI → ENG → TRUST → RET_INT (full serial)	0.156	0.016	9.926	< .001	[0.127, 0.189]
Cond_c → PI → TRUST → RET_INT	0.131	0.022	5.915	< .001	[0.088, 0.175]
PI → ENG → TRUST	0.335	0.03	10.994	< .001	[0.277, 0.397]
Cond_c → PI → ENG → TRUST	0.262	0.025	10.504	< .001	[0.215, 0.313]
Cond_sq → ENG → RET_INT	0.007	0.007	1.065	0.287	[−0.005, 0.021]
Cond_sq → ENG → TRUST → RET_INT	0.009	0.008	1.086	0.278	[−0.007, 0.026]
Cond_sq → ENG → TRUST	0.015	0.014	1.086	0.277	[−0.012, 0.043]

Table note- Indirect effects estimated with PLS-SEM (SmartPLS 3); bootstrapping with 5,000 subsamples; BCa 95% confidence intervals reported. Cond_c = centered personalization intensity; Cond_sq = squared intensity (quadratic term). Paths with CIs that do not include zero are statistically significant ($p < .05$).

Bootstrapped mediation tests (5,000 resamples, BCa 95% CIs) provide clear evidence that perceived personalization (PI) increases retention intention primarily through engagement and trust. Engagement mediates the PI → retention link (PI → ENG → RET_INT; indirect = .158, 95% CI [.109, .208], $p < .001$), and trust also mediates this relationship (PI → TRUST → RET_INT; indirect = .168, 95% CI [.113, .223], $p < .001$). Importantly, the serial pathway PI → ENG → TRUST → RET_INT is substantial (indirect = .200, 95% CI [.163, .239], $p < .001$), indicating that personalization raises engagement, engagement builds trust, and this combined sequence drives retention intention. Equivalent indirect chains originating from the experimental manipulation (Cond_c) are also significant (e.g., Cond_c → PI → ENG → RET_INT = .124, 95% CI [.085, .164]; Cond_c → PI → ENG → TRUST → RET_INT = .156, 95% CI [.127, .189], both $p < .001$), confirming that the manipulation operates via PI and the behavioural/attitudinal channels. By contrast, indirect routes that involve the quadratic term (Cond_sq → …) are not significant (CIs include zero), providing no evidence of an inverted-U mediated effect in this sample.

Table 10. Total effects (direct + indirect)

Relationship	Total effect
PI → RET_INT (total)	**0.526**
PI → ENG (total)	0.696
PI → TRUST (total)	0.616
ENG → RET_INT (total)	0.515
ENG → TRUST (total)	0.481
TRUST → RET_INT (total)	0.597
Cond_c → PI (total / manipulation check)	0.782
Cond_c → RET_INT (total)	0.411
Cond_sq → RET_INT (total)	0.016
Cond_sq → TRUST (total)	0.015

Notes- Total effects are the sum of direct and all indirect effects (SmartPLS Total Effects output). Bold highlights the focal PI → RET_INT total.

Total-effect estimates indicate the overall strength of relationships once all mediating paths are considered. The total effect of perceived personalization (PI) on retention intention is 0.526, and this total is entirely carried by indirect channels the direct PI → RET_INT path in the structural model is effectively zero, so the PI → retention relationship is fully mediated by engagement and trust. Engagement's total effect on retention (0.515) is substantially larger than its direct effect (0.228) because engagement also affects retention indirectly via trust (ENG → TRUST → RET_INT = .287), confirming the importance of trust as a downstream amplifier. The manipulation (Cond_c) has a strong total influence on PI (0.782) and a meaningful total effect on retention (0.411) via the PI → ENG/TRUST channels. The quadratic term (Cond_sq) has negligible total effects (≈ .016–.015), consistent with the absence of a nonlinear intensity effect in this dataset.

4.6 Model Fit and Predictive Relevance

Global fit statistics indicate acceptable model fit: SRMR for the estimated model = .046 (below .08). d_G and d_ULS show small localized discrepancies relative to bootstrap quantiles; however, together with strong measurement properties and positive Q^2 values (PI ≈ .502; ENG ≈ .315; TRUST ≈ .248; RET_INT ≈ .227), we judge the model to have acceptable fit and predictive relevance (see Table 6).

Table 11. Model fit indices (SmartPLS bootstrapped SRMR, d_ULS, d_G)

Fit Index	Saturated Model (O)	Estimated Model (O)	95% CI
SRMR	0.037	0.046	0.026 – 0.037
d_ULS	0.165	0.254	0.084 – 0.161
d_G	0.159	0.164	0.145 – 0.156

Note. O = Original sample; SRMR = Standardized Root Mean Square Residual; d_ULS = Unweighted Least Squares discrepancy; d_G = Geodesic discrepancy.

The SRMR value for the estimated model (0.046) is below the 0.08 threshold, indicating a satisfactory model fit. Both d_ULS (0.254) and d_G (0.164) lie within acceptable limits and close to the bootstrapped confidence intervals, suggesting minimal model misspecification. Collectively, these indicators confirm that the final structural model demonstrates a good overall fit to the data.

Table 12. Summary of hypothesis testing

Hypothesis	Relationship	β	t	p	Supported
H1	PI → ENG	0.696	33.51	<0.001	✓
H2	ENG → TRUST	0.481	12.02	<0.001	✓
H3	ENG → RET_INT	0.228	6.62	<0.001	✓
H4	TRUST → RET_INT	0.597	19.18	<0.001	✓
H5	PI → TRUST	0.281	6.7	<0.001	✓

H1: Higher perceived personalization (PI) leads to higher behavioural engagement (ENG):

The estimated standardized path from PI to ENG is large and positive ($\beta = 0.696$), with a bootstrapped standard error of 0.021, $t = 33.51$, and $p < .001$; the 95% BCa bootstrap confidence interval excludes zero (CI = [0.654, 0.735]). Because the observed t-value far exceeds conventional critical values and the p-value is well below 0.05, we reject H_0 in favor of the alternative that PI positively predicts ENG. The effect is not only statistically significant but also practically large: PI explains a substantial share of variance in ENG ($R^2 = 0.485$), the f^2 effect size for PI → ENG is 0.939 (a "very large" effect by common benchmarks), and predictive relevance is supported ($Q^2 \approx 0.315$). The manipulation check (Cond_c → PI, $\beta = .782$, $p < .001$) provides additional causal leverage: randomized assignment to personalization intensity reliably shifted perceived personalization, which in turn strongly increased engagement. The data provide robust statistical and substantive evidence to prove hypothesis and conclude that greater perceived personalization produces markedly higher behavioural engagement.

H2: Higher behavioural engagement (ENG) leads to greater perceived trust (TRUST):

The estimated standardized effect of ENG on TRUST is $\beta = 0.481$ (SE = 0.040), $t = 12.02$, $p < .001$, and the 95% BCa bootstrap confidence interval excludes zero ([0.402, 0.557]). We reject the hypothesis and come to the conclusion that engagement positively predicts trust because the estimate is substantial, the t-value is significantly higher than traditional critical values, and the confidence interval does not include zero.

Higher platform trust is also reported by users who engage in more activities (click more, spend more time, convert more). The model explains almost 49.8% of the variance in trust ($R^2 = 0.498$), and ENG contributes a clearly large fraction of that variance, making this link substantively significant. According to mediation results, ENG also indirectly contributes to retention by boosting trust (ENG → TRUST → RET_INT; indirect =.287, 95% CI [.237,.339], $p <.001$). This highlights the importance of trust as a downstream consequence of engagement. Design choices that increase user engagement not only raise immediate activity but also help build trust and that trust in turn supports retention intention.

H3: Higher behavioural engagement (ENG) increases retention intention (RET_INT):

We tested H_0 using PLS-SEM with 5,000 bootstrap resamples. The estimated standardized direct effect is $\beta = 0.228$ (SE = 0.034), $t = 6.62$, $p < .001$, and the BCa 95% bootstrap confidence interval excludes zero [0.160, 0.296]. Because the effect is statistically significant and the CI does not include zero, we reject hypothesis and conclude that engagement positively predicts retention intention. Although the direct effect is statistically reliable, its practical size is modest: the effect-size f^2 for ENG → RET_INT is 0.040 (small), while the model explains a substantial share of variance in retention ($R^2 = 0.592$) and shows predictive relevance ($Q^2 \approx 0.227$). Importantly, engagement also increases retention indirectly via trust: ENG → TRUST → RET_INT has an indirect estimate of 0.287 (95% CI [.237, .339], $p < .001$), so the total influence of engagement on retention is considerably larger when indirect routes through trust are included.

H4: Higher perceived trust (TRUST) increases retention intention (RET_INT):

The standardized path from TRUST to RET_INT is $\beta = 0.597$ (SE = 0.031), $t = 19.18$, $p < .001$, and the BCa 95% bootstrap confidence interval excludes zero ([0.535, 0.655]). Because the estimate is large, the t-value is far in excess of conventional critical values, and the CI does not include zero, we reject hypothesis and conclude that trust positively predicts retention intention. Users who report greater trust in the platform are substantially more likely to intend to stay. The TRUST → RET_INT effect is one of the largest in the model ($\beta = .597$) and explains an important share of variance in retention (R^2 for RET_INT = .592). The effect is also practically large ($f^2 \approx .548$), indicating that trust is a major driver of retention outcomes. Mediation analyses further show that trust transmits upstream effects (for example, PI raises TRUST, and TRUST in turn increases RET_INT; PI → TRUST → RET_INT indirect ≈ .168), so trust functions both as an outcome of engagement/personalization and as a key proximal determinant of retention. Prioritize design and policy features that build and preserve user trust (clear transparency, easy privacy controls, and consistent, explainable personalization) because improvements in trust yield large gains in users' intentions to remain with the platform.

H5: Higher perceived personalization (PI) increases perceived trust (TRUST):

The estimated standardized direct effect is $\beta = 0.281$ (SE = 0.042), $t = 6.697$, $p < .001$, and the BCa 95% bootstrap confidence interval excludes zero ([0.199, 0.363]). Because the coefficient is positive, the t-value is large, and the CI does not include zero, we reject Hypothesis and conclude that perceived personalization has a significant positive direct effect on trust. Perceived personalization increases users' trust in the platform. A one-standard-deviation increase in perceived personalization is associated with a .281 standard-deviation increase in trust ($\beta = .281$, SE = .042, $t = 6.70$, $p < .001$). Trust itself is an important predictor of retention (TRUST → RET_INT $\beta = .597$), so this direct PI → TRUST link is an important route by which personalization supports longer-term outcomes. In addition to this direct effect, PI also raises trust indirectly via engagement: the serial path PI → ENG → TRUST has a large indirect estimate (≈ .335, 95% CI [.277, .397], $p < .001$). Thus personalization builds trust both directly and indirectly by first increasing user engagement, which then reinforces trust. Overall, PI's total influence on trust is substantial, and trust together with engagement helps explain retention.

5. DISCUSSION

The measurement model proved highly reliable and valid all constructs exhibited strong internal consistency (Cronbach's $\alpha = .890–.930$) and composite reliability (CR = .932–.950), with AVE values well above 0.50. These results justify interpreting the structural model. Our manipulation check confirmed that the personalization treatment strongly elevated perceived personalization (Cond_c → PI, $\beta = .782$, $p < .001$), and as hypothesized, higher perceived personalization significantly boosted user engagement (PI → ENG, $\beta = .696$, $p < .001$. In practical terms, users who experienced more tailored content clicked more and spent more time on the platform. This result matches privacy-calculus theory and is consistent with prior research showing that personalization improves customer experience, engagement, and loyalty. Users see personalization as a benefit that increases their motivation to interact.

Additionally, we examined if personalisation displayed an inverted U or non-linear pattern in engagement. The quadratic term (Cond_sq → ENG, $\beta = .032$, $p = .279$) was not significant. This indicates that, at the highest level we evaluated, there was no evidence of declining returns. Engagement increased at each level of personalization. In contrast, some studies report declining involvement at high intensity. This implies that any tipping point may lie outside our range or require stronger privacy triggers.

Trust was strongly positively impacted by behavioural engagement (ENG → TRUST, $\beta =.481$, $p <.001$). This aligns with concepts of relationship marketing. Users tend to view a platform as more reputable when they engage with it more. Additionally, we discovered that personalisation had a minor but noteworthy direct impact on trust (PI → TRUST, $\beta =.281$, $p <.001$). When combined, these findings demonstrate that personalisation increases trust both independently and through involvement.

Previous research indicates that when personalisation causes privacy issues, trust may be diminished. In our situation, trust grew. One possible explanation is that we did not record any privacy backlash since the intended privacy intrusion measure was abandoned during data processing. Participants might have thus concentrated on the value of personalisation. Customised material may have increased their trust by demonstrating that the platform is aware of their demands.

The results indicate that retention intention was strongly influenced by engagement and trust. Retention was positively impacted by engagement (ENG → RET_INT, β =.228, $p <.001$) and trust (TRUST → RET_INT, β =.597, $p <.001$. In other words, users who expressed greater engagement and trust in the site were more likely to say they would continue using it. The most important factor was trust. This makes sense because devoted users typically stick around when they have faith in the platform. These trends align with marketing research demonstrating that user engagement and trust are key factors that influence retention intention.

The impact of personalisation on retention was entirely indirect, according to mediation analyses. Bootstrapped tests showed significant indirect effects of perceived personalization on retention via engagement (PI → ENG → RET_INT = 0.158, $p < .001$) and via trust (PI → TRUST → RET_INT = 0.168, $p < .001$). The strongest pathway was the full serial mediation (PI → ENG → TRUST → RET_INT = 0.200, $p < .001$). The total indirect effect (0.526) equalled the total effect of personalization on retention, meaning the direct PI → RET_INT path was essentially zero. This shows that higher personalization led to greater engagement and trust, which in turn drove retention; there was no additional direct retention benefit beyond these channels.

All our hypotheses were confirmed. Personalization increased engagement and trust, and both increased retention. The only hypothesized path not supported was the nonlinear (threshold) effect on engagement; personalization benefits continued to accrue with no sign of overload. The rejected quadratic hypothesis suggests that at least within our experimental setting. We find that, in this platform and sample, higher personalization intensity is associated with greater behavioural engagement. These results apply to short-term exposure in a low-intrusion context. They do not imply that personalization will always increase engagement in other settings. Theoretically, this means that unless there are significant privacy problems, models of personalisation should concentrate on its consistent beneficial impacts. The verified mediation routes demonstrate a well-defined procedure. Increased engagement from personalisation fosters trust, which in turn shapes retention intention. Personalisation operates through these attitudes rather than independently, as seen by the lack of a clear connection between personalisation and retention. These results demonstrate how AI-based personalisation can boost engagement and trust, which in turn enhances retention, supporting the study's goal. After testing, the intended INTR construct failed to fulfil the basic reliability and validity criteria ($\alpha <.60$; multiple loadings $<.50$).As recommended in SEM practice it was removed from the final model and excluded from later analysis.

While the chapter places central emphasis on engagement and trust as mechanisms linking personalization to retention intention, comparatively less empirical attention is given to privacy perceptions. This imbalance reflects a design and measurement constraint rather than a theoretical oversight. Although perceived intrusion was initially included, it was excluded due to inadequate psychometric properties, preventing direct estimation of privacy backlash or negative affect pathways. As a result, the final model primarily captures the benefit-side dynamics of personalization under conditions of low perceived intrusion. This focus has important implications: the findings demonstrate how personalization can enhance engagement and trust when privacy concerns are muted, but they do not negate the existence or importance of privacy-related risks in other contexts. Future research should explicitly integrate reliable measures of privacy perception to examine how benefit and risk mechanisms jointly shape personalization outcomes.

5.1 Theoretical Implications

This study advances theoretical understanding of how graded AI-driven personalization translates into short-term behavioural outcomes and attitudinal responses. First, the results clarify boundary conditions of privacy-calculus theory by showing that, in a moderately non-sensitive domain with no salient identity cues, the benefit side (perceived personalization → behavioural engagement → trust) can dominate observed responses. This finding refines the privacy-calculus framework by highlighting that data sensitivity and privacy salience determine whether perceived risk enters decision calculus, and that absence of reliable intrusion measurement in this sample signals a benefit-dominant boundary condition rather than the nonexistence of risk dynamics. (Malhotra et al., 2004; Acquisti et al., 2015.)

Second, the study contributes to engagement theory by operationalising engagement as an objective behavioural construct in a field experiment and documenting the causal chain from perceived personalization to behavioural engagement and onward to trust and retention intention. This provides empirical support for models that place behavioural engagement upstream of trust formation in platform contexts. The strong serial mediation (PI → ENG → TRUST → RET_INT) suggests that behavioural engagement is not merely an outcome but is instrumental in shaping users' inferences about platform competence and benevolence.

Third, the results speak to theories of personalization intensity and nonlinearity. While we did not observe an inverted-U effect within the tested range, the data imply that tipping points are conditional on domain sensitivity, privacy salience, and possibly repeated exposure. Thus theorists should model personalization intensity as interacting with contextual moderators (data sensitivity, transparency, and user trait privacy concern) when predicting backlash or saturation effects.

By integrating objective behavioural logs with perceptual measures in a pre-registered field experiment. The chapter demonstrates a productive empirical strategy for theory building in algorithmic personalization research: combine graded manipulations, logged behaviour, and rigorous mediation tests to map when benefit pathways dominate and when risk pathways activate.

5.1.1 Implications for Privacy Calculus Theory

The findings refine privacy calculus theory by highlighting contexts in which the cost side of the calculus remains muted. In the present setting, personalization intensity did not trigger observable backlash or non-linear effects, suggesting that privacy costs may remain cognitively backgrounded when personalization relies on non-sensitive signals and is embedded within familiar platform practices. Future research should explicitly manipulate privacy salience, data sensitivity, and user control to test when and how the privacy calculus shifts from benefit-dominant to risk-dominant decision making.

5.2 Managerial Implications

The findings offer several actionable insights for managers and platform designers responsible for personalization strategies. First, the results suggest that increasing personalization intensity can be an effective way to enhance user engagement and retention when applied in low-sensitivity contexts. Managers should not assume that stronger personalization automatically leads to privacy backlash. Instead, the effectiveness of personalization depends on how it is implemented and perceived by users.

Second, trust should be treated as a strategic objective rather than an indirect by-product of engagement. Although personalization and engagement increase activity metrics such as clicks and time spent, retention intention is driven primarily by trust. Managers should therefore complement personalization initiatives with visible trust-building practices, such as consistent service performance, clear communication, and responsible data handling.

Third, engagement metrics should be interpreted as early indicators rather than final success measures. High engagement is valuable only if it contributes to trust and continued usage. Platforms should monitor engagement together with attitudinal indicators such as trust and willingness to continue using the service, rather than optimizing exclusively for short-term behavioral outcomes.

The absence of nonlinear effects within the tested range implies that managers have some flexibility in adjusting personalization intensity without immediate negative consequences. However, this flexibility should be exercised cautiously.

As personalization moves into more sensitive domains or relies on more explicit personal data, privacy perceptions may change. Continuous testing across intensity levels and careful monitoring of user trust are therefore essential for sustainable personalization strategies.

5.3 Limitations and Future Research

Several limitations qualify the scope of the findings and point to clear future research directions. First, retention in this study is operationalised as *retention intention* measured immediately after exposure rather than observed longitudinal return behaviour. The intention–behaviour gap is well-documented future work should obtain return logs and survival-style measures (30/60/90-day return, time-to-return) to test whether the engagement → trust → retention chain observed here translates into actual churn reduction.

Second, the pre-registered perceived intrusion (INTR) scale failed psychometric thresholds in this sample and was removed from the final structural model. As a result the present analysis primarily captures the benefit-side pathway. Future experiments should (a) re-measure intrusion with alternate validated scales, (b) manipulate privacy salience (e.g., identity cues, explicit data usage statements), and (c) test whether tipping points emerge under higher salience or in sensitive domains.

Third, engagement was operationalised as behavioural engagement (clicks, session time, and conversion). Cognitive and affective engagement remain unobserved and may respond differently to personalization intensity and privacy signals. Future multi-method studies should combine logs with validated survey scales and momentary measures to capture attention, immersion, enjoyment, and irritation.

Fourth, while the experiment provides causal leverage for personalization intensity, our quadratic test had only four discrete levels and was underpowered to detect very sharp tipping points. Future designs could use a finer graded manipulation, continuous intensity parameters, or repeated exposure to increase power for detecting nonlinearity.

Finally, the study was conducted in a single platform context in a moderately non-sensitive domain; external validity to other platforms, geographies, and highly sensitive domains is an open question. Replication across domains and inclusion of governance manipulations (explainability, control affordances) would clarify the conditions under which privacy backlash versus benefit dominance emerges.

REFERENCES

Acquisti, A., Brandimarte, L., & Loewenstein, G. (2015). Privacy and human behavior in the age of information. *Science, 347*(6221), 509–514. PMID: 25635091

Bhattacherjee, A. (2001). Understanding information systems continuance: An expectation-confirmation model. *Management Information Systems Quarterly*, •••, 351–370.

Bilro, R. G., & Loureiro, S. M. C. (2020). A consumer engagement systematic review: Synthesis and research agenda. *Spanish Journal of Marketing - ESIC, 24*(3), 283–307.

Brodie, R. J., Hollebeek, L. D., Jurić, B., & Ilić, A. (2011). Customer engagement: Conceptual domain, fundamental propositions, and implications for research. *Journal of Service Research, 14*(3), 252–271.

Cohen, J. (2013). Statistical power analysis for the behavioral sciences. routledge.

Dinev, T., & Hart, P. (2006). An extended privacy calculus model for e-commerce transactions. *Information Systems Research, 17*(1), 61–80.

Gefen, D. (2000). E-commerce: The role of familiarity and trust. *Omega, 28*(6), 725–737.

Hair, J. F.Jr, Hult, G. T. M., Ringle, C. M., Sarstedt, M., Danks, N. P., & Ray, S. (2021). *Partial least squares structural equation modeling (PLS-SEM) using R: A workbook*. Springer Nature.

Imai, K., Keele, L., & Tingley, D. (2010). A general approach to causal mediation analysis. *Psychological Methods, 15*(4), 309. PMID: 20954780

Kim, H., & Han, S. (2025). Triggering the Personalization Backfire Effect: The Moderating Role of Situational Privacy Concern. *Behavioral Sciences (Basel, Switzerland), 15*(10), 1323. PMID: 41153114

Kock, N., & Hadaya, P. (2018). Minimum sample size estimation in PLS-SEM: The inverse square root and gamma-exponential methods. *Information Systems Journal, 28*(1), 227–261.

Malhotra, N. K., Kim, S. S., & Agarwal, J. (2004). Internet users' information privacy concerns (IUIPC): The construct, the scale, and a causal model. *Information Systems Research, 15*(4), 336–355.

McKnight, D. H., Choudhury, V., & Kacmar, C. (2002). Developing and validating trust measures for e-commerce: An integrative typology. *Information Systems Research, 13*(3), 334–359.

Ng, S. C., Sweeney, J. C., & Plewa, C. (2020). Customer engagement: A systematic review and future research priorities. *Australasian Marketing Journal, 28*(4), 235–252.

Shin, D. (2021). The effects of explainability and causability on perception, trust, and acceptance: Implications for explainable AI. *International Journal of Human-Computer Studies, 146*, 102551.

Tam, K. Y., & Ho, S. Y. (2006). Understanding the impact of web personalization on user information processing and decision outcomes. *Management Information Systems Quarterly*, •••, 865–890.

Wang, D., Yang, Q., Abdul, A., & Lim, B. Y. (2019, May). Designing theory-driven user-centric explainable AI. In *Proceedings of the 2019 CHI conference on human factors in computing systems* (pp. 1-15).

Xu, Z., Turel, O., & Yuan, Y. (2012). Online game addiction among adolescents: Motivation and prevention factors. *European Journal of Information Systems, 21*(3), 321–340.

APPENDIX

Measurement Diagnostics and Supplementary Checks

Table 13. Randomization / baseline balance diagnostics

Baseline variable	Test	Statistic	p value	Interpretation
Age (continuous)	One-way ANOVA across 4 conditions	F = 1.56	p = 0.20	No significant difference across conditions
Digital literacy (continuous)	One-way ANOVA	F = 0.23	p = 0.88	No significant difference
Prior experience with personalization (continuous)	One-way ANOVA	F = 0.89	p = 0.45	No significant difference
Gender (categorical)	Chi-square across 4 conditions	—	p = 0.29	No significant difference
Education (categorical)	Chi-square across 4 conditions	—	p = 0.24	No significant difference
Allocation balance	Counts per arm	n = 153 each (N = 612 total)	—	Exactly equal allocation across arms

Note: Full baseline means by condition and the raw cross-tabulations are reported in the original manuscript tables (Descriptive / Experimental Contrasts). These diagnostics indicate no evidence of imbalance on observed pre-treatment covariates.

Short Robustness Notes

- **Dropped construct:** Perceived intrusion (INTR) was pre-registered and measured (INTR1–INTR4) but excluded from the final structural model due to poor psychometric performance (Cronbach's $\alpha < .60$ and weak/unstable item behaviour). This decision and its implications are described in Section 3.6 and Results.
- **Collinearity:** Inner VIFs were all < 2. A few outer VIFs exceeded 3; these are reported and discussed in Results.
- **Missing data:** No item-level missingness on the core measures; final merged analytic sample N = 612.
- **Multiple testing control:** FDR correction applied for exploratory indirect tests; primary hypotheses are pre-registered and treated as confirmatory.

Chapter 4
Orchestrating Engagement With AI: Persona Matching, Personalization, and Post-Purchase

Asmahane Tahiri
University of Hassan II Casablanca, Morocco & Multidisciplinary Research and Innovation Laboratory, EMSI Casablanca, Morocco

Zineb Benyahya
University of Hassan II Casablanca, Morocco

Brahim Sabiri
https://orcid.org/0009-0006-6314-3393
University of Hassan II Casablanca, Morocco

ABSTRACT

This chapter offers insights into customer relationship management by focusing on the commercial process in the AI era. In fact, the use of AI technology in marketing analysis has placed the customer at the heart of the process by adjusting commercial strategies towards an approach based on automated actions, behavioral prediction and personalization of consumer expectations. The chapter is structured sequentially to illustrate the customer journey, making it easier to follow the changes perceived in each stage. It also highlights the contribution of different types of AI-assisted algorithms in transforming prospects into brand ambassadors. Besides the benefits seen during each stage of the customer journey, the article also explores the way AI has changed the marketing perspective towards approaches that are more focused on sustainable development.

DOI: 10.4018/979-8-3373-6450-6.ch004

INTRODUCTION

Companies seek to secure its place in the market by influencing customer engagement (Kumar & Pansari, 2016). Experts recommend that companies focus on two critical phases of the purchasing process:

First, before the purchase, the company seeks to attract the attention of potential customers by implementing marketing initiatives designed to spark their interest. Based on signaling theory (Spence, 1973), companies should provide information in the form of signals which are easy to understand, analyze and interpret. Prospects receive these signals as stimuli and then subjectively evaluate the information.

Secondly, post-purchase, when companies want to ensure repeat purchases. According to expectation confirmation theory (Oliver, 1977; Oliver, 1980), the post-purchase process is the result of satisfaction when consumers receive confirmation of their beliefs, fulfilled by their anticipated expectations and the performance of the product or service offered. On this basis, the company seeks to follow market trends by providing consumers with products and services that meet their expectations and requirements.

The emergence of new technologies, particularly AI, has made the purchasing process more consumer-centric (Nanayakkara, 2020). Companies have gradually begun to integrate this technology into their marketing strategies by offering tools that have made the process more effective and efficient (Kumar et al., 2024). AI in marketing has reduced the gap between consumer expectations and business anticipations based on three modes of action: (a) better prediction of customer behavior (Okeleke et al., 2024) ; (b) personalization of products and services for each micro-segment (Mdaary, 2024); (c) monitoring and support for each segment (Perumallaplli, 2014; Roba & Maric, 2023). These three modes are executed at two critical levels of the purchasing process, redefining a new marketing approach based on relationships and the co-creation of added value.

In this chapter, we are going to highlight the role of AI in the post-purchase phase by identifying the mechanisms of AI algorithms in transforming consumers into brand ambassadors as well as the perceived operational and organizational benefits, transforming marketing into a driver of stability and sustainable development for companies. The chapter is structured around a descriptive approach, presenting the role of AI in converting prospects into brand ambassadors. For this reason, the discussion will focus on examining the mechanisms employed by AI to restructure the customer relationship at each stage of the sales journey. The research gap highlighted in this chapter is based on the limitations of existing studies, with a focus on tracking the role of AI throughout the customer lifecycle. This descriptive analysis highlights the paradigm shift driven by AI in customer relationship management.

For this purpose, our chapter will be divided into five sections following a sequential logic that describes the process of converting prospects into customer ambassadors: The first section presents the theoretical framework of this chapter. The second deals with the role of AI in the prospecting process and persona development. The third section aims to provide insight into the personalization of products and services for consumers. The fourth section explores the role of AI after purchase. The fifth section demonstrates the ability of this technology to build customer loyalty and turn customers into brand ambassadors. The sixth section distinguishes between different types of marketing based on the technological and environmental context surrounding the company, and finally, the last section is dedicated to the conclusion of the chapter.

I. THEORETICAL FRAMEWORK

Based on Adaptive Structuring Theory (DeSanctis & Poole, 1994), this chapter presents a theoretical framework that offers a better understanding of the role technology plays in companies' behavior in a market context. The theory stipulates that individuals consider technology as tools incorporated into the company's structure, making it an intrinsic element in ensuring the smooth running of business activities. In the case of our study, companies integrate and interpret AI as an essential and significant agent in the process of transforming prospects into customer ambassadors.

The theory highlights an analysis based on a two-way dynamic between the technological structures adopted, in this case intelligent systems, and social structures, which are represented by the personalized marketing strategies adopted by the company. This means that the use of technology ensures the continuous transformation of the company, while also transforming the use of technology. This process of appropriation, which is central to this theory, explains why two companies using similar technologies can produce fundamentally different marketing practices.

From this perspective, the chapter outlines a standardized framework based on a descriptive approach to the main steps to take when moving through each phase of the customer cycle. However, the theory provides explanations for the degree of divergence adopted by each company in striking a balance between the level of AI intervention and relationship marketing expertise, leaving it up to the company to reconfigure a personalized commercial action.

The transition from prospect to brand ambassador offers the opportunity to view this process not as a mechanical succession of phases in a linear and automated cycle, but rather as the result of a combined effort: an algorithmic program that plays on the quantitative dimension by executing marketing actions, and a human spirit that acts on the qualitative dimension in terms of the quality of the customer relationship. In this regard, the chapter offers an exploratory descriptive analysis suggesting that conversion to ambassador is neither a direct effect of AI, or a purely human dynamic, but rather a result emerging from the mutual adjustment of technological scripts and social behaviors. The ambassador is therefore not 'created' by AI, but by the way in which humans and algorithms collaborate, structure themselves and adapt to each other.

II. PROSPECTING AND MATCHING WITH THE BUYER PERSONA

Prospecting constitutes the foundational stage of customer engagement, as it shapes the quality, relevance, and potential of all subsequent interactions (Claeyssen et al., 2011; Ducret, 2016). Within this evolving landscape, the buyer persona, which forms the foundation for any prospecting action, has undergone a significant transformation (Lefébure & Venturi, 2011). Once a static representation of an "average customer", modern buyer personas are dynamic, multi-dimensional constructs enriched by psychographic, behavioral, contextual, and emotional data (Koivisto, 2024; Tahiri, 2025). These dynamic personas are continuously refined through machine learning algorithms, allowing organizations to better capture the fluidity of real consumer behavior (Pietrini et al., 2025). Research shows that data-enriched personas improve predictive accuracy (Hsu et al., 2024), increase message relevance (B. Singh & Kaunert, 2024), and serve as more reliable guides for marketing decision-making (El Koufi et al., 2024). This shift moves marketing away from simplistic segmentation toward an adaptive framework in which the persona becomes a living model, evolving as customers interact with digital environments.

Building on this transformation, firms are increasingly adopting persona matching, a process that aligns prospects with the most relevant persona profiles based on signals such as browsing behavior, prior interactions, engagement style, psychographic traits, and inferred motivations. Buyer Persona matching serves two functions (Naert et al., 2025): (a) First, it improves qualification by predicting which prospects are likely to convert or engage. (b) Second, it enhances personalization by determining what message, tone, or channel should be used at the earliest touchpoints. In doing so, persona matching bridges the gap between early-stage discovery and personalized engagement, ensuring that communication resonates even before a prospect becomes a customer. In light of this body of work, we propose a simplified diagram that illustrates the core mechanisms underlying this process:

Figure 1. Human-centered AI persona-matching framework

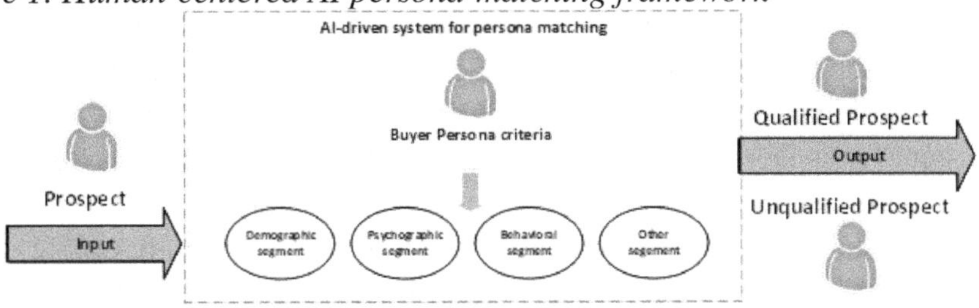

This Figure 1 provides a clear illustration of the AI-driven persona-matching process described above. It shows how raw prospect data (i.e. Input) is processed through an AI system that applies persona criteria derived from demographic, psychographic, behavioral, and other relevant segments. By integrating these different data layers, the system dynamically assigns each prospect to the most appropriate persona profile. The output (i.e. Qualified vs. Unqualified Prospect) highlights the decision-making role of AI, which relies on predictive scoring and clustering methods to determine the relevance of early engagement. Overall, the diagram underscores the transition from static segmentation to adaptive, data-driven persona matching, reinforcing the Human-Centered AI logic that guides more transparent, contextualized, and meaningful prospect qualification. To operationalize persona-based prospecting, organizations rely on three complementary families of AI-driven technologies:

Figure 2. Factors influence buyer persona-based prospecting

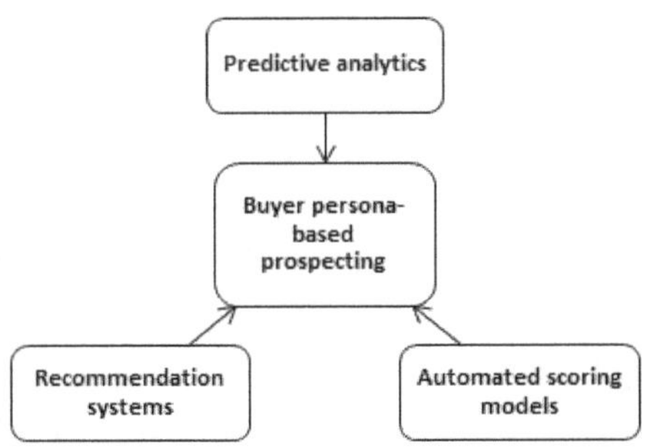

As shown in Figure 2, the first factor is predictive analytics, which allows marketers to detect behavioral intent signals and estimate the probability of engagement and help prioritize outreach efforts (Bhattacharya et al., 2025). The second factor is automated scoring systems to classify prospects based on similarity to ideal personas or likelihood to respond to specific types of messages. Traditional lead scoring relied on predefined rules, but modern AI-driven scoring adapts in real time, recalibrating weights as new behavioral data emerges (Beenders, 2023; Okonkwo, 2024). The third factor encompasses recommendation technologies, which determine not only which content to display but also when and through which channels (Chowdary et al., 2024). These systems infer consumer preferences and adjust outreach strategies accordingly, ensuring greater alignment with emotional and cognitive states at the point of contact. These technological advances significantly enhance the efficiency and relevance of prospecting; their effectiveness depends on more than algorithmic sophistication.

According to Nizamani et al., (2026), Human-Centered AI (HCAI) principles become essential to maintain trust, transparency, and fairness. HCAI places human values at the center of AI design, ensuring that automated decisions remain understandable, respectful, and aligned with the psychological needs of consumers (Bingley et al., 2023). In prospecting, this means ensuring that recommendation systems do not reinforce harmful stereotypes, that predictive models remain explainable to marketers and consumers, and that decisions involving high-impact communication maintain human oversight.

Moreover, the complexity of digital ecosystems introduces new ethical and operational challenges (Pastor-Escuredo & Vinuesa, 2022; Tabaghdehi & Foroudi, 2024). AI-driven prospecting relies on large volumes of personal and behavioral data, raising concerns about consent, data governance, and potential biases embedded in training datasets (IPSOS, 2023). Mehrabi et al. (2022) have shown that models trained on historical data can unintentionally reproduce discrimination, skew qualification processes and reducing fairness in customer engagement. Therefore, organizations must adopt robust governance frameworks that include bias-detection protocols, fairness metrics, and transparent communication about how user data is analyzed. These practices reinforce human oversight, supporting AI systems rather than replacing human judgment.

Aguirre et al, (2016) discuss about another key dimension relates to consumers' evolving perceptions of personalization. While personalization is associated with greater satisfaction and engagement, it can also trigger feelings of intrusiveness when perceived as overly targeted or misaligned with expectations. Research on the "personalization paradox" demonstrates that consumers appreciate tailored content up to the point where it begins to feel invasive. This insight highlights the importance of balance: predictive models must optimize relevance without compromising user comfort. Buyer Persona matching should create resonance, not pressure. Human-centered design helps maintain this balance by emphasizing transparency, control, and consent as integral components of the user experience.

Operationally, human-centered prospecting also involves enabling employees to work collaboratively with AI systems. Sales and marketing teams often resist automated scoring or predictive recommendations when they perceive them as opaque or disjointed from their expertise (Longoni et al., 2019; Van den Broek et al., 2021). To address this, organizations should integrate explainability tools that clarify why a prospect is assigned a particular score, persona, or outreach strategy. Explainable AI not only strengthens internal trust but enhances employee performance by providing actionable insights that augment professional judgment (Arrieta et al., 2020; Komiak & Benbasat, 2006; Rai, 2020). Thus, AI-supported prospecting succeeds when it empowers human decision-makers rather than constraining them.

This human–machine synergy is particularly important given the increasing complexity of consumer journeys. Digital pathways are no longer linear; consumers move fluidly across platforms, compare options, and engage in self-directed research before interacting with brands. AI-driven prospecting helps decode this complexity, identifying micro-moments of intent and enabling timely engagement. Yet, the goal is not simply to automate outreach faster or cheaper. Instead, AI should help organizations understand the contextual, emotional, and motivational layers that underpin consumer decisions. Persona matching, when grounded in human-centric principles, becomes a tool for empathy as much as for efficiency.

In this sense, AI-enabled prospecting marks not a shift away from human connection but an opportunity to deepen it. By augmenting organizational capacity to understand prospects at scale, AI strengthens the foundations of trust that define meaningful customer relationships. As AI systems predict interests, detect needs, and suggest communication pathways, human oversight ensures that these technologies remain guided by fairness, respect, and user well-being. The result is a hybrid prospecting approach that combines analytical precision with human sensitivity.

III. PRODUCT AND SERVICE PERSONALIZATION THROUGH HUMAN-CENTERED INTERACTIVE AI

Following the initial stage of AI-driven prospect qualification and persona matching described in Section 1, personalization becomes the next strategic layer in the customer engagement (Teepapal, 2025). Once individuals are classified as qualified or unqualified prospects, AI systems adjust their role from prediction and segmentation to the orchestration of tailored value propositions. The transition illustrated in the schema, where qualified and unqualified prospects are routed into differentiated personalization paths, captures the essence of Human-Centered Interactive AI: personalization must be meaningful, context-aware, and aligned with human motivations.

Human-centered technologies extend the value of buyer persona matching by continuously adapting product attributes, content, and service elements. Through this adaptive framework, AI transforms the 10 Ps of Marketing into a dynamic set of levers that can be customized at scale to deliver unique, experience-driven engagement. This section explores how these technologies operate, why they matter, and how they reinforce the continuity between user identity (Section 1) and tailored experience (Section 2).

3.1. Human-Centered Personalization: A Continuity of the Persona-Matching Process

The personalization stage relies on the buyer persona criteria identified earlier, demographic attributes, psychographic insights, behavioral tendencies, and contextual factors. These insights form the foundation upon which AI systems build differentiated experiences. The goal is not simply to adjust product recommendations, but to configure a multi-dimensional value proposition that reflects each user's motivational drivers.

Figure 3. Conceptual model of human-centered AI personalization

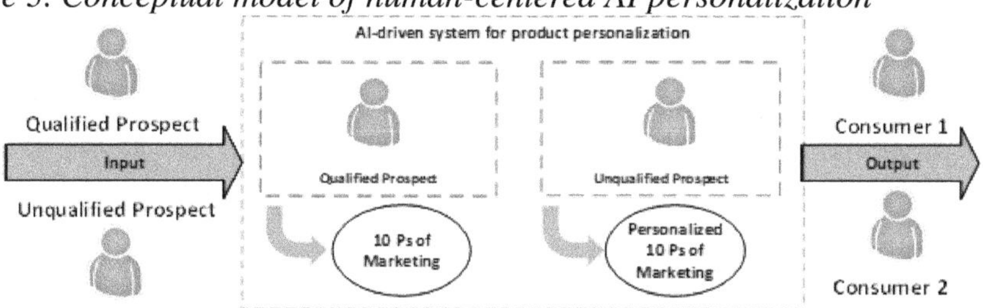

In this model, qualified prospects follow a direct personalization path, where the system activates finely tuned adjustments (the "10 Ps of Marketing") consistent with their persona profile. Unqualified prospects, in contrast, enter a more exploratory pathway—receiving broader recommendations, educational content, or trial-based interactions that help clarify their latent needs. Both paths converge toward the transformation of prospects into Consumer 1 or Consumer 2, each benefiting from a personalized set of marketing levers.

This process aligns with recent research highlighting that personalization is most effective when grounded in cognitive and emotional characteristics rather than surface-level traits (Salminen et al., 2022). By connecting persona structure to real-time adaptation, the system avoids generic approaches and instead delivers experiences that feel both relevant and respectful of users' decision-making styles.

3.2. Recommendation Engines as the Core of Adaptive Product Personalization

Recommendation engines constitute the central mechanism through which AI personalizes products and services (Nguyen et al., 2024). Three major types are particularly relevant in a human-centered context:

- **Collaborative filtering:** This model infers preferences by comparing users with similar behavioral patterns. It is effective for qualified prospects whose persona mapping has already identified clear motivational proximities. Studies by Linden et al. (2003) show that collaborative filtering significantly increases conversion and satisfaction when aligned with high-quality input data, exactly the situation created after prospect qualification.
- **Content-based recommendations:** These systems analyze product attributes and match them with explicit user interests, making them suitable for unqualified prospects who lack sufficient behavioral history. By highlighting product features, benefits, and contextual use cases, the system guides these individuals toward more refined preferences (Brusilovski et al., 2007).
- **Hybrid models:** Combining both approaches, hybrid engines provide flexibility across diverse persona types. They dynamically adjust recommendations based on uncertainty levels, psychological drivers, and consumption contexts, making them particularly aligned with human-centered principles (Burke, 2002).

In the figure 3, this entire process is represented in the differentiated pathways leading to tailored outputs for Consumer 1 and Consumer 2. The recommendation system acts as the engine of personalization transforming buyer persona insights into real-time adaptive suggestions.

3.3. Adaptive Interfaces: Designing Experiences That Respond to Human Diversity

Personalization extends beyond product suggestions to the interface itself. Adaptive interfaces use behavioral data, cognitive indicators, and emotional cues to modify how information is presented. This approach is rooted in the unified theory of acceptance and use of technology (Venkatesh et al., 2003; Venkatesh & Bala,

2008), which personalization must adapt to how people behave and think, not only what they want. We distinguished three forms of adaptation:

Figure 4. Type of adaptations

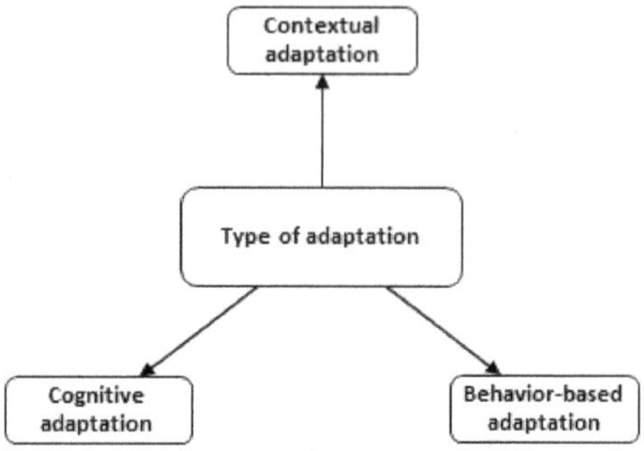

Interfaces personalized adjustments enhance usability and reduce cognitive load, contributing to a smoother transition from prospect to consumer (Montazer & Ahmadi, 2024). For analytic buyer personas may simplify decision pathways or comparison matrices for rational, detail-oriented users. For emotional buyer personas may prefer visually rich, experiential layouts (Alves et al., 2020). Similarly, by analyzing clickstreams, scroll depth, dwell time, and navigation patterns, AI can interpret behavioral intent and adjust interface complexity, timing of recommendations, or decision aids (Black, 2024; Wang et al., 2017). Referring back to Figure 3, the differentiation between qualified and unqualified prospects is reflected here: qualified prospects receive optimized, streamlined interactions, while unqualified ones encounter supportive, educational flows. Both aim to maximize comfort, autonomy, and clarity.

3.4. NLP and Semantic Personalization: Understanding Meaning, Emotion, and Intent

Natural Language Processing is a kind of algorithms used to understand, generate and interact with human languages of users (Chowdhary, 2020; Fanni et al., 2023; Nadkarni et al., 2011). According to Joshi et al. (2021), this technique enhances personalization by interpreting the semantic and emotional content behind user-generated texts in several ways:

Table 1. NLP algorithm for prospect engagement

NLP item	Presentation
Intent detection (Ferrera et al., 2025; Jbene et al., 2025)	NLP identifies whether the user is exploring, comparing, complaining, or preparing to purchase. This is particularly useful for unqualified prospects who need progressive guidance.
Sentiment analysis (Ismail et al., 2024; Rane et al., 2024)	The emotional tone extracted from text helps organizations adjust communication style-supportive, enthusiastic, reassuring—according to user mood and expectation.
Conversational personalization (Cho et al., 2022; Huang et al., 2023)	AI-powered chat interfaces can respond in ways that align with persona traits. For instance, analytical personas receive precise, data-driven responses, whereas social-driven personas may appreciate relational, empathetic messaging.

Recent research (Favour et al., 2025; Pandian et al., 2025) emphasizes that linguistic personalization significantly strengthens trust and reduces friction in digital environments. NLP thus acts as a bridge between technological intelligence and human communication needs.

3.5. The 10 Ps of Marketing as a Framework for AI-Driven Personalization

Figure 3 introduces the "10 Ps of Marketing" as the core mechanism through which personalization is operationalized. AI systems modulate each P differently depending on whether the prospect is qualified or unqualified.

Table 2. Mix Marketing analysis for qualified and unqualified prospect

Nature of prospects	Mix Marketing	Analysis
For qualified prospects	Product	Advanced configurations aligned with persona needs
	Price	Personalized discounts or value bundles
	Place	Preferred channels and delivery modes
	Promotion	Targeted messages rooted in psychographic motivations
	People	Human-assisted touchpoints when needed
	Process	Streamlined paths with minimal friction
	Physical evidence	Trust cues adapted to risk perception
	Personalization	Hyper-tailored experiences
	Participation	Co-creation opportunities
	Performance	Metrics aligned with user expectations

Nature of prospects	Mix Marketing	Analysis
For unqualified prospects	Product	Introductory or exploratory suggestions
	Promotion	Educational content and trust-building narratives
	Process	Guided experiences reducing ambiguity
	Participation	Surveys, quizzes, or needs-assessment tools

This dual approach mirrors the model's logic and maintains coherence with the persona-matching findings from Section 1.

3.6. Convergence: From Personalized Pathways to Consumer Transformation

Ultimately, the personalization ecosystem aims to transform prospects, qualified or unqualified, into engaged consumers (Theraiyan, 2025; Wijethilak et al., 2025). As shown in Figure 4, the algorithms transform every kind of prospect to consumer with his own specificities. What differentiates them is not their initial qualification score, but the personalization strategy applied.

This reflects a core principle of Human-Centered Interactive AI: every user, regardless of initial categorization, receives a pathway designed to enhance autonomy, relevance, and satisfaction (Tkalčič & Ferwerda, 2025). The personalization system becomes not merely a recommendation tool but an adaptive journey builder, orchestrating meaningful experiences across cognitive, emotional, and contextual dimensions (Gujar, 2024). According to Asli & Bensassi (2025), the personalization becomes a strategic tool to attract persona-based prospect qualification.

By using AI-enabled recommendation systems (Taneja & Tripathi, 2020), adaptive interfaces (Cen & Zhao, 2024) and NLP technologies (BAE & Park, 2025) organizations can transform segmented prospects to a real customers and enhances theirs preferences and decision-making style. Figure 4 provided illustrates this continuity, showing how qualified and unqualified prospects converge toward personalized consumer states through differentiated 10 Ps of Marketing pathways. By orchestrating engagement in this way, Human-Centered Interactive AI ensures that personalization enhances the human foundations of customer experience.

IV. POST-PURCHASE AND SUSTAINED ENGAGEMENT

Each company's goal is to ensure that buyers repeat the purchasing process multiple times. In order to achieve this, it is necessary to implement loyalty and targeting strategies on a permanent basis. AI acts as a mediator, capturing buyers' behavioral and emotional signals and then developing other signals that are designed to attract their attention and meet their expectations, making it possible to build consumer loyalty by increasing the likelihood of repeat purchases. Indeed, research has identified the causal effect of this technology on products and services in various fields, such as banking (Armutcu et al., 2024), e-commerce (Aktaş & Durmaz, 2025), hotel services (Lei et al., 2023), and health services (Sharma et al., 2023).

Naeimi & Family (2025) highlight that, globally, companies are using this technology for three specific reasons: (a) to personalize offers; (b) to predict expectations and preferences; (c) to enhance the customer experience. Similarly, Usmonov (2025) emphasizes that the application of technical solutions based on generative AI improves buyers' satisfaction by providing proactive and rapid responses to their questions and expectations. The author also points out that AI-driven strategies offer the ability to convert prospects into buyers by leveraging emotional connections through personalized interactions. Bilal et al. (2024) found that the use of AI in the commercial process improves consumer satisfaction by influencing their shopping experience and strengthening their engagement through personalized recommendations and targeted suggestions. The authors point out that satisfaction becomes a key factor in supporting purchase intention. These results were also observed by Nazir et al. (2023). These authors emphasized that the use of AI at the operational stage, by optimizing conversion rates from prospects to consumers and by using social media to support their engagement, makes it easy to boost their satisfaction, which facilitates their intention to repurchase.

Although this technology encourages companies to take advantage of several benefits, it also helps to avoid problems that affect the quality of services provided. The study conducted by Hu et al. (2024) demonstrated that integrating AI, which interacts with consumers like a human being, into customer service enhances customer satisfaction and increases the likelihood of repeat purchases. Similarly, Adekunle et al. (2023) found that the use of machine learning models on commercial data makes it possible to better determine which marketing actions to implement for each consumer (e.g. optimization of commercial offers, personalization of commercial offers, prediction of commercial offers), which reduces their dropout rate and increases their engagement.

Based on this research, we propose a simplified diagram describing the AI-assisted algorithmic system responsible for ensuring consumer engagement after online purchases (Figure 5).

Figure 5. Simplified diagram of the AI-driven system for post-purchase engagement

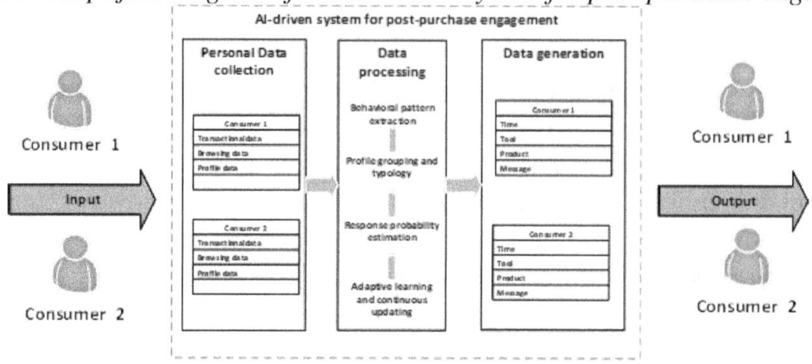

Since any algorithmic system depends on the availability of data to function properly, algorithmic systems designed to analyze post-purchase actions rely on collecting the following types of data:

- **Transactional data:** includes numerical parameters recorded at the time the customer makes the purchase (e.g. purchase history, item returned, amount spent, purchase frequency, time spent on purchase, etc.);
- **Browsing data:** includes technical parameters collected based on the browsing behavior of the customer (e.g. pages visited, duration of visit, traffic source, device used, items added to basket, forms filled in, etc.);
- **Profile data:** includes qualitative and quantitative parameters on regular and occasional buyers voluntarily provided by them as part of the purchase process (e.g. name, age, location, email address, telephone number, etc.).

Using this data, algorithmic models generate learning and prediction models to analyze, classify and target consumers once again through personalized actions. This involves a sequential four-step process:

- **Extraction of behavioral patterns:** this first step consists of profiling consumers based on commonalities identified in the collected data. This involves establishing mathematical models for consumer clustering based on behavioral, demographic and psychosocial criteria.
- **Clustering and profiling:** the aim of this second step is to group the profiles identified into sub-segments based on unique criteria, before creating scalable micro-profiles that are updated according to the interactions recorded by the company.

- **Estimating the probability of response:** the aim of this third stage is to estimate the probability that a sub-segment will respond positively to a personalized marketing action recommended by the company. Mathematical prediction models are used to construct a personalized equation based on the weighting of the parameters that most influence the behavior or decision-making of each sub-segment.
- **Adaptive learning and continuous updating:** this final step relies on sophisticated algorithmic models designed as a self-learning process to increase the relevance of marketing actions and gradually improve the suggestions sent to each sub-segment.

Once processing is complete, the system can then generate personalized data based on the characteristics of each sub-segment. The potential marketing action takes the form of a message sent to each individual as an incentive to restart the purchasing process. Four parameters can be configured to ensure personalized communication:

- **The time of sending:** the company relies on AI-assisted predictive models to identify the best times to retarget consumers.
- **The nature of the action:** the company sends personalized messages to consumers. It uses intelligent recommendation systems or chatbots powered by NLP algorithms to facilitate interaction with consumers.
- **The message content:** the company uses two methods to develop the message content: The 'What?' takes the form of the personalized product designed for consumers, and the 'How?' reflects the style of verbal language used to address the consumer.
- **The communication channel:** represents the communication devices used to send the message. These tools are automatically programmed to send messages, usually by e-mail, mobile app, text message or other channels.

V. CUSTOMERS AS BRAND AMBASSADORS AND THE ROLE OF INFLUENCER MARKETING

The use of artificial intelligence to improve the customer experience (Sahut & Laroche, 2025) has led to increased satisfaction, engagement, and loyalty (P. Singh & Singh, 2024). As a result, loyal customers have become true ambassadors with a mission to promote their experiences with the brand.

5.1. The Use of AI in the Process of Transforming Customers Into Ambassadors

Brand ambassador refers to a customer who spontaneously shares information based on a positive perception of a brand (Chabry et al., 2020). According to the literature, companies use customer relationship management strategies to convert prospects into customers and then into brand ambassadors (Lefébure & Venturi, 2011). These actions offer an economic advantage for two reasons: (a) ambassador customers are loyal to the brand, which provides a steady cash flow for the company; (b) these ambassador customers act as a sales force, relying on word of mouth to spread the word about the brand, which allows the company to reduce its advertising budget or use influencers.

The integration of AI has accelerated this process of converting consumers into loyal customers by offering a range of digital tools to promote the brand. The diagram below provides a simplified overview of AI's contribution to transforming customers into brand ambassadors (Figure 6).

Figure 6. Simplified diagram showing the role of AI in training customer ambassadors

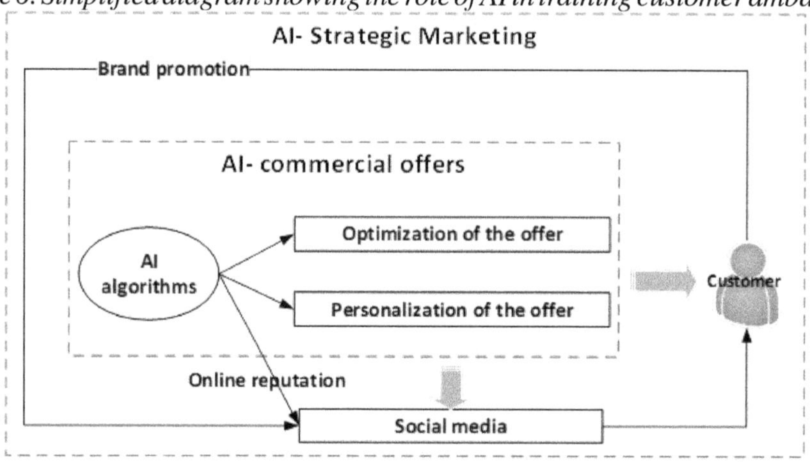

Companies are turning to AI to make their commercial content more appealing and attractive to consumers. This technology is also being used to improve brand image by influencing the quality and quantity of information shared on social media through two distinct mechanisms: (a) online reputation involves using digital media to promote an ethically acceptable image of a brand (Boistel, 2014; Boistel & Laroutis, 2019). AI algorithms are used to analyze comments made by internet users, filtering out inappropriate messages or those that could damage the brand's reputation (Ami, 2021; Dietrich, 2025). Similarly, they are used by marketers in order to automate content publication (Al-Harbi, 2025). These actions improve brand perception (Vij et al., 2024) and strengthen its credibility, which increases customer loyalty (Sun, 2025). (b) Loyal customers who express an emotional attachment to the brand become ambassadors for the company (El-Merabet et al., 2025). Companies use AI to target and attract these types of customers. The table below provides a detailed list of the main technologies used for this purpose:

Table 3. Technologies used to detect and target customer advocates

AI Technology	Role
AI-based recommendation detection systems (Chaudhry & Dhawan, 2020; Leblanc & Roux, 2025)	Analyze suggestions and recommendations made by customers who spontaneously mention the brand and positively recommend it to their network
Sentiment analysis and text mining (Drus & Khalid, 2019; Tarnowska& Ras, 2019)	Scan shared reviews and comments to identify customers with strong brand loyalty who express positive and intense emotions
E-reputation and social monitoring tools (Zahran & Rolando, 2025; Zhou et al., 2023)	Detect highly active customers on social media who show a high level of engagement and defend the brand
Predictive models of customer behavior (Nkomo & Mupa, 2024; Zulaikha et al., 2025)	Predict the likelihood that a customer will share and recommend the brand to their network

The objective of the company is to find profiles that are highly attached to the brand in order to offer them adapted content or sponsorship programs. The mission of customer ambassadors is to share their consumer experiences and positive perceptions of the brand on social media. This is a form of influencer marketing that relies on social influence to promote the company's products and services.

5.2. Influencer Marketing in the Age of AI

Influencer marketing is a type of marketing that relies on opinion leaders to promote a product, service or even an idea (Haji & Bouziane, 2021). Based on the concept of homophily, companies often target influencers who share the same criteria as their personas in order to simplify their targeting (Bu et al., 2022). The integration of artificial intelligence in the influencer marketing field has taken two forms:

AI as an Influencer Assistant

The intense competitiveness among influencers leads them to maintain a stable presence on social media by constantly posting content (Galante et al., 2024). Since this requires their full availability, most of them rely instead on a delegation system to ensure a constant supply of attractive content for their social media accounts. While mega-influencers often rely on communication agencies to manage their social media accounts, influencers with lesser notoriety choose technological solutions to automate content creation and distribution (Hurley, 2024). AI solutions provide several features that make influencers' work smoother and easier to accomplish. The table below lists some of the advantages cited by Dhiman & Bhati (2025). Based on a review of the literature, we explored the technological aspects behind the way these solutions work:

Table 4. The advantages of using AI technology for influencers

Advantages	Operating mechanism
Identify trendy content	Text mining algorithms can be used to scan posts that receive more interaction in order to detect trends (Bhatnagr, 2025)
Create personalized content to meet audience expectations	Sentiment analysis models analyze underlying emotions in audience comments to identify their preferences/fears (Wicaksono & Sudarmiatin, 2025)
Target specific segments for influencer campaigns	Clustering models create audience segments based on their social media activity (e.g. active, passive) (Johansson, 2016)
Anticipate audience engagement	Predictive algorithms determine the probability that content will successfully generate interest and interaction among audiences (Aishwarya et al., 2025)
Enhance the effectiveness of advertising messages	Optimization algorithms make messages more effective, easier to understand (Wen et al., 2022).

AI as an Influencer

Marketing agencies are becoming more reliant on AI-assisted solutions to enhance promotional activities (Lachmann et al., 2024). Recently, AI-generated digital avatars have emerged to play the role of influencers (Yu, 2025).

Allal-Chérif et al. (2024) point out that the popularity of this new form of influencer marketing is due to four key criteria: Firstly, the non-human nature of AI influencers helps to maintain a good social image and avoid human error (e.g. avoiding scandals and controversies, preventing unpredictable behavior). Secondly, the appeal of these virtual influencers lies in the credibility and creativity of the narrative universe proposed by their owners, using storytelling techniques. Thirdly, the integration of virtual influencers improves marketing campaigns by producing creative and visually perfect content. Fourthly, virtual influencers inspire greater trust and authenticity as they are less likely to engage in deceptive behavior (e.g. lying, hypocrisy, concealment of interests).

Yu et al. (2024) have also shown that virtual influencers programmed to perfectly replicate human emotions are more likely to engage users through captivating content similar to that produced by humans. Rehman et al. (2025) base their argument on the idea that virtual influencers who succeed in making consumers more emotionally attached to the brand are those who have managed to show similarities to human characteristics and have been able to take advantage of their trust. On the other hand, other studies have found that virtual influencers can be harmful to a brand's image. Zhang & He (2025)found that consumers tend to have less trust and express less interest in the brand because AI is still very limited in terms of acting independently, intentionally, or credibly. The authors concluded that the use of AI influencers can reduce the effectiveness of marketing actions. The systemic study conducted by Hewapathirana &Perera (2024) shows that virtual influencers are less authentic than human influencers, as users consider these avatars to be nothing more than pre-programmed robots designed to perform specific tasks and actions.

VI. FROM AGILE MARKETING TO SUSTAINABLE MARKETING

The use of AI is not limited to an operational context, which only aims to improve marketing actions, but is a true strategic transformation approach capable of establishing sustainable and innovative practices. Garg et al. (2025) conducted a systematic literature review where they found that customers showed greater loyalty to a company's brand and gave it more credibility when companies adopted environmentally friendly practices (e.g. green branding, sustainable packaging), especially when these practices used artificial intelligence to reinforce these initiatives.

Before exploring these different marketing approaches, it is important to remember that the purpose of marketing analysis is to answer three essential questions: what to sell, where to sell, and to whom to sell. In light of the principles of contingency theory (Burns & Stalker, 1961; Lawrence & Lorsch, 1967), such analysis does not follow a standard model, as each company must adjust to specific intrinsic factors (e.g. management style and level of technology adoption) and extrinsic factors (e.g. the dynamism of the environment).

We suggest a matrix comparing different types of marketing based on two dynamics: first, the company's responsiveness to market changes; second, the level of AI tool implementation within the company. These two parameters define the type of marketing that is appropriate for the company, as shown in the diagram below:

Figure 7. Classification of marketing approaches

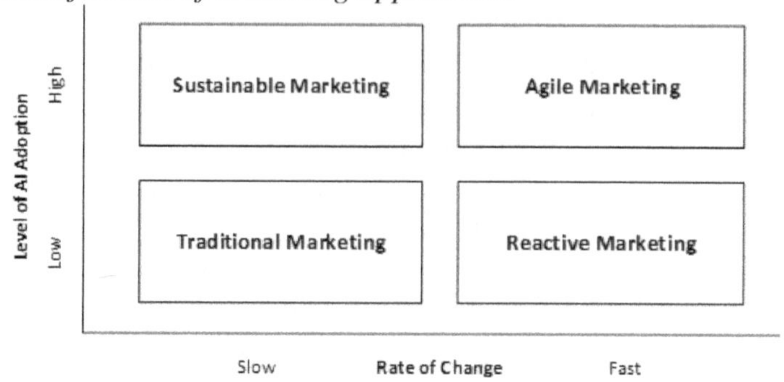

In a stable and technology-savvy environment, companies rely on traditional marketing techniques. These techniques are based on standardized market analysis methods and traditional tools and approaches. When these companies are exposed to a dynamic environment, they develop a reactive marketing approach. They tend to follow trends and adjust their actions, often in an improvised manner. Marketing teams then rely on their expertise and intuition to anticipate or anticipate changes.

The integration of AI at both organizational and strategic levels in a dynamic environment is pushing companies to adopt agile marketing. They are constantly seeking signals from the market, which explains why their operating mode is based on continuous adaptation. Data analysis makes this adaptation faster and more accurate. Furthermore, in a stable environment, companies are more inclined to choose sustainable marketing. The degree of control over market changes pushes them to strengthen their relationships with stakeholders by adopting more responsible practices. Emon & Khan (2024) analysis shows that companies that are able to successfully adapt to market changes through technology are succeeding in transforming their marketing approach, moving from a purely opportunistic approach towards a responsible value creation approach. We propose a simplified model to illustrate this transition (Figure 8).

Figure 8. From agile marketing to sustainable marketing

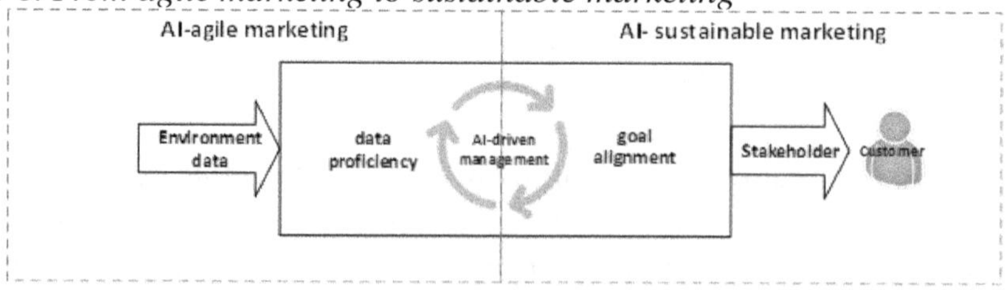

Based on an efficient AI-assisted management approach, the company, operating under an agile logic, adopts marketing actions based on continuous collection of data flows from the market, to ensure rapid adaptation to changes and anticipate future actions. AI, through its big data processing algorithms and prediction models, is capable of keeping pace with rapid market changes and proposing appropriate action plans. Once this ability to adapt has been mastered, companies move towards a management approach based on sustainable objectives. In this case, AI is used again, focusing on reorienting the company's strategic goals through the principles of sustainable marketing in order to better meet the expectations of stakeholders, particularly customers.

CONCLUSION

The integration of artificial intelligence has revolutionized marketing strategies by introducing a new approach that places the customer at the center of marketing analysis. Algorithmic systems have in fact begun to assume the role of marketers, by manipulating data and selecting the most effective and optimal actions, as well as the role of influencers, by offering personalized and direct content for each target audience. These changes define a new marketing paradigm based on the hyper-personalization of marketing offers and the minimization of human intervention.

Based on the human-AI cooperation approach, this descriptive work highlights the way AI works in the commercial process, from prospecting to customer loyalty. There are two main reasons why companies rely on this technology: (a) to optimize financial, cognitive and technical resources; (b) to ensure relevant results. Currently, companies are sharing very positive feedback, indicating a very promising future for this technology.

However, some ethical questions need to be asked regarding the application of this new technology, especially when it comes to managing personal data, since the results are based on algorithmic models trained on historical or very personal data. Also, the quality of the data is a challenge for companies, considering the fact that biased, false, or misused data can reduce the relevance of the models' results or even provide incorrect results. Companies must therefore interact with AI very carefully in order to ensure maximum benefits without suffering any of its inconveniences. In order to make this technology a tool for sustainable economic and social progress, future work should focus on exploring the ethical dimension of AI models.

Consequently, the chapter provides a clear overview of the role of AI throughout the customer journey, however there is limited reference to interdisciplinary debates. Seeking to broaden the scope of the study, the chapter could be enhanced by exploring several research angles. A more assertive embrace of these perspectives would allow the chapter to move beyond a strictly descriptive dimension and position itself as an integrative contribution reflecting the complexity of human-AI interactions in contemporary digital environments.

REFERENCES

Adekunle, B. I., Chukwuma-Eke, E. C., Balogun, E. D., & Ogunsola, K. O. (2023). Improving customer retention through machine learning : A predictive approach to churn prevention and engagement strategies. *International Journal of Scientific Research in Computer Science. Engineering and Information Technology*, *9*(4), 507–523.

Aguirre, E., Roggeveen, A. L., Grewal, D., & Wetzels, M. (2016). The personalization-privacy paradox : Implications for new media. *Journal of Consumer Marketing*, *33*(2), 98–110.

Aishwarya, K. M., Hemanth, K., & Ashwini, P. J. (2025). Predictive Analytics for Social Media Engagement. *International Journal of Advanced Research in Computer and Communication Engineering*, *14*(8), 155–162. DOI: 10.17148/IJARCCE.2025.14816

Aktaş, M., & Durmaz, Y. (2025). The Mediating Role of Customer Satisfaction in the Effect of Artificial Intelligence-Enabled Chatbots on Online Shopping Experience and Repurchase Intention. *REFLEKTİF Sosyal Bilimler Dergisi*, *6*(3), 969–990.

Allal-Chérif, O., Puertas, R., & Carracedo, P. (2024). Intelligent influencer marketing : How AI-powered virtual influencers outperform human influencers. *Technological Forecasting and Social Change*, *200*, 123113. DOI: 10.1016/j.techfore.2023.123113

Alves, T., Natálio, J., Henriques-Calado, J., & Gama, S. (2020). Incorporating personality in user interface design : A review. *Personality and Individual Differences*, *155*, 109709. DOI: 10.1016/j.paid.2019.109709

Ami, R. (2021). AI in Automated Content Moderation on Social Media. *International Journal of Artificial Intelligence and Machine Learning*, *4*(3). https://itaimle.com/index.php/ijaiml/article/download/249/26

Armutcu, B., Tan, A., Ho, S. P. S., Chow, M. Y. C., & Gleason, K. C. (2024). The effect of bank artificial intelligence on consumer purchase intentions. *Kybernetes*, *54*(10), 5529–5553. DOI: 10.1108/K-01-2024-0145

Arrieta, A. B., Díaz-Rodríguez, N., Del Ser, J., Bennetot, A., Tabik, S., Barbado, A., García, S., Gil-López, S., Molina, D., & Benjamins, R. (2020). Explainable Artificial Intelligence (XAI) : Concepts, taxonomies, opportunities and challenges toward responsible AI. *Information Fusion*, *58*, 82–115.

Asli, I., & Bensassi, H. N. (2025). Intelligence Artificielle et Stratégies de Marketing Personnalisé : Une Revue Systématique de la Littérature. *Revue Française d'Economie et de Gestion*, *6*(7). Advance online publication. DOI: 10.5281/zenodo.16374934

BAE, K. P., & Park, H. (2025). Optimizing Personalized Marketing Strategies with NLP and Machine Learning on Customer Review Data. *Cuestiones de Fisioterapia*, *54*(1), 151–159.

Beenders, C. (2023). *How to Approach the Development Process of a Lead Scoring Model* [Bachelor's thesis, Oulu University of Applied Sciences]. https://www.theseus.fi/handle/10024/812465

Bhatnagr, P. (2025). Virtual influencers on Instagram : A text mining study of consumer sentiments in China. *Journal of Modelling in Management*. Advance online publication. DOI: 10.1108/JM2-01-2025-0024

Bhattacharya, C., Parasar, A., Sudhakar, P. K., Kumar, S., & Bakshi, S., & Shinde, Sonal. B. (2025). AI-Powered Predictive Models Transforming the Future of Digital Marketing and Customer Engagement. *Journal of Informatics Education and Research*, *5*(1). Advance online publication. DOI: 10.52783/jier.v5i1.2015

Bilal, M., Zhang, Y., Cai, S., Akram, U., & Halibas, A. (2024). Artificial intelligence is the magic wand making customer-centric a reality! An investigation into the relationship between consumer purchase intention and consumer engagement through affective attachment. *Journal of Retailing and Consumer Services*, *77*, 103674.

Bingley, W. J., Curtis, C., Lockey, S., Bialkowski, A., Gillespie, N., Haslam, S. A., Ko, R. K., Steffens, N., Wiles, J., & Worthy, P. (2023). Where is the human in human-centered AI? Insights from developer priorities and user experiences. *Computers in Human Behavior*, *141*, 107617.

Black, J. J. (2024). *Predictors of Online Purchase Conversions Using Clickstream Data and Sentiment Analysis* [PhD Thesis, University of South Alabama]. https://search.proquest.com/openview/7d2a048972585e4ff973097e0f66ea0e/1?pq-origsite=gscholar&cbl=18750&diss=y

Boistel, P. (2014). Réputation : Un concept à définir. *Communication et organisation. Revue scientifique francophone en Communication organisationnelle*, *46*, Article 46. DOI: 10.4000/communicationorganisation.4796

Boistel, P., & Laroutis, D. (2019). E-réputation et réputation : Similitudes et différences. Une analyse comparative conceptuelle. *RIMHE : Revue Interdisciplinaire Management. Homme & Entreprise*, *368*(3), 104–120. DOI: 10.3917/rimhe.036.0104

Brusilovski, P., Kobsa, A., & Nejdl, W. (2007). *The adaptive web : Methods and strategies of web personalization* (Vol. 4321). Springer Science & Business Media.

Bu, Y., Parkinson, J., & Thaichon, P. (2022). Influencer marketing : Homophily, customer value co-creation behaviour and purchase intention. *Journal of Retailing and Consumer Services, 66*, 102904. DOI: 10.1016/j.jretconser.2021.102904

Burke, R. (2002). Hybrid Recommender Systems : Survey and Experiments. *User Modeling and User-Adapted Interaction, 12*(4), 331–370. DOI: 10.1023/A:1021240730564

Burns, T., & Stalker, G. M. (1961). The management of innovation. London. *Tavistock Publishing. Cited in Hurley, RF and Hult, GTM (1998). Innovation, Market Orientation, and Organisational Learning: An Integration and Empirical Examination. Journal of Marketing, 62*(4), 42–54.

Cen, Z., & Zhao, Y. (2024). Enhancing user engagement through adaptive interfaces : A study on real-time personalization in web applications. *Journal of Economic Theory and Business Management, 1*(6), 1–7.

Chabry, L., Gillet-Goinard, F., & Jourdan, R. (2020). Outil 46. Le client ambassadeur. In *La Boîte à Outils* (p. 192). Dunod. https://shs.cairn.info/article/DUNOD_CHABR_2020_01_0126

Chaudhry, S., & Dhawan, S. (2020). AI-Based Recommendation System for Social Networking. In Pant, M., Sharma, T. K., Verma, O. P., Singla, R., & Sikander, A. (Eds.), *Soft Computing : Theories and Applications* (Vol. 1053, pp. 617–629). Springer Singapore., DOI: 10.1007/978-981-15-0751-9_58

Cho, I., Wang, D., Takahashi, R., & Saito, H. (2022). *A Personalized Dialogue Generator with Implicit User Persona Detection* (arXiv:2204.07372). arXiv. /arXiv.2204.07372DOI: 10.48550

Chowdary, K. M. T., Vallepu, M., Purushotham, A. N. S., & Kumari, N. (2024). Personalized Marketing and Recommendation Systems. In *Predictive Analytics and Generative AI for Data-Driven Marketing Strategies* (1re éd., p. 82-89). Chapman and Hall/CRC. https://www.taylorfrancis.com/chapters/edit/10.1201/9781003472544-7/personalized-marketing-recommendation-systems-mani-teja-chowdary-maniteja-vallepu-naga-sai-purushotham-neelam-kumari

Chowdhary, K. R. (2020). Natural Language Processing. In K. R. Chowdhary, *Fundamentals of Artificial Intelligence* (p. 603-649). Springer India. DOI: 10.1007/978-81-322-3972-7_19

Claeyssen, Y., Deydier, A., & Riquet, Y. (2011). *Le Marketing client multicanal. Prospection, fidélisation et reconquête du client.* Dunod., DOI: 10.3917/dunod.claey.2011.01

DeSanctis, G., & Poole, M. S. (1994). Capturing the Complexity in Advanced Technology Use : Adaptive Structuration Theory. *Organization Science*, *5*(2), 121–147. DOI: 10.1287/orsc.5.2.121

Dhiman, R., & Bhati, N. S. (2025). When AI meets influencers : Role of AI-powered instagram influencers driving consumers' purchase intentions: An integration of SMIV & SOR framework. *Journal of Open Innovation, 11*(3), 100591. DOI: 10.1016/j.joitmc.2025.100591

Dietrich, F. (2025). AI-based removal of hate speech from digital social networks : Chances and risks for freedom of expression. *AI and Ethics*, *5*(3), 2943–2953. DOI: 10.1007/s43681-024-00610-7

Drus, Z., & Khalid, H. (2019). Sentiment analysis in social media and its application : Systematic literature review. *Procedia Computer Science*, *161*, 707–714.

Ducret, G. (2016). Outil 37. La prospection commerciale. In *La Boîte à outils de la TPE* (Dunod, p. 114-115). Dunod. https://shs.cairn.info/article/DUNOD_DUCRE_2016_01_0114

El Koufi, N., & Belangour, A., & sadiq, M. (2024). Toward a decision-making system based on artificial intelligence for precision marketing : A case study of Morocco. *Journal of Open Innovation*, *10*(1), 100250. DOI: 10.1016/j.joitmc.2024.100250

El-Merabet, O., Kinani, S., El-Merabet, Z., & El-Merabet, O. (2025). Enhancing eWOM Intention Through Social Media-based Brand Communities in the Higher Education Sector : The Mediating Effect of Brand Attachment. *Micro & Macro Marketing*, *2/2025*. Advance online publication. DOI: 10.1431/114094

Emon, M. M. H., & Khan, T. (2024). A systematic literature review on sustainability integration and marketing intelligence in the era of artificial intelligence. *Review of Business and Economics Studies*, *12*(4), 6–28.

Fanni, S. C., Febi, M., Aghakhanyan, G., & Neri, E. (2023). Natural Language Processing. In Klontzas, M. E., Fanni, S. C., & Neri, E. (Eds.), *Introduction to Artificial Intelligence* (pp. 87–99). Springer International Publishing., DOI: 10.1007/978-3-031-25928-9_5

Favour, A., Kunle, A., Oladele, S., & Timileyin, J. (2025). *The Role of Natural Language Processing (NLP) in Enhancing Customer Experience in Fintech : Applications in Chatbots and Virtual Assistants.* https://www.researchgate.net/profile/Sunday-Oladele-2/publication/390454097_The_Role_of_Natural_Language_Processing_NLP_in_Enhancing_Customer_Experience_in_Fintech_Applications_in_Chatbots_and_Virtual_Assistants/links/67ee55069b1c6c4877726d7d/The-Role-of-Natural-Language-Processing-NLP-in-Enhancing-Customer-Experience-in-Fintech-Applications-in-Chatbots-and-Virtual-Assistants.pdf

Ferrera, A., Mezzotero, G., & Ursino, D. (2025). A linguistics-based approach to refining automatic intent detection in conversational agent design. *Information Sciences*, *689*, 121493.

Galante, F., Garetto, M., & Leonardi, E. (2024). Competition of Influencers : A Model for Maximizing Online Social Impact. *ACM Web Science Conference*, 343-353. DOI: 10.1145/3614419.3644031

Garg, V., Bohara, S., & Srivastav, A. (2025). AI-driven sustainability marketing transforming consumers' perception toward eco-friendly brands. *Discover Sustainability*, *6*(1), 984. DOI: 10.1007/s43621-025-01934-y

Gujar, V. (2024). New age marketing : AI personalization strategies in digital world. *International Advanced Research Journal in Science, Engineering and Technology, 11*(3). https://www.researchgate.net/profile/Vivek-Gujar/publication/379512526_New_Age_Marketing_AI_Personalization_Strategies_In_Digital_World/links/660d0c2d390c214cfd310d61/New-Age-Marketing-AI-Personalization-Strategies-In-Digital-World.pdf

Haji, I., & Bouziane, A. (2021). Le marketing d'influence au Maroc, entre perception et professionnalisme des acteurs. *Alternatives Managériales Economiques, 3*(2), 23-42. DOI: 10.48374/IMIST.PRSM/ame-v3i2.27506

Hewapathirana, I. U., & Perera, N. (2024). Navigating the age of AI influence : A systematic literature review of trust, engagement, efficacy and ethical concerns of virtual influencers in social media. *Journal of Infrastructure. Policy and Development*, *8*(8), 1–46. DOI: 10.24294/jipd.v8i8.6352

Hsu, P.-F., Lu, Y.-H., Chen, S.-C., & Kuo, P. P.-Y. (2024). Creating and validating predictive personas for target marketing. *International Journal of Human-Computer Studies*, *181*, 103147. DOI: 10.1016/j.ijhcs.2023.103147

Hu, Y., Xiao, Y., Hua, Y., Fan, Y., & Li, F. (2024). The More Realism, the Better? How Does the Realism of AI Customer Service Agents Influence Customer Satisfaction and Repeat Purchase Intention in Service Recovery. *Behavioral Sciences (Basel, Switzerland)*, *14*(12), 1182. DOI: 10.3390/bs14121182 PMID: 39767323

Huang, Q., Zhang, Y., Ko, T., Liu, X., Wu, B., Wang, W., & Tang, H. (2023). Personalized dialogue generation with persona-adaptive attention. *Proceedings of the AAAI Conference on Artificial Intelligence*, *37*(11), 12916–12923. https://ojs.aaai.org/index.php/AAAI/article/view/26518

Hurley, Z. (2024). Understanding Social Media Marketing Managers' Intermediary Role : A Middle Eastern Case Study. *The Sage Handbook of Promotional Culture and Society*, 151.

IPSOS. (2023). *World Mental Health Day 2023 : A Global Advisor Survey* (p. 15). IPSOS. https://www.ipsos.com/sites/default/files/ct/news/documents/2023-10/Ipsos-World_Mental_Health_Day_Survey_2023.pdf

Ismail, W. S., Ghareeb, M. M., & Youssry, H. (2024). Enhancing customer experience through sentiment analysis and natural language processing in e-commerce. *Journal of Wireless Mobile Networks, Ubiquitous Computing and Dependable Applications*, *15*(3), 60–72.

Jbene, M., Chehri, A., Saadane, R., Tigani, S., & Jeon, G. (2025). Intent detection for task-oriented conversational agents : A comparative study of recurrent neural networks and transformer models. *Expert Systems: International Journal of Knowledge Engineering and Neural Networks*, *42*(2), e13712. DOI: 10.1111/exsy.13712

Johansson, A. (2016). *Clustering user-behavior in a collaborative online social network : A case study on quantitative user-behavior classification* [Master's Thesis, KTH ROYAL INSTITUTE OF TECHNOLOGY]. https://www.diva-portal.org/smash/record.jsf?pid=diva2:945762

Joshi, R., Patel, N., Iyer, M., & Iyer, S. (2021). Leveraging reinforcement learning and natural language processing for AI-driven hyper-personalized marketing strategies. *International Journal of AI ML Innovations*, *10*(1). http://ijoaimli.com/index.php/v1/article/view/19

Koivisto, T. (2024). *The Use of AI in B2B Sales And Prospecting* [Bachelor's Thesis, Aalto University School of Business]. https://aaltodoc.aalto.fi/items/f22d33cb-2daa-41a4-b4be-7c945ea1842e

Komiak, S. Y., & Benbasat, I. (2006). The effects of personalization and familiarity on trust and adoption of recommendation agents. *Management Information Systems Quarterly*, ●●●, 941–960.

Kumar, V., Ashraf, A. R., & Nadeem, W. (2024). AI-powered marketing : What, where, and how? *International Journal of Information Management*, *77*, 102783. DOI: 10.1016/j.ijinfomgt.2024.102783

Kumar, V., & Pansari, A. (2016). Competitive Advantage through Engagement. *JMR, Journal of Marketing Research*, *53*(4), 497–514. DOI: 10.1509/jmr.15.0044

Lachmann, H., Schneider, T., & Wagner, L. (2024). AI Revolution : Evolving Skills in Marketing Agency Jobs. *Special Issue Innovative Brand Management*, *IV*, 53–74.

Lawrence, P. R., & Lorsch, J. W. (1967). *Organization and environment : Managing differentiation and integration* (1re éd.). Harvard University Press. https://cir.nii.ac.jp/crid/1970867909784112773

Leblanc, C., & Roux, A. (2025). AI and Social Media : An Integrative Literature Review. *Communication Management*. https://hal.science/hal-05041614

Lefébure, R., & Venturi, G. (2011). *Gestion de la relation client (2e* (Eyrolles, E., Ed.).

Lei, C., Hossain, M. S., & Wong, E. (2023). Determinants of repurchase intentions of hospitality services delivered by artificially intelligent (AI) service robots. *Sustainability*, *15*(6), 4914.

Linden, G., Smith, B., & York, J. (2003). Amazon. com recommendations : Item-to-item collaborative filtering. *IEEE Internet Computing*, *7*(1), 76–80.

Longoni, C., Bonezzi, A., & Morewedge, C. K. (2019). Resistance to medical artificial intelligence. *The Journal of Consumer Research*, *46*(4), 629–650.

Mdaary, S. (2024). Artificial Intelligence and organizational performance : A literature review. *American Scientific Journal*, *3*(23), 726–726. DOI: 10.5281/zenodo.11160590

Mehrabi, N., Morstatter, F., Saxena, N., Lerman, K., & Galstyan, A. (2022). A Survey on Bias and Fairness in Machine Learning. *ACM Computing Surveys*, *54*(6), 1–35. DOI: 10.1145/3457607

Montazer, F., & Ahmadi, M. (2024). Designing Adaptive Interfaces in the Metaverse : Reducing Cognitive Load for Enhanced User Experience. *International Journal of Advanced Human Computer Interaction*, *2*(2), 44–54.

Nadkarni, P. M., Ohno-Machado, L., & Chapman, W. W. (2011). Natural language processing : An introduction. *Journal of the American Medical Informatics Association : JAMIA, 18*(5), 544–551. PMID: 21846786

Naeimi, M., & Family, Q. (2025). AI and Post-Purchase Behavior : Personalization, Behavioral Insights, and Ethical Challenges. *Behavioral Insights, and Ethical Challenges (September 07, 2025).* https://papers.ssrn.com/sol3/papers.cfm?abstract_id=5460815

Naert, S., Puleston, J., Mayou, S., & Bardon, Y. (2025). *Personas in the age of AI : Promises and limitations* (IPSOS Views, p. 11). IPSOS. https://www.ipsos.com/sites/default/files/ct/news/documents/2025-07/ipsos-views-personas-in-the-age-of-AI.pdf

Nanayakkara, N. W. O. K. D. S. P. (2020). *Application of Artificial Intelligence in Marketing Mix : A Conceptual Review* (SSRN Scholarly Paper 3862936). Social Science Research Network. DOI: 10.2139/ssrn.3862936

Nazir, S., Khadim, S., Ali Asadullah, M., & Syed, N. (2023). Exploring the influence of artificial intelligence technology on consumer repurchase intention : The mediation and moderation approach. *Technology in Society, 72*, 102190. DOI: 10.1016/j.techsoc.2022.102190

Nguyen, D.-N., Nguyen, V.-H., Trinh, T., Ho, T., & Le, H.-S. (2024). A personalized product recommendation model in e-commerce based on retrieval strategy. *Journal of Open Innovation, 10*(2), 100303. DOI: 10.1016/j.joitmc.2024.100303

Nizamani, M. M., Zhang, H.-L., & Lai, Z. (2026). Human-centered AI : Advancing ethical, transparent, and context-aware systems for sustainable development. *Technology in Society, 84*, 103121. DOI: 10.1016/j.techsoc.2025.103121

Nkomo, N., & Mupa, M. N. (2024). The Impact of Artificial Intelligence on Predictive Customer Behaviour Analytics in E-commerce : A Comparative Study of Traditional and AI-driven Models. *Iconic Research and Engineering Journals, 8*(5), 432–451.

Okeleke, P. A., Ajiga, D., Folorunsho, S. O., & Ezeigweneme, C. (2024). Predictive analytics for market trends using AI : A study in consumer behavior. *International Journal of Engineering Research Updates, 7*(1), 36–49.

Okonkwo, K. (2024). *Using Artificial Intelligence (AI) to Manage Buyer Persona in E-commerce based on Kotler & Keller's 2016 Model of Consumer Behaviour : Archival Research based on Secondary Data in form of Relevant Publications* [Bachelor's thesis]. Jamk University of Applied Sciences.

Oliver, R. L. (1977). Effect of expectation and disconfirmation on postexposure product evaluations : An alternative interpretation. *The Journal of Applied Psychology*, *62*(4), 480.

Oliver, R. L. (1980). A Cognitive Model of the Antecedents and Consequences of Satisfaction Decisions. *JMR, Journal of Marketing Research*, *17*(4), 460–469. DOI: 10.1177/002224378001700405

Pandian, A., Mohankumar, K. P., Padmini, S., Amaran, S., & Sreekumar, K. (2025). Enhancing Trust and Collaboration Using Explainability in Natural Language Processing for AI-Driven Healthcare. In A. Kumar, T. Ananth Kumar, P. Das, C. Sharma, & A. K. Dubey (Éds.), *Explainable Artificial Intelligence in the Healthcare Industry* (1re éd., p. 619-650). Wiley. DOI: 10.1002/9781394249312.ch26

Pastor-Escuredo, D., & Vinuesa, R. (2022). Towards an Ethical Framework in the Complex Digital Era. *AI*, *3*(4), 961–974. DOI: 10.3390/ai3040057

Perumallaplli, R. (2014). Conversational AI for Customer Support : Automation in Large Enterprises. *SSRN*, *5228517*, •••. https://papers.ssrn.com/sol3/papers.cfm?abstract_id=5228517

Pietrini, R., Galdelli, A., Mancini, A., Frontoni, E., & Zingaretti, P. (2025). Machine Learning-Driven Marketing Personas for the Luxury Fashion Market. In A. Del Bue, C. Canton, J. Pont-Tuset, & T. Tommasi (Éds.), *Computer Vision – ECCV 2024 Workshops* (Vol. 15623, p. 402-416). Springer Nature Switzerland. DOI: 10.1007/978-3-031-91569-7_25

Rai, A. (2020). Explainable AI : From black box to glass box. *Journal of the Academy of Marketing Science*, *48*(1), 137–141. DOI: 10.1007/s11747-019-00710-5

Rane, N., Paramesha, M., Choudhary, S., & Rane, J. (2024). Artificial intelligence in sales and marketing : Enhancing customer satisfaction, experience and loyalty. *Experience and Loyalty (May 17, 2024)*. https://papers.ssrn.com/sol3/papers.cfm?abstract_id=4831903

Rehman, A., Kumar, S., Salam, M. A., & Virmani, N. (2025). How does AI-powered virtual influencer's anthropomorphism impact trust and brand love? The moderating role of opinion leadership. *Technological Forecasting and Social Change*, *219*, 124198. DOI: 10.1016/j.techfore.2025.124198

Roba, G. B., & Maric, P. (2023). AI in Customer Relationship Management. In Kryvinska, N., Greguš, M., & Fedushko, S. (Eds.), *Developments in Information and Knowledge Management Systems for Business Applications* (Vol. 462, pp. 469–487). Springer Nature Switzerland., DOI: 10.1007/978-3-031-25695-0_21

Sahut, J.-M., & Laroche, M. (2025). Using artificial intelligence (AI) to enhance customer experience and to develop strategic marketing : An integrative synthesis. *Computers in Human Behavior*, *170*, 108684. DOI: 10.1016/j.chb.2025.108684

Salminen, J., Kandpal, C., Kamel, A. M., Jung, S. G., & Jansen, B. J. (2022). Creating and detecting fake reviews of online products. *Journal of Retailing and Consumer Services*, *64*, 102771.

Sharma, V., Gupta, M., Jangir, K., Chopra, P., & Pathak, N. (2023). The Impact of Post-Use Consumer Satisfaction on Smart Wearables Repurchase Intention in the Context of AI-Based Healthcare Information. In *Enhancing Customer Engagement Through Location-Based Marketing* (pp. 77–101). IGI Global Scientific Publishing., DOI: 10.4018/978-1-6684-8177-6.ch007

Singh, B., & Kaunert, C. (2024). Future of Digital Marketing : Hyper-Personalized Customer Dynamic Experience with AI-Based Predictive Models. In *Revolutionizing the AI-Digital Landscape* (1re éd., p. 189-203). Productivity Press.

Singh, P., & Singh, V. (2024). The power of AI : Enhancing customer loyalty through satisfaction and efficiency. *Cogent Business & Management*, *11*(1), 2326107. DOI: 10.1080/23311975.2024.2326107

Spence, M. (1973). Job Market Signaling. *The Quarterly Journal of Economics*, *87*(3), 355–374. DOI: 10.2307/1882010

Sun, W. (2025). Artificial Intelligence in Branding : The Influence of AI-Quality on Brand Perception and Consumer Loyalty. *International Journal of Advanced AI Applications*, *1*(8), 39–64.

Tabaghdehi, S. A. H., & Foroudi, P. (2024). Introduction : Business Strategies and Ethical Challenges in the Digital Ecosystem. In *Business Strategies and Ethical Challenges in the Digital Ecosystem* (p. 1-4). Emerald Publishing Limited. https://www.emerald.com/insight/content/doi/10.1108/978-1-80455-069-420241001/full/html

Tahiri, A. (2025). Marketing stratégique et intelligence artificielle : Vers un nouveau paradigme algorithmique. *Revue Française d'Economie et de Gestion*, *6*(9). https://www.revuefreg.fr/index.php/home/article/view/2341

Taneja, A. K., & Tripathi, C. (2020). AI-powered recommender systems : Personalization and bias. *Turkish Journal of Computer and Mathematics Education*, *11*(1), 1090–1094.

Tarnowska, K. A., & Ras, Z. W. (2019). Sentiment analysis of customer data. *Web Intelligence*, *17*(4), 343–363. DOI: 10.3233/WEB-190423

Teepapal, T. (2025). AI-driven personalization : Unraveling consumer perceptions in social media engagement. *Computers in Human Behavior*, *165*, 108549. DOI: 10.1016/j.chb.2024.108549

Theraiyan, E. (2025). A Study on the Impact of Personalization in Increasing Customer Engagements. *International Journal for Research in Applied Science and Engineering Technology*, *13*(4), 10–22214.

Tkalčič, M., & Ferwerda, B. (2025). Adaptation and Personalization in Human-Centered AI. In Germanakos, P., Juhasz, M., Kongot, A., Marathe, D., & Sacharidis, D. (Eds.), *Human-Centered AI: An Illustrated Scientific Quest* (pp. 493–511). Springer Nature Switzerland., DOI: 10.1007/978-3-031-61375-3_7

Usmonov, M. (2025). Crafting Connections : Generative AI's Impact on Post-Purchase Communication in E-Commerce. *Contemporary Issues of Communication*, *4*(1), 288–310.

Van den Broek, E., Sergeeva, A., & Huysman, M. (2021). When the machine meets the expert : An ethnography of developing AI for hiring. *Management Information Systems Quarterly*, *45*(3), 1557–1580.

Venkatesh, V., & Bala, H. (2008). Technology Acceptance Model 3 and a Research Agenda on Interventions. *Decision Sciences*, *39*(2), 273–315. DOI: 10.1111/j.1540-5915.2008.00192.x

Venkatesh, V., Morris, M. G., Davis, G. B., & Davis, F. D. (2003). User acceptance of information technology : Toward a unified view. *Management Information Systems Quarterly*, **•••**, 425–478.

Vij, A., Vij, M., Farouk, M., & Kumar, P. (2024). Evaluating the Effectiveness of AI-Integrated Digital Marketing on Consumer Behavior, Brand Perception, and Sales Performance. *2024 2nd International Conference on Cyber Resilience (ICCR)*, 1-6. DOI: 10.1109/ICCR61006.2024.10533049

Wang, G., Zhang, X., Tang, S., Wilson, C., Zheng, H., & Zhao, B. Y. (2017). Clickstream User Behavior Models. *ACM Transactions on the Web*, *11*(4), 1–37. DOI: 10.1145/3068332

Wen, L., Lin, W., & Guo, M. (2022). Study on Optimization of Marketing Communication Strategies in the Era of Artificial Intelligence. *Mobile Information Systems*, *2022*, 1–11. DOI: 10.1155/2022/1604184

Wicaksono, A. T. S., & Sudarmiatin, S. (2025). Social Media Sentiment Analysis : Customer Perception of Digital Marketing. *Asian Journal of Applied Business and Management*, *4*(2), 437–450.

Wijethilak, H. P., Singh, S. K., & Dhand, S. (2025). AI for personalizing customer interactions : Improving engagement and satisfaction. In *AI, Corporate Social Responsibility, and Marketing in Modern Organizations* (p. 221-244). IGI Global Scientific Publishing. https://www.igi-global.com/chapter/ai-for-personalizing-customer-interactions/362263

Yu, J. (2025). AI-Generated Influencers. In *Encyclopedia of Artificial Intelligence in Marketing* (pp. 1–7). Springer., DOI: 10.1007/978-3-031-75316-9_18-1

Yu, J., Dickinger, A., So, K. K. F., & Egger, R. (2024). Artificial intelligence-generated virtual influencer : Examining the effects of emotional display on user engagement. *Journal of Retailing and Consumer Services, 76*, 103560. DOI: 10.1016/j.jretconser.2023.103560

Zahran, A. M., & Rolando, B. (2025). Understanding the Influence of Online Reviews on Brand Reputation in the Digital Age. *International Journal of Economics And Business Studies*, *2*(1), 72–94. DOI: 10.1234/ijebs.v2i1.109

Zhang, Y., & He, A.-Z. (2025). The impact of AI influencer endorsements on consumers' purchase intentions : The serial mediating roles of mind perception and brand trustworthiness. *Journal of Product and Brand Management*, *34*(5), 754–765. DOI: 10.1108/JPBM-02-2024-4974

Zhou, A., Men, L. R., & Tsai, W.-H. S. (2023). The power of AI-enabled chatbots as an organizational social listening tool. *Organizational listening for strategic communication*, 63-80.

Zulaikha, S., Mohamed, H., Kurniawati, M., Rusgianto, S., & Rusmita, S. A. (2025). Customer Predictive Analytics Using Artificial Intelligence. *The Singapore Economic Review*, *70*(04), 1009–1020. DOI: 10.1142/S0217590820480021

Chapter 5
Investigating the Influence of Digital Strategies on Consumer Engagement and Conversion:
The Mediating Role of Engagement.

Mohamed Bouaddi
https://orcid.org/0009-0009-0951-0203
Faculty of Legal, Economic, and Social Sciences, Moulay Ismail University, Meknes, Morocco

ABSTRACT

This study aims to investigate the impact of digital strategies on consumer engagement and the mediating role of engagement in driving conversion behaviors, such as purchases and sign-ups. Focusing on content strategy, digital communication channels, and user experience (UX), a quantitative survey of 500 Moroccan consumers was conducted. Structural equation modeling (SEM) revealed that all three strategies positively influence engagement, which in turn significantly impacts conversion. Engagement acts as a key mediator, linking digital efforts to desired consumer actions. The findings underscore the importance of delivering high-quality content, leveraging multiple communication channels, and optimizing UX. Practical implications suggest that marketers should adopt integrated, customer-centric digital strategies to enhance engagement, drive conversions, and build long-term loyalty in a competitive digital environment.

DOI: 10.4018/979-8-3373-6450-6.ch005

INTRODUCTION

In today's rapidly evolving economic and technological landscape, the integration of digital technologies into marketing practices has become both a necessity and a catalyst for transformation (Nwabekee et al., 2024). Businesses are increasingly operating in an environment characterized by heightened competition, fast-changing consumer behaviors, and rising expectations for immediacy, personalization, and value (Pascucci et al., 2023). In this context, digital marketing has emerged as a strategic imperative, enabling firms to reach their audiences in more targeted, efficient, and interactive ways than ever before (Parveen et al.,2024).

The digital era offers organizations unprecedented access to real-time data, which can be leveraged to craft personalized, adaptive, and consumer-centric strategies (Nuseir et al., 2023). Through tools such as social media, content marketing, mobile applications, and search engine optimization, businesses can now engage with consumers across multiple touchpoints, creating immersive and dynamic experiences (Darvidou, 2024). However, simply having a digital presence is no longer sufficient (Dwivedi et al., 2021). To remain competitive and build meaningful relationships, companies must go further, developing strategies that do not just inform or persuade, but engage and convert (Fernández & Oliver, 2025).

Consumer engagement has thus become a cornerstone of effective digital strategy. It reflects the emotional, cognitive, and behavioral investment of consumers in their interactions with brands (Rowi et al., 2024). Engagement is no longer a passive reaction but an active, ongoing relationship that can influence brand loyalty, customer satisfaction, and ultimately, conversion outcomes, whether these be purchases, subscriptions, downloads, or other desired actions (Van Asperen et al., 2017). As a performance metric, engagement also serves as a proxy for brand relevance in an increasingly saturated digital marketplace (Dessart et al., 2015).

Despite the growing emphasis on engagement, the mechanisms through which digital strategies influence both engagement and conversion remain insufficiently explored, particularly in emerging markets. While existing literature has examined digital marketing tools in isolation, there is a lack of integrated research that explains how specific strategic components, such as content strategy, digital communication channels, and user experience (UX, collectively shape consumer engagement, and how that engagement, in turn, mediates conversion behavior.

Understanding this dynamic is particularly relevant in emerging digital markets like Morocco, where the pace of digital transformation has accelerated in recent years (Elhazziti et al., 2023). The Moroccan population is increasingly connected through mobile devices and active on social media platforms, creating new opportunities for brands to engage with consumers in meaningful ways (Ben Youssef & Dahmani, 2023; Tobi, 2023). Social media, in particular, plays a central role in shaping consumer awareness, preferences, and purchasing behavior, providing firms with channels to build relationships, deliver personalized content, and drive engagement (Bouaddi et al., 2024).

Despite this growing digital presence, there remains a limited body of empirical research exploring how Moroccan consumers respond to different digital marketing strategies, such as content quality, multi-channel communication, and user experience optimization. This gap underscores the need for targeted studies to understand the mechanisms through which digital initiatives influence consumer engagement and conversion in the Moroccan context

This study aims to address that gap by adopting a quantitative research design based on data collected from Moroccan consumers who interact with brands online. Specifically, the study investigates the impact of three core digital marketing components, content strategy, communication channels, and user experience, on consumer engagement, and evaluates the mediating role of engagement in driving conversion outcomes.

By exploring these relationships, the research contributes to both academic literature and business practice. From a theoretical perspective, it offers a more nuanced understanding of the interconnectedness of digital marketing elements and their effects on consumer behavior. From a practical standpoint, it provides evidence-based recommendations for businesses aiming to enhance the effectiveness of their digital campaigns. The findings will enable marketers to design more targeted, engaging, and conversion-driven strategies, ensuring that every aspect of the digital experience, from content creation to platform usability, serves to deepen engagement and improve commercial performance.

1. LITERATURE REVIEW

1.1. Exploring Key Concepts

Before exploring the interrelationships between digital strategies, consumer engagement, and conversion, it is important to first establish a clear understanding of each key concept. The following sections define and examine the main components, digital strategies, content, communication channels, user experience, consumer engagement, and conversion, that underpin the study's analytical framework.

1.1.1. Digital Strategies

Digital strategies are comprehensive, coordinated plans that organizations develop to leverage digital technologies and platforms effectively to achieve specific business objectives, such as enhancing brand awareness, acquiring new customers, and driving sales growth (Ologunebi, 2023). These strategies go beyond simple marketing campaigns or ad hoc digital activities; they are carefully designed frameworks that align organizational goals with the digital tools and platforms most appropriate for reaching and engaging target audiences (Wild Ali & Ortega-Gutierrez, 2025).

Rather than being a collection of isolated actions, digital strategies consist of interconnected components that must function cohesively to create meaningful and measurable outcomes in the digital landscape (Osemeike et al., 2024). These components include content strategy, digital communication channels, user experience, analytics, and performance monitoring (Vij & Taneja, 2022). Each element interacts with and supports the others, ensuring that messaging is consistent, user journeys are seamless, and engagement leads to tangible results such as conversions, customer retention, or brand loyalty (Habib & Jha, 2025).

By integrating various digital tools, platforms, and processes, organizations can optimize performance across all touchpoints, ensuring that every interaction reinforces the brand promise and contributes to overarching business objectives (Ruggieri et al., 2018). This holistic approach allows companies to respond dynamically to changing market conditions, personalize experiences for diverse audience segments, and maintain a competitive edge in increasingly saturated digital markets (Pascucci et al., 2023). Ultimately, a well-executed digital strategy ensures that the organization's digital presence is coherent, efficient, and strategically aligned to deliver measurable value (Habib & Jha, 2025).

In the context of our study digital strategies concern three crucial elements: content strategy, digital communication channels and user experience (UX).

1.1.1.1. Content Strategy

A core pillar of any digital strategy is content strategy, which entails the deliberate and systematic planning, creation, delivery, and governance of digital content to effectively engage target audiences and advance broader organizational objectives (Darvidou, 2024). This involves not only producing high-quality content but also ensuring that it aligns with the brand's overall goals, communicates consistent messaging, and maintains a unified tone across diverse digital platforms such as websites, social media, email campaigns, and mobile applications (Baltes, 2015). By establishing a coherent and structured approach, content strategy transforms information into a meaningful connection between the brand and its audience, guiding perceptions, stimulating interactions, and fostering long-term relationships (Lopes & Casais, 2022).

Furthermore, an effective content strategy considers the context, preferences, and specific needs of different audience segments (Isibor et al.,2025). By tailoring content to resonate with particular user groups, whether through informative articles, engaging visuals, interactive media, or personalized messaging, organizations can enhance relevance, capture attention, and increase the likelihood of active engagement (Liu, 2024). This audience-centric approach ensures that content does not simply exist for visibility but becomes a catalyst for meaningful user interactions and sustained interest in the brand (Du Plessis, 2017).

Finally, content strategy functions as a bridge connecting brand objectives with user experience (Bailie & Urbina, 2013). Beyond attracting attention, well-planned content guides users through the digital journey, supports decision-making processes, and encourages desired actions such as subscriptions, inquiries, or purchases (Evania et al., 2023). In this sense, content strategy is both a strategic and operational tool: it not only communicates value but also shapes consumer behavior, strengthens brand credibility, and amplifies the effectiveness of other digital strategy components, including communication channels and UX design (Clark, 2016).

1.1.1.2. Digital Communication Channels

However, content alone is insufficient without the support of effective digital communication channels, which serve as the essential conduits through which brands connect with their audiences. These channels encompass a wide range of platforms, including social media networks such as Facebook, Instagram, and LinkedIn, company websites, email marketing campaigns, mobile applications, and emerging digital touchpoints that facilitate direct interaction between brands and consumers (Jeswani, 2023). The strategic selection, integration, and management of these channels are critical for determining not only the reach of digital content but also its resonance and overall impact on target audiences (Feng et al., 2009).

Digital communication channels play a pivotal role in amplifying the visibility of content while simultaneously shaping the nature and quality of consumer engagement (Sashi, 2021). Through these channels, users are able to interact with the brand by liking, sharing, commenting, or participating in discussions, which fosters a more active, two-way relationship between the consumer and the organization (George et al., 2023). Moreover, channels serve as pathways that guide consumers along the journey from initial awareness to deeper engagement and eventual conversion, highlighting the importance of carefully matching content types with the platforms most appropriate for the intended audience (Mou, 2024).

Effective channel management also involves understanding the characteristics, behaviors, and preferences of different user segments to ensure messages are delivered at the right time, in the right format, and within the context most relevant to their needs (Lamm et al., 2019). By integrating content strategy with an optimized channel strategy, organizations can enhance the efficiency and effectiveness of their digital communications, ensuring that each interaction contributes to stronger engagement, improved brand perception, and measurable business outcomes (Penga & Li, 2024).

1.1.1.3. User Experience (ux)

Complementing both content and channel strategy is user experience (UX), a critical dimension of digital strategy that focuses on the overall quality and effectiveness of interactions users have with digital platforms (Luther et al., 2020). UX encompasses every touchpoint a user encounters, from the ease of navigation and loading speed to the visual design, layout, and responsiveness of a platform (Pal, 2024). Regardless of how compelling the content or strategically chosen the channels are, a poorly designed interface can frustrate users, diminish engagement, and ultimately hinder the achievement of desired outcomes (Umoren et al., 2025).

A positive UX prioritizes usability, visual appeal, responsiveness, personalization, and accessibility, ensuring that users can efficiently and enjoyably navigate digital platforms (Ghosh & Dubey, 2025). For example, intuitive navigation structures, clear calls to action, mobile-friendly design, and fast-loading pages contribute to seamless interactions that encourage users to explore content, engage with features, and complete tasks without unnecessary friction (Hristov, 2024). Personalization, such as tailored recommendations or adaptive interfaces, makes users feel valued and understood, further enhancing satisfaction and fostering loyalty (Sudirjo et al., 2024).

Beyond immediate usability, UX acts as the connective tissue that integrates content and communication channels into a coherent, engaging, and meaningful digital experience (Karthikeyan & Aruna, 2025). By delivering consistent, intuitive, and enjoyable interactions, UX not only builds trust and satisfaction but also reduces bounce rates, encourages repeat visits, and supports critical conversion behaviors such as purchases, subscriptions, or other key actions (Bhaskaran, 2024). In essence, an effective UX strategy ensures that digital touchpoints work harmoniously, maximizing engagement and enabling organizations to achieve their broader strategic objectives efficiently (Anitha, 2024).

1.1.2. Consumer Engagement

After defining the main components of digital strategies, it becomes essential to understand how these strategies translate into meaningful consumer interactions. Consumer engagement is a multifaceted concept that encompasses cognitive, emotional, and behavioral dimensions of a consumer's relationship with a brand (Bowden, 2009). The cognitive dimension involves the awareness, attention, and mental investment that consumers devote to understanding a brand's messages, values, and offerings. The emotional dimension reflects the feelings and attachments consumers develop toward the brand, such as trust, excitement, or loyalty. Meanwhile, the behavioral dimension manifests in tangible actions, including interactions with digital content, participation in brand initiatives, and repeated purchasing behavior. Together, these dimensions illustrate that consumer engagement goes beyond mere exposure to marketing messages; engaged consumers actively participate in the brand experience. They seek opportunities to interact with, contribute to, and derive meaning from their relationship with the brand, making engagement a dynamic, reciprocal process (Harrigan et al., 2017). This shift from passive audience to active participant marks a significant change in how brands must approach communication and relationship-building in the digital age.

In digital environments, consumer engagement can take multiple forms, ranging from observable online actions to more participatory behaviors. Liking, commenting, and sharing content on social media platforms are some of the most visible indicators of engagement. At the same time, consumers may contribute by writing product reviews, participating in online forums or brand communities, or generating their own content related to the brand (user-generated content) (Cao et al., 2021). These behaviors indicate not only interest but also a willingness to invest time and effort in the brand relationship. Such active involvement is closely linked with higher levels of satisfaction, trust, and long-term loyalty, demonstrating that engagement is both a process and an outcome of meaningful brand interactions (Ooko et al., 2023).

The depth and quality of engagement are strongly influenced by drivers such as personalization, relevance, interactivity, and trust (Casaca & Miguel, 2024). Digital consumers respond more positively to experiences tailored to their specific needs, preferences, and behaviors (Efendioğlu, 2024). Interactive content, timely and responsive communication, and transparency enhance engagement by making consumers feel recognized and valued. Brands that facilitate dialogue rather than merely broadcasting messages are better positioned to cultivate authentic relationships that encourage repeated interactions and long-term loyalty (Hollebeek & Macky, 2019). Importantly, high levels of consumer engagement translate into measurable business benefits (Raeisi, 2017). Engaged consumers are more likely to return to a brand, advocate for it to others, and progress from interest to concrete actions, including purchases, subscriptions, or other forms of conversion (Khan et al., 2020). As such, consumer engagement not only strengthens brand equity but also serves as a strategic lever for driving business performance and sustaining competitive advantage in the digital marketplace (Vo Minh Sang et al., 2022).

1.1.3. Conversion

Beyond engagement, conversion constitutes the ultimate objective of digital marketing efforts, reflecting the successful transformation of consumer interest into concrete action. It refers to the moment when a user completes a predefined action that aligns with the organization's strategic goals (Huang et al., 2019). These actions can include purchasing a product, subscribing to a newsletter, downloading a whitepaper, requesting a demo, or even spending a specific amount of time on a page (Lamrhari et al., 2022). Each of these outcomes signals a successful progression through the digital marketing funnel, from awareness and interest to decision and action. Thus, conversion represents a tangible outcome of user engagement and is essential for measuring the effectiveness of digital efforts (Bag et al., 2022).

In the context of digital strategies, conversion is more than just an endpoint, it is a key performance indicator (KPI) that reflects how well a digital experience has been designed and executed (Saura et al., 2017). Marketers often employ Conversion Rate Optimization (CRO) strategies to enhance consumer actions, such as purchases, sign-ups, or downloads. CRO involves the systematic use of tools and techniques to better understand user behavior, identify friction points, and refine calls to action (Al Khaldy, 2024).

There is many common CRO methods including, firstly, A/B testing, which compares two versions of a webpage or element, such as headlines, images, or buttons, to determine which performs better, secondly, heatmaps, which visually show where users click, scroll, or hover on a page, revealing which content attracts attention and which is overlooked, thirdly, session recordings, which track individual user interactions in real time, helping identify navigation issues or drop-off points and analytics, which provide quantitative insights into user behavior, traffic patterns, and conversion trends (Dingre, 2024). By leveraging these tools, marketers can continuously improve digital experiences, reduce obstacles in the user journey, and make it easier for users to engage and complete desired actions (Hnylyakevych & Zinkova, 2024). The goal is to remove obstacles that prevent users from taking the desired actions, thereby increasing the likelihood of conversion (Purnomo, 2023).

A high conversion rate generally indicates that a brand's digital presence effectively aligns with user expectations and needs (Wan, 2023). It suggests that the user experience is intuitive, the content is persuasive, and the digital channels are successfully supporting the customer journey. Conversely, low conversion rates often point to issues such as poor site usability, irrelevant messaging, or lack of trust, prompting marketers to revisit and adapt their strategies (McDowell et al., 2016). In this way, conversion serves not only as a measurement of success but also as a diagnostic tool for continuous optimization (Miikkulainen et al., 2017).

Ultimately, conversion metrics are fundamental for assessing the return on investment (ROI) of digital marketing campaigns (Ramachandran, 2023). They provide insights into which strategies are most effective at turning engagement into action and help justify resource allocation across different digital initiatives (Ahmad et al., 2021). By focusing on improving conversions, businesses can achieve greater marketing efficiency, strengthen customer acquisition, and foster long-term profitability in an increasingly competitive digital environment (Denga et al., 2022).

1.2. The Influence of Digital Strategies on Conversion and the Mediating Role of Consumer Engagement

After having explored the individual components of digital strategies, including content strategy, digital communication channels, and user experience, as well as the key concepts of consumer engagement and conversion, the next step is to examine how these elements interact. Understanding these relationships is critical, as the effectiveness of digital strategies in driving conversion often depends on the mediating role of consumer engagement. The following sub-sections discuss these dynamics, highlighting the ways in which specific digital strategies influence engagement and, ultimately, conversion outcomes.

1.2.1. The Impact of Content Strategies on Consumer Engagement

Content plays a pivotal role in digital marketing strategies, serving as the primary means by which brands capture consumer attention and drive engagement. According to Rani (2022), high-quality, relevant, and personalized content is crucial for encouraging user interaction with a brand. The relevance of content directly influences consumers' willingness to engage actively, whether through commenting, sharing, or liking posts, as emphasized by Bazi et al. (2023). These authors highlight that informative and consumer-tailored content creates an environment conducive to deeper engagement.

Another important factor in sustaining consumer interest is diversifying content formats. Cuevas-Molano (2021) points out that combining articles, videos, infographics, and podcasts helps reach different audience segments and caters to their varied preferences. Alongside format diversity, maintaining a consistent posting frequency is critical; regular content updates ensure that the brand remains top-of-mind and fosters an ongoing relationship with consumers.

Furthermore, Rahman et al. (2022) stress the value of interactive content in strengthening user engagement. Incorporating interactive elements such as polls, quizzes, or live videos encourages active participation rather than passive consumption. This participatory experience builds a sense of community and closeness with the brand, not only boosting engagement but also fostering lasting trust between consumers and the brand.

Implementing content strategies that are diverse, high-quality, consistent, and interactive proves to be a powerful driver in enhancing consumer engagement within digital ecosystems.

Hypothesis 1: Content strategy positively impacts consumer engagement.

1.2.2. Digital Communication Channels and Their Influence on Engagement

The effectiveness of digital communication channels plays a vital role in optimizing consumer engagement in today's digital landscape. Wahyudi et al. (2024) emphasize that integrating multiple communication channels is essential for maximizing brand-consumer interaction. This integration ensures that consumers can engage with brands through their preferred platforms, enhancing overall engagement levels.

Santoso & Sudarmiatin (2024) highlight the importance of a multichannel approach, which combines both traditional digital channels, such as email marketing and search engine optimization (SEO), with more modern platforms like social media and mobile applications. This combination not only broadens the reach of marketing efforts but also enables brands to engage with diverse audience segments in more meaningful ways.

Channel diversity also allows for personalized messaging targeted at specific consumer groups, increasing the relevance and impact of communication. By tailoring messages to the preferences and behaviors of different segments, brands can foster stronger emotional connections and encourage more active participation.

Supporting this, Laroche et al. (2014) found that multichannel marketing campaigns enhance consumer engagement by delivering coherent and personalized experiences across various platforms. Consistency in messaging and user experience across channels helps build trust and reinforces brand identity.

Furthermore, Eslami et al. (2022) reveal that consumers who engage with brands across multiple channels, such as social media, websites, and email, are more likely to exhibit active behaviors like sharing content, commenting, and recommending products to others. This multichannel engagement creates a more immersive brand experience that drives deeper consumer loyalty.

> **Hypothesis 2.** Digital communication channels positively impact consumer engagement.

1.2.3. User Experience (UX) and Its Role in Consumer Engagement

User Experience (UX) is a crucial factor in driving consumer engagement on digital platforms. An optimized UX, characterized by smooth navigation, intuitive interfaces, and fast loading times, is consistently linked to higher levels of user interaction and satisfaction (Liu et al., 2024). When users find a platform easy and enjoyable to use, they are more likely to stay longer, explore more content, and engage actively with the brand.

Nielsen et al. (2018) highlight that a well-designed website significantly reduces bounce rates, which means users are less likely to leave immediately and more inclined to visit multiple pages. This increased interaction enhances opportunities for engagement, such as clicking on calls to action, commenting, or sharing content.

Mobile optimization is another essential aspect of UX, especially considering the growing number of users accessing digital content through smartphones. Pereira et al. (2020) emphasize that a seamless mobile experience is vital to retain and engage users who predominantly use mobile devices. Poor mobile UX can lead to frustration, disengagement, and lost conversions (Okonkwo, 2024).

Moreover, personalizing the user experience plays a powerful role in boosting engagement. Features like product recommendations based on users' browsing history or preferences create a sense of relevance and value, encouraging users to interact more deeply with the platform. Personalization fosters a connection between the consumer and brand, enhancing loyalty and repeat interactions.

Hypothesis 3. A better user experience enhances consumer engagement.

1.2.4. Consumer Engagement and Its Relationship With Conversion

Consumer engagement is widely acknowledged as a critical driver of conversion intentions. According to Homburg et al. (2017), high levels of engagement, reflected through actions such as clicks, likes, shares, or comments, are strongly associated with an increased likelihood of conversion. Conversions can take various forms, including purchases, subscriptions, or other meaningful actions that benefit the brand.

The more engaged consumers are with a brand, the higher the probability they will take desired actions like completing a purchase, signing up for a service, or participating in campaigns (Helme-Guizon et al., 2019). This relationship highlights the importance of nurturing engagement to move consumers along the conversion funnel.

Research by Jiang et al. (2019) emphasizes the significant role of social media engagement in driving conversion rates. When consumers interact with social media posts or advertisements, they develop a stronger connection with the brand. This interaction not only solidifies brand-consumer relationships but also enhances consumer trust, a key factor that positively influences purchase intentions and other conversion behaviors (Yang et al., 2016).

In essence, fostering active consumer engagement increases the likelihood of conversion and supports the brand's growth objectives.

Hypothesis 4. Consumer engagement positively impacts conversion.

1.2.5. The Mediating Role of Engagement in the Relationship Between Digital Strategies and Conversion

Consumer engagement frequently acts as a vital mediator linking digital strategies, such as content creation, communication channels, and user experience, to conversion outcomes. Research by Tomar et al. (2024) highlights how well-executed content strategies foster higher levels of engagement, which in turn lead to increased conversion rates. Their findings demonstrate that engagement is not merely a by-product but an essential mechanism that activates conversion behaviors, including repeat purchases and service subscriptions, underscoring its critical role in translating digital marketing efforts into tangible business results.

Further, Schulz et al. (2020) emphasize that engagement on digital platforms transcends being a simple measure of consumer interest. Instead, it serves as a key driver of customer loyalty and retention, which are fundamental to sustaining long-term brand success. Similarly, Rudy et al. (2021) stress that engagement cultivates deeper, more enduring relationships between brands and consumers, reinforcing brand affinity and trust over time.

Therefore, digital marketing initiatives, whether focused on crafting engaging content, leveraging diverse communication channels, or enhancing user experience, indirectly contribute to higher conversion rates by promoting sustained consumer interaction and building stronger trust with the brand (Alfiyahsari et al., 2023). This mediating role of engagement is pivotal in ensuring that digital strategies effectively influence consumer behavior and drive business growth.

Therefor the following hypotheses are proposed:

Hypothesis 5. Content strategy has an indirect impact on conversion, through consumer engagement.
Hypothesis 6. Digital communication channels have an indirect impact on conversion, via consumer engagement.
Hypothesis 7. A better user experience leads to greater conversion, through consumer engagement.

Subsequently, the conceptual model of this research is presented in Figure 1 based on the literature review and the hypotheses formulated.

Figure 1. The conceptual model of the research

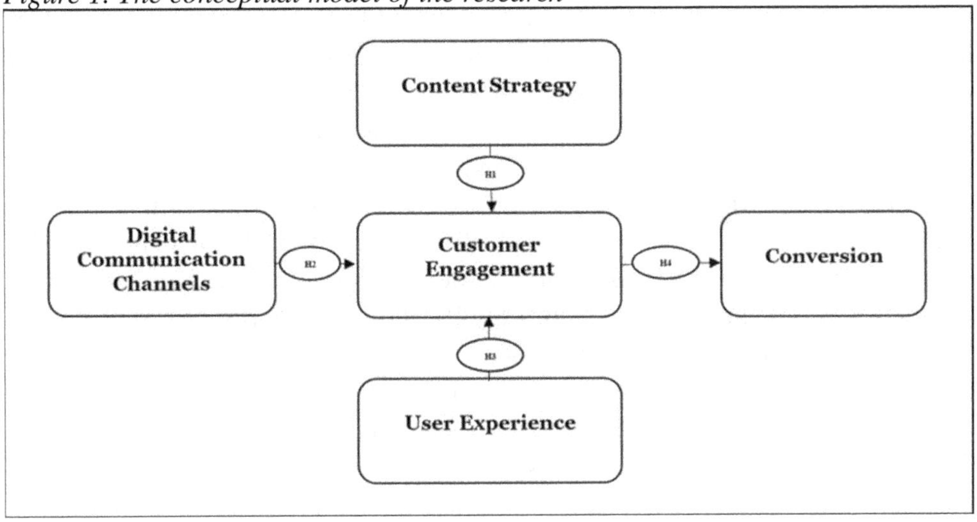

2. RESEARCH METHODOLOGY

To empirically validate the conceptual framework, a quantitative research design was implemented. The following section presents the methodology adopted in this study, detailing the population, sampling method, data collection process, and analytical techniques used to test the hypothesized relationships.

Our study adopts a quantitative approach to analyze the impact of digital strategies on consumer engagement and conversion in the Moroccan context. The quantitative approach was preferred because it allows for objective measurement of the relationships between various variables and testing of the hypotheses formulated from the conceptual model (Ghanad, 2023). By using this method, measurable data were collected, enabling in-depth statistical analysis to determine the magnitude and direction of the effects of digital strategies on consumer behaviors. This approach also provides the possibility of generalizing findings from a representative sample, essential for a better understanding of consumer behaviors in a specific digital market such as Morocco (Kumo, 2023).

The sample for our study consists of 500 active Moroccan consumers in the digital realm, particularly on social media platforms and in interactions with online brands. This target population was chosen due to the rise of digital marketing and e-commerce in Morocco, as well as the high level of technology usage by consumers (Bouaddi et al., 2024). The sample was selected using stratified random sampling, ensuring adequate representation based on criteria such as age, gender, education level, and technology usage. This sample size was selected to ensure sufficient statistical reliability and allow for a robust analysis of the relationships between the variables in the research model (Mokkink et al., 2022).

At this level, primary results (Table 1) have indicated that the majority of respondents are young, with 40% of participants in the age group of 18-25 years (200 individuals), highlighting the strong representation of young adults in the survey. The 26-35 age group follows closely with 30% (150 individuals). In contrast, older age groups make up a smaller portion: 20% of respondents are aged between 36-45 years, 8% are between 46-60 years, and only 2% of respondents are 60 years or older. This suggests that the survey predominantly attracted a young and adult population, which may reflect these groups' heightened interest in digital tools.

Next, 58% of the respondents are male (290 participants), while 42% are female (210 individuals). Although males are slightly more numerous, the gender difference is not significant, indicating a relatively balanced distribution between genders in the sample.

In terms of digital tool usage, 40% of respondents (200 participants) use digital tools between 3 and 5 hours per day, reflecting regular use of digital tools in their daily lives. Furthermore, 30% of participants use digital tools between 5 and 10 hours per day, indicating a relatively high level of engagement with digital technologies. Another 20% of respondents use digital tools between 1 and 3 hours daily, suggesting moderate usage. Lastly, 10% of respondents spend more than 10 hours per day using these tools, indicating a group that is more intensively connected to technology.

Table 1. Respondents profile

Demographic variable	Category	Frequency	Percentage (%)
Age	18-25	200	40%
	26-35	150	30%
	36-45	100	20%
	46-60	40	8%
	60+	10	2%
Sex	Male	290	58%
	Female	210	42%
Frequency of Digital Tool Usage	1-3 Hours/day	100	20%
	3-5 Hours/day	200	40%
	5-10 Hours/day	150	30%
	More than 10 Hours/day	50	10%

Source: Survey Conducted with Respondents

Data were collected using a structured online questionnaire. The questionnaire included closed-ended questions on a 1-to-5 Likert scale to measure consumer perceptions of the digital strategies employed by brands (Ha, 2022). The questionnaire covered five key variables: content strategy, digital communication, user experience (UX), consumer engagement, and conversion. Each variable was measured using five specific items (Seee table 2), that were adapted from prior research to ensure content validity (DeVellis, 2017). The questionnaire was administered online through Google Forms, and links to the questionnaire were distributed primarily via social media, facilitating access to a wide range of Moroccan consumers.

Table 2. Measurement scales

Construct	Item Code	Item Statement	Sources
Content Strategy	CS1	The brand provides content that is relevant to my interests.	Waqas et al., (2021); Lee and Johar. (2025); Bouaddi et al. (2024); Darvidou (2024).
	CS2	The content from the brand is informative.	
	CS3	The content encourages me to interact with the brand.	
	CS4	The content is personalized according to my preferences.	
	CS5	The brand uses engaging multimedia content like videos, infographics, etc.	
Digital Communication Channels	DCC1	The brand communicates effectively through social media.	Tsimonis and Dimitriadis (2014) ; Karafuto et al. (2015); Pedrero-Esteban and Barrios-Rubio (2024); Lussak et al. (2024).
	DCC2	The brand's emails and notifications are relevant to me.	
	DCC3	The brand provides consistent communication across multiple channels.	
	DCC4	The brand's digital communication encourages me to take action.	
	DCC5	I feel the brand reaches me through my preferred digital channels.	
User Experience (UX)	UX1	The website is easy to navigate.	Sandesara et al. (2022) ; Huma et al. (2025) ; Naumann et al. (2007).
	UX2	The mobile version of the website/app is user-friendly.	
	UX3	The website/app loads quickly without delays.	
	UX4	The interface is intuitive and easy to use.	
	UX5	The website/app experience is personalized according to my preferences.	

continued on following page

Table 2. Continued

Construct	Item Code	Item Statement	Sources
Consumer Engagement	CE1	I actively like, share, or comment on the brand's content.	Lourenço et al. (2022) ; Yoo (2024) ; Santos et al. (2022).
	CE2	I frequently interact with the brand online.	
	CE3	I follow the brand on social media and check updates regularly.	
	CE4	I participate in online discussions or polls hosted by the brand.	
	CE5	I feel connected to the brand through its online presence.	
Conversion	CNV1	I have purchased products/services of the brand after engaging online.	Yang (2024) ; Martínez-López et al. (2021) ; Gudigantala et al. (2016) ; Di Fatta et al. (2018).
	CNV2	I am likely to subscribe to the brand's offers after interacting online.	
	CNV3	My interactions with the brand influence my purchase decisions.	
	CNV4	I recommend the brand to others based on my online interactions.	
	CNV5	Online engagement with the brand leads me to take desired actions like purchase, sign-up, etc.	

The collected data were analyzed using the SmartPLS 4 method (Partial Least Squares Structural Equation Modeling), which allows for the simultaneous analysis of relationships between multiple latent variables and evaluation of direct and indirect effects in a model (Stein et al., 2012). This method was chosen due to its ability to handle complex models and its flexibility for exploratory research, particularly in the field of digital marketing (Guenther et al., 2023). The analysis process involved initial steps of testing the reliability of items using Cronbach's alpha, as well as assessing the convergent and discriminant validity of the scales used. Subsequently, the measurement model was evaluated to verify the quality of relationships between latent variables. Finally, structural relationships were examined to assess the validity of the research hypotheses.

3. RESULTS

The results section reports the empirical findings derived from data analysis using the SmartPLS 4 software. It begins with the evaluation of the measurement model to ensure reliability and validity, followed by the assessment of the structural model to test the proposed hypotheses and determine the strength of the relationships between variables.

3.1. Evaluation of the Measurement Model

The measurement model was evaluated using SmartPLS 4, and the results, as presented in Table 3, indicate that the validity and reliability values meet the required criteria. The Average Variance Extracted (AVE) values are greater than the reference threshold of 0.5 (Hair et al., 2017), indicating good convergent validity for the constructs. Furthermore, the Cronbach's Alpha (CA) exceeds the threshold of 0.7, while the Composite Reliability (CR) also meets the consistency threshold. These values ensure the robustness of the measurement model, validating the items used in the study for the different constructs. The details of the CA, CR, and AVE values are presented in Table 3.

Table 3. Validity and reliability values

Construct	Cronbach's Alpha (CA)	Composite Reliability (CR)	Average Variance Extracted (AVE)
Content strategy (CS)	0.912	0.947	0.818
Digital Communcation Channels (DCC)	0.905	0.938	0.804
User Experience (UX)	0.920	0.949	0.826
Customer Engagement (CE)	0.930	0.951	0.871
Conversion (CNV)	0.912	0.945	0.853

Source: Results extracted from SmartPls 4

The results in Table 3 show that the values of the Average Variance Extracted (AVE) are all above 0.5, indicating good convergent validity for the latent variables used in the model. In fact, an AVE value greater than 0.5 means that each latent variable adequately explains the items associated with it. This suggests that the items measuring each latent variable are well correlated with each other, and that the constructs are adequately represented in the model. Consequently, these results validate the items' ability to measure the latent variables consistently.

Next, the values for Cronbach's Alpha (CA) and Composite Reliability (CR) are both above 0.7, demonstrating high internal reliability for each latent variable. A Cronbach's Alpha greater than 0.7 is often considered a good indicator of internal consistency of the items, meaning that these items reliably measure the same characteristic or concept (Nunnally & Bernstein, 1994). Furthermore, the Composite Reliability (CR), ranging from 0.938 to 0.951 for the different latent variables, reinforces this observation by indicating a high level of consistency in the relationships between the items and latent variables.

In summary, these indices suggest that the model is reliable, with items consistently measuring the latent variables. Finally, the Composite Reliability (CR), ranging from 0.938 to 0.951, indicates excellent internal consistency for the latent variables. This means that the items consistently measure the same underlying concept, and the relationship between items within each latent variable is strongly connected. A high Composite Reliability value ensures that the results obtained are robust and reliable for testing the structural relationships in the model.

Table 4 presents the factor loadings for the various constructs in the study. The factor loadings are significant, exceeding the threshold of 0.5, and ideally above 0.7 (Hair et al., 2017), confirming that the items used in our study have achieved satisfactory discriminant validity.

Table 4. Factor loadings (outer loadings)

Items	CS	DCC	UX	CE	CNV
CS1	0.870				
CS2	0.923				
CS3	0.906				
CS4	0.912				
CS5	0.921				
DCC1		0.890			
DCC2		0.931			
DCC3		0.906			
DCC4		0.884			
DCC5		0.912			
UX1			0.934		
UX2			0.920		
UX3			0.905		
UX4			0.916		
UX5			0.924		
CE1				0.944	
CE2				0.931	
CE3				0.912	
CE4				0.905	
CE5				0.916	

continued on following page

Table 4. Continued

Items	CS	DCC	UX	CE	CNV
CNV1					0.902
CNV2					0.917
CNV3					0.921
CNV4					0.902
CNV5					0.922

Source: Results extracted from SmartPls 4

The results values of the outer loadings in table 4 for each item are all greater than 0.7, which is an excellent indicator of the quality of the scales used in our study. These high values confirm that each item is a strong representative of the latent variable to which it is associated, ensuring a reliable measurement of the theoretical constructs. Additionally, each item is clearly associated with its corresponding latent variable (for example, CS1 with Content Strategy, DCC1 with Digital Communication Channels, etc.). This strong association between items and their respective latent variables indicates the convergent validity of the model, meaning that the items are indeed measuring what they are supposed to measure. Furthermore, discriminant validity is also confirmed, as all factor loadings exceed 0.7. This indicates that the latent variables are clearly distinguishable from one another. In other words, each latent variable measures a distinct concept without significant overlap with other variables in the model. These results strengthen the overall validity of the model and ensure that the different dimensions are correctly captured and differentiated.

3.2. Evaluation of the Structural Model

After having established that the measurement model is both reliable and valid, we can now proceed to evaluate the structural model. This step examines the hypothesized relationships between the latent variables, determining the strength and significance of the paths connecting content strategy (CS), digital communication channels (DCC), user experience (UX), consumer engagement (CE), and conversion (CNV). For this purpose, we have examined the path coefficients (See table 5), which measure the strength and direction of the relationships between the latent variables in the model. These coefficients are calculated through PLS-SEM (Partial Least Squares Structural Equation Modeling) analysis. The path coefficients help to determine if the relationships between variables are statistically significant (Deng & Yuan, 2023).

Table 5. Results of hypothesis testing

Relation	Path Coefficient	t-Value	p-Value	Hypothesis	Conclusion
CS - CE	0.390	6.112	<0.001	H1: CS influences CE	Supported
DCC - CE	0.417	5.817	<0.001	H2: DCC influences CE	Supported
UX - CE	0.342	5.560	<0.001	H3: UX influences CE	Supported
CS - CNV	0.318	5.345	<0.001	H4: CS influences CNV	Supported
DCC - CNV	0.282	5.120	<0.001	H5: DCC influences CNV	Supported
UX - CNV	0.243	4.042	<0.001	H6: UX influences CNV	Supported
CE - CNV	0.402	6.254	<0.001	H7: CE influences CNV	Supported

Source: Results extracted from SmartPls 4

Figure 2. The conceptual model of the study

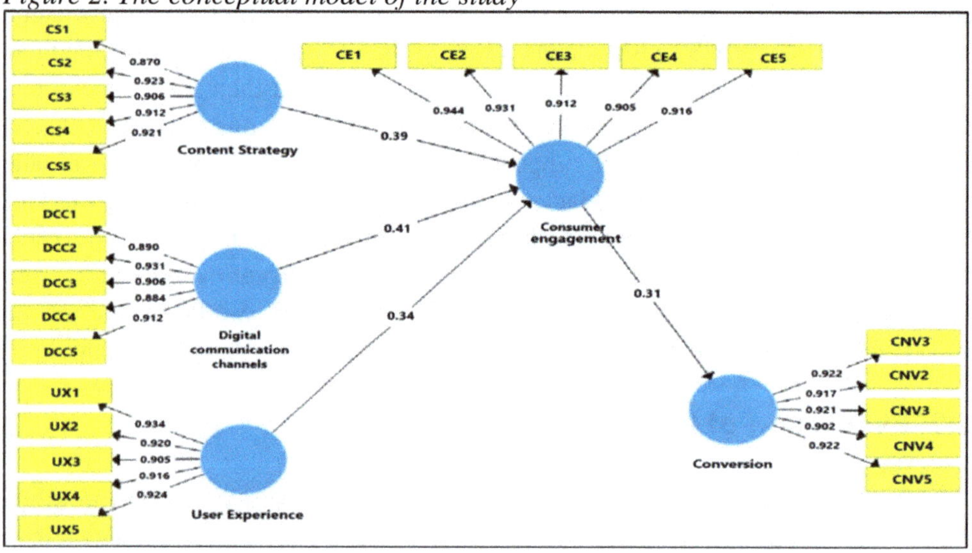

The results of the conceptual model, based on the analysis of path coefficients (See table 5 and Figure 2), provide valuable insights into the relationships between the latent variables of the study, namely Content Strategy (CS), Digital Communication Channels (DCC), User Experience (UX), Consumer Engagement (CE), and Conversion (CNV).

The influence of Content Strategy (CS) on Consumer Engagement (CE)

The path coefficient of 0.390 between Content Strategy (CS) and Consumer Engagement (CE) is statistically significant with a t-value of 6.112 ($p < 0.001$). This indicates that the quality and relevance of the content provided by the company play a crucial role in consumer engagement. In other words, the more interesting and relevant the content is perceived, the more likely consumers are to actively engage with the brand. This relationship confirms the importance of content strategy in consumer engagement, a key element in digital marketing strategies.

The influence of Digital Communication Channels (DCC) on Consumer Engagement (CE)

Digital Communication Channels (DCC) have a path coefficient of 0.417, with a t-value of 5.817 ($p < 0.001$). This means that effectively using digital channels such as social media, email marketing, and online advertising plays a significant role in consumer engagement. Companies that select and use these channels effectively are more likely to capture the attention of their target audience and maintain an ongoing relationship, thus fostering higher engagement.

The influence of User Experience (UX) on Consumer Engagement (CE)

User Experience (UX) also shows a significant effect on Consumer Engagement, with a path coefficient of 0.342, t-value = 5.560, and $p < 0.001$. This result highlights the importance of offering a smooth and pleasant experience to users on digital platforms. When consumers find a company's website or app easy to navigate, fast, and well-designed, they are more likely to engage actively with the brand. In summary, UX is a key factor in consumer engagement, emphasizing the need for businesses to prioritize an intuitive and efficient interface.

The influence of Content Strategy (CS) on Conversion (CNV)

The path coefficient of 0.318 between Content Strategy (SC) and Conversion (CNV) shows that marketing content also impacts consumer conversion (t-value = 5.345, $p < 0.001$). This suggests that high-quality, relevant, and well-targeted content can positively influence consumers' purchasing behaviors. Consumers who engage with convincing content are more likely to take action, resulting in a higher conversion rate.

The influence of Digital Communication Channels (DCC) on Conversion (CNV)

The effect of Digital Communication Channels (CND) on Conversion (CNV) is also significant, with a path coefficient of 0.282 (t-value = 5.120, $p < 0.001$). This shows that digital channels not only engage consumers but also contribute to converting that engagement into concrete actions, such as purchases or sign-ups. Companies that optimize the use of digital channels, especially by creating targeted and relevant campaigns, can therefore increase their conversion rate.

The influence of User Experience (UX) on Conversion (CNV)

User Experience (UX) also plays a crucial role in consumer conversion, with a path coefficient of 0.243 (t-value = 4.042, $p < 0.001$). A well-designed and functional site not only increases consumer engagement but also facilitates the transition from interaction to conversion. When the shopping experience is simple, fast, and frictionless, consumers are more likely to complete a purchase, directly impacting conversion rates.

The influence of Consumer Engagement (CE) on Conversion (CNV)

Finally, Consumer Engagement (CE) has a direct effect on Conversion (CNV), with a path coefficient of 0.402 (t-value = 6.254, $p < 0.001$). This highlights that the more engaged consumers are with the brand, the more likely they are to make a conversion. Engagement can manifest in various forms, such as interactions on social media, comments on posts, or repeat purchases. This result underscores the importance of consumer engagement not only for establishing a long-term relationship with them but also for driving conversion.

4. DISCUSSION

The results of this study confirm the hypotheses regarding the influence of digital strategies on consumer conversion and the mediating role of engagement. Overall, the findings validate that content strategy, digital communication channels, and user experience (UX) significantly affect consumer engagement, which, in turn, drives conversion. While these results align with prior studies conducted primarily in Western and Asian contexts, examining them within the Moroccan digital ecosystem offers new insights into how these theoretical relationships operate in emerging digital markets.

The finding that content strategy positively influences consumer engagement confirms established digital marketing theories (Rani, 2022; Bazi et al., 2023), which emphasize that personalized, relevant, and interactive content fosters user involvement. However, in Morocco, engagement is influenced not only by content relevance but also by cultural resonance and authenticity. Moroccan consumers often prefer content that reflects collective values, community identity, and social narratives, rather than purely individualistic appeals. This refines Western-centric theories by suggesting that content effectiveness in emerging markets is both informational and culturally interpretive, adding a nuanced layer to engagement theory.

Similarly, the impact of digital communication channels (DCC) on engagement and conversion corroborates prior findings (Wahyudi et al., 2024; Santoso & Sudarmiatin, 2024). Yet, in the Moroccan context, channel accessibility, trust, and social validation play a particularly important role. Unlike Western markets where multichannel strategies assume universal digital literacy, Moroccan consumers rely heavily on mobile-based and social media platforms, such as WhatsApp, Facebook, and Instagram. This highlights that effective digital communication in emerging markets depends not only on channel integration but also on ease of access and perceived reliability, refining multichannel theory for diverse digital landscapes.

The positive influence of user experience (UX) on engagement and conversion is consistent with prior research (Liu et al., 2024; Nielsen et al., 2018), but with local nuances. Moroccan consumers place particular emphasis on mobile optimization, simplicity, and bilingual interfaces (Arabic and French). While UX principles of usability and intuitive design are largely universal, their operationalization in Morocco requires attention to local technological and cultural constraints, demonstrating that context-specific UX design is critical for maximizing engagement.

The study also confirms that consumer engagement directly impacts conversion, aligning with research by Homburg et al. (2017) and Zheng et al. (2022). Interestingly, while the engagement-to-conversion pathway appears cross-culturally consistent, Moroccan engagement drivers are often community-based and socially validated, rather than algorithmically personalized alone. This finding suggests that while engagement reliably predicts conversion, its antecedents are shaped by cultural and infrastructural factors, adding depth to global engagement-conversion theory.

One of the study's key contributions lies in confirming the mediating role of engagement between digital strategies and conversion in an emerging market context. While prior models (Tomar et al., 2024; Schulz et al., 2020) established engagement as a mediator, evidence from Morocco demonstrates that engagement also functions as a trust-building mechanism, bridging digital exposure and actual consumer actions. This extends existing mediation models by emphasizing the role of cultural trust and social validation in transforming engagement into measurable business outcomes in emerging markets.

From a theoretical perspective, these findings refine Western-centric models of digital marketing by emphasizing contextual adaptation. While structural relationships between digital strategies, engagement, and conversion are largely universal, the mechanisms underlying engagement, including cultural resonance, accessibility, and trust, differ across markets. This contributes to a more globally inclusive theory of digital consumer behavior, particularly relevant for researchers studying non-Western or hybrid cultural environments.

Building on these findings, it is clear that the results not only deepen our theoretical understanding of the relationships between digital strategies, consumer engagement, and conversion but also offer actionable insights for practitioners. By translating these empirical conclusions into concrete practices, businesses can enhance the effectiveness of their digital initiatives and better leverage engagement to drive conversions. The results of our study offer several practical implications for businesses looking to improve their digital strategies and maximize conversion rates.

First, brands should invest in high-quality, personalized, and relevant content strategies for their target audiences. Content should not only be informative but also engaging, using various formats (articles, videos, infographics, etc.) to maintain consumer interest and encourage interaction. The use of interactive content, such as polls, quizzes, or live videos, could be particularly effective in fostering deep and lasting engagement.

Second, a multichannel approach is essential to reach a wider audience and interact with them across multiple platforms. Companies need to combine traditional channels (such as email marketing and SEO) with more modern channels (social media, mobile apps) to offer a consistent and personalized experience. Integrating diverse communication channels not only increases the reach of campaigns but also encourages continuous and authentic interactions with consumers, thus strengthening their engagement.

Third, optimizing the user experience (UX) on websites and mobile apps must be a priority. Businesses need to ensure that their digital platforms offer smooth navigation, an intuitive interface, quick response times, and effective personalization. Mobile optimization is especially crucial given the prevalence of platform access through smartphones. Well-designed and personalized UX can significantly reduce bounce rates, encourage users to engage more, and bring them back to platforms, thereby promoting the conversion process.

Finally, consumer engagement, which proves to be a key factor in conversion, must be actively nurtured. Companies need to put mechanisms in place to encourage frequent and meaningful interactions, whether it be likes, shares, comments, or other forms of participation. The more engaged a consumer is, the more likely they are to take action, whether it's making a purchase, subscribing, or performing another form of conversion.

5. RESEARCH LIMITATIONS AND FUTURE DIRECTIONS

While this study provides valuable insights into the impact of digital strategies on consumer engagement and conversion, several limitations should be acknowledged. First, the research was conducted exclusively among Moroccan consumers. Cultural, economic, and technological differences may limit the generalizability of the findings to other countries or regions.

Second, the study employed a cross-sectional survey design, capturing data at a single point in time. This approach restricts the ability to draw causal conclusions regarding the relationships between digital strategies, engagement, and conversion. Third, the reliance on self-reported measures introduces potential biases, such as social desirability or inaccurate recall, meaning that respondents' reported engagement may not fully reflect actual online behaviors.

Additionally, although the study examined content strategy, digital communication, user experience, engagement, and conversion, other influential factors, such as brand trust, price sensitivity, or competitive positioning, were not included. Finally, each variable was measured using five items. While concise and practical, this may not fully capture all the nuances of complex constructs like engagement or user experience.

Building on these limitations, several avenues for future research are proposed. Future studies could expand the sample to include larger, more diverse, and cross-cultural populations, enhancing generalizability and allowing for the exploration of regional differences in digital strategy effectiveness. Longitudinal research designs could track consumer engagement and conversion over time, providing stronger evidence of causality and the temporal effects of digital strategies.

Incorporating additional variables, such as brand trust, perceived value, and customer loyalty, could offer a more comprehensive understanding of the factors driving conversion. Experimental and behavioral approaches, including controlled experiments or analyses of behavioral data (e.g., clickstream, purchase history), could complement survey findings and provide more objective insights into consumer interactions with digital content. Moreover, future research could explore the impact of emerging technologies, such as AI-driven personalization, chatbots, and immersive media (AR/VR), on engagement and conversion.

By addressing these limitations and pursuing these research directions, future studies can provide deeper, more generalizable insights into the role of digital strategies in enhancing consumer engagement and driving business outcomes.

CONCLUSION

The results of this study highlight the significant role of digital strategies in shaping consumer engagement and driving conversions. Content strategy, emphasizing high-quality, relevant, and engaging material, was found to be a crucial factor in attracting consumer attention and encouraging active interaction with brands. This suggests that well-crafted content not only informs consumers but also fosters meaningful engagement that can lead to actionable outcomes, such as purchases or sign-ups.

Digital communication channels, including social media, email marketing, and other online platforms, also play an essential role in building consumer engagement. Effective use of these channels enables brands to reach their target audiences consistently, maintaining ongoing interactions that strengthen the consumer-brand relationship. Similarly, user experience emerged as a key determinant of engagement and conversion, with smooth, intuitive, and frictionless digital interfaces encouraging consumers to explore, interact, and ultimately take desired actions.

Consumer engagement itself was identified as a central mediator in the relationship between digital strategies and conversion. Brands that succeed in fostering engagement are more likely to see that interest translated into tangible actions, highlighting the importance of viewing engagement as an ongoing, interactive process rather than a short-term outcome.

From a theoretical perspective, this study contributes to the literature by demonstrating the interconnectedness of content strategy, digital communication channels, and user experience, and how these elements collectively influence consumer behavior. It also reinforces the mediating role of engagement, providing a more integrated understanding of how digital marketing strategies affect conversion outcomes.

Practically, the findings offer actionable insights for businesses seeking to optimize their digital marketing efforts. Companies are encouraged to adopt a holistic approach that combines high-quality content, multi-channel communication, and user-centered design. Prioritizing sustained engagement through personalized interactions, seamless experiences, and consistent messaging can strengthen brand loyalty and enhance conversion rates.

Finally, this study provides valuable evidence from the Moroccan market, an emerging digital context where empirical research on integrated digital strategies is still limited. It shows that strategies that emphasize content, communication, and user experience can effectively engage consumers and drive conversion, offering guidance for businesses operating in similar emerging market environments.

REFERENCES

Ahmad, A., Alshurideh, M., Al Kurdi, B., Aburayya, A., & Hamadneh, S. (2021). Digital transformation metrics: A conceptual view. *Journal of Management Information and Decision Sciences*, *24*(7), 1–18. https://www.abacademies.org/articles/digital-transformation-metrics--a--conceptual--view-11806.html

Al Khaldy, I. A. (2024). Impact of digital marketing techniques in increasing effectiveness of conversion rate optimization (CRO) among telecommunication organizations in Jordan. *International Research Journal of Economics and Management Studies*, *3*(2), 251–259. DOI: 10.56472/25835238/IRJEMS-V3I2P131

Alfiyahsari, R., Taurina, R. A., & Priyanka, G. (2023). The effectiveness of using digital marketing communication strategies and their conversion effects (Case study on DatascripMall.ID). [JoSS]. *Journal of Social Sciences*, *2*, 507–522. DOI: 10.57185/joss.v2i6.96

Anitha, M. V. (2024). *Enhancing customer experience through digital transformation: Strategies and impact*. Today's Multidisciplinary Research Perspectives.

Bag, S., Srivastava, G., Al Bashir, M. M., Kumari, S., Giannakis, M., & Chowdhury, A. H. (2022). Journey of customers in this digital era: Understanding the role of artificial intelligence technologies in user engagement and conversion. *Benchmarking*, *29*(7), 2074–2098. DOI: 10.1108/BIJ-07-2021-0415

Bailie, R. A., & Urbina, N. (2013). *Content strategy: Connecting the dots between business, brand, and benefits*. XML Press.

Baltes, L. P. (2015). Content marketing-the fundamental tool of digital marketing. *Bulletin of the Transilvania University of Brasov. Series V, Economic Sciences*, ●●●, 111–118. https://www.scirp.org/reference/referencespapers?referenceid=4034107

Bazi, S., Filieri, R., & Gorton, M. (2023). Social media content aesthetic quality and customer engagement: The mediating role of entertainment and impacts on brand love and loyalty. *Journal of Business Research*, *160*, 113778. DOI: 10.1016/j.jbusres.2023.113778

Ben Youssef, A., & Dahmani, M. (2023). Examining the drivers of e-commerce adoption by Moroccan firms: A multi-model analysis. *Information (Basel)*, *14*(7), 1–19. DOI: 10.3390/info14070378

Bhaskaran, V. (2024). Designing for trust: The crucial role in digital user experiences. *Journal of User Experience*, *19*(2), 53–59. https://uxpajournal.org/wcontent/uploads/sites/7/2024/02/JUX_Bhaskaran_Feb-2024.pdf

Bouaddi, M., Sanaa, M., & Siham, K. (2024). The effect of using social media by brands on customer engagement: Content quality, personalization, and constant presence as key factors. In Proceedings of the International Conference on Information Technology, Multimedia, Architecture, Design, and E-Business (Vol. 3, pp. 533-545).

Bowden, J. L.-H. (2009). The process of customer engagement: A conceptual framework. *Journal of Marketing Theory and Practice*, *17*(1), 63–74. DOI: 10.2753/MTP1069-6679170105

Cao, D., Meadows, M., Wong, D., & Xia, S. (2021). Understanding consumers' social media engagement behaviour: An examination of the moderation effect of social media context. *Journal of Business Research*, *122*, 835–846. DOI: 10.1016/j.jbusres.2020.06.025

Casaca, J., & Miguel, L. P. (2024). The influence of personalization on consumer satisfaction: Trends and challenges. In *Data-driven marketing for strategic success* (pp. 256–292). IGI Global., DOI: 10.4018/979-8-3693-3455-3.ch010

Clark, D. (2016). Content strategy: An integrative literature review. *IEEE Transactions on Professional Communication*, *59*(1), 7–23. DOI: 10.1109/TPC.2016.2537080

Cuevas-Molano, E., Matosas-López, L., & Bernal-Bravo, C. (2021). Factors increasing consumer engagement of branded content in Instagram. *IEEE Access : Practical Innovations, Open Solutions*, *9*, 143531–143548. DOI: 10.1109/ACCESS.2021.3121186

Darvidou, K. (2024). Content marketing strategy and development. *Technium Business and Management*, *10*, 55–67. DOI: 10.47577/business.v10i.11902

Deng, L., & Yuan, K. H. (2023). Which method is more powerful in testing the relationship of theoretical constructs? A meta comparison of structural equation modeling and path analysis with weighted composites. *Behavior Research Methods*, *55*(4), 1460–1479. DOI: 10.3758/s13428-022-01838-z PMID: 35653013

Denga, E. M., Vajjhala, N. R., & Rakshit, S. (2022). The role of digital marketing in achieving sustainable competitive advantage. In Digital transformation and internationalization strategies in organizations (pp. 44-60). https://doi.org/DOI: 10.4018/978-1-7998-8169-8.ch003

Dessart, L., Veloutsou, C., & Morgan-Thomas, A. (2015). Consumer engagement in online brand communities: A social media perspective. *Journal of Product and Brand Management*, *24*(1), 28–42. DOI: 10.1108/JPBM-06-2014-0635

DeVellis, R. F. (2017). *Scale development: Theory and applications* (4th ed.). Sage.

Di Fatta, D., Patton, D., & Viglia, G. (2018). The determinants of conversion rates in SME e-commerce websites. *Journal of Retailing and Consumer Services*, *41*, 161–168. DOI: 10.1016/j.jretconser.2017.12.008

Dingre, S. (2024). An approach to optimize conversion rate using behavioral economics. *Journal of Marketing Studies*, *7*(1), 8–14. DOI: 10.47941/jms.1680

Du Plessis, C. (2017). The role of content marketing in social media content communities. *South African Journal of Information Management*, *19*(1), 1–7. DOI: 10.4102/sajim.v19i1.866

Dwivedi, Y. K., Ismagilova, E., Hughes, D. L., Carlson, J., Filieri, R., Jacobson, J., Jain, V., Karjaluoto, H., Kefi, H., Krishen, A. S., Kumar, V., Rahman, M. M., Raman, R., Rauschnabel, P. A., Rowley, J., Salo, J., Tran, G. A., & Wang, Y. (2021). Setting the future of digital and social media marketing research: Perspectives and research propositions. *International Journal of Information Management*, •••, 1–37. DOI: 10.1016/j.ijinfomgt.2020.102168

Efendioğlu, İ. H. (2024). Digital consumer behavior: A systematic literature review. *Prizren Social Science Journal*, *8*(1), 67–80. DOI: 10.32936/pssj.v8i1.479

Elhazziti, M. A., Ferraz, D., Elazzouzi, E., Mastere, M., & Gomes, J. S. (2023). Digital transformation in Morocco: Challenges and perspectives. *Journal of US-China Public Administration*, *20*(2), 83–97. DOI: 10.17265/1548-6591/2023.02.001

Eslami, S. P., Ghasemaghaei, M., & Hassanein, K. (2022). Understanding consumer engagement in social media: The role of product lifecycle. *Decision Support Systems*, *162*, 113707. DOI: 10.1016/j.dss.2021.113707

Evania, S., Listiana, E., Rosnani, T., & Fahruna, Y. (2023). The effect of influencer marketing and content marketing on customer engagement and purchase decisions on followers. Asian Journal of Economics. *Business and Accounting*, *23*(2), 12–20. DOI: 10.9734/ajeba/2023/v23i2917

Feng, Y., Guo, Z., & Chiang, W. Y. K. (2009). Optimal digital content distribution strategy in the presence of the consumer-to-consumer channel. *Journal of Management Information Systems*, *25*(4), 241–270.

Fernández, D. L., & Oliver, M. (2025). Methodology, strategies, and factors for business innovation in large companies. *International Journal of Innovation Studies*, *9*(2), 91–115. DOI: 10.1016/j.ijis.2025.02.002

George, O. O., Dosumu, R. E., & Makata, C. O. (2023). Integrating multi-channel brand communication: A conceptual model for achieving sustained consumer engagement and loyalty. *International Journal of Management and Organizational Research*, *2*(1), 254–260. DOI: 10.54660/IJMOR.2023.2.1.254-260

Ghanad, A. (2023). An overview of quantitative research methods. *International Journal of Multidisciplinary Research and Analysis*, *6*(8). Advance online publication. DOI: 10.47191/ijmra/v6-i8-52

Ghosh, S., & Dubey, S. (2025). The field of usability and user experience (UX) design. In *Navigating usability and user experience in a multi-platform world* (pp. 117–154). IGI Global.

Gudigantala, N., Bicen, P., & Eom, M. T. (2016). An examination of antecedents of conversion rates of e-commerce retailers. *Management Research Review*, *39*(1), 82–114. DOI: 10.1108/MRR-05-2014-0112

Guenther, P., Guenther, M., Ringle, C. M., Zaefarian, G., & Cartwright, S. (2023). Improving PLS-SEM use for business marketing research. *Industrial Marketing Management*, *111*, 127–142. DOI: 10.1016/j.indmarman.2023.03.010

Ha, M.-T. (2022). Data collection using online questionnaires in marketing. In *Doing research online* (pp. 1–12). SAGE Publications., DOI: 10.4135/9781529603569

Habib, A., & Jha, A. N. (2025). A critical review of "Digital marketing strategies - Through websites, digital funnels, social media and digital tools.". *EPH-International Journal of Business & Management Science*, *11*(1). Advance online publication. DOI: 10.53555/eijbms.v11i1.203

Hair, J. F., Hult, G. T. M., Ringle, C. M., & Sarstedt, M. (2017). *A primer on partial least squares structural equation modeling (PLS-SEM)* (2nd ed.). Sage Publications.

Harrigan, P., Evers, U., Miles, M. P., & Daly, T. M. (2017). Customer engagement and the relationship between involvement, engagement, self-brand connection and brand usage intent. *Journal of Business Research*, *88*, 388–396. DOI: 10.1016/j.jbusres.2017.11.046

Helme-guizon, A., & Magnoni, F. (2019). Consumer brand engagement and its social side on brand-hosted social media: How do they contribute to brand loyalty? *Journal of Marketing Management*, *35*, 1–26. DOI: 10.1080/0267257X.2019.1599990

Hnylyakevych, I. Z., & Zinkova, S. V. (2024). Role of conversion rate optimisation (CRO) in marketing. *Market Economy Modern Management Theory and Practice*, *23*(1(56)), 36–53. DOI: 10.18524/2413-9998.2024.1(56).309063

Hollebeek, L. D., & Macky, K. (2019). Digital content marketing's role in fostering consumer engagement, trust, and value: Framework, fundamental propositions, and implications. *Journal of Interactive Marketing*, *45*, 27–41. DOI: 10.1016/j.intmar.2018.07.003

Homburg, C., Jozić, D., & Kuehnl, C. (2017). Customer experience management: Toward implementing an evolving marketing concept. *Journal of the Academy of Marketing Science*, *45*(3), 377–401.

Hristov, I. (2024). Web design for small businesses: Enhancing user experience [Bachelor's thesis, Haaga-Helia University of Applied Sciences]. Retrieved from https://www.theseus.fi/handle/10024/869156

Huang, N., Sun, T., Chen, P., & Golden, J. M. (2019). Word-of-mouth system implementation and customer conversion: A randomized field experiment. *Information Systems Research*, *30*(3), 805–818. DOI: 10.1287/isre.2018.0832

Huma, S., Ahmed, W., Ikram, M., & Najmi, A. (2025). Influence of mobile application service quality and convenience on young customer retention. *Spanish Journal of Marketing - ESIC*, *29*(4), 402–424. DOI: 10.1108/SJME-11-2023-0310

Isibor, N. J., Attipoe, V., Oyeyipo, I., Ayodeji, D. C., Mayienga, B. A., Alonge, E., & Onwuzulike, O. C. (2025). Analyzing successful content marketing strategies that enhance online engagement and sales for digital brands. *International Journal of Advanced Multidisciplinary Research and Studies*, *5*(2), 842–851. DOI: 10.62225/2583049X.2025.5.2.3906

Jeswani, R. (2023). The role and importance of social media marketing in brand building. *Irish Interdisciplinary Journal of Science & Research*, *7*(4), 1–9. DOI: 10.46759/IIJSR.2023.7401

Karthikeyan, G., & Aruna, P. (2025). User experience optimization in immersive technologies: Techniques, challenges, and opportunities. In *2025 International Conference on Intelligent Computing and Control Systems (ICICCS)* (pp. 908-917). IEEE.

Khan, I. A., Hollebeek, L. D., Fatma, M., Islam, J. U., & Rahman, Z. (2020). Brand engagement and experience in online services. *Journal of Services Marketing*, •••, 1–34. DOI: 10.1108/JSM-03-2019-0106

Kumo, W. (2023). Leveraging consumer behavior research for effective marketing strategies. *Advances in Business & Industrial Marketing Research*, *1*(3), 117–129. DOI: 10.60079/abim.v1i3.196

Lamm, K. W., Borron, A., Holt, J., & Lamm, A. (2019). Communication channel preferences: A descriptive audience segmentation evaluation. *Journal of Applied Communications, 103*(3). Advance online publication. DOI: 10.4148/1051-0834.2238

Lamrhari, S., El Ghazi, H., Oubrich, M., & El Faker, A. (2022). A social CRM analytic framework for improving customer retention, acquisition, and conversion. *Technological Forecasting and Social Change, 174*, 1–19. DOI: 10.1016/j.techfore.2021.121275

Laroche, M., Kiani, I., Economakis, N., & Richard, M.-O. (2014). Effects of multichannel marketing on consumers' online search behavior: The power of multiple points of connection. *Journal of Advertising Research, 53*, 431–443. DOI: 10.2501/JAR-53-4-431-443

Lee, B. C., & Johar, G. V. (2025). The effect of personalized content in media entertainment on engagement with the domain. *The Journal of Consumer Research*. Advance online publication. DOI: 10.1093/jcr/ucaf018

Liu, X. (2024). Research on the strategy of content innovation and audience experience improvement in media programs in the digital age. *Media and Communication Research, 5*(4), 104–111. DOI: 10.23977/mediacr.2024.050414

Liu, Y., Tan, H., Cao, G., & Xu, Y. (2024). Enhancing user engagement through adaptive UI/UX design: A study on personalized mobile app interfaces. *Computer Science & IT Research Journal, 5*, 1942–1962. DOI: 10.51594/csitrj.v5i8.1457

Lopes, A. R., & Casais, B. (2022). Digital content marketing: Conceptual review and recommendations for practitioners. *Academy of Strategic Management Journal, 21*(2), 1–17. https://www.scirp.org/reference/referencespapers?referenceid=3710429

Lourenço, C. E., Hair, J. F.Jr, Zambaldi, F., & Canniatti Ponchio, M. (2022). Consumer brand engagement concept and measurement: Toward a refined approach. *Journal of Retailing and Consumer Services, 68*. Advance online publication. DOI: 10.1016/j.jretconser.2022.103053

Lussak, A., Ramadhan, R., & Darmawan, I. (2024). Personalized digital marketing perspectives and practices in education industry. *Multidisciplinary Science Journal, 6*(12), 1–7. DOI: 10.31893/multiscience.2024268

Luther, L., Tiberius, V., & Brem, A. (2020). User experience (UX) in business, management, and psychology: A bibliometric mapping of the current state of research. *Multimodal Technologies and Interaction, 4*(2), 1–18. DOI: 10.3390/mti4020018

Martínez-López, F. J., Aguilar-Illescas, R., Molinillo, S., Anaya-Sánchez, R., Coca-Stefaniak, J. A., & Esteban-Millat, I. (2021). The role of online brand community engagement on the consumer-brand relationship. *Sustainability, 13*(7), 1–17. DOI: 10.3390/su13073679

McDowell, W. C., Wilson, R. C., & Kile, C. O.Jr. (2016). An examination of retail website design and conversion rate. *Journal of Business Research, 69*(11), 4837–4842. DOI: 10.1016/j.jbusres.2016.04.040

Miikkulainen, R., Iscoe, N., Shagrin, A., Cordell, R., Nazari, S., Schoolland, C., . . . Lamba, G. (2017). Conversion rate optimization through evolutionary computation. In Proceedings of the Genetic and Evolutionary Computation Conference (pp. 1193-1199). GECCO '17. https://doi.org/DOI: 10.1145/3071178.3071312

Mokkink, L. B., de Vet, H., Diemeer, S., & Eekhout, I. (2022). Sample size recommendations for studies on reliability and measurement error: An online application based on simulation studies. *Health Services and Outcomes Research Methodology, 23*(24), 242–265. DOI: 10.1007/s10742-022-00293-9

Mou, A. J. (2024). Marketing capstone insights: Leveraging multi-channel strategies for maximum digital conversion and ROI. *Review of Applied Science and Technology, 3*(04), 1–28. DOI: 10.63125/5w76qb87

Naumann, A., Hurtienne, J., Israel, J. H., Mohs, C., Kindsmüller, M. C., Meyer, H. A., & Husslein, S. (2007). Intuitive use of user interfaces: Defining a vague concept. In A. Holzinger (Ed.), Engineering psychology and cognitive ergonomics: 7th International Conference, EPCE 2007, Beijing, China, July 22-27, 2007, Proceedings (Lecture Notes in Computer Science, Vol. 4559, pp. 123-132). Springer. https://doi .org/DOI: 10.1007/978-3-540-73331-7_14

Nunnally, J. C., & Bernstein, I. H. (1994). *Psychometric theory* (3rd ed.). McGraw-Hill.

Nuseir, M., El-Refae, G., Aljumah, A., Alshurideh, M., Urabi, S., & Al Kurdi, B. (2023). Digital marketing strategies and the impact on customer experience. *Systematic Reviews.*

Nwabekee, S. U., Abdul-Azeez, O. Y., Agu, E. E., & Ijomah, T. (2024). Digital transformation in marketing strategies: The role of data analytics and CRM tools. International Journal of Finance. *Risk and Strategic Trends, 3*(2), 56–72. DOI: 10.56355/ijfrst.2024.3.2.0047

Okonkwo, C. (2024). Assessment of user experience (UX) design trends in mobile applications. *Journal of Technology and Systems, 6*, 29–41. DOI: 10.47941/jts.2147

Ologunebi, J. O. (2023). Digital marketing strategies, plan and implementations: A case study of JumiaGroup and ASDA UK (MPRA Paper No. 118771) [Working paper]. MPRA. https://mpra.ub.uni-muenchen.de/118771/

Ooko, J. A., Aila, F. O., & Odondo, A. (2023). Relationship between customer satisfaction and brand loyalty. The International Journal of Business & Management, 11(9), Article BM2309-005. https://doi.org/DOI: 10.24940/theijbm/2023/v11/i9/BM2309-005

Osemeike, G. E., Okpeke, P. P., & Ijomah, T. (2024). Strategic approaches for successful digital transformation in project management across industries. *International Journal of Frontiers in Engineering and Technology Research*, *7*(1), 1–11. DOI: 10.53294/ijfetr.2024.7.1.0037

Pal, A. (2024). Enhancing customer experience: Creating new touchpoints for experience-centric mobile services. Retrieved from https://helda.helsinki.fi/server/api/core/bitstreams/09e1fd78-f29d-40f0-87f3-47f56758b3b0/content

Parveen, N., Othman, R. O. M., Abbadi, D. M. A., Al-Lobani, E. M., Skhawat, H., Ali, M. S., & Mejdi, K. (2024). Digital marketing strategies in the age of social media: A comparative study of global brands. *Nanotechnology Perceptions*, *20*(S13), 212–242. DOI: 10.62441/nano-ntp.vi.2771

Pascucci, F., Savelli, E., & Gistri, G. (2023). How digital technologies reshape marketing: Evidence from a qualitative investigation. *Italian Journal of Marketing*, *2023*(1), 27–58. DOI: 10.1007/s43039-023-00063-6

Pedrero-Esteban, L. M., & Barrios-Rubio, A. (2024). Digital communication in the age of immediacy. *Digital*, *4*(2), 302–315. DOI: 10.3390/digital4020015

Penga, X., & Li, L. (2024). Optimization strategies for enterprise brand communication from the perspective of digital marketing communication. *Proceedings of the 8th International Conference on Education Technology, Management and Humanities Science (ETMHS 2024)* (pp. 368-373). Francis Academic Press.

Pereira, R. S., Lieira, D. D., Silva, M. A. D., Pimenta, A. H., da Costa, J. B., Rosário, D., & Meneguette, R. I. (2020). RELIABLE: Resource allocation mechanism for 5G network using mobile edge computing. *Sensors (Basel)*, *20*(19), 5449. PMID: 32977383

Purnomo, Y. J. (2023). Digital marketing strategy to increase sales conversion on e-commerce platforms. [ADMAN]. *Journal of Contemporary Administration and Management*, *1*(2), 54–62. DOI: 10.61100/adman.v1i2.23

Raeisi, S. (2017). The importance of customer engagement and service innovation in value co-creation. World Academy of Science, Engineering and Technology, International Journal of Social, Behavioral, Educational, Economic. *Business and Industrial Engineering*, *11*(4). 775-780.Scholar.waset.org/1999.10/10006723

Rahman, W. N., Mutum, D. S., & Ghazali, E. M. (2022). Consumer engagement with visual content on Instagram: Impact of different features of posts by prominent brands. [IJESMA]. *International Journal of E-Services and Mobile Applications*, *14*(1), 1–21. DOI: 10.4018/IJESMA.295960

Ramachandran, K. K. (2023). Evaluating ROI in digital marketing campaigns: Metrics, measurement, and insights. *International Journal of Management*, *14*(7), 190–204. https://iaeme.com/Home/issue/IJM?Volume=14&Issue=7

Rani, A. (2022). The role of content marketing in the era of digitalization. *International Journal of Advanced Research*, *10*, 1355–1362. DOI: 10.21474/IJAR01/14349

Rowi, A. S., Wahyudi, M. A., & Oswari, T. (2024). Role of digital marketing strategies in enhancing customer engagement and brand loyalty: A study of e-commerce platforms. *International Journal of Business Law and Education*, *5*(2), 2778–2788. DOI: 10.56442/ijble.v5i2

Rudy, R., Prabowo, H., Furinto, A., & Hamsal, M. (2021). The influence of digital technology, customer experience, and customer engagement on e-commerce customer loyalty. *Journal of Theoretical and Applied Information Technology*, *99*, 1149–1161.

Ruggieri, R., Savastano, M., Scalingi, A., Bala, D., & D'Ascenzo, F. (2018). The impact of digital platforms on business models: An empirical investigation on innovative start-ups. *Management & Marketing*, *13*(4), 1210–1225. DOI: 10.2478/mmcks-2018-0032

Sandesara, M., Bodkhe, U., Tanwar, S., Alshehri, M. D., Sharma, R., Neagu, B.-C., Grigoras, G., & Raboaca, M. S. (2022). Design and experience of mobile applications: A pilot survey. *Mathematics*, *10*(14), 1–20. DOI: 10.3390/math10142380

Sang, V. M., Hương, N., & Giang, D. N. H. (2022). The role of social brand engagement on brand equity and purchase intention for fashion brands. *Cogent Business & Management*, *9*(1), 1–21. DOI: 10.1080/23311975.2022.2143308

Santos, Z. R., Cheung, C. M. K., Coelho, P. S., & Rita, P. (2022). Consumer engagement in social media brand communities: A literature review. *International Journal of Information Management*, *63*. Advance online publication. DOI: 10.1016/j.ijinfomgt.2021.102457

Santoso, F., & Sudarmiatin, S. (2024). Analysis of the influence of multichannel marketing strategy in the 5.0 era: Integrating online and offline for optimal results. *Journal of Business Management and Economic Development*, *2*, 979–997. DOI: 10.59653/jbmed.v2i02.843

Sashi, C. M. (2021). Digital communication, value co-creation and customer engagement in business networks: A conceptual matrix and propositions. *European Journal of Marketing*, *55*(6), 1643–1663. DOI: 10.1108/EJM-01-2020-0023

Saura, J. R., Palos-Sánchez, P., & Cerdá Suárez, L. M. (2017). Understanding the digital marketing environment with KPIs and web analytics. *Future Internet*, *9*(4), 1–13. DOI: 10.3390/fi9040076

Schulz, T., Böhm, M., Gewald, H., & Krcmar, H. (2020). Smart mobility–an analysis of potential customers' preference structures. *Electronic Markets*, *31*(1), 105–124.

Stein, C. M., Morris, N. J., & Nock, N. L. (2012). Structural equation modeling. In Hinrichs, A. R. (Ed.), *Methods in molecular biology* (Vol. 850, pp. 495–512). Humana Press., DOI: 10.1007/978-1-61779-555-8_27

Sudirjo, F., Fajariana, D. E., Vandika, A. Y., & Sagena, U. (2024). The effect of digital transformation, user experience, and user interface on customer loyalty in technology startups in Bandung. *West Science Interdisciplinary Studies*, *2*(09), 1850–1856. DOI: 10.58812/wsis.v2i09.1305

Tobi, Y. (2023). *E-commerce and the digital economy in Morocco, a factor of social inclusivity and employment: Context, approach and limits (EuroMeSCo Paper No. 58)*. European Institute of the Mediterranean.

Tomar, G., Pandey, L., & Journals, C. (2024). Influence of personalized advertising on consumer engagement and conversion rates. https://doi.org/DOI: 10.13140/RG.2.2.30689.31844

Tsimonis, G., & Dimitriadis, S. (2014). Brand strategies in social media. *Marketing Intelligence & Planning*, *32*(3), 328–344. DOI: 10.1108/MIP-04-2013-0056

Umoren, P., Ukpe, A. P., & Akpolome, D. (2025). Digital communication in organizations: Trends, strengths, and weaknesses. *Direct Research Journal of Management and Strategic Studies*, *6*(1), 55–64. DOI: 10.26765/DRJMSS354001347

Van Asperen, M., de Rooij, P., & Dijkmans, C. (2017). Engagement-based loyalty: The effects of social media engagement on customer loyalty in the travel industry. *International Journal of Hospitality & Tourism Administration*, *19*(3), 1–17. DOI: 10.1080/15256480.2017.1305313

Vij, S., & Taneja, G. (2022). Digital marketing strategies: A comprehensive guide. In *Dynamics of management in a digital world* (pp. 1–22). Seema Sahitya Bhawan., DOI: 10.5281/zenodo.14483877

Wahyudi, M., Oswari, T., & Purwoko, B. (2024). Role of digital marketing strategies in enhancing customer engagement and brand loyalty: A study of e-commerce platforms. *International Journal of Business, Law, and Education*, *5*, 2778–2788. DOI: 10.56442/ijble.v5i2.936

Wan, Y. (2023). Investigating the impact and effectiveness of digital marketing on brand awareness, sales and customer engagement. *Advances in Economics Management and Political Sciences*, *51*(1), 146–152. DOI: 10.54254/2754-1169/51/20230651

Waqas, M., Hamzah, Z. L., & Mohd Salleh, N. A. (2021). Customer experience with branded content: A social media perspective. *Online Information Review*, *45*(5), 964–982. DOI: 10.1108/OIR-10-2019-0333

Wild Ali, M. M., & Ortega-Gutierrez, J. (2025). Digital marketing: Strategies, challenges, and opportunities in the digital technology. *Global Journal of Economics and Business*, *15*(1), 40–52. DOI: 10.31559/GJEB2025.15.1.3

Yang, S., Lin, S., Carlson, J., & Jr, W. (2016). Brand engagement on social media: Will firms' social media efforts influence search engine advertising effectiveness? *Journal of Marketing Management*, •••, 1–32. DOI: 10.1080/0267257X.2016.1143863

Yang, W. (2024). Research on the influence of brand interaction on social media platforms and consumers' purchasing decision-making process. *RSM*, *7*, 622. Advance online publication. DOI: 10.61173/rsm7b622

Yoo, J. (2024). Can consumer engagement on social media affect brand extension success? The case of luxury fashion brands and restaurants. *Journal of Retailing and Consumer Services*, *79*. Advance online publication. DOI: 10.1016/j.jretconser.2024.103885

Zheng, R., Li, Z., & Na, S. (2022). How customer engagement in live-streaming affects purchase intention and customer acquisition, E-tailer's perspective. *Journal of Retailing and Consumer Services*, *68*, 103015. DOI: 10.1016/j.jretconser.2022.103015

Chapter 6
Influencing the Future:
Exploring the Impact of YouTube Advertising on Youth

Afef Sahli
https://orcid.org/0000-0002-5290-893X
University of Tunis El Manar, Tunisia

Hajer Bellalouna
https://orcid.org/0000-0002-3526-4423
University of Manouba, Tunisia

ABSTRACT

This study examines children's involvement in purchasing decisions, focusing on children aged 8 to 12 after viewing YouTube advertisements. The research explores the influence of two contrasting emotional appeals-fear and humor-on children's behavioral intentions. By analyzing 85 schoolchildren's reactions, the study employs a probabilistic approach using the LOGIT model to assess the likelihood of purchase decisions based on emotional responses. The findings aim to identify which emotional appeal has a greater effect on children's decision-making processes, highlighting the role of various factors in shaping their purchasing intentions. This research offers insights into the emotional impact of advertising on young audiences, contributing to understanding how different types of ads influence children's consumer behavior.

INTRODUCTION

As children mature within a consumer-centric culture, they navigate a landscape defined by commodities they must navigate. Their consumption habits not only mirror economic and social ties with objects and their environment but also signify avenues

DOI: 10.4018/979-8-3373-6450-6.ch006

for learning, value formation, self-realization, and social integration. Since today's children are tomorrow's adults, several studies have chosen children as their main target (Mertala, 2020; Lichy et al., 2023) to analyze and understand their views on consumption. We focus on "pre-adolescents" (aged 8-12) with the study by Bauman and Tatum (2009). Most of the research carried out focused on the socialization of this target group through various means of communication (Bénédict, 2022; Bonnéry & Pasquali, 2023; Frangieh & Akiki, 2023).

Since their emergence, the media have been known to occupy an important place in social life, as small screens increasingly attract consumers and influence their lifestyles and consumption behaviors (Hubermont & Masset, 2023). This also applies to children, who spend more time in front of screens than their families and communities (Turcotte, 2022; Parent, 2023). While various media transmit a kind of advertising bombardment, some authors have explored the relationship between children and advertising on YouTube. In this sense, humor, fear, surprise, etc., can be used in hyperbolic advertising to further influence recipients' emotional, cognitive, and conative responses.

Based on the literature, we have concluded that studies on the effects of advertising on decision-making behavioral intentions tend to target adults. However, there is a clear lack of research to understand their evolving role in the context of the new commercial revolution (Moati, 2011). According to Naat (2022), the social and consumption practices of young people tend to evolve more rapidly. As the most connected population, this age group is increasingly demanding when it comes to consumption, we therefore need to provide an answer to our problem:

To what extent do humorous/threatening YouTube ads influence children's behavioral intention?

Our research is divided into two parts. The first part presents a review of the literature on humorous/threatening advertising to children on YouTube, and the second part presents the research methodology and results obtained.

1. LITERATURE REVIEW

1.1. Children's Sensitivity to Purchasing Decisions

Studies of children's buying behavior show that they actively participate in certain stages of the family's purchasing decision process (Rigaux-Bricmont, 1986; Brée, 1993). Their influence is greater during the formation of purchase ideas than during the search for information and final decisions (Brée, 1990). According to Ward

(1974), socialization is “the set of processes by which young people acquire skills, knowledge, and attitudes that strongly influence their buying behavior.”

Researchers have analyzed children's behavior, examining their perceptions and purchases (Brée, 2021; Bartels et al., 2023), their impact on their parents' purchasing decisions (Berey & Pollay, 1968; Wells & Losciuto, 1966), and the impact of parents and peers on their own consumption patterns (Brée, 1993). On the other hand, some researchers have sought to understand the processes that each child goes through, enabling them to see their world from several angles (Carlson, 2001). This process is traced by developments in the child consumer's cognitive and social behavior, passing through three different consecutive stages, each marked by a particular cognitive process and a very specific way of thinking. The socialization of the child consumer can have repercussions on the decision-making process.

The work of Hajtaieb and El Aoud (2003), Durand-Mégret et al. (2012), and Buijzen et al. (2023) reveals the role played by children in family prescriptions, especially with the advent of the Internet, which has altered purchasing behavior and “given rise to profound mutations” (Vanheems, 2010). “As these young people undergo a process of identity and social construction that pushes them to seek their own identity while conforming to those around them, consumption contributes significantly and presents an integral part in their quest for identity” (Naat, 2022). Social media use has become a normative element of adolescent behavior. As a result, Lichy et al. (2023) assert that “Facebook, TikTok, Instagram, YouTube, and Snapchat are widely used by children under 13, who circle the political minimum age for opening an account » (De Veirman et al., 2020; Martínez & Olsson, 2019).

The following table summarizes relevant research focusing on children/adolescents and social media.

Table 1. Summary of relevant literature focusing on children and social media

Authors	Age Group	Theory or Underpinning	Methodology
Hou et al. (2014)	7-10	Online identity: behaviors and motivations	Ethnography and field study
Hook et al. (2016)	6-14	Brand network and social identity	Ethnography
Huk (2016)	10-12	UGT	Surveys and Interviews
Livingstone et al. (2017)	6-14	Mediation, digital literacy	Survey
Lagínová & Fornálová (2018)	Children	Parental mediation	Secondary data analysis
Mertala (2020)	3-6	Childhood perception of digital technology	Qualitative

continued on following page

Table 1. Continued

Authors	Age Group	Theory or Underpinning	Methodology
Pasquale et al. (2020)	8-13	Accessibility	Experiment
Lichy et al. (2023)	8-12	Social-identity and self-identity	Interviews

Source: Lichy et al. (2023)

This table presents some surveys that are carried out with children and their uses of social media. The majority of this research emphasizes positive communication and the important role played by parents in influencing their children's online behavior.

1.2. Emotion in the Advertising Persuasion Process

Guitouni (2000) defines emotion "as a set, a form of paradigm, including feelings, thoughts, psychological and biological states and the whole range of action tendencies that they arouse."

In the field of communication, researchers have attributed three different functions to emotion during the advertising persuasion process, namely: the adaptive function, the motivational function, and the communicative function.

- **Adaptive function**: The individual's attention is often directed towards the stimuli. To do this, this function creates balance and offers the possibility of adapting to changes linked to the environment by generating new psychological and behavioral manifestations (Lombardot, 2007). Additionally, this adaptive function allows individuals to process new information and modify their responses accordingly, ensuring effective interaction with the environment. It promotes resilience by encouraging flexible thinking and behavior, enabling individuals to overcome challenges, improve coping strategies, and enhance problem-solving abilities in the face of unexpected circumstances. This ongoing process supports both psychological stability and the ability to thrive in dynamic environments.
- **Motivational function**: Emotions represent an innate primary motivational mechanism, inscribed in the biological structure of the human being. Thanks to its hedonic and disruptive nature, emotion facilitates the process of adopting behaviors by the individual (Lombardot, 2007). Emotions drive the individual to act in accordance with their needs and desires, influencing decisions and actions that are aligned with survival, well-being, and social bonding. This motivational function not only helps the individual react quickly to environmental stimuli but also strengthens the learning process by associating emotional experiences with specific outcomes, thus guiding future behaviors.

- **Communicative function**: Emotional expressions are not only what they are to us, but also what they are to others, and their meaning depends on the reception they receive. In this case, emotion can be considered as a form of communication through which the individual brings out bodily manifestations that reveal his internal state (Scherer et al., 2004). These emotional expressions allow individuals to convey complex feelings and intentions non-verbally, facilitating social interactions and building connections with others. They serve as a universal language, often transcending cultural barriers, enabling empathy and understanding. By observing and interpreting these emotional cues, others can respond appropriately, which fosters social harmony and cooperative behaviors. Emotional communication is thus an essential tool in navigating relationships and maintaining social bonds.

1.3. The Use of Humor and Fear in Hyperbolic Advertising

According Smith (2024), Rhetoric can be defined as "the art of pretend speech," often finds a good refuge in the world of advertising, thanks to its diversity and the multiple figures of style that allow advertising to display its conventions and stimulate a public, whose duty is to discern amply between the truth and the pretense. There are many rhetorical figures used in the advertising field with the aim of implicitly influencing the behavior of the recipient of the message. Among these figures, we can talk about hyperbole, a figure intrinsically linked to rhetorical marks in the advertising field (Bonhomme, 2014). Hyperbole is a rhetorical figure made explicit by the demarcation of a neutral formulation, to result in the creation of special effects in the recipient of the advertising message, thus rhetorized, while resorting to exaggeration (Kerbrat-Orecchioni, 2015).

1.3.1. The Use of Humor in Hyperbolic Advertising

Day by day, the use of humorous strategies in the world of advertising communication is becoming more and more frequent on the part of advertisers, with the aim of attracting more attention, fulfilling a factitive and persuasive aim (Soulages, 2006). Today, advertisers consider that the use of humor is an appropriate process, which will enable the objectives to be achieved through communication. Hyperbole in this case can be an important figure of speech, allowing for the accentuation of humor in a television advertisement and thus promoting stronger positive affective reactions in the receiver.

This exaggerated humor helps to create memorable moments, increasing the likelihood of the advertisement being shared or discussed, which further amplifies its reach and effectiveness. Furthermore, hyperbolic humor can make a brand appear more approachable and relatable, helping to build a stronger emotional connection with the audience. By employing humor and exaggeration, advertisers can tap into the emotions of their audience, making their message not only entertaining but also persuasive.

Humor has become a powerful tool in advertising, particularly when combined with hyperbolic exaggeration. Hyperbolic advertising relies on exaggerated claims or situations to attract attention, create memorable experiences, and influence consumer attitudes. Understanding the theoretical foundations of humor in advertising helps marketers design effective campaigns that not only entertain but also persuade.

The following table presents key theories and models explaining the use of humor in hyperbolic advertising.

Table 2. The use of humor in hyperbolic advertising: Theories and models

Theory/Model	Key Mechanism	Role of Humor	Role of Hyperbole	Advertising Impact
Humor Processing Model McGhee (1979)	3-stage processing	Triggers emotional response	Sets up incongruity	Engagement and enjoyment
Superiority Theory Morreall (1983)	Feeling superior	Ridicule/absurdity	Exaggerated failures	Brand differentiation
Affect Transfer Model Weinberger & Gulas (1992)	Emotional conditioning	Generates positive affect	Amplifies humor	Positive brand attitude
Dual-Process Theories Chaiken & Trope (1999)	Cognitive + affective	Enjoyment + thinking	Stimulates both routes	Stronger attitude formation
Rhetorical Perspective Perloff (2017)	Stylistic device	Entertains	Linguistic figure	Memorability and distinctiveness
Relief Theory Meyer (2000)	Emotional release	Tension reduction	Builds playful tension	Positive affect

Source: Adapted by authors

In conclusion, hyperbolic humor in advertising leverages cognitive and emotional mechanisms to capture attention, engage audiences, and positively influence brand perception. The combination of exaggeration and humor works through various psychological and rhetorical pathways, as highlighted by the theories and models presented above. Marketers can use these insights to design campaigns that are not only entertaining but also persuasive and memorable.

1.3.2. The Use of Fear in Hyperbolic Advertising

Marketing research carried out in the field of communication strategies, and more precisely in advertising persuasion, has shown that appealing to strongly negative emotions, such as fear, ensures greater influence on the affective, cognitive, and conative reactions of the receiver of the advertising message. Hyperbole in this case is a rhetorical figure that can play a considerable role in the effectiveness of a threatening television advertisement as well as in advertising persuasion, by amplifying the negative emotions that may be felt following a threatening advertisement (Lim, 2023).

Based on a model inspired by the work of Godener (1999), the value of the use of fear in a television advertisement is explained by the following three points:

1. The emotions of fear felt following exposure to a threatening television advertisement are initiated first of all by cognitive processing of the information presented relating to the danger presented.
2. The power of advertising persuasion is determined through a cognitive process, reflecting the threat perceived in the television advertisement as well as the negative emotions experienced.
3. Advertising persuasion can be adaptive, that is to say rational and cognitive in nature, promoting a desire to move away from the danger communicated and the adoption of the recommended behavior. It can still be non-adaptive and therefore affective, caused by the emotion of fear felt, subsequently favoring the appearance of protective reactions whose goal is the reduction of the fear and not the danger communicated.

These emotional responses may lead to avoidance behaviors or temporary relief measures that are not directly related to the original danger but focus on alleviating the fear itself.

The strategic use of fear has long been recognized as a powerful persuasive technique in advertising, designed to capture attention, stimulate emotional responses, and influence consumer attitudes and behaviors. When combined with hyperbolic messaging characterized by deliberate exaggeration to intensify perceptions fear appeals can significantly amplify the perceived severity of threats and the urgency of response. Over the decades, several communication and marketing theories have been developed to explain how individuals process fear-based messages and how exaggeration shapes these responses.

The following table synthesizes key theories and models, both classical and contemporary, that provide conceptual foundations for understanding the mechanisms, roles, and limitations of fear appeals within hyperbolic advertising strategies.

Table 3. Theories and models of fear in hyperbolic advertising

Theory / Model	Key Mechanism	Role of Hyperbole	Risk / Limitation
Fear Appeal Theory Hovland et al (1953)	Fear + solution	Raises fear intensity	Defensive avoidance
Protection Motivation Theory Rogers (1975)	Protection motivation	Exaggerates severity/ vulnerability	Effectiveness depends on credibility
Elaboration Likelihood Model Petty & Cacioppo (1986)	Peripheral vs central processing	Grabs attention via emotion	Skepticism under central route
Extended Parallel Process Model Witte (1992)	Threat + efficacy appraisal	Amplifies threat	Low efficacy → fear control
Hyperbole Models McQuarrie & Mick (1996)	Rhetorical exaggeration	Emotional salience	Credibility erosion
Integrated Threat–Emotion–Action Model Kim & Hall (2021)	Threat → Emotion → Action	Amplifies sharing/ purchase	Over-hyperbole leads to backlash

Source: Adapted by authors

These theoretical perspectives provide a comprehensive lens through which to analyze and evaluate contemporary fear-driven hyperbolic advertising practices.

1.4. Advertising on YouTube

The 2000s were marked by the development of the Internet at home, "digital convergence," and digital commerce (Benbouja & Cavalli, 2010; Schmitt & De Jouvenel, 2022). Young people's acceptance of the Internet as a means of commercial communication is borne out by all the research on the subject. According to a study by Net Observer (2021), a significant percentage of 8- to 15-year-olds are online for an average of more than 3 hours a day. Over 50% say they have made online purchases in the last 6 months. In recent years, there has been an increase in awareness and appreciation of advertising.

In general, advertising on the Internet, and YouTube in particular, is totally unpredictable and can appear at any time on many different types of sites for utilitarian or hedonistic reasons (Chouk & Guiot, 2014). In this context, several researchers refer to the rhetorical figure in advertising communication (Bud, 2022; Razkaoui, 2022). It occupies a significant place in advertising persuasion thinking and in the generation of emotions in children, considered to be a very important target to work on (Attruia, 2021; Spector, 2022). Rhetoric is defined as "the art of feigned speech", or as "a cunning deviation from audience expectations that conforms to models regardless of the specifics of the occasion in which it takes place" (Laamouri & Gharbi, 2008).

Still, on a purely theoretical basis, the emotional component is exploited more than the informational component in children. Consistent with the research of Prochaska et al. (1988), change represents two hierarchical factors: "experiential" and "behavioral." For this reason, among the performance strategies adopted, aimed at arousing feelings and emotions, is fear (La Tour & Zahra, 1988). Fear is considered to be a negative emotion felt, in the majority of cases, in the presence of a threat, and this can, of course, be associated with the environment, to speak of a social threat (Gallopel et al., 2006). Researchers have also shown that fear and threat are two distinct concepts, but there is a strong reciprocal relationship between the two (Gallopel et al., 2006). The process of advertising persuasion is explained by the public's attitude to advertising, and research in this field (Preston, 2005) is used to understand how advertising persuasion can bring about a change in attitude towards the individual. Indeed, this change in attitude will, in turn, provoke a certain social influence, resulting in a change in consumer behavior (Fointiat & Barbier, 2015).

1.5. Theories and Models of Advertising on YouTube

Advertising on YouTube is a powerful tool for marketers, leveraging the platform's wide reach and diverse audience. Several theories and models explain how advertising on YouTube influences consumer behavior and decision-making. Here are some of the key theories related to advertising on YouTube

Table 4. Theories and models of advertising on YouTube

Theory/Model	Theory Overview	Application to YouTube
AIDA Model (Attention, Interest, Desire, Action) Strong (1925)	The AIDA model explains the stages that a consumer goes through during the process of buying a product: Attention, Interest, Desire, and Action.	YouTube ads need to grab attention quickly (through engaging visuals or an intriguing hook), spark interest (perhaps through storytelling or addressing a need), build desire (by highlighting benefits), and prompt action (like visiting a website or purchasing directly).
Social Influence Theory Deutsch & Gerard (1955)	This theory explores how individuals' behaviors and attitudes are influenced by the opinions and behaviors of others in their social environment.	Social influence is powerful on YouTube, where users often follow influencers or celebrities they admire. Advertisements that use these figures can leverage their influence to sway consumer behavior, especially if the influencer is seen as authentic and trustworthy.
Cognitive Dissonance Theory Festinger (1957)	Cognitive dissonance occurs when individuals experience discomfort due to conflicting beliefs or behaviors, prompting them to resolve the inconsistency.	Ads on YouTube can create cognitive dissonance by highlighting discrepancies between a viewer's current behavior and the ideal behavior. This discomfort motivates viewers to make changes, such as purchasing the product, to restore consistency.
Social Cognitive Theory (SCT) Bandura (1963)	SCT emphasizes the role of observational learning and modeling. People learn behaviors and attitudes by observing others, particularly when those others are seen as relatable or admirable.	YouTube ads often feature influencers or celebrities who model behaviors, showing how a product is used and how it benefits them. Viewers, especially those who identify with the influencer, are more likely to emulate those behaviors and purchase the product.
Fear Appeal Theory Janis (1967)	This theory argues that presenting a threat or fear can motivate individuals to change their behavior, especially when a solution is offered to mitigate the danger.	Ads on YouTube that highlight risks (e.g., health risks, missing out on opportunities) can use fear appeals. These ads can motivate viewers to take action to avoid the feared outcome, such as buying a product.
Uses and Gratifications Theory (UGT) Katz et al. (1973)	UGT focuses on why people actively seek out specific media and content to fulfill their needs, such as entertainment, information, or social interaction.	YouTube viewers often seek out content that entertains or informs. Ads that align with these needs (e.g., funny or educational content) are more likely to be well-received.
Theory of Reasoned Action (TRA) Fishbein & Ajzen (1975)	TRA suggests that an individual's behavior is determined by their intention to perform the behavior, which is influenced by their attitudes and subjective norms (what others think they should do).	YouTube ads can influence viewers' intentions to purchase by shaping their attitudes toward a product and by presenting social proof (such as showing how many others use the product or showcasing positive reviews).
Dual Process Model Kahneman & Tversky (1979)	This model suggests that people process information through two systems: System 1 (fast, automatic, emotional) and System 2 (slow, deliberate, logical).	YouTube ads often target both systems. For example, a quick, emotional ad may appeal to System 1, prompting instant reactions, while a more detailed ad with product information targets System 2, leading to rational decision-making.

continued on following page

Table 4. Continued

Theory/Model	Theory Overview	Application to YouTube
Elaboration Likelihood Model (ELM) Petty & Cacioppo (1986)	ELM posits that there are two routes to persuasion: the central route (involving thoughtful, logical processing of information) and the peripheral route (based on superficial cues like attractiveness or music).	YouTube ads can either engage viewers through deep, rational content (central route) or appeal to emotions and superficial aspects (like humor or celebrity endorsements) for a quick, emotional reaction (peripheral route).
Priming Theory Bargh et al. (1996)	Priming refers to the psychological phenomenon where exposure to one stimulus influences the response to a subsequent stimulus, often without conscious awareness.	YouTube ads can prime viewers by repeatedly exposing them to certain ideas, products, or emotions. A brand that associates itself with happiness or luxury may influence viewers to view it in a positive light.
Humor in Advertising Weitz et al. (2003)	Humor is an effective tool in advertising, as it captures attention, creates positive emotions, and makes the brand more memorable.	Many successful YouTube ads incorporate humor, making them more engaging and shareable. The use of humor can make a brand seem more relatable, encourage viral sharing, and improve brand recall.

Source: Adapted by authors

Advertising on YouTube is a dynamic and multifaceted process that draws from various psychological, emotional, and social theories. By understanding these theories, marketers can design ads that not only capture attention but also engage viewers at deeper cognitive and emotional levels, ultimately driving desired behaviors like brand loyalty, subscriptions, and purchases.

2. RESEARCH HYPOTHESES

2.1. Threatening Advertising

With regard to the various theoretical findings made by researchers, it turns out that exposure to an advertising communication can engender the need for commitment to the new desirable behavior transmitted in the spot, by reinforcing the receiver's intention to adopt this behavior (Zidouri, 2023). On the other hand, it's preferable for the threat applied in the YouTube ad to present, in some way, a real occurrence, while at the same time offering a possibility of resolving the problem communicated, intending to annihilate the danger transmitted by the threatening ad and prompt the child to act according to the recommended behavior (Charry & Pecheux, 2008). Indeed, having a conative reaction, as a result, demonstrates a definite advertising effectiveness, prompting us to take a closer look at the impact that a threatening ad could have, and thus to focus on understanding the intention of purchase behavior and the modification of undesirable behavior in children.

On the other hand, it's obvious to remember that children rely more on their affective side than their cognitive side when processing an advertising message. In other words, the child does not counter-argue the threatening ad in-depth, but is capable of challenging the solution or behavior proposed in the ad, and even intends to react to it based on purely affective mechanisms (Charry & Pecheux, 2008).

Following exposure to a threatening advertisement, the intensity of the emotional reactions of fear felt by the child can have a positive impact on the persuasiveness of the advertisement and thus act on the child's purchase decision intention (Lavoisier-Mérieux, 2002). Moreover, Gallopel et al. (2006) and Sassi-Chamsi (2022) have stated that beliefs about the behavior recommended and communicated in an ad also contribute to the formation and influence of an individual's behavioral intention. Based on these findings, we formulate our first hypothesis:

> **H1:** Exposure to a threatening advertisement on YouTube increases the probability of the child's behavioral intention.

This hypothesis gives rise to two sub-hypotheses that will enable us to understand the relationship between affective and cognitive factors and exposure to threatening advertising, in favor of preoccupation with purchase.

The first sub-hypothesis is then posed as follows:

> **H1.1:** There is a positive effect between exposure to a threatening advertisement on YouTube and the likelihood of the creation of negative emotions in children.

The second sub-hypothesis is as follows:

> **H1.2:** There is a positive effect between exposure to threatening advertising on YouTube and children's beliefs about preoccupied shopping behavior.

2.2. A Humorous Advertisement

Far from fear and threatening advertising, it has been shown that humor is highly appreciated by children in advertising communication (Cottin, 2022; Raschel, 2022). In fact, a humorous message can be more effective in terms of advertising persuasion than a humorless one (De Pelsmacker et al., 2013).

Congruent with previous work, the effectiveness of an advertising communication is strongly linked to the effectiveness of the behavior recommended in the ad. The aim of communicating this behavior is to encourage its adoption to operate differently in society, leading to a change in certain habits and behaviors that contribute to the purchase decision (Brée & Pantin-Sohier, 2023). Moreover, when the recommended behavior aligns with the values, aspirations, and lifestyles of the target audience, the likelihood of it being embraced increases. This alignment fosters a sense of relevance and personal connection, making the advertising message not only persuasive but also impactful. Additionally, the more tangible and achievable the behavioral change seems, the more effective the ad will be in motivating action, creating a deeper, lasting influence on the consumer's decision-making process.

As we've already mentioned, it's obvious to remember that children are targets who, unlike adults, focus on affective rather than cognitive bases when processing the advertisements to which they are exposed. The dominance of affect can, in this case, help to influence the child's behavioral intention, and even change his or her behavior and the appearance of new manners and habits.

The effective use of humor provokes emotions of joy and pleasure and influences the receiver's psychological side, and it is the triggering of these pleasant emotions that breaks with the stable routine of any situation (Belch et al., 2005).

In other words, the presence and increase in the level of humor in a YouTube ad promotes a cheerful, pleasant atmosphere, and thus facilitates advertising persuasion, especially in cases where the recommendations presented by the ad prove apt at amplifying the emotions felt (Belch et al., 2005).

Following the example of some marketing research, we can talk about the role that advertising communication can play in influencing the beliefs of the individual exposed to it. Exposure to a hyperbolic and humorous advertising message may contribute to the influence of the individual's beliefs about the behavior recommended by the ad (Derbaix et al., 2004). The exaggerated nature of hyperbolic humor amplifies emotional responses, making the message more memorable and engaging. This emotional impact can shift the individual's perceptions and attitudes towards the product or behavior being advertised. Furthermore, humor often reduces resistance to the message, making the viewer more open to adopting the recommended behavior. When combined with hyperbole, humor can create a sense of urgency or importance, further reinforcing the likelihood of the individual embracing the behavior promoted in the ad. Consequently, this type of advertising not only influences immediate reactions but can also shape long-term beliefs and consumer attitudes.

Based on this theoretical review, we propose our second hypothesis:

> **H2:** Exposure to a humorous YouTube ad increases the probability of a child's behavioral intention.

This hypothesis gives rise to two sub-hypotheses.

The first sub-hypothesis is as follows:

H2.1: There is a positive effect between exposure to humorous advertising on YouTube and the likelihood of positive emotions being created in children.

We can then cite our second sub-hypothesis:

H2.2: There is a positive effect between exposure to humorous advertising on YouTube and children's beliefs about recommended behavior.

This figure presents our research model.

Figure 1. Research model

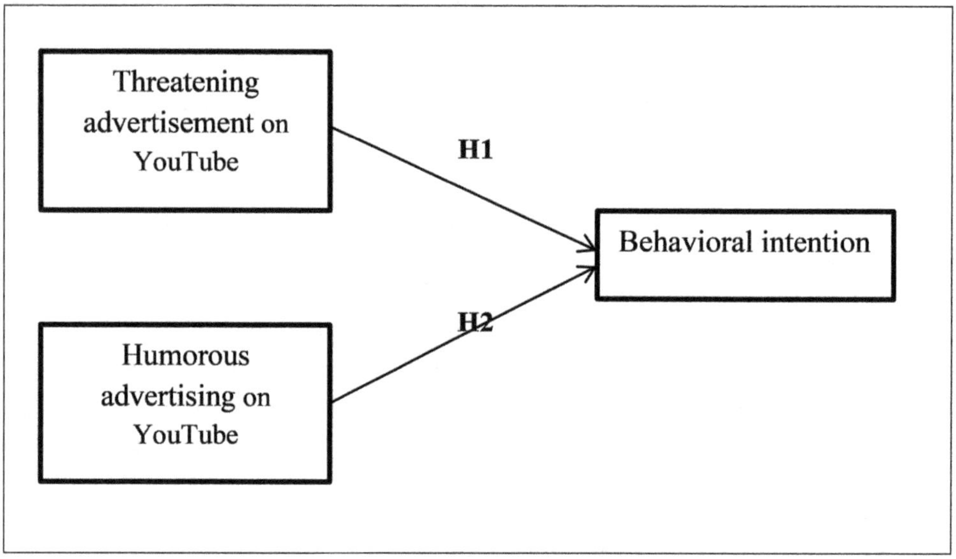

This figure explains the different relationships between the different variables.

3. RESEARCH METHODOLOGY

3.1. Population Selection

To guarantee results, it's obvious to define the population from which we're sorting our sample. Given that our research focuses on children's purchasing decisions, and based on our review of the literature, which showed that there is an age range that must be respected for our survey to be a success, we have targeted 85 children between the ages of 8 and 12 who attend private schools. This age range (8-12 years) is justified by the work of Lichy et al. (2023). They were selected to view two different advertisements, to answer a questionnaire that was administered face-to-face in the classroom after permission from the parents, school principal, and teacher. Data collection lasted two months (every day after school). The following table describes the main characteristics of the sample.

Table 5. Sample characteristics

Variable (N = 85)	Number	Percentage
Type		
Girl	52	61.18%
Boy	33	38.82%
Age		
[8; 9] years	10	11.76%
[9; 10] years	17	20%
[10; 11] years	24	28.24%
[11; 12] years	34	40%
Education		
3rd Year	10	11.76%
4th Year	17	20%
5th Year	24	28.24%
6th Year	34	40%

3.2. Choice of Measuring Instruments

Having set out the various hypotheses of our research, we now turn to the measurement instruments chosen, enabling us to continue our data collection and analysis work. These constructs are evaluated on a binary scale (0 = No; 1 = Yes), on which the response elements are provided. The choice of the binary scale is justified by the "age" criterion of the target group, which is clearly children.

For hypotheses H1 and H2, we opted to measure the individual's behavioral intention construct recommended by Prochaska et al. (1991).

Table 6. Measurement scale for the intention to adopt the recommended ecological behavior (Prochaska et al., 1991)

	Yes	No
I should be concerned about the ecological environment.		
I will try to be concerned about the ecological environment.		
I will really try to be concerned about the ecological environment.		

Regarding hypothesis H1.1, the review of the literature highlighted a measurement instrument with psychometric qualities, through which it has proven its effectiveness in various fields such as advertising (Allen et al., 1988), consumer behavior (Laverie and Kleine, 1993; Westbrook & Oliver, 1991), and social marketing (Allen et al., 1992).

This is the 'Differential Emotions Scale,' referred to in French as 'the scale for measuring negative affective reactions triggered by the advertisement,' which gives significant prominence to negative emotion. The aim is to highlight the persuasive impact of the negative emotions experienced during the viewing of the threatening advertisement.

Table 7. Measurement scale for negative affective reactions triggered by the advertisement (Izard, 1977)

Emotions	Items	Yes	No
Sadness	I felt sadness		
	I felt depressed		
Anger	I was furious		
	I felt anger		
Guilt	I felt guilty		
Disgust	I felt a sense of revulsion		
	I felt disgust		
Fear	I felt fear		
	I felt tense		
	I felt nervous		
	I was frightened		
Shame	I felt shame		

To test hypotheses H1.2 and H2.2, it is inevitable to use a measurement scale for the individual's beliefs about the behavior conveyed in the television advertisement. This will help to understand the importance of beliefs regarding the recommended behavior following this communication. This is why we used a measurement scale to study the impact that an advertising communication could have on the individual's beliefs about the desired behavior they should adopt.

Table 8. Measurement scale for beliefs regarding social behavior

	Items	Yes	No
Overall Effectiveness I believe that the preservation of wildlife and plants,	- It is beneficial		
	- It is useful		
	- It helps increase the safety of our planet against various dangers		
Ability to Initiate the Behavior Personally, concern for the environment,	- It requires a lot of effort		
	- I find it burdensome		
	- I find it easy		
Social Benefits When I keep my environment clean,	- It shows adult behavior		
	- It shows civic-mindedness		
	- It shows responsible behavior		
Specific Effectiveness When I protect and preserve nature,	- I reduce the severity of the problems our planet faces		
	- I reduce the risk of damage to wildlife and plants		

In order to verify hypothesis H2.1, there is an expressed need for a tool to measure the emotions experienced following exposure to an advertisement. The emotions and feelings experienced could, in a way, reflect the effectiveness of an advertisement featuring humor compared to one that does not. In this context, and following a review of the theory, we were able to find a measurement scale that allows us to carry out our work.

Table 9. Scales of positive and negative affective reactions according to Pham (2001)

Items	Yes	No
How did you feel when watching this advertisement?		
This advertisement made me happy.		
With this advertisement, I felt good.		
This advertisement made me joyful.		
I enjoyed watching this advertisement.		
I did not enjoy watching this advertisement.		
I was disgusted by this advertisement.		
I was scared while watching this advertisement.		

continued on following page

Table 9. Continued

Items	Yes	No
With this advertisement, I felt bad.		
This advertisement made me furious.		
This advertisement made me sad.		

After outlining the different hypotheses of our research, we now focus on the measurement tools selected, which will allow us to proceed with data collection and analysis. For hypotheses H1 and H2, we chose to assess the construct of behavioral intention using the scale proposed by Prochaska et al. (1991). Additionally, we utilized Izard's (1977) scale for evaluating negative affective reactions triggered by the advertisement, the scale for measuring beliefs about social behavior, and Pham's (2001) scale for positive and negative affective reactions. These constructs are assessed using a binary scale (0 = No; 1 = Yes), with the corresponding response options. The use of a binary scale is based on the "age" criterion of the target group, which specifically refers to children.

3.3. Choosing the LOGIT Model

A research methodology must be put in place to properly address the problem and verify the research hypotheses. To this end, and given the nature of the data, the method adopted is logistic regression. The use of the Binary Logit model can be justified by its flexibility and specific features, as well as its predictive and descriptive capacities, enabling us to respond adequately to the object of our research. The aim is to measure the probability of a child, aged between 8 and 12, having a purchase intention after viewing a hyperbolic YouTube advert with a threatening or humorous title. Then, in a comparative approach, the results obtained will enable us to detect which, between humor and fear, is better to adopt in a YouTube ad to have a greater influence on behavioral intention.

4. RESEARCH RESULTS

4.1. Reliability of Results

The data collected were analyzed in this table, and the research hypotheses were tested using SPSS software to investigate the different types of relationships. The factorial analysis of the variables shows a satisfactory KMO index with a value > 0.5, as well as a significant Bartlett's sphericity test with a p-value = 0.000. Cronbach's alpha is accepted with a value > 0.5. All results show good reliability.

Table 10. Scale reliability

Variable	KMO	Bartlett Test	Cronbach's Alpha
Negative Affective Reactions	0.599	0.914	0.625
Negative Beliefs About Recommended Behavior	0.777	0.883	0.761
Intention to Adhere to Social Behavior (Negative)	0.644	0.928	0.672
Positive Affective Reactions	0.733	0.917	0.797
Positive Beliefs About Recommended Behavior	0.673	0.901	0.674
Intention to Adhere to Social Behavior (Positive)	0.703	0.872	0.769

In this preliminary stage, we began by analyzing the dimensionality and reliability of the measurement scales used for the entire sample.

4.2. Hypothesis Testing and Discussion

At the end of this data analysis and interpretation, the results obtained enable us to deduce the probability that a child, aged between 8 and 12, will have a behavioral intention to buy (Norin et al., 2024), based on the emotions triggered and the beliefs regarding this behavior following exposure to a YouTube ad, once threatening and once humorous. Given that we are working on two different emotional effects, fear and humor, in a YouTube ad, we proceeded doubly to accomplish our investigation.

Concerning threatening advertising, our results show that the probability of a child aged between 8 and 12 having a behavioral intention to make a purchase decision following a YouTube ad depends solely on the negative affective reactions triggered by the ad. Specifically, the greater the level of fear or anxiety evoked by the threatening ad, the stronger the child's intention to purchase, provided that the ad effectively conveys a solution to mitigate the perceived threat. On the other hand, in humorous advertising, the child's behavioral intention to buy is significantly influenced by the positive emotions elicited, such as joy and amusement, which enhance the appeal of the product and make it more desirable (Ghouse et al., 2025 ; Lawal, 2025 ; Lad & Nayak, 2024).

Our results suggest that while fear-based ads primarily lead to a purchase decision through the emotional discomfort they create, humorous ads engage children more effectively by fostering positive associations with the product, ultimately increasing their intent to purchase (Eisend, 2021 ; Nabi et al., 2020). Thus, both emotional strategies-fear and humor-play distinct roles in shaping purchase intentions, with humor likely to have a more lasting and positive effect on children's attitudes towards the advertised products.

4.2.1. Case of a Threatening Advertisement

Model Prediction Rate

From this table, we can see that the correct percentage is equal to 72.3%, which corresponds to the model's prediction rate following the introduction of the predictor variables. This shows that the introduction of the explanatory variables contributes to the prediction of the variable to be explained, and therefore to the probability that the child intends to engage in the behavior of concern for the environment, given the negative affective reactions triggered by viewing the threatening advertisement and the child's beliefs regarding the behavior of concern for the environment following exposure to the advertisement.

Table 11. Classification table

Observed		**Previsions**		
		BI		**Correct pourcentage**
		Defavorable	**Favorable**	
Step1 BI	Defavorable	10	19	34.5
	Favorable	4	50	92.6
Global pourcentage				72.3

a.The cut value is .500
BI: Behavioral intentions

The Overall Meaning of the Model

According to this table, the chi-square value and its significance, with $P < 0.05$, being equal to 0.007, confirm the contribution of the variables to the improvement of the model, thereby demonstrating the overall significance of the model.

Table 12. Composite tests of the model coefficients

		Chi-square	**ddl**	**Sig.**
Step 1	**Step**	**10.035**	**2**	**0.007**
	Block	10.035	2	0.007
	Model	10.035	2	0.007

The Model's Goodness of Fit

The strength of the relationship between the dependent and independent variables is given by the two estimates: Cox and Snell's R-squared and Nagelkerk's R-squared. The latter is an adjusted version of Cox and Snell's R-squared and is therefore closer to reality. Thus, our model explains 15.7% of the variance in the dependent variable, which may be considered acceptable but is not strong enough.

Table 13. Summary of models

Step	Log Likelihood 2	Cox and Snell's R-squared	R-two of Nagelkerke
1	97.379a	0.114	0.157

The Individual Significance of the Model

Beliefs about the recommended behavior are not influenced by exposure to this advertising and therefore do not play a role in adherence to purchase decision-making behavior. The results indicate that B = 0.785 and that the Wald test is not significant, with a value of 0.444, at a margin of error of 5%. Since the B coefficient is positive and the Wald test is not significant, we can conclude that the child's beliefs about purchase decision-making do not influence the target's intention to adopt this recommended behavior. H1.2 is therefore invalidated.

Table 14. Variables of the equation

		B	E.S	Wald	ddl	Sig.	Exp(B)
Step 1a	BB	0.785	1.025	0.586	1	0.444	2,192
	AR	128	0.655	7.784	1	0.005	6.221
	Constant	-106	1.099	2.135	1	0.144	0.201

BI: Behavioral intentions

BB: Belief toward the behavior

AR: Affective reactions

B is the utility weight parameter that describes the contribution of each predictive variable in explaining the intention to engage in environmentally concerned behavior.

Exp(B) is an odds indicator that reflects the odds ratio for each unit increase in the predictive variable.

According to theory (De Pelsmacker et al., 2013), the invalidation of our second sub-hypothesis can be explained by the process of fear control, which leads to a non-adaptive reaction favoring a protective response on the part of the child. In this case, under the effect of fear, there is a certain absence of beliefs about the behavior recommended by the threatening ad on the part of the child, who will react to reduce his fear and not the danger communicated in the ad. This fear control process diverts the child's focus from the product or behavior being promoted and instead triggers coping mechanisms aimed at alleviating the emotional discomfort caused by fear (Shen & Dillard, 2021). As a result, the child may engage in avoidance behaviors, such as ignoring the ad or disengaging from the recommended action, as they prioritize emotional relief over adopting the proposed behavior. Therefore, while the threatening ad may succeed in evoking fear, it fails to encourage the desired behavioral change or purchase decision, as the child's primary objective is to reduce the negative emotions, rather than address the threat or engage with the product being advertised.

4.2.2. Case of a Humorous Advertisement

Model Prediction Rate

This table shows that the correct percentage is equal to 83.1%, which correspondsto the model's prediction rate following the introduction of the predictor variables. This then expresses that the introduction of the explanatory variables, which are the positive affective reactions triggered by viewing the humorous ad and the child's beliefs regarding the behavior of concern for the environment following exposure to the humorous ad, contributes to the prediction of the variable to be explained and therefore to the probability that the child intends to engage in the behavior of concern for the environment.

Table 15. Classification table

Observed		**Previsions**		
		Bih		**Correct pourcentage**
		0	**1**	
Step1 bih	0	3	14	17.6
	1	0	66	100.0
Global pourcentage				83.1

a.The cut value is .500
bih: behavioral intention in the case of humor.

The Overall Meaning of the Model

The chi-square value and its significance, with $P < 0.05$, being equal to 0.002, are clearly shown in this table, confirming the contribution of the variables to the improvement of the model and thereby demonstrating the overall significance of the model.

Table 16. Composite tests of the model coefficients

		Chi-square	Ddl	Sig.
Step 1	**Step**	**12.608**	**2**	**0.002**
	Block	12.608	2	0.002
	Model	12.608	2	0.002

The Model's Goodness of Fit

Nagelkerke's R-squared explains 22.1% of the dependent variable, the probability of a behavioral intention toward environmental concern, through the explanatory variables "positive affective reactions triggered in the child when viewing a humorous ecological advertisement and the child's beliefs regarding environmentally concerned behavior following a humorous ecological advertisement.

Table 17. Summary of models

Step	Log Likelihood 2	Cox and Snell's R-squared	R-two of Nagelkerke
1	71.556a	0.141	0.221

The Individual Significance of the Model

This table explains the impact and weight of each explanatory variable in the model, namely positive affective reactions triggered in the child when viewing a humorous ecological advertisement and the child's beliefs regarding environmentally concerned behavior following a humorous ecological advertisement, in predicting the intention to adopt environmentally concerned behavior.

For the first explanatory variable, the results show that the coefficient B is positive and that the Wald test is significant at a 5% error margin, with B = 1.025 and sig = 0.003. This indicates that the positive affective reactions triggered in the child when viewing a humorous advertisement positively influence the intention of the same target to adopt environmentally concerned behavior.

Table 18. Variables of the equation

		B	E.S	Wald	Ddl	Sig.	Exp(B)
Step 1a	BB	1.025	0.608	2.754	1	0.003	1.786
	AR	0.479	0.168	6.201	1	0.002	1.253
	Constant	0.213	0.159	2.113	1	0.157	0.802

Children's beliefs about the purchase decision-making behavior recommended by advertising. The results obtained show that the B coefficient is positive and that the Wald test is significant, with values of B = 0.479 and sig = 0.002. H2.2 is confirmed.

These results seem logical from the theoretical underpinning consulted. The analysis of the data collected in this research work will be carried out by a logistic regression of the variable to explain "the behavioral intention", depending on two explanatory variables, namely "the affective reactions triggered following the viewing of the advertisement" as well as "beliefs towards this behavior" (Ghosh, 2022). Humor is also one of the elements of advertising that appeals to children. Indeed, humor's ability to create a cheerful, upbeat atmosphere encourages the creation of positive emotions and reinforces the child's belief in the behavior communicated by the humorous ad (Paine et al., 2025 ; Nicolini, 2022). According to the probabilistic analysis carried out using the Logit model, and as part of a comparative approach, the equations expressing the probability of adopting a purchase decision-making behavior show that a humorous advert on YouTube would have a greater influence than a threatening advert on the child's purchase decision-making intention communicated in both types of adverts (Table 19).

Table 19. Summary of assumptions

Assumptions	Check
H1: Exposure to a threatening advertisement on YouTube increases the probability of the child's behavioral intention.	Partially confirmed
H1.1: There is a positive effect between exposure to a threatening advertisement on YouTube and the likelihood of the creation of negative emotions in children.	Confirmed
H1.2: There is a positive effect between exposure to threatening advertising on YouTube and children's beliefs about preoccupied shopping behavior.	Invalidated
H2: Exposure to a humorous YouTube ad increases the probability of a child's behavioral intention.	Confirmed
H2.1: There is a positive effect between exposure to a humorous advert on YouTube and the likelihood of positive emotions being created in children.	Confirmed
H2.2: There is a positive effect between exposure to humorous advertising on YouTube and children's beliefs about recommended behavior.	Confirmed

Thus, we can conclude that the results obtained support the literature review we conducted, and the tests of the relationships have contributed to achieving the objective of our research work, enabling us to put forward certain recommendations.

CONCLUSION

Through this research work, we have focused on the behavior of concern for the environment that children, aged between 8 and 12, could have, as recommended in the theory. This age group, being at a developmental stage where they are forming beliefs and values, is particularly susceptible to messages that highlight environmental issues. According to the theory, children of this age are influenced by external stimuli, such as advertising, which can shape their attitudes and behaviors toward environmental sustainability. By analyzing their reactions to ads promoting eco-friendly products or actions, we aimed to understand how emotional appeals, like humor or fear, might affect their willingness to engage in environmentally responsible behaviors. Our findings suggest that children's concern for the environment is not only influenced by their immediate emotional responses but also by their growing awareness of environmental issues, which is often reinforced through educational content. The study also highlighted the importance of tailoring messages that resonate with children's values, helping them internalize environmentally conscious behaviors, and promoting positive attitudes towards sustainability.

Our work presents several theoretical contributions. Firstly, we looked at the study of advertising persuasion after discovering that children today spend more time in a virtual world through small screens than in their real world with members of their entourage and society. In this case, the media and the world of communication are seen as opportune actors in the ecological socialization of the child. In addition, the study of advertising persuasion has shown that the use of figures of speech is effective in advertising communication.

Next, we thought it would be interesting to study a child's behavioral intention, using a YouTube ad as a starting point. Unlike adults, children function on an emotional level. We found that negative and/or positive emotions can have a very strong influence on our target's affective reactions. On this basis, our research focused on the study of children's decision-making following exposure to hyperbolic and commercially-oriented YouTube ads, whether threatening or humorous, using two explanatory variables for the phenomenon in each case, namely: the affective reactions triggered and the child's beliefs about the recommended behavior following viewing of these two different ads.

Then, an empirical analysis, using the Logit model, was favored in this research work, enabling us to verify the hypotheses formulated and provide elements of an answer to our research problem. To do this, we opted for logistic regression as the working technique in our methodological section, since this technique will enable us to develop a prediction model in which we will predict the variable to be explained by the various explanatory variables drawn from the theory.

Finally, these findings were supported by theoretical justifications, stating that the fear control process can undertake the path of non-adaptive reactions, resulting in an absence of advertising persuasion and a protective reaction against the fear present in the ad and not the danger communicated.

Humor, on the other hand, is one of the main determinants that appeal to children and positively attract their attention. Humorous ecological advertising would then have a greater influence on the likelihood of children adopting environmentally-conscious behavior, through the positive affective reactions triggered and the target group's beliefs in the ecological behavior recommended by the ad.

Our work also makes several managerial contributions. On the one hand, the role of consumer associations is to inform Internet users, especially children, about the tools and techniques that enable them to choose whether or not to be exposed to advertising. In addition to this informative role, consumer associations can mobilize public opinion to change the law for better consumer protection, or at least force a debate on better management for better protection of advertising.

On the other hand, we should invest in the children who constitute the future generations of our society. Indeed, the research carried out always shows the existence of a certain sensitivity of the child to advertising, which requires the intervention of the Ministry of Education by setting up a model of subjects including and ensuring learning reserved for his concerns.

We can also talk about the Ministry of Information Technologies and Communications as well as all types of companies involved in the subject by designing advertising campaigns aimed at raising awareness and influencing children's behavior.

As with all research, however, our study has its limitations, which may give rise to future avenues of investigation. A sample of 85 respondents is insufficient and raises a problem regarding the generalizability of the results. Also, Our sample was selected for convenience and was made up of children attending a private elementary school. This choice does not guarantee external validity, and so a generalization of the results obtained cannot be possible under any circumstances. It would therefore be interesting to conduct this study with a broader target group of children, including children from different regions of the country, from backgrounds that are less exposed to advertising, and from different types of schools.

REFERENCES

Allen, C. T., Machleit, K. A., & Kleine, S. S. (1992). A comparison of attitudes and emotions as predictors of behavior at diverse levels of behavioral experience. *The Journal of Consumer Research, 18*(4), 493–504.

Allen, C. T., Machleit, K. A., & Marine, S. S. (1988). On assessing the emotionality of advertising via Izard's differential emotions scale. *Advances in Consumer Research. Association for Consumer Research (U. S.), 15*(1), 226–231.

Attruia, F. (2021). L'autorité des jeunes influenceurs du Web dans le genre de l'«unboxing»: un cas d'étude français/italien. *Argumentation et Analyse du Discours, 26*.

Bandura, A. (1963). Social reinforcement and behavior change—Symposium, 1962: 1. Behavior theory and identificatory learning. *The American Journal of Orthopsychiatry, 33*(4), 591. PMID: 13966305

Bargh, J. A., Chen, M., & Burrows, L. (1996). Automaticity of social behavior: Direct effects of trait construct and stereotype activation on action. *Journal of Personality and Social Psychology, 71*(2), 230. PMID: 8765481

Bartels, M., Drummond, P., & Carrigan, M. (2023). The persuasive influence of branded content on children's purchase intentions. *Journal of Business Ethics, •••*, 1–17.

Bauman, S., & Tatum, T. (2009). Web sites for young children: Gateway to online social networking?. *Professional School Counseling, 13*(1), 2156759X0901300102.

Belch, M. A., Krentler, K. A., & Willis-Flurry, L. A. (2005). Teen internet mavens: Influence in family decision making. *Journal of Business Research, 58*(5), 569–575.

Benbouja, A., & Cavalli, P. (2010). Les 15-17 ans internautes et le comportement de consommation des parents: Le cas des Français et des Italiens. *9Th International Marketing Trends Conference*, Venice, January.

Bénédict, T. M. (2022). Usage des réseaux sociaux Facebook et WhatsApp et leur impact sur l'éducation des jeunes en ville de Butembo.

Berey, L. A., & Pollay, R. W. (1968). The influencing role of the child in family decision making. *JMR, Journal of Marketing Research, 5*, 70–72.

Bonhomme, M. (2014). *Pragmatique des figures du discours*. Honoré Champion.

Bonnéry, S., & Pasquali, P. (2023). Le "métier d'enfant" 50 ans après: Penser l'éducation et la socialisation avec Jean-Claude Chamboredon. *Revue Française de Pédagogie*, •••, 5–15.

Brée, J. (1990). Les enfants et la consommation: Un tour d'horizon des recherches. *Revue et Applications en Marketing*, *1/90*, 43–69.

Brée, J. (1993). *Les enfants, la consommation et le marketing* (1ère éd.). Paris, Presses Universitaires de France.

Brée, J. (2021). *Kids Marketing* (3e éd.). Éditions EMS.

Brée, J., & Pantin-Sohier, G. (2023). Chapitre 1. De l'importance de comprendre le consommateur. *Les Topos*, *5*, 9–40.

Bud, I. (2022). La rhétorique publicitaire. *Annales Universitatis Apulensis. Series Philologica*, *23*(1), 369–376.

Buijzen, M., Cleeren, M., & Valkenburg, P. M. (2023). Understanding children's online advertising literacy: A framework and review of the literature. *Journal of Communication*, *73*(1), 74–98.

Carlson, D. R. J. C. L. (2001). Sélection Internationale. *Recherche et Applications en Marketing*, *16*(1), 87.

Chaiken, S., & Trope, Y. (Eds.). (1999). *Dual-process theories in social psychology*. Guilford Press.

Charry, K., & Pecheux, C. (2008). Enfance, alimentation et publicité: quels rôles pour le marketing?. *Reflets et perspectives de la vie économique*, (2), 9-17.

Chouk, I., & Guiot, D. (2014). *Publicité intrusive sur Internet: une étude exploratoire des profils de résistance. In 13ème journée de recherche sur le e-marketing/marketing digital.*

Cottin, J. (2022). Les symboles bibliques dans la publicité: développement, contextes, conflits. *Communiquer. Revue de communication sociale et publique, 34*, 21-32.

De Pelsmacker, P., Geuens, M., & Bergh, J. (2013). Humor in advertising: A framework for understanding its effectiveness. *Journal of Marketing*, *77*(2), 3–20.

De Veirman, M., De Jans, S., Van den Abeele, E., & Hudders, L. (2020). Unravelling the power of social media influencers: a qualitative study on teenage influencers as commercial content creators on social media. In *The regulation of social media influencers* (pp. 126–166). Edward Elgar Publishing.

Derbaix, C., Gregory, P., Lavoisier, L. M., Lehu, J. M., Pecheux, C., Poncin, I., ... & Vanhamme, J. (2004). La Théorie de l'irrationalité retreinte, fondement de la communication persuasive.

Deutsch, M., & Gerard, H. B. (1955). A study of normative and informational social influences upon individual judgment. *Journal of Abnormal and Social Psychology, 51*(3), 629. PMID: 13286010

Durand-Mégret, B., Ezan, P., & Vanheems, R. (2012). Quand le cross-canal devient familial… Un nouveau pouvoir d'influence des adolescents au sein de la famille. *In Acte de conférence Etienne Thil.*

Eisend, M. (2021). Humor in advertising: A meta-analysis. *Journal of the Academy of Marketing Science, 49*, 649–669.

Festinger, L. (1957). Social comparison theory. *Selective Exposure Theory, 16*(401), 3.

Fishbein, M., Ajzen, I., & Belief, A. (1975). *Intention and Behavior: An introduction to theory and research.*

Fointiat, V., & Barbier, L. (2015). Persuasion et Influence: changer les attitudes, changer les comportements. Regards de la psychologie sociale. *Journal d'interaction personne-système, 4*(1), 1-18.

Frangieh, B., & Akiki, J. (2023). L'accompagnant scolaire des élèves à besoins éducatifs particuliers en situation d'intermétiers. *La nouvelle revue-Éducation et société inclusives, 95*(3), 43-56.

Gallopel, K., Rieunier, S., Debenedetti, S., Dion, D., & Le Gall-Ely, M. (2006). Impact des avertissements sanitaires dans la lutte contre le tabagisme: synthèse théorique ET résultats D'UNE étude qualitative. *Revue française du marketing*, (206).

Ghosh, P. (2022). Reliability as a moderator in the relationship between the general attitude toward advertising and purchase intention. *South Asian Journal of Management, 29*(2), 97–116.

Ghouse, S. M., Durrah, O., & Chaudhary, M. (2025). Children as consumers: Influence strategies and decision-making roles in Arab households. *Journal of Islamic Marketing.*

Godener, V. (1999). L'efficacité du stress en publicité (Doctoral dissertation, Paris 1).

Guitouni, M. (2000). Au cœur de l'identité. *L'intelligence émotionnelle.*

Hajtaieb El Aoud, N. (2003). La contribution de l'adolescent dans la prise de décision d'achat de la famille: un essai de modélisation. *Université Pierre Mendès-France, Grenoble, Thèse de doctorat en sciences de gestion.*

Hovland, C. I., Janis, I. L., & Kelley, H. H. (1953). Communication and persuasion.

Hubermont, A., & Masset, J. (2023). Est-ce possible que Twitch devienne l'un des médias les plus influents d'ici 2035, comparable voire surpassant la télévision traditionnelle?

Izard, C. E. (1977). Differential emotions theory. In *Human emotions* (pp. 43–66). Springer US.

Janis, I. L. (1967). Effects of fear arousal on attitude change: Recent developments in theory and experimental research. *Advances in Experimental Social Psychology, 3*, 166–224.

Kahneman, D., & Tversky, A. (1979). Prospect theory: An analysis of decisions under risk. *Econometrica, 47*(2), 263–291.

Katz, E., Blumler, J. G., & Gurevitch, M. (1973). Uses and gratifications research. *Public Opinion Quarterly, 37*(4), 509–523.

Kerbrat-Orecchioni, C. (2015). Dialogue théâtral et interactions médiatiques: Le fonctionnement du «trope communicationnel». *Littérature, linguistique et didactique du français: Les travaux Pratiques d'André Petitjean, 125.*

Kim, M. J., & Hall, C. M. (2021). Do perceived risk and intervention affect crowdfunder behavior for the sustainable development goals? A model of goal-directed behavior. *Journal of Cleaner Production, 311*, 127614.

Laamouri, L. K., & Gharbi, J. E. (2008). L'impact de l'imagerie mentale générée par un site Web marchand sur la valeur perçue et l'intention de comportement. *7éme congrès sur les tendances Marketing.*

Lad, K. S., & Nayak, A. (2024). Impact of Emotional Response of Youth on Pester Power Advertising. Library of Progress-Library Science, *Information Technology & Computer*, 44(3).

Lavoisier-Mérieux, L. M. (2002). De l'efficacité des stratégies de communication publicitaires menaçantes: une étude de la relation entre émotions négatives et persuasion dans le domaine de la lutte contre l'insécurité routière. *Actes du, 2.*

Lawal, K. (2025). Advertising Targeted at Children: Effects on Materialism and Brand Loyalty Formation.

Lichy, J., McLeay, F., Burdfield, C., & Matthias, O. (2023). Understanding pre-teen consumers' social media engagement. *International Journal of Consumer Studies*, *47*(1), 202–215.

Lim, Y. (2023). Emotional exaggeration and consumer resistance in digital advertising. *International Journal of Advertising*, *42*(5).

Lombardot, É. (2007). La nudité en publicité: Quelle influence sur l'attention portée à l'annonce et la fonction mémorielle de la marque? [French Edition]. *Recherche et Applications en Marketing*, *22*(4), 23–41.

Martínez, C., & Olsson, T. (2019). Making sense of YouTubers: How Swedish children construct and negotiate the YouTuber Misslisibell as a girl celebrity. *Journal of Children and Media*, *13*(1), 36–52.

McGhee, P. E. (1979). The role of laughter and humor in growing up female. In *Becoming female: Perspectives on development* (pp. 183–206). Springer US.

McQuarrie, E. F., & Mick, D. G. (1996). Figures of rhetoric in advertising language. *The Journal of Consumer Research*, *22*(4), 424–438.

Mertala, P. (2020). Young children's perceptions of ubiquitous computing and the Internet of Things. *British Journal of Educational Technology*, *51*(1), 84–102.

Meyer, J. C. (2000). Humor as a double-edged sword: Four functions of humor in communication. *Communication Theory*, *10*(3), 310–331.

Moati, P. (2011). *La nouvelle révolution commerciale*. Odile Jacob.

Morreall, J. (1983). *Taking laughter seriously*. SUNY press.

Nabi, R. L., Myrick, J. G., & Kim, S. C. (2020). Feeling scared, happy, or both? The effects of mixed emotional appeals in advertising on attitudes and behavioral intentions. *Journal of Advertising*, *49*(4), 435–449.

Nicolini, V. (2022). Fear vs humor appeals: A comparative study of children's responses to anti-smoking advertisements. *Asia Pacific Journal of Marketing and Logistics*, *34*(2), 166–184.

Norin, A., Ishfaq, H., Shaheen, W. A., & Abbas, Z. (2024). Advertising Effects on Young Minds: Probing into Environmental Awareness, Purchasing Patterns, and Attitudinal Shifts in Children. *Research Journal for Societal Issues*, *6*(1), 272–292.

Paine, A. L., Hashmi, S., Fink, E., Mitchell, P., & Howe, N. (2025). Humorous peer play and social understanding in childhood. *Communications Psychology*, *3*, 76. PMID: 40355511

Parent, E. (2023). «Ça dépend»: Converser, publier et scroller sur les réseaux sociaux à l'adolescence.

Perloff, M. (2017). Eliot the Young Reviewer: The Formation of Aesthetic Judgment. *Literary Imagination*, *19*(2), 135–142.

Petty, R. E., & Cacioppo, J. T. (1986). Message elaboration versus peripheral cues. In *Communication and persuasion: Central and peripheral routes to attitude change* (pp. 141–172). Springer New York.

Preston, C. (2005). *Thomas Browne and the writing of early modern science*. Cambridge University Press.

Prochaska, J. O., Fairhurst, S. K., Velicer, W. F., Velasquez, M. M., & Rossi, J. S. (1991). The process of smoking cessation: An analysis of precontemplation, contemplation, and preparation stages of change. *Journal of Consulting and Clinical Psychology*, *59*(2), 295–304. PMID: 2030191

Prochaska, J. O., Rossi, J. S., & Wilcox, N. S. (1991). Change processes and psychotherapy outcome in integrative case research. *Journal of Psychotherapy Integration*, *1*(2), 103.

Prochaska, J. O., Velicer, W. F., DiClemente, C. C., & Fava, J. (1988). Measuring processes of change: Applications to the cessation of smoking. *Journal of Consulting and Clinical Psychology*, *56*(4), 520. PMID: 3198809

Prochaska, J. O., Velicer, W. F., Guadagnoli, E., Rossi, J. S., & DiClemente, C. C. (1991). Patterns of change: Dynamic typology applied to smoking cessation. *Multivariate Behavioral Research*, *26*(1), 83–107. PMID: 26782613

Raschel, E. (2022). Peut-on rire de tout? Réflexions sur les « lois du genre » des expressions humoristiques. *Recueil Dalloz*, *27*, 1367.

Razkaoui, Y. (2022). Les rhétoriques de la publicité: Les figures de style. *Revue des Etudes Multidisciplinaires en Sciences Economiques et Sociales*, *7*(1).

Rigaux-Bricmont, B. (1986). L'avenir de la recherche en matière de décision collective d'achat. *Recherche et Applications en Marketing*, *1*(2), 17–26.

Rogers, R. W. (1975). A protection motivation theory of fear appeals and attitude change1. *The Journal of Psychology*, *91*(1), 93–114. PMID: 28136248

Sassi-Chamsi, H. (2022). Les effets du ton d'un message persuasif en santé sur la motivation et l'intention de changer de comportement: Regards croisés de la Théorie de l'Auto-Détermination et de la Théorie des Niveaux de Représentation (Doctoral dissertation, Université Grenoble Alpes).

Scherer, K. R., Wranik, T., Sangsue, J., Tran, V., & Scherer, U. (2004). Emotions in everyday life: Probability of occurrence, risk factors, appraisal and reaction patterns. *Social Sciences Information. Information Sur les Sciences Sociales*, *43*(4), 499–570.

Schmitt, M., & de Jouvenel, M. (2022). *Le baromètre du numérique-édition 2022. Mondes virtuels–Perspectives et enjeux*, 112.

Shen, L., & Dillard, J. P. (2021). Fear appeals and children: Understanding affective and cognitive responses to threatening messages. *Journal of Consumer Behaviour*, *20*(6), 1571–1583. DOI: 10.1002/cb.1987

Smith, E. E. (2024). Building critical digital literacies for social media through educational development. *Journal of Contemporary Issues in Education*, *19*(2), 64–89.

Soulages, J. C. (2006). Les stratégies humoristiques dans le discours publicitaire. *Questions de Communication*, *10*, 103–118.

Spector, C. (2022). Rhétorique et pratique morale.

Strong, E. K.Jr. (1925). Theories of selling. *The Journal of Applied Psychology*, *9*(1), 75–98.

Turcotte, C. (2022). Les écrans chez les enfants d'âge préscolaire et leurs habiletés socioémotionnelles: Exploration de différents types d'utilisation des écrans et du rôle modérateur de la médiation parentale (Doctoral dissertation, Université Laval).

Vanheems, R. (2010). Quand le client multi-canal invite à réinventer le marketing du point de vente. *9ème Journées Normandes de Recherches sur la Consommation*, Session 5, 25 et 26 Mars, Rouen.

Ward, S. (1974). Consumer socialization. *The Journal of Consumer Research*, *1*, 1–14.

Weinberger, M. G., & Gulas, C. S. (1992). The impact of humor in advertising: A review. *Journal of Advertising*, *21*(4), 35–59.

Weitz, J., D'Angelica, M., Gonen, M., Klimstra, D., Coit, D. G., Brennan, M. F., & Karpeh, M. S. (2003). Interaction of splenectomy and perioperative blood transfusions on prognosis of patients with proximal gastric and gastroesophageal junction cancer. *Journal of Clinical Oncology*, *21*(24), 4597–4603. PMID: 14673048

Wells, W. D., & Lo Sciuto, L. A. (1966). Direct observation of purchasing behavior. *JMR, Journal of Marketing Research*, *3*, 227–283.

Westbrook, R. A., & Oliver, R. L. (1991). The dimensionality of consumption emotion patterns and consumer satisfaction. *The Journal of Consumer Research*, *18*(1), 84–91.

Witte, K. (1992). Putting the fear back into fear appeals: The extended parallel process model. *Communication Monographs*, *59*(4), 329–349.

Zidouri, C. (2023). La médiation pédagogique et le développement de la compétence interculturelle dans l'enseignement du FLE au secondaire algérien (Doctoral dissertation, Université IBN KHALDOUN-Tiaret).

KEY TERMS AND DEFINITIONS

Behavioral Intention: The likelihood or probability that an individual will engage in a specific behavior, such as purchasing a product, influenced by various emotional or cognitive factors.

Decision-Making Process: The series of steps an individual takes to make a choice, including recognizing a need, gathering information, evaluating options, and making a decision, often influenced by emotional, cognitive, and social factors.

Emotional Appeal: A marketing technique that seeks to influence consumer behavior by triggering an emotional response, such as fear or joy, through advertisements to create stronger engagement with the product or service.

Humorous: Advertising that utilizes humor to engage viewers, aiming to create positive emotions, make the content memorable, and increase the likelihood of favorable consumer behavior through enjoyment and laughter.

School Children: Children within the age group typically attending primary or elementary school, usually aged 8 to 12, who are the target group in studies examining their consumer behavior and responses to advertisements.

Threatening: A form of advertising that uses fear or warnings about potential negative outcomes to motivate a viewer to act in a specific way, often by presenting a danger or threat that requires a response.

YouTube Advertising: The use of video advertisements on YouTube to promote products or services, targeting specific demographics and interests through tailored content shown before, during, or after video content.

Chapter 7
From Co-Design to Commitment

Olfa Ammar
https://orcid.org/0000-0001-6270-9435
University of Sfax, Tunisia

ABSTRACT

As firms increasingly rely on co-design platforms to involve consumers in early-stage innovation, important questions remain regarding how different co-design activities shape consumer engagement and consumer–product relationships. Drawing on the Stimulus–Organism–Response framework and activity and engagement theories, this study examines how participation in two distinct co-design activities (prototype customization vs. prototype evaluation), affects consumers' cognitive, emotional, and physical engagement, and how these engagement states vary with co-design taskstranslate into psychological ownership and purchase intention. A cross-cultural between-subjects experiment was conducted in the context of olive oil packaging design. Results reveal that engagement dimensions diverge systematically across co-design activities. From a human–computer interaction perspective, the findings underscore the importance of designing co-design platforms that balance cognitive load, emotional stimulation, and user control, all are very important to build a strong consumer-product relationship.

INTRODUCTION

At the heart of today's shift toward user-centric innovation, product design development is no longer the exclusive domain of designers. Crowdsourcing and co-creation activities emphasized the user-centric approaches and have become central to modern product development strategies (Mathew et al., 2025). Guided by

DOI: 10.4018/979-8-3373-6450-6.ch007

Service-Dominant Logic, value co-creation is increasingly seen from an experience-centric perspective, where consumers are active co-creators rather than passive recipients of product or brand value (Prahalad & Ramaswamy, 2004; Vargo et al., 2008; Varshneya et al., 2017). With advances in technology and web-based platforms enabling consumers to ideate, share their preferences, evaluate, and influence design decisions, the question is no longer *if* they should be involved, but *how deeply*.

To translate this involvement into concreate and effective outcomes, firms must provide appropriate tools that facilitate resource exchange, support collaboration, and allow consumers to contribute meaningfully. Prior research highlights that consumer involvement in early design stages strengthens person–object relationships (Atakan et al., 2014) and ensures that solutions meet consumer needs (López-Mas et al., 2022). For example, firms can empower consumers to generate, evaluate, and vote on product ideas, which improves product-market fit and promises product success (Fuchs & Schreier, 2011). Building on Booz, Allen, and Hamilton's (1982) seven-phase model of new product development, these phases can be approached as distinct co-design activities in which consumers could be actively involved. These distinct co-design activities act as initial contact point between the product and the target consumer, as well as, as different stimuli, potentially shaping consumers' psychological and behavioral responses toward the product. However, the differential effects of these activities on consumer–product relationships remain largely unexplored in the existent literature.

Positioned within the broader evolution of human-centered interactive technologies, this chapter examines virtual co-design activities as key mechanisms through which consumer engagement is shaped and enacted. By focusing on consumer participation in prototype generation and evaluation, both activities take place at the initial stage of packaging development, this chapter shows how different technology-enabled interaction modes transforms users from passive recipients into active co-creators, influencing their cognitive, emotional, and behavioral relationships with products. In doing so, the chapter aligns with the book's objective of understanding how interactive, user-centric systems foster meaningful engagement and value co-creation.

The chapter begins with a literature review to present and define the research concepts and outline the main indicators of the consumer–product relationship. This is followed by hypothesis development, the detailed research methodology and, then, data analysis and results are presented and followed by a discussion. The chapter concludes with limitations and directions for future research, highlighting implications for both theory and practice in co-design and consumer engagement.

LITERATURE REVIEW

Co-Design Experience

Design is always considered as a strategic tool for competitive advantage and product differentiation, especially in competitive industries (Hendrayanti & Nurauliya, 2021). Putting priority on consumer's needs when developing the product design, creates value for both of firm and consumers. This enhanced the emergence of the concept of user-centered design that entails end-user involvement in the development process in order to develop a product design that meets the needs and preferences of users who end up consuming it (Christensen et al., 2017).

Today, with the advancement of Web techniques and AI technologies, empowering people in the design process changed the landscape of design practices and the optimization of the design results (Sanders & Stappers, 2014). At the early stage of the democratization of the design process, Piller and Salvador (2016, p. 4) defined, "*customer co-design describes a process that allows customers to express their product requirements and carry out product realization processes by mapping the requirements into the physical domain of the product [...] During these co-designing processes, users sometimes even take over the role of being the innovators*". Consumers active participation vary according to the specific objective of co-design, either to develop ideas, create designs concepts and/or evaluate/select developed designs (Füller et al., 2011). Today, with the rapid advancement of the AI technologies, co-design process is increasingly assisted allowing consumers' inputs to shape the outcome of this participatory process more significantly than ever before. This was attested with Allen's et al., (2018) qualitative study when every manager interviewed stated "*design crowdsourcing serves as a resource-supplement strategy that simplifies and accelerates the flow of NPD.*" Indeed, establishing interactive processes that leverage consumers' experiential knowledge enhances firms' resources and increases new product success. In this research, co-design broadly refers to consumers' active participation in packaging design stages,

Co-Design Activity

From activity theory perspective, Nardi (1996, pp.38) maintained "*what takes place in an activity system composed of object, actions, and operation, is the context [...]. Context is both internal to people—involving specific objects and goals—and, at the same time, external to people, involving artifacts, other people, specific settings.*" Therefore, the co-design activity provides the framework that guides the extent of participants' engagement, the tools they use, and the way they reason and behave during the activity performance.

This research focuses on packaging design, highlighting the importance of involving consumers in the early "fuzzy front end" of the development process to understand their needs and ensure effective solutions (Simms & Trott, 2010). Consumer could be engaged throughout the design process, but this study concentrates on the idea-generation stage, which, following Booz, Allen, and Hamilton's (1982) model, comprises two key activities: prototype generation and prototype evaluation.

- Prototype generation: it presents the creative process that serves to produce and generate a variety and a "treasure" of ideas. Each prototype is very welcomed and is considered as a 'can do basis'.
- Prototype evaluation: it represents consumer evaluation of all gathered designs during idea generation stage to select the promising ones. This helps us restrict the number of generated ideas and have a deep vision of consumer's thoughts and preferences.

Each phase involves a specific co-design activity with a clear objective and outcome (i.e., generated prototype or prototypes' ratings). Drawing on Nardi's assumption (1996), we argue that these activities possess distinct properties that contextualize consumer participation. This research focuses on virtual co-design experiences for prototype generation and evaluation, which differ in objectives, levels of involvement, and human-computer interaction environments. While co-design defines the overall context, specific tasks shape how consumers think and act within it.

Co-Design Task

In the framework of the activity theory, Leont'ev (1974) denotes activity's components as subject, object, actions, and operations. A subject is a person or a group of persons engaged in an activity. An object motivates the subject and gives a specific direction to the activity. Actions are goal-directed, coordinated, and conscious (Nardi, 1996). A given situation helps situate these actions and guide participants' reflections. Building on Coughlan's and Duff (1994) assumption regarding the role of tasks in defining an activity's parameters and boundaries, this study considers co-design tasks as situations that structure consumers' actions during the co-design activity. Consequently, a single activity may involve multiple tasks that orient participants' thinking and behavior in distinct ways.

From the cognitive side, when performing an activity, the process entails information processing, logical reasoning, drawing inferences, evaluating alternatives, comparing, contrasting and synthesizing ideas (Xie, 2023). Drawing on concept–

knowledge (C–K) theory (Hatchuel & Weil, 2003), each design activity follows a logical reasoning process that connects new concepts to existing knowledge. Involving consumers in packaging design requires them to apply prior product knowledge in new ways. Since knowledge is organized as an associative network (Lawson, 2002), tracing consumers' reasoning and cognitive flow during a specific design task is essential. In other words, assigning a specific packaging co-design task frames the product category in consumers' minds and shapes the rules governing the design context.

Consumer Engagement

The concept of engagement has long attracted attention in sociology and psychology. Early socio-psychological work defined engagement as a psychological state reflecting the relationship between individuals and their actions, shaped by both situational characteristics and the personal significance of the act (Kiesler, 1971; Joule & Beauvois, 1989; Joule & Beauvois, 2002). In organizational psychology, Kahn (1990) extended this view by conceptualizing engagement as the cognitive, emotional, and physical investment individuals bring to their roles, emphasizing personal involvement, self-expression, and connection to work and others.

From a relationship marketing perspective, engagement emerges as a relational factor that enhances consumer–firm/brand connections and indicates relationship strength and quality (Vivek et al., 2012). More recently, the focus has shifted from relational exchange to value in exchange and value in use through active firm–consumer interaction (Eggert et al., 2018; Abid et al., 2022). Within this logic, value creation is founded on consumers' engagement in interactive experiences that illustrate the active roles of individuals and other partners in the exchange relationship (Prahalad & Ramaswamy, 2004; Ramaswamy & Ozcan, 2018). Building on these foundations, Brodie et al. (2011), drawing on S-D logic principles (premises 6, 8, 9, and 10), outlined the conceptual roots of customer engagement in value co-creation, emphasizing its emergence through interactive and co-creative experiences. Engagement thus describes basic forms of service exchange (e.g., interaction, co-creation, product/solution development) and illustrates value co-creators' connections to brands, firms, products, communities, and co-creation activities (Brodie et al., 2011; Vivek et al., 2012).

From relationship marketing, the engagement concept emerges as a relational factor that enhances consumer-firm/brand connection and an important indicator of this relationship strength and quality (Vivek et al., 2012). More recently, the relationship marketing's focus moves from "*relational exchange*" to "*value in exchange*" and "*value in use*" through firm-consumer active interaction (Eggert et al., 2018; Abid et al., 2022). Building on relationship marketing and interactive experiences,

Brodie et al., (2011) were based on four S-D logic principles to outline and explain the conceptual roots of customer engagement in the context of value co-creation. The concept describes the basic forms of service exchange (e.g. interaction, co-creation, product/solution development, etc.) and/ or to illustrate value co-creator's connection to the brand, the firm, the product, the community and/or to the co-creation activity (Brodie et al.,2011; Vivek et al., 2012). In value co-creation and crowdsourcing literatures (Zhang, 2022; Herter et al., 2023), consumer engagement has been widely considered as an essential concept to recognize and interpret the effectiveness of these participatory activities. Moreover, research emphasized that effective consumer engagement in value co-creation requires supportive ecosystems and interactive platforms that facilitate participation and resource exchange. Digital technologies have expanded virtual platforms as central engagement touchpoints, enhancing the ease and effectiveness of consumer involvement (Claffey & Brady, 2014).

These contexts diversity come up with various engagement definitions. Hollebeek (2011, p.790) defined the engagement concept as "*the level of an individual customer's motivational, brand-related and context-dependent state of mind characterized by specific levels of cognitive, emotional and behavioral activity in direct brand interactions*". This definition underlines the interactive, context-dependent, subjective and multifaceted natures of the engagement construct. Across disciplines, engagement is commonly conceptualized as a multidimensional construct comprising cognitive, emotional, and behavioral dimensions (Martinez, 2015). Cognitive engagement reflects attentiveness, information processing, and deep interest in the focal object (Ashley & Tuten, 2015; Tarute et al., 2017), while emotional engagement captures affective responses such as enjoyment, enthusiasm, and a sense of belonging (Brodie et al., 2011; Hollebeek, 2011; Tarute et al., 2017). Behavioral engagement refers to effort, participation, persistence, and energy invested in the engagement relationship (Griffin et al., 2008; Van Doorn et al., 2010; Tarute et al., 2017). Consumer engagement is understood as a "context-dependent state of mind" (Hollebeek, 2011), meaning that situational factors shape how individuals invest cognitively, emotionally, and behaviorally in an activity. In this research, we further explore this context-dependent perspective.

Consumer-Product Relationship (R)

Fritzsche et al., (2015) asserted in their work within open innovation field that the co-design platforms play the role of a necessary medium that establish a relationship between a subject and an object. Interaction throughout the co-design process fosters close consumer–product relationships, making co-design a powerful driver of meaningful connections. Previous research on person-object relationship (Pierce et al., 2003; Orth, 2019) maintained that active participation in the realization process of an object (e.g. product) results in a strong and deep association between individual self and the resulted product. Atakan et al., (2014) maintained that individuals' effort, time and attention invested when producing a product yield them to exhibit cognitive and/or affective, and/or behavioral responses toward the output. As Atakan et al., (2014) stated, "*during the self-production process, the product is formed in the image of its creator, revealing his tastes, preferences, and identity*" (pp. 2). To this extent, consumers perceive the product they participated in its development as a definition, expression and reflection of their selves and find themselves psychologically and emotionally connected and tied to it. This serve as a starting point for the development of the sense of belongingness and psychological ownership feeling toward the target product (Pierce et al., 2003). Indeed, Hair et al., (2016, pp.199) maintained, "*psychological ownership arises when spending time and effort with an object, independent from any buying decision*". Pierce et al., (2001) introduced psychological ownership theory in the organization field and define the concept as the "*state where an individual feels as though the target of ownership or a piece of that target is 'theirs' (i.e., it is MINE!)*" (2003, pp. 5). Accordingly, we adopt psychological ownership to capture consumers' emotional attachment and cognitive identification with the packaging prototypes they customize or evaluate. This construct allows us to frame the emotional and cognitive dimensions of the consumer–product relationship.

As a way to shed the light on the behavioral manifestation of consumer-product relationship, we call attention to consumers' purchase intention toward the product. Indeed, "*purchase behavior is a key point for consumers to access and evaluate the specific product*" (Mirabi et al., 2015, pp. 268) and purchase intention is a popular construct that helps in predicting consumers' actual purchase behavior. Therefore, consumers' intention to purchase the product points toward extending consumer associations with the product beyond the space of the co-design experience.

Hypothesis Development

The S-O-R Model

The S-O-R paradigm, introduced by Mehrabian and Russel in 1974, has been employed in different research in co-creation experiences as it helps in linking the effect of different contexts of co-creation to the participant's behavioral and attitudinal responses through his internal states (e.g. cognition, emotion, etc.) (Kamboj et al., 2018). Particularly, the advanced S-O-R model explains how various environmental characteristics and features (Stimuli) affect people's cognitive and affective states (Organism) and, subsequently, their behavioral responses (Response) in an approach/avoidance frame. This model has been applied in different research streams, such as retail environment and online shopping (Kim and Lennon, 2013), social commerce (Liu et al., 2016; Wu and Li, 2018), online brand communities (Kamboj et al., 2018) and virtual reality (Kim et al., 2020) by adjusting its building blocks according to their research contexts. Across these studies, evidence consistently shows that the S-O-R model is effective for explaining how external factors, such as environmental features and experiential cues (S), shape individuals' internal states (O) and, in turn, their behavioral responses (R) (Claffey and Brady, 2014; Kim et al., 2020). In this research, the S-O-R framework helps to link the co-design stimuli factors to consumers' internal and external responses. In the following, we display these effects into the sequential S-O-R modeling.

The Effect of Co-Design Experience on Consumer Engagement

The latent state-trait (LST) theory maintains that individual psychological variance (his cognition, emotion and behavior) does not only depends on the person but also on the remaining situation (Steyer et al., 1999). Based on this theory, various studies (Geiser et al., 2015) emphasized on specific-situation-trait and proved that changing contexts and experimental manipulations leads to individual intra state variations. In co-creation research, activities vary widely in environment, tools, requirements, outputs, and participant involvement (Piller & Salvador, 2016; Hamdi-Kidar et al., 2019). For example, previous research (Franke & Piller, 2004; Davis et al., 2023) showed that co-design toolkits offering greater freedom and autonomy enhance participants' sense of contribution. Similarly, engagement theory suggests that meaningfulness, responsibility, and contribution drive task engagement (Kahn, 1990). Building on this, different co-design activities shape distinct forms and levels of consumer engagement, influenced by virtual environment characteristics.

Prototype customization and evaluation differ not only in objectives but also in experience, tools, interactive platform, and participant control. Customization activity uses an attribute-based toolkit, offering multiple design options and autonomy to create preferred prototypes. Evaluation, in contrast, uses an alternative-based system with a limited set of designs, resulted from the customization phase, restricting participants' control and choices. Participants in the prototype customization activity would not share similar engagement state with those who participate in the design evaluation activity with restricted interactivity and control levels over the prototypes. Building on the discussion above, the activity that requires higher resources integration and involves greater interactivity is likely to generate higher engagement level. Accordingly, we hypothesize the following:

H1: Consumers who participate in prototype customization activity (vs. prototype evaluation activity) would achieve higher (vs. lower) engagement state in the activity.

H1a: Consumers who participate in prototype evaluation activity (vs. prototype customization activity) would achieve higher (vs. lower) cognitive eengagement state in the activity.

H1b: Consumers who participate in prototype customization activity (vs. prototype evaluation activity) would achieve higher (vs. lower) emotional engagement state in the activity.

H1c: Consumers who participate in prototype customization activity (vs. prototype evaluation activity) would achieve higher (vs. lower) physical engagement state in the activity.

From the engagement perspective, previous research highlighted that setting an explicit goal to attain when performing an activity is an important motivational factor. Indeed, Sonnentag (2017, pp.8) attested that "*engagement becomes most obvious while working on a task.*" Matta et al., (2015) employed role theory in their study on work engagement and organizational behavior to prove that employees are more engaged with their work when they are more conscious about their own positions and when processing and accomplishing a specific purposeful and meaningful task. Accordingly, task-oriented co-design activities provide greater insight into participants' engagement levels. Research in learning and gaming shows that engagement increases with non-routine, thought-provoking tasks that demand cognitive, interactive, or physical effort (Hoffman & Nadelson, 2010; Hamari et al., 2016). However, it's very important to highlight that challenging tasks, encourage broader thinking, while overly difficult ones can cause anxiety and burnout (Sonnentag, 2017). Building on this, we argue that consumer engagement in co-design activities is shaped not only by activity features but also by the specific outlined tasks.

Importantly, engagement is influenced by the cognitive demands of the task. Typical, familiar packaging prototypes require low cognitive effort, as consumers can rely on prior knowledge. In contrast, atypical or unusual prototypes demand higher cognitive effort to discern deviations from category norms (Rosch & Mervis, 1975). Thus, moderately challenging co-design tasks are likely to elicit the strongest engagement. Therefore, we hypothesize the following:

H2: Consumers who participate in atypical (vs. typical) prototypes customization (vs. prototypes evaluation) would reach higher (vs. lower) engagement in the activity.

H2a: Consumers who participate in atypical (vs. typical) prototypes customization (vs. prototypes evaluation) would reach higher (vs. lower) cognitive engagement in the activity.

H2b: Consumers who participate in atypical (vs. typical) prototypes customization (vs. prototypes evaluation) would reach higher (vs. lower) emotional engagement in the activity.

H2c: Consumers who participate in atypical (vs. typical) prototypes customization (vs. prototypes evaluation) would reach higher (vs. lower) physical engagement in the activity.

The Effect of Consumer Engagement on Consumer-Product Relationship

The Effect of Consumer Engagement on Psychological Ownership. According to Joule and Beauvois (1998), engagement links individuals not just to their acts but to the meaning they assign to them. Action identification theory (Vallacher & Wegner, 2012) suggests that this perceived identity can evolve with context and task challenges (Meineri & Guéguen, 2014). Consumers' engagement in co-design reflects their interest in the activity, shaping the perceived value of its outcomes. Pierce et al. (2003) identified three routes to psychological ownership: control, intimate knowledge, and self-investment. When consumers influence, interact deeply with, and dedicate effort to a product, they develop a stronger sense of ownership. In co-creation, active consumer participation cultivates psychological ownership of co-created outcomes (Yuksel et al., 2019; Chen et al., 2021). In co-design, participants actively choose, modify, and evaluate packaging prototypes, experiencing the consequences of their decisions and exercising some control over the outcome. Building on this, we hypothesize the following:

H3: Consumer engagement in co-design activity positively influence his psychological ownership.

The effect of Consumer Engagement on his Purchase Intention. Purchase intention, a key behavioral intention, is a strong predictor of actual purchase behavior (Ajzen, 1991). Research shows that consumer engagement in product development increases interest in self-created products and boosts purchase intention (Franke & Piller, 2004). Even non-participants show higher interest when a product is co-designed or "customer-ideated" (Fuchs and Schreier, 2011; Ammar et al., 2017). Participation also fosters satisfaction and repeat engagement with the brand (Brodie et al., 2011), reinforcing purchase intentions (Hsieh & Chang, 2016; Martinez & Seock, 2017). From the engagement theory and the foot-in-the-door (FITD) technique (Joule & Beauvois, 1989) suggest that initial engagement encourages consistent subsequent behaviors. Thus, consumers involved in packaging generation or evaluation are more likely to develop purchase intentions toward the co-created product. Accordingly, we hypothesize:

H4: Consumer engagement in co-design activity positively influence his purchase intention.

Psychological ownership reflects consumers' cognitive and emotional connection to an object, influencing attention, motivation, and behavior. Research shows that stronger ownership increases product valuation and drives willingness to pay and purchase (Franke & Piller, 2004; Jussila et al., 2015; Stoner et al., 2018). The sense of identification and belonging created through ownership gives the customized packaging symbolic value, satisfying personal needs such as self-expression and possession, which in turn drives purchase intention. Therefore, we hypothesize:

H5: Consumers psychological ownership positively influence their purchase intention.

Figure 1.

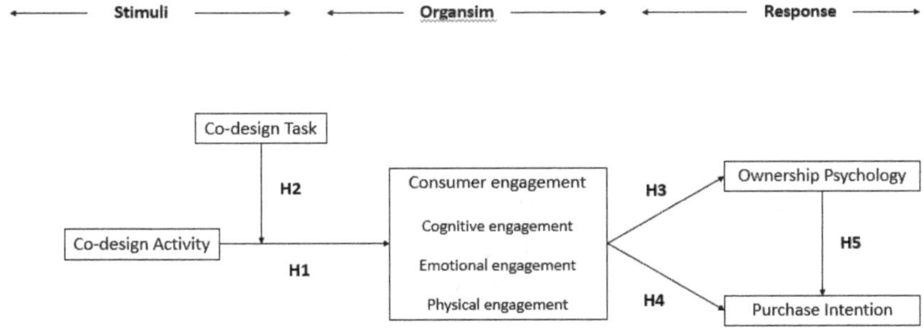

METHODOLOGY

Data Collection

In the present research, we conducted a between subject experiment with the independent variable (co-design activity) at two levels: prototype customization and prototype evaluation. Each activity included two tasks engaging participants with typical or atypical prototypes, resulting in four experimental groups. To support the design, we developed tailored toolkits for each activity and that could be seen from this video link.

We focused on olive oil packaging for our co-design activities. Indeed, while packaging strongly influences consumer perception and purchase decisions in low-involvement products (Silayoi & Speece, 2004), it is often less important than price, type, or origin in the case of olive oil product (Chrysochou et al., 2021). This study examines whether co-designing packaging helps consumers express and recognize their preferences and potentially enhancing purchase intention.

To enhance generalizability, we conducted a cross-cultural study with 608 participants from the United States and 495 from Tunisia via a web-based Qualtrics survey. The US is the world's second-largest olive oil importer, reflects high consumer demand and health awareness, while Tunisia is a major exporter with a deep-rooted olive oil tradition, highlights the product's cultural and nutritional significance. All participants were randomly assigned to one of the four experimental groups. Before attributing participants to their specific treatment, they answered questions related to their knowledge and involvement toward the product category. Sample characteristics, after data cleaning, are presented in table 1.

The present research adopts measures instruments developed in previous studies. Consumers' purchase intention was assessed using single-item measure with 7-point Likert Scale, where 1 means "extremely unlikely" and 7 means "extremely likely". Particularly, right after completing the assigned activity, participants respond to the following question *"considering that an olive oil product with the packaging you have designed (with the packaging design that you rated as the best) would be available in the market, how likely it is that you would buy it?."*. Next, for consumer engagement we adopted Martinez's (2015) measurement scale. To measure consumer psychological ownership, we adapted Cui, Ye and Teo, (2011) measurement scale (4 items). In order to reduce error variance and improve the observed effect size (Meyvis and Van Osselaer, 2017), we employed control variables including consumer innovativeness (Ailawadi, Neslin and Gedenk, 2001), consumer familiarity (d'Astous and Gargouri, 2001) toward olive oil and their past purchase behavior of olive oil using single item question stating that *"Have you bought olive oil during the past 12 months"* with yes or no as answers. Finally, participants reported their age and gender.

Table 1. Sample characteristics

	US		TN	
Items	**Frequency/Mean**	**Percentage**	**Frequency/Mean**	**Percentage**
Gender				
Male	270	47.3%	149	31.4%
Female	301	52.7%	326	68.6%
Age				
18-25	74	13%	147	30.9%
26-35	237	41.5%	191	40.2%
36-45	135	23.6%	91	19.2%
46-55	76	13.3%	34	7.2%
56 ≤	49	8.6%	12	2.5%
Education				
High school or below	181	31.7%	42	8.8%
Bachelor degree	316	55.3%	153	32.2%
Masters degree or above	74	13%	280	58.9%
Olive oil purchase during the past 12 months				
Yes	499	87.4%	455	95.8%
No	72	12.6%	20	4.2%
Consumer characteristics				
Consumer innovativeness	M_{US}= 5.18 (SD= 1.11)		M_{TN}= 5.21 (SD= 1.12)	
Consumer familiarity toward olive oil	M_{US}= 5.15 (SD= 1.35)		M_{TN}= 6.41 (SD= 0.6)	

Data Analysis and Results

Constructs' Psychometrics Properties

We performed a confirmatory factor analysis that provided us with great quality of the adjustment indices and confirmed the stability of the global measurement models of both samples.

Test of the Established Hypotheses and Results Interpretation

Before testing the established hypothesis, we checked the manipulation of co-design task by conducting a one-way Anova in order to investigate whether consumers' perception toward the generated/evaluated packaging typicality deviates across the co-design tasks to which they were assigned. We employed one item measurement scale of typicality perception going from 1= extremely dissimilar to 7= extremely similar to olive oil packaging. The findings of both samples (see table 4) showed significant differences between treatments, which validate tasks manipulation.

Table 2. One way Anova results of manipulation check

	US sample					TN sample				
	N	**Mean**	**SD**	*F*	*p*	**N**	**Mean**	**SD**	*F*	*p*
Typical design	286	4.39	1.65			239	5.26	1.97		
Atypical design	285	3.41	1.75	47.23	<.000	236	2.63	1.94	213.516	<.000
Total	571	3.90	1.77			475	3.95	2.35		

Subsequently, we move to test the established hypothesis and we start by MANCOVA analysis using SPSS to examine the deviation of consumers' responses when manipulating the different co-design factors.

Testing the Effects of co-Design Activities' Factors on Consumer Engagement

The overall model for consumer engagement was significant for both the US ($R^2_{adj} = .177$, $F(5, 565)=25.57$, $p<0.001$) and TN samples ($R^2_{adj} = .181$, $F(5, 469)=21.96$, $p<0.001$). The results revealed non-significant main effect on the overall consumer engagement state in both samples (F_{US} (1, 565) =3.055, p= .081>.05; F_{TN} (1, 469) =3.12, p= .078>.05). The insignificant mean differences between consumers engagement in packaging prototype customization ($M_{US^-Customization}$= 6.04, *se*= .043; $M_{TN^-Customization}$= 5.37, *se*= .045) and prototypes evaluation ($M_{US^-Evaluation}$= 5.93, *se*= .045; $M_{TN^-Evaluation}$= 5.25, *se*= .046) activities asserted the between subjects test's findings. Considering consumer engagement dimensions, consumers in both samples showed greater cognitive engagement in packaging prototypes evaluation ($M_{US^-Evaluation}$= 6.5, *se*= .039; $M_{TN^-Evaluation}$= 6, *se*= .051) than in prototype customization activity ($M_{US^-Customization}$= 6.35, *se*= .037; $M_{TN^-Customization}$= 5.83, *se*= .051). These findings attest that the cognitive efforts needed when evaluating the packaging prototypes are much demanding than when customizing them. Therefore, we approve the stated hypothesis H1a in both samples. Besides, the results showed that co-design activity significantly affects US and TN consumers' emotional engagement (F_{US} (1, 565) =9.365, p= .002<.01; F_{TN} (1, 469) =5.4, p= .021<.05). In both samples, consumers' revealed higher affective reactions and enjoyment when participating in packaging prototype customization ($M_{US^-Customization}$= 5.87, *se*= .056; $M_{TN^-Customization}$= 5.4, *se*= .058) than when evaluating the prototypes ($M_{US^-Evaluation}$= 5.62, *se*= .059; $M_{TN^-Evaluation}$= 5.2, *se*= .059). However, co-design activity has non-significant effect on US consumers' physical engagement (F_{US} (1, 565) =.006, p= .94>>>.05). This is in contrast to TN consumers who invested greater physical effort when customizing the packaging prototype ($M_{TN-Customization}$= 4.72, *se*= .084) than when evaluating the prototypes ($M_{TN-Evaluation}$= 4.38, *se*= .085).

According to co-design factors' interaction effects on consumer engagement, the findings in both samples revealed insignificant interaction effects. However, from visual perspective, the profile plots presented in the following figures, show non-parallel and, in some cases, intersect lines of the main effects, which yields to think that some potential interactions exist (see Figure 2 and Figure 3). Indeed, the difference in level between the two lines, which could be clearly observed in TN and US consumers' cognitive engagement profile plot and in US consumers' emotional and physical engagement profile plots, indicate a potential effect of co-design activity task.

Figure 2. Profile plots of the interaction effects between co-design activity and co-design task on US consumer engagement construct and its various dimensions

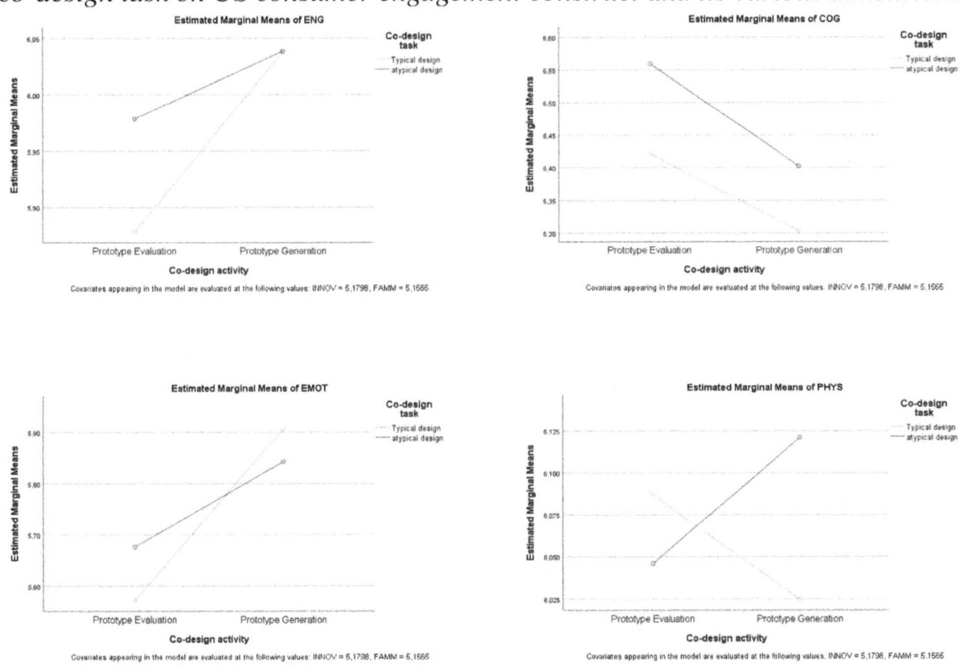

Figure 3. Profile plots of the interaction effects between co-design activity and co-design task on TN consumer engagement construct and its various dimensions

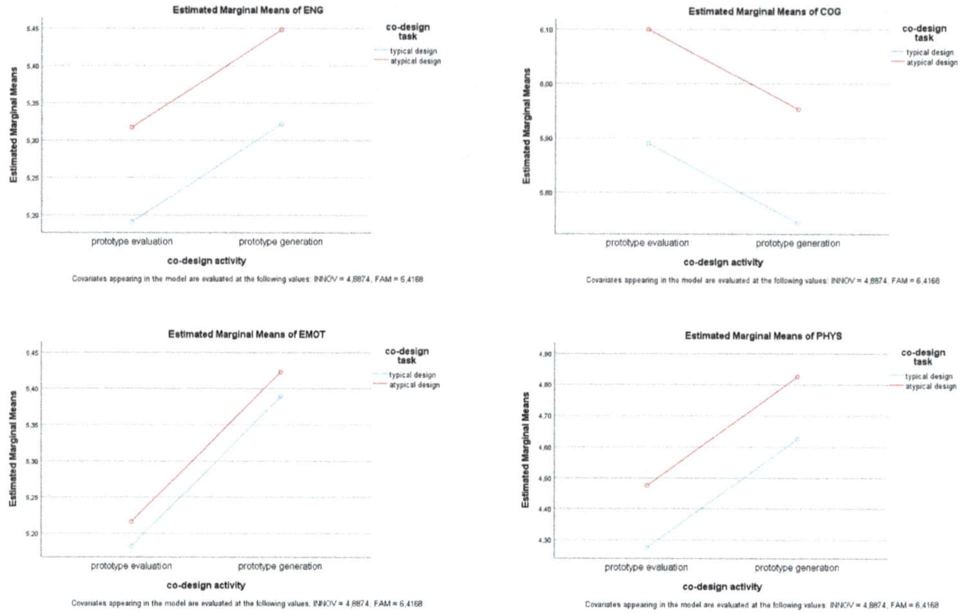

We performed a moderation analysis using PROCESS Macro (Model 1) and we got insignificant influence of the direct effect of co-design activity on US and TN consumers' engagement (β_{US} = -.110, t $_{US}$ = 1.75, p=.081>.05; β_{TN} = .116, t $_{TN}$= 1.77, p=.077>.05) (see table 3). These findings approve means' indifferences obtained with MANCOVA analysis and yield to disapprove the established hypothesis H1 across both samples. The results for the co-design activity and co-design task interaction (X×W) and the corresponding changes in R^2 showed no statistical significant effects even when looking narrowly to the effect of each of co-design task. Indeed, either to deal with typical (β_{US} = .16, t $_{US}$ = 1.8, p=.07>.05; β_{TN} = .167, t $_{TN}$= 1.84, p=.06>.05) or atypical packaging prototype(s) (β_{US} = .06, t $_{US}$ = .676, p=.5>>>.05; β_{TN} = .065, t $_{TN}$= .700, p=.48>>>.05), there is no significant difference of consumer engagement across different co-design activities. This disapproves H2 for both samples.

However, across both samples, the findings indicated that at a specific task, consumers' cognitive, emotional and physical engagement states significantly differ across co-design activities. Indeed, for both samples, the results showed significant influence of the task of evaluating atypical packaging prototypes on consumers' cognitive state (β_{US} = -.157, t $_{US}$ = -2.08, p=.04<.05; β_{TN} = -.300, t $_{TN}$= -2.9, p=.00<.01). Thus, consumers' participation in atypical prototype(s) evaluation stimulates great extent of cognitive effort than when participating in atypical prototype customization ($M_{US\text{-}Atypical\ evaluation}$ = 6.56 vs. $M_{US\text{-}Atypical\ customization}$ = 6.4; $M_{TN\text{-}Atypical\ evaluation}$ = 6.17 vs. $M_{TN\text{-}Atypical\ customization}$ = 5.87). However, as there is no statistically significant difference in cognitive engagement when dealing with typical prototypes, we disconfirm the hypotheses H2a.

In regards consumers' emotional engagement, the results (β_{US} = .251, t_{US} = 3.06, p=.00<.01; β_{TN} = .194, t_{TN} = 2.32, p=.021<.05) confirmed the means differences obtained with MANCOVA analysis, thus, we approve H1b in both samples. However, the results showed non-significant interaction effect (β_{US} = -.17, t_{US} = -1.03, p=.3>>>.05; β_{TN} = -.028, t_{TN} = -.17, p=.86>>>.05). When examining each of the co-design tasks separately, we notice that only when it is about dealing with typical design(s) (β_{US} = .335, t_{US} = 2.9, p=.00<.01) US consumers exhibited greater emotional engagement in customization than in evaluation activity ($M_{US\text{-}Typical\ evaluation}$ = 5.57 vs. $M_{US\text{-}Typical\ customization}$ = 5.9). This wasn't the case with TN sample. Hence, we disapprove H2b among TN consumers, but we partially confirm it among US consumers.

According to consumer's physical engagement, we got insignificant influence of co-design activity on US consumers (β_{US} = .006, t_{US} = .076, p=.94>>>.05) but positive and significant effect on TN consumers (β_{TN} = .338, t_{TN} = 2.78, p=.00<.01). These findings yield to disconfirm H1c among US sample and to confirm it among TN sample. However, for both samples, the results showed non-significant interaction effect. When examining closely each of the co-design tasks, we realize that only when it is about dealing with typical design(s) (β_{TN} = .356, t_{TN} = 2.12, p=.035<.05) TN consumers invest significant physical effort and energy when customizing typical packaging prototypes than when evaluating them ($M_{TN\text{-}Typical\ evaluation}$ = 4.26 vs. $M_{TN\text{-}Typical\ customization}$ = 4.62). In contrast, the results obtained among US consumers, showed insignificant difference between co-design tasks. Hence, we disapprove H2c among US sample and we partially confirm it among TN sample.

Effect of Consumer Engagement on Consumer-Product Relationship

At this level of analysis, we controlled for the effect of consumers' innovativeness and familiarity toward olive oil. The results are shown in table 3. In both samples, the findings revealed significant positive influence of consumers' overall engagement state on consumers' psychological ownership (β_{US} = .295, t_{US} = 6.85, p=.00<.01; β_{TN} = .255, t_{TN} = 5.3, p=.00<.01). Thus, consumers' engagement in packaging prototype customization/evaluation activity induces their feelings of ownership toward that packaging prototype. Additionally, consumers' emotional (β_{US} = .346, t_{US} = 8.18, p=.00<.01; β_{TN} = .288, t_{TN} = 6.06, p=.00<.01) and physical (β_{US} = .108, t_{US} =

2.606, p=.00<.01; β_{TN} = .186, t_{TN}= 3.97, p=.00<.01) engagement states positively influence their ownership psychology toward the resulting packaging prototype. The results confirmed that consumers' self-investment when customizing/evaluating a packaging prototype build up the feeling of ownership toward that packaging. Accordingly, for both samples, we confirm H3, H3b and H3c and we disconfirm H3a.

To test the effect of consumer engagement on his intention to purchase the product, we controlled for the effect of consumer's innovativeness and familiarity toward olive oil, as well as, his previous purchase behavior of this product. The results presented in table 3 show that US consumers' overall engagement (β_{US} = .185, t_{US} = 4.24, p=.00<.01), cognitive engagement (β_{US} = .118, t_{US} = 2.84, p=.00<.01) and emotional engagement (β_{US} = .182, t_{US} = 4.17, p=.00<.01) positively and significantly influence their purchase intention toward the product they participated in its packaging customization/evaluation. However, devoting physical effort in packaging prototype customization/evaluation has no effect on consumers' purchase intention (β_{US} = .07, t_{US} = 1.708, p>.05). Therefore, for US sample we confirm H4, H4a and H4b, but we disapprove the H4c. According to TN sample, the results indicate insignificant overall models. Accordingly, we disapprove the established hypothesis H4, H4a, H4b and H4c for TN sample.

We continued the analysis by testing the fifth hypothesis. In both samples, the findings revealed significant positive influence of consumers' psychological ownership on consumers' purchase intention (βUS = .178, t US (569) = 4.37, p=.00<.01; βTN = .403, t TN (473) = 9.55, p=.00<.01). In other words, consumers feeling of ownership toward the packaging prototype they customized/highly evaluated induce to great extent his purchase intention toward the product. Hence, we confirm H5 for both samples.

Additional Tests to Explore the Co-Design–Commitment Mechanism

After testing and validating this research core hypotheses, we aim to expand this research analytical scope to deepen our understanding of how engagement in co-design activities shapes consumers' relationship with the product.

Direct effect of co-design activity on consumer-product relationship. We conducted univariate analysis (ANOVA) for means' differences between treatment groups followed by linear regression analysis. For both samples, consumers showed great ownership feeling toward their customized packaging prototype ($M_{US\text{-}Customization}$= 5.06, *se*= .067; $M_{TN\text{-}Customization}$= 5.56, *se*= .048) than toward the prototype they highly evaluated ($M_{US\text{-}Evaluation}$= 4.30, *se*= .043; $M_{TN\text{-}Evaluation}$= 4.96, *se*= .049). These mean differences are supported by linear regression results, showing a significant positive effect of co-design activity on consumers' feelings of ownership in both the U.S. (β = .308, t = 7.73, p < .01) and Tunisia (β = .369, t = 8.64, p < .01), highlighting the importance of engaging consumers in packaging prototype customization to foster a sense of possession toward the output.

According to co-design activity effect on consumers' purchase intention; we got different results across both samples. Indeed, the findings revealed insignificant direct effect of co-design activity on US consumers' intention to purchase the product ($F(1, 569)=.147$, $p>>>0.5$), in contrast to TN consumers activities ($F(1, 473)=28.62$, $p<0.001$). Indeed, TN consumers are more intend to purchase olive oil packed in a packaging they participated in its prototype customization (M_{TN}-$_{Customization}$= 5.36, *se*= .057) more than in a packaging they participated in its prototype evaluation (M_{TN}-$_{Evaluation}$= 5.19, *se*= .058). Linear regression analysis indicated significant positive effect ($\beta_{TN} = .239$, $t_{US} = 5.35$, $p=.000<.01$) indorsing the relevance of involving consumers in packaging prototype customization to provoke their intention to purchase the product.

Indirect effect of co-design activity on consumer-product relationship. For mediation analysis, we used PROCESSv3.3 Macro method (Hayes, 2017). Precisely, the main reason of PROCESS Macro usage is to test which of the indirect effects of co-design activity (X) on consumers' psychological ownership and purchase intention (Y) through consumer engagement (M) were significant. Based on previous results, we take into account the insignificance of some direct relationships as a reasonable precondition of explaining the presence or absence of indirect effect of co-design activity on consumer-product relationship through consumers' engagement states. Indeed, the absence of simple causal relation between independent variable (X) and mediator variable (M) or between mediator variable and dependent variable (Y) imposes evidence of absence of indirect relationship between X and Y.

The direct positive and significant effect of co-design activity on consumers' psychological ownership is estimated as $c'= .687$ ($t_{US}(566)= 7.6$; $p<<<.01$, [.509; .864]) for US sample and $c'= .502$ ($t_{TN}(470)= 7.317$; $p<<<.01$, [.636; .621]) for TN sample. The findings revealed significant positive indirect effect of co-design activity on US and TN consumers' ownership psychology through their emotional engagement ($ab_{US} = .087$; $Boot.LLCI_{US}= .026$, $Boot.ULCI_{US}= .118$; $ab_{TN} = .041$; $Boot.LLCI_{TN}= .003$, $Boot.ULCI_{TN}= .091$). Specifically, these results indicated that regarding US and TN consumers' who participated in packaging prototypes customization, those who were emotionally engaged in the activity, they were, respectively, on average, 0.087 and 0.041 unit higher in their ownership feeling toward the packaging. The results of the total effect of co-design activity on US ($c= .773$, $t_{US}(566)= 8.23$; $p<<<.01$, [.589; .958) and TN ($c= .542$, $t_{TN}(470)= 7.71$; $p<<<.01$, [.404; .680]) consumers' psychological ownership indicated that those who were emotionally engaged in packaging customization activity were, on average and respectively, 0.773 and 0.542 units higher in their ownership feeling than those who participated in prototypes evaluation. Looking closely to the difference of indirect effect between the TN and US sample, it is obvious that being emotionally engaged in the co-design activity count greatly for US consumers' ownership feeling development toward the activity outcome than for TN consumers (ab_{US} = .087> ab_{TN} = .041).

For TN sample, previous analysis shed the light on the potential existence of indirect effect of co-design activity on consumers' psychological ownership through their physical engagement state. The mediation analysis revealed significant positive indirect effect (ab_{TN} = .028; Boot.LLCI$_{TN}$= .005, Boot.ULCI$_{TN}$= .061) demonstrating that devoting great extent of physical effort and determination induces consumers' feeling of ownership toward the developed prototype with 0.028 units higher than their ownership feeling toward the favorably evaluated packaging prototype. Moreover, the significance of the indirect effect of co-design activity on US consumers' purchase intention through their cognitive engagement (ab_{US} = -.035; Boot.LLCI$_{US}$= -.083, Boot.ULCI$_{US}$= -.004) indicates that, consumers' cognitive engagement perfectly mediates the effect of co-design activity on consumers' purchase intention toward an olive oil packed in the customized/favorably evaluated packaging prototype. The negative sign of this indirect effect, resulting from the product of opposite signs of the coefficients of the direct paths (a_{US}= -.137, p= .011; b_{US} = .256, p=.005), designates that consumers' cognitive engagement negatively mediates the effect of co-design activity on consumers' purchase intention. In other words, as path *a* is negative for the reason that prototype customization activity reduces cognitive effort devotion and path *b* is positive as intensifying the reduction of cognitive effort increases consumer purchase intention, both of these signs create negative indirect effect. Particularly, these results indicated that consumers who experienced lower cognitive effort are, on average, 0.015 unit higher in their purchase purchase intention. The findings confirm the full mediator role of cognitive engagement in the relationship between co-design activity and US consumers' purchase intention.

Similarly, the findings revealed insignificant direct negative effect of co-design activity on US consumers' purchase intention as *c'*= -.082 (t_{US} (565)= -.714; p>>>.05, [-.307; .143]). Interestingly, the significance of the indirect effect (ab_{US} = .062; Boot.LLCI$_{US}$= .017, Boot.ULCI$_{US}$= .121) indicate that customizing the prototype boosts enjoyment, enthusiasm, and emotional involvement, which in turn increase consumers' intention to purchase the product with a .062-unit.

Table 3. Results of liner regression analysis

	US sample						TN sample					
	Overall model			Model parameters			Overall model			Model parameters		
	R^2	F	p	β	t	p	R^2	F	P	β	T	P
Consumer engagement												
Own.Psy→P. Int	.055	19.10	.000	.178	4.37	.000	.163	91.28	.000	.403	9.55	.000
Eng→Own.Psy	.136	46.92	.000	.295	6.850	.000	.103	28.07	.000	.255	5.3	.000
Cog.Eng→Own.Psy	.065	.367	n.s.	.026	.606	n.s.	.049	.015	n.s.	.006	.124	n.s.
Emot.Eng→Own.Psy	.163	66.95	.000	.346	8.18	.000	.118	36.57	.000	.288	6.06	.000
Phys.Eng→Own.Psy	.076	6.8	.009	.108	2.606	.009	.080	15.8	.000	.186	3.97	.000
Eng→P. Int	.117	18.012	.000	.185	4.24	.000	.010	.004	n.s.	-.003	-.063	n.s.
Cog.Eng→P. Int	.102	8.09	.000	.118	2.84	.005	.011	.484	n.s.	-.032	-.696	n.s.
Emot.Eng→P. Int	.116	17.38	.000	.182	4.17	.000	.012	1.04	n.s.	.051	1.02	n.s.
Phys.Eng→P. Int	.094	2.92	n.s.	.07	1.708	n.s.	.012	.961	n.s.	-.048	-.980	n.s.
Consumer-product relation												
CA→Own.Psy	.095	59.81	.000	.308	7.73	.000	.136	74.7	.000	.369	8.64	.000
CA→ P. Int	.000	.147	n.s.	-.016	-.383	n.s.	.057	28.62	.000	.239	5.35	.000

DISCUSSION

Through the S-O-R framework, this study offers a fresh perspective on how consumer engagement in different co-design contexts shape consumer-product relationship. Across both samples, consumers showed similar engagement whether customizing or evaluating packaging prototypes, challenging the assumption that engagement is strongly context-dependent. A closer look at engagement's dimensions helps explain this pattern: evaluation demanded more cognitive effort, emotional engagement peaked during customization, and physical effort varied by sample. TN consumers, more familiar with olive oil, invested more physical effort in customization, while US consumers showed similar effort across tasks. From a human–computer interaction perspective, these findings highlight how cultural familiarity and product meaning shape user interaction with co-design interfaces, extending HCI research by demonstrating that engagement with interactive systems is culturally situated rather than uniform. This underscores the need for culturally adaptive co-design toolkits that align task structure, feedback, and interaction complexity with users' contextual knowledge and experiential backgrounds.

The non-significant interaction effect of co-design activity and design task was unexpected. Across both samples, engagement and its dimensions remained largely unchanged. Looking at the consumer–product relationship, our findings show that psychological ownership reliably boosts purchase intention in both samples. Customized or highly evaluated prototypes carry symbolic meaning that resonates with consumers' preferences and identification. As consumers identify more strongly with the prototype, their motivation to acquire the product increases.

The hands-on, autonomous nature of customization deepened both US and TN consumers' stronger psychological ownership when customizing the packaging prototype. Their sense of control and self-expression, fostering a closer emotional connection than simple evaluation. This made the customized prototype feel personally theirs. However, the effect on purchase intention differed across samples. For TN consumers, customization significantly increased purchase intention, while for US consumers it did not, instead, their purchase intention rose when they were cognitively and emotionally engaged in the activity. In the US case, to drive willingness to buy the product, mental effort, enthusiasm, and enjoyment mattered far more than physical effort devoted in participatory activity. For TN consumers, engagement didn't shape purchase intention. Their choices rely more on habitual or product-related factors, with psychological ownership being the main influence identified in this study.

In general, this study showed that strengthening the U.S. consumer–olive oil relationship requires engaging consumers in packaging prototype customization through emotionally rich experiences. At this level, based on recent research assumptions, we believe that AI-driven personalization (Witkowski & Wodecki, 2025), gamified design elements (lopes et al., 2024), and real-time visual or social feedback can enhance immersion, enjoyment, and perceived agency, thereby compensating for lower cultural familiarity with the product (Li & Sun, 2025). In contrast, the Tunisian consumer–olive oil relationship is already grounded in strong symbolic and cultural meanings; thus, simple involvement in packaging customization is sufficient, regardless of the level of experiential intensity. These findings suggest that advanced interactive technologies should be deployed strategically rather than uniformly, supporting the design of adaptive co-design systems that calibrate emotional stimulation and technological sophistication to users' cultural context and prior product relationships.

CONCLUSION

From a human–computer interaction perspective, this chapter highlights how technology-mediated co-design platforms function as interactive environments that shape consumer cognitive, emotional and behavioral engagement. By examining prototype generation and evaluation as distinct interaction modes, our results suggest that effective co-design toolkits should provide intuitive interfaces that reduce cognitive load, and integrate feedback mechanisms that reinforce users' sense of contribution and control. By aligning interaction design with users' cognitive, emotional, and behavioral engagement, firms can transform co-design platforms into human-centered systems that foster meaningful participation, experiential value, and innovation outcomes. In addition, this study highlights how co-design effects differ across cultures. For example, physical engagement is critical for Tunisian consumers, whereas emotional engagement drives US consumers' connection with the product. Managerially, firms should ensure the difference between samples and make sure that co-design activities are engaging, enjoyable, and emotionally stimulating.

Theoretical Implications

This research established several interesting theoretical contributions. First, we enriched the co-design and value co-creation literatures with the activity theory by examining how different co-design activities differentially shape engagement. By distinguishing between co-design activities and co-design tasks, the study demonstrates that co-design is not a monolithic experience but a set of heterogeneous interaction modes with distinct psychological consequences. In addition, rather than treating engagement as a single latent state, this study confirms the multidimensionality of consumer engagement and revealed that cognitive, emotional, and physical engagement states respond differently to design stimuli and tasks. This nuanced perspective explains why overall engagement levels may appear similar across activities, while their underlying mechanisms diverge. Moreover, prior research has paid limited attention to how participatory and interactive co-creation experiences contribute to the development of consumer–product relationships. This study addresses this gap by demonstrating how co-design experiences shape this relationship through both emotional and behavioral mechanisms. Finally, this research extends HCI literature with cross-cultural lenses highlighting to contextualize this interactivity within cultural and product-specific contexts.

Managerial Implications

From a managerial perspective, this study offers various practical insights. First, we demonstrated that not all co-design activities serve the same strategic objective. For instance, prototype customization is particularly effective for fostering emotional engagement and psychological ownership, whereas prototype evaluation is better suited for eliciting cognitive involvement and thoughtful comparison. Therefore, practitioners should align co-design activities with specific objectives, such as relationship building versus insight generation. In addition, this study's findings highlighted the importance of cultural adaptation in co-design strategies. For example, for markets where the co-design product is not familiar, firms must actively stimulate emotional and cognitive engagement to drive buying decisions. Finally, from technological perspective, the study highlights the value of human-centered co-design toolkits that minimize cognitive overload while maximizing user autonomy, real-time responses, gamified elements, or AI-driven recommendation systems may further enhance engagement and strengthen consumer–product relationships.

Limitations and Future Research

While this study provides initial insights into how co-design factors influence consumer–product relationship, it has some limitations. We focused on cognitive, emotional, and physical engagement, but behavioral engagement was not captured. Future research could explore this path.

This study treated consumers broadly. We highlight the value of examining specific groups (e.g. lead users, brand communities, or skilled versus less-skilled participants) could reveal how different types of consumers respond to customization and evaluation tasks. Similarly, with the development of AI technologies, integrating analytical tools to track choices in customization platforms would allow deeper insight into attribute selection and decision processes. In addition, caution is needed in generalizing results to products with more technical or manufacturing complexities. Extending research across countries, product categories, and different stages of packaging development would further enrich understanding of how co-design shapes consumer–product relationships globally.

ACKNOWLEDGMENTS

I would like to sincerely thank Prof. Polymeros Chrysochou from Aarhus University for his valuable support during the data collection process. His assistance and collaboration were instrumental to the successful completion of this research.

Declaration of AI use. The author acknowledge the use of ChatGPT (version 2024-03) for language refinement in this manuscript. The tool was employed exclusively to enhance readability and clarity. The authors affirm that all idea generation, intellectual content, analysis, and interpretations are entirely their own.

REFERENCES

Abid, M. F., Shamim, A., Khan, Z., & Khan, I. (2022). Value creation or value destruction: Conceptualizing the experiential nature of value-in-use. *Journal of Consumer Behaviour*, *21*(3), 583–601.

Ajzen, I. (1991). The theory of planned behavior. *Organizational Behavior and Human Decision Processes*, *50*(2), 179–211.

Allen, B. J., Chandrasekaran, D., & Basuroy, S. (2018). Design crowdsourcing: The impact on new product performance of sourcing design solutions from the "Crowd". *Journal of Marketing*, *82*(2), 106–123.

Ammar, O., Chrysochou, P., & Trabelsi Trigui, I. (2017, May). Consumer Perceptions And Response Toward Co-Designed Packaging. In *22nd International Conference on Corporate and Marketing Communications*, Zaragoza, Spain, May 4-5

Ashley, C., & Tuten, T. (2015). Creative strategies in social media marketing: An exploratory study of branded social content and consumer engagement. *Psychology and Marketing*, *32*(1), 15–27.

Atakan, S. S., Bagozzi, R. P., & Yoon, C. (2014). Consumer Participation in the Design and Realization Stages of Production: How Self production Shapes Consumer Evaluations and Relationships to Products. *International Journal of Research in Marketing*, *31*(4), 395–408.

Booz, Allen, & Hamilton (1982), New Products Management for the 1980s.

Brodie, R. J., Hollebeek, L. D., Jurić, B., & Ilić, A. (2011). Customer engagement: Conceptual domain, fundamental propositions, and implications for research. *Journal of Service Research*, *14*(3), 252–271.

Christensen, B. T., Ball, L. J., & Halskov, K. (2017). *Analysing design thinking: Studies of cross-cultural co-creation*. CRC Press.

Chrysochou, P., Tiganis, A., Trigui, I. T., & Grunert, K. G. (2021). A Cross-Cultural Study on Consumer Preferences for Olive Oil. *Food Quality and Preference*, •••, 104460.

Claffey, E., & Brady, M. (2014). A model of consumer engagement in a virtual customer environment. *Journal of Customer Behaviour, 13*(4), 325–346.

Coughlan, P., & Duff, P. A. (1994). Same task, different activities: Analysis of SLA task from an Activity Theory perspective. *Vygotskian approaches to second language research*, 173-193.

Cui, T., Ye, H., & Teo, H. H. (2011). Value co-creation with customers through design toolkits: The importance of preference fit and *psychological* ownership. In the 9th European Conference on Information Systems, ECIS

Davis, A., Tuckey, M., Gwilt, I., & Wallace, N. (2023). Understanding co-design practice as a process of "welldoing". *International Journal of Art & Design Education, 42*(2), 278–293.

Eggert, A., Ulaga, W., Frow, P., & Payne, A. (2018). Conceptualizing and communicating value in business markets: From value in exchange to value in use. *Industrial Marketing Management, 69*, 80–90.

Franke, N., & Piller, F. (2004). Value creation by toolkits for user innovation and design: The case of the watch market. *Journal of Product Innovation Management, 21*(6), 401–415.

Fuchs, C., & Schreier, M. (2011). Customer empowerment in new product development. *Journal of Product Innovation Management, 28*(1), 17–32.

Füller, J., Hutter, K., & Faullant, R. (2011). Why co-creation experience matters? Creative experience and its impact on the quantity and quality of creative contributions. *R & D Management, 41*(3), 259–273.

Geiser, C., Litson, K., Bishop, J., Keller, B. T., Burns, G. L., Servera, M., & Shiffman, S. (2015). Analyzing person, situation and person× situation interaction effects: Latent state-trait models for the combination of random and fixed situations. *Psychological Methods, 20*(2), 165. PMID: 25528499

Griffin, M. A., Parker, S. K., & Neal, A. (2008). Is behavioral engagement a distinct and useful construct? *Industrial and Organizational Psychology: Perspectives on Science and Practice, 1*(1), 48–51.

Hamari, J., Shernoff, D. J., Rowe, E., Coller, B., Asbell-Clarke, J., & Edwards, T. (2016). Challenging games help students learn: An empirical study on engagement, flow and immersion in game-based learning. *Computers in Human Behavior, 54*, 170–179.

Hamdi-Kidar, L., Keinz, P., Le Nagard, E., & Vernette, E. (2019). Comparing lead users to emergent-nature consumers as sources of innovation at early stages of new product development. *Journal of Product Innovation Management, 36*(5), 616–631.

Hatchuel, A., & Weil, B. (2003). A new approach of innovative Design: an introduction to CK theory. *In the 14th International Conference on Engineering Design*, Stockholm.

Hendrayanti, S., & Nurauliya, V. (2021). Building competitive advantage through innovation, creativity, product quality. *BASKARA: Journal of Business and Entrepreneurship, 4*(1), 85–94.

Herter, M. M., Shuqair, S., Pinto, D. C., Mattila, A. S., & Zandonai Pontin, P. (2023). Does crowdsourcing necessarily lead to brand engagement? The role of crowdsourcing cues and relationship norms on customer-brand relationships. *Journal of Product and Brand Management, 32*(7), 988–1004.

Hoffman, B., & Nadelson, L. (2010). Motivational engagement and video gaming: A mixed methods study. *Educational Technology Research and Development, 58*(3), 245–270.

Hollebeek, L. (2011). Exploring customer brand engagement: Definition and themes. *Journal of Strategic Marketing, 19*(7), 555–573.

Hsieh, S. H., & Chang, A. (2016). The psychological mechanism of brand co-creation engagement. *Journal of Interactive Marketing, 33*(1), 13–26.

Joule, R. V., & Beauvois, J. L. (1989). Une théorie psychosociale: La théorie de l'engagement. Perspectives commerciales. [French Edition]. *Recherche et Applications en Marketing, 4*(1), 79–90.

Joule, R. V., & Beauvois, J. L. (2002). *Petit traité de manipulation à l'usage des honnêtes gens*. Presses Universitaires de Grenoble.

Jussila, I., Tarkiainen, A., Sarstedt, M., & Hair, J. F. (2015). Individual psychological ownership: Concepts, evidence, and implications for research in marketing. *Journal of Marketing Theory and Practice, 23*(2), 121–139.

Kahn, W. A. (1990). Psychological conditions of personal engagement and disengagement at work. *Academy of Management Journal, 33*(4), 692–724.

Kamboj, S., Sarmah, B., Gupta, S., & Dwivedi, Y. (2018). Examining branding co-creation in brand communities on social media: Applying the paradigm of Stimulus-Organism-Response. *International Journal of Information Management*, *39*, 169–185.

Kiesler, C. A. (1971). *The psychology of commitments: Experiments linking behavior to belief.* Academic Press.

Kim, J., & Lennon, S. J. (2013). Effects of reputation and website quality on online consumers' emotion, perceived risk and purchase intention: Based on the stimulus-organism-response model. *Journal of Research in Interactive Marketing*, *7*(1), 33–56.

Kim, M. J., Lee, C. K., & Jung, T. (2020). Exploring consumer behavior in virtual reality tourism using an extended stimulus-organism-response model. *Journal of Travel Research*, *59*(1), 69–89.

Lawson, R. (2002). Consumer knowledge structures: Background issues and introduction. *Psychology and Marketing*, *19*(6), 447–455.

Leont'ev, A. (1974). The problem of activity in psychology. *Social Psychology*, *13*(2), 4–33.

Li, Y., & Sun, M. (2025). The impact of perceived interactivity on purchase intention in interactive video: A CAB-based chain mediation model of empathy, immersion, and arousal. *Frontiers in Communication*, *10*, 1615509.

Liu, H., Chu, H., Huang, Q., & Chen, X. (2016). Enhancing the flow experience of consumers in China through interpersonal interaction in social commerce. *Computers in Human Behavior*, *58*, 306–314.

Lopes, J. M., Gomes, S., & Rodrigues, I. (2024). Playing the gamification and co-creation game: A bibliometric literature review. *Management Review Quarterly*, *74*(1), 353–376.

López-Mas, L., Claret, A., Bermúdez, A., Llauger, M., & Guerrero, L. (2022). Co-creation with consumers for packaging design validated through implicit and explicit methods: Exploratory effect of visual and textual attributes. *Foods*, *11*(9), 1183. PMID: 35563908

Martinez, B., & Seock, Y. K. (2017). Crowdsourcing the design process: The influence of consumer characteristics on participation and behavioral intentions. *Journal of Marketing Management and Consumer Behavior*, *2*(1).

Martinez, M. G. (2015). Solver engagement in knowledge sharing in crowdsourcing communities: Exploring the link to creativity. *Research Policy*, *44*(8), 1419–1430.

Mathew, S. M., Nayak, S., & Rao, V. (2025). Determinants of online apparel mass customization: A decade in review. *Journal of Fashion Marketing and Management*, *29*(1), 113–136.

Mehrabian, A., & Russell, A. (1974). *An approach to environmental psychology*. MIT Press.

Meineri, S., & Guéguen, N. (2014). Foot-in-the-door and action identification. Binding communication applied to environmental conservation. *European Review of Applied Psychology*, *64*(1), 3–11.

Mirabi, V., Akbariyeh, H., & Tahmasebifard, H. (2015). A study of factors affecting on customers purchase intention. [JMEST]. *Journal of Multidisciplinary Engineering Science and Technology*, *2*(1).

Nardi, B. A. (1996). Activity theory and human-computer interaction. *Context and consciousness: Activity theory and human-computer interaction, 436*(1), 7-16.Chen, T., Dodds, S., Finsterwalder, J., Witell, L., Cheung, L., Falter, M., ... & McColl-Kennedy, J. R. (2021). Dynamics of wellbeing co-creation: a psychological ownership perspective. *Journal of Service Management*, *32*(3), 383–406.

Orth, D. (2019). *Designing meaningful objects*. University of Technology Sydney.

Pierce, J. L., Kostova, T., & Dirks, K. T. (2003). The state of psychological ownership: Integrating and extending a century of research. *Review of General Psychology*, *7*(1), 84–107.

Piller, F., & Salvador, F (2016) Design toolkits, organizational capabilities, and firm performance. *Revolutionizing Innovation: Users, Communities, and Open Innovation*, 1.

Prahalad, C. K., & Ramaswamy, V. (2004). Co-creation experiences: The next practice in value creation. *Journal of Interactive Marketing*, *18*(3), 5–14.

Ramaswamy, V., & Ozcan, K. (2018). What is co-creation? An interactional creation framework and its implications for value creation. *Journal of Business Research*, *84*, 196–205.

Rosch, E., & Mervis, C. B. (1975). Family resemblances: Studies in the internal structure of categories. *Cognitive Psychology*, *7*(4), 573–605.

Sanders, E. B. N., & Stappers, P. J. (2014). Probes, toolkits and prototypes: Three approaches to making in codesigning. *CoDesign*, *10*(1), 5–14.

Silayoi, P., & Speece, M. (2004). Packaging and purchase decisions: An exploratory study on the impact of involvement level and time pressure. *British Food Journal*.

Simms, C., & Trott, P. (2010). Packaging development: A conceptual framework for identifying new product opportunities. *Marketing Theory*, *10*(4), 397–415.

Sonnentag, S. (2017). A task-level perspective on work engagement: A new approach that helps to differentiate the concepts of engagement and burnout. *Burnout Research*, *5*, 12–20.

Steyer, R., Schmitt, M., & Eid, M. (1999). Latent state–trait theory and research in personality and individual differences. *European Journal of Personality*, *13*(5), 389–408.

Stoner, J. L., Loken, B., & Stadler Blank, A. (2018). The name game: How naming products increases psychological ownership and subsequent consumer evaluations. *Journal of Consumer Psychology*, *28*(1), 130–137.

Tarute, A., Nikou, S., & Gatautis, R. (2017). Mobile application driven consumer engagement. *Telematics and Informatics*, *34*(4), 145–156.

Vallacher, R. R., & Wegner, D. M. (2012). Action identification theory. *Handbook of theories of social psychology*, 1, 327-348.

Van Doorn, J., Lemon, K. N., Mittal, V., Nass, S., Pick, D., Pirner, P., & Verhoef, P. C. (2010). Customer engagement behavior: Theoretical foundations and research directions. *Journal of Service Research*, *13*(3), 253–266.

Vargo, S. L., Maglio, P. P., & Akaka, M. A. (2008). On value and value co-creation: A service systems and service logic perspective. *European Management Journal*, *26*(3), 145–152.

Varshneya, G., Das, G., & Khare, A. (2017). Experiential value: A review and future research directions. *Marketing Intelligence & Planning*, *35*(3), 339–357.

Vivek, S. D., Beatty, S. E., & Morgan, R. M. (2012). Customer engagement: Exploring customer relationships beyond purchase. *Journal of Marketing Theory and Practice*, *20*(2), 122–146.

Witkowski, A., & Wodecki, A. (2025). Where does AI play a major role in the new product development and product management process?. *Management Review Quarterly*, 1-38.

Wu, Y. L., & Li, E. Y. (2018). Marketing mix, customer value, and customer loyalty in social commerce: A stimulus-organism-response perspective. *Internet Research*, *28*(1), 74–104.

Xie, X. (2023). The cognitive process of creative design: A perspective of divergent thinking. *Thinking Skills and Creativity*, *48*, 101266.

Yuksel, M., Darmody, A., & Venkatraman, M. (2019). When consumers own their work: Psychological ownership and consumer citizenship on crowdsourcing platforms. *Journal of Consumer Behaviour*, *18*(1), 3–11.

Zhang, J. (2022). Knowledge learning with crowdsourcing: A brief review and systematic perspective. *IEEE/CAA Journal of Automatica Sinica*, 9(5), 749-762.

Chapter 8
Exploring Guest Experiences With Virtual Reality in Hospitality:
Insights on Engagement and Emotional Well-Being

Sihem ben Saad
https://orcid.org/0000-0003-3034-9206
Higher School of Sciences and Technology of Design, University of Manouba, Tunis, Tunisia

ABSTRACT

This chapter examines the adoption of virtual reality (VR) in hospitality and its impact on guest experiences, expectations, and emotional well-being. Using qualitative methods, semi-structured interviews were conducted with 15 participants navigating VR simulations of hotel environments, including rooms, common areas, and leisure spaces. Thematic analysis reveals that VR offers both functional and emotional value, enhancing planning, cognitive engagement, and informed decision-making. Interactivity supports focused attention and meaningful social experiences, while immersive visual and auditory cues promote relaxation and psychological restoration. Individual differences, such as technology familiarity and gender, could influence engagement and perceptions. Findings highlight VR's dual role in facilitating cognitive exploration and fostering emotional well-being, offering actionable insights for designing guest-centered, immersive experiences.

DOI: 10.4018/979-8-3373-6450-6.ch008

1. INTRODUCTION

The hospitality industry is undergoing a profound transformation driven by immersive technologies. These tools are reshaping how guests experience, evaluate, and interpret hotel services. Modern travelers increasingly seek personalized, emotionally engaging, and meaningful experiences rather than purely functional services (Barta, Gurrea, & Flavián, 2023–2025; Buhalis et al., 2023; Bretos et al., 2024). In this context, virtual reality (VR) has emerged as a powerful innovation. It allows guests to explore hotel facilities, visualize room layouts, and interact with virtual environments before their stay (Cucinella et al., 2025; Flavián et al., 2021; Luan & Phan, 2024; Valmorisco et al., 2024).

Beyond these functional advantages, VR can also generate emotional and restorative benefits. Prior work shows that VR environments may promote relaxation, psychological recovery, and stress reduction. These effects are particularly relevant for individuals facing geographic, financial, or mobility constraints, as well as during crisis situations such as pandemics or natural disasters (Flavián et al., 2019; Kim et al., 2021; Riches et al., 2024). Leading hotel brands have recognized these opportunities. Marriott's "VRoom" and Hilton's VR tours illustrate how immersive experiences can support decision-making while also creating emotional engagement (Fan et al., 2022; Abou-Shouk et al., 2024; AAnter, 2025).

Despite growing interest, research in hospitality remains largely focused on functional or transactional outcomes, including satisfaction, purchase intentions, and trust in digital systems (Buhalis et al., 2023; Fan et al., 2022; Flavián et al., 2019; Kim et al., 2021; Luan & Phan, 2024; Loureiro et al., 2021). Emotional and psychological experiences are still understudied. Clinical research, however, has demonstrated VR's relaxing potential in various populations, including palliative care patients and young adults (Riches et al., 2024). Emerging studies in leisure and tourism also highlight this potential, but the evidence remains limited (Cieślik, 2025; Cho et al., 2024; Martínez-Molés et al., 2022; Tussyadiah et al., 2018). Moreover, relaxation is often treated as a short-lived state leading to outcomes such as purchase decisions, rather than as a meaningful emotional experience on its own (Suntornteerasut et al., 2024).

Individual differences may also shape immersive experiences. Gender and technological familiarity can influence perceptual, cognitive, and emotional responses to VR environments (Martínez-Molés et al., 2022; Loureiro et al., 2021). These factors suggest the need for qualitative exploration. Quantitative approaches alone cannot capture the depth, nuance, and personal meaning of guests' emotional responses to VR.

Flow theory provides a relevant lens to analyze these experiences. It conceptualizes immersive activities as moments of deep engagement, intrinsic enjoyment, and emotional balance, which may promote relaxation and psychological restoration (Csikszentmihalyi, 1990). This perspective shifts the focus from purely functional outcomes to users' lived experiences.

This qualitative and exploratory study aims to understand how guests perceive VR hotel experiences, how these interactions may foster relaxation and well-being, and which factors support or hinder emotional impact. By emphasizing subjective experiences, personal interpretations, and emotional responses, this research enriches hospitality and human–computer interaction literature. It also offers practical insights for designing VR experiences that are engaging, restorative, and inclusive.

An overview of the chapter's structure is as follows. It first presents the literature and conceptual foundations, with particular attention to flow theory and its relevance to immersive technologies. It then explores the use of VR in hospitality, focusing on guest engagement and relaxation. The methodology section follows, outlining the sampling strategy, data collection process, and analytical approach. The results section details participants' perceptions, experiences, and well-being outcomes. The chapter concludes with the main theoretical contributions, managerial implications, and a discussion of limitations and future research directions.

2. LITERATURE REVIEW AND CONCEPTUAL FOUNDATIONS

2.1 Flow Theory

Flow theory serves as the primary theoretical foundation for this study, providing insights into how individuals experience deep engagement and satisfaction during immersive activities (Csikszentmihalyi, 1990). The theory posits that individuals enter a state of flow when they are fully absorbed in an activity. This state is characterized by high levels of enjoyment, concentration, and intrinsic motivation. Flow emerges when individuals perceive a balance between the challenges of the activity and their skill level. This balance creates a seamless and gratifying experience.

In the context of immersive technologies such as virtual reality (VR), flow theory is particularly relevant. VR environments are designed to foster deep engagement by stimulating users' sensory and cognitive capacities. When guests interact with VR, such as navigating virtual hotel tours or exploring destination simulations, they invest time and effort. This investment is rewarded by the immersive and enjoyable nature of the experience (Gaggioli et al., 2020).

Prior research has applied flow theory in multiple domains, including e-learning platforms (Chen et al., 2018), video games (Sweetser & Wyeth, 2005), and digital marketing (Hoffman & Novak, 2009). In these contexts, flow has been linked to positive outcomes such as engagement, satisfaction, and loyalty (Akar, 2021). In

VR, flow manifests through users' perceptions of pleasure and stimulation. It drives deeper exploration and emotional connection to the content.

Despite its relevance, few studies have examined the interplay between flow and psychological well-being in VR experiences, especially in service sectors like hospitality. This study addresses this gap by exploring how flow can explain positive outcomes from VR experiences, including perceived pleasure, sensory stimulation, and relaxation.

While models such as the Technology Acceptance Model (TAM) and the Stimuli-Organism-Response (SOR) framework are widely used in technology research, they have limitations for this study. TAM focuses on determinants of technology adoption, such as perceived ease of use and perceived usefulness (Davis et al., 1989). Although TAM offers insights into VR adoption, it does not fully capture experiential and affective dimensions such as engagement and intrinsic enjoyment. Similarly, the SOR model explains how external stimuli are processed to generate behavioral responses (Flavián et al., 2019). However, it often emphasizes a sequential process, without deeply exploring the psychological mechanisms that underlie immersive experiences (Mehrabian & Russell, 1974; Scherer et al., 2010).

In contrast, flow theory specifically addresses the experiential and emotional dimensions of VR. It is essential for understanding how VR transforms user experiences and contributes to well-being. This theory provides a robust framework for investigating how guests attain deep engagement, and how this engagement leads to emotional satisfaction and psychological enrichment (Csikszentmihalyi, 1997; Anderson et al., 2017). By choosing flow theory, this study goes beyond functional and behavioral outcomes to investigate the immersive, pleasurable, and transformative nature of VR experiences.

Flow theory aligns closely with the study's qualitative focus on subjective guest experiences. It emphasizes how VR environments foster emotional connection, engagement, and well-being, areas not fully addressed by TAM or SOR (Hoffman & Novak, 2009). Overall, flow theory offers a nuanced and holistic perspective on consumer experiences, highlighting the psychological states that lead to meaningful and impactful interactions with VR technology (Choi & Kim, 2022).

This study leverages flow theory to explore how VR hotel experiences may enhance guests' engagement, enjoyment, and emotional well-being. The qualitative, exploratory approach allows for an in-depth understanding of participants' perceptions, interpretations, and emotional responses. By focusing on lived experiences, this research contributes to hospitality literature and human–computer interaction studies. It also provides practical insights for designing VR experiences that are immersive, engaging, and restorative.

2.2. Enhancing User Experience Through Immersive Technologies

Immersive technologies (ImTs), including Virtual Reality (VR), Augmented Reality (AR), and Mixed Reality (MR), are transforming how users experience services across industries (Calvet et al., 2019). VR refers to a computer-generated, three-dimensional environment that allows users to interact with digital simulations of real-world scenarios through wearable devices such as head-mounted displays (HMDs) (Freina & Ott, 2015; Negut et al., 2016). Fully immersive VR experiences can be delivered via HMDs or multi-projected screens, while non-immersive setups using desktops or smartphones are also possible (Buttussi & Chittaro, 2023). These environments often consist of entirely computer-generated visuals or 360-degree imagery, viewable through VR HMDs (Araiza-Alba et al., 2021). The ability to track users' movements and provide sensory feedback creates a strong sense of immersion (Saghafian et al., 2020).

AR enhances the real world by overlaying virtual elements in real time, allowing interaction with both physical and digital objects simultaneously (Rodríguez-Abad et al., 2021). MR extends this interaction further by merging real-world components with virtual environments, producing a semi-virtual experience. Together, these technologies form the umbrella term extended reality (XR), which includes all forms of virtual and real environments and human–machine interactions enabled by wearable and computing technologies. Each immersive technology provides different levels of user engagement. VR offers full immersion into virtual environments, limiting real-world interactions. AR allows interaction with both virtual and physical elements. MR balances these aspects, integrating real-world components while maintaining virtual immersion.

Although these technologies are not new, their adoption has accelerated, especially in sectors like tourism (Mora-Serrano et al., 2021). ImTs are increasingly used in education and training through serious games that simulate real-life scenarios that are otherwise hard to reproduce safely (Gamberini et al., 2021). These applications prioritize learning and skill development rather than entertainment (Giessen, 2015; Feng et al., 2018; Saghafian et al., 2020). Organizations recognize that immersive technologies can reduce training time, lower infrastructure costs, improve productivity, and ensure safety (Saghafian et al., 2020). Software tools such as Unreal Engine (Dhalmahapatra et al., 2021), Unity (Matsas & Vosniakos, 2017), and Blender (Isleyen & Duzgun, 2019) are widely used to develop these virtual environments (Çakiroğlu & Gökoğlu, 2019).

In tourism, VR has reshaped how users experience destinations. VR allows tourists to explore destinations virtually, which enhances decision-making and perceptions of products or services (Guttentag, 2010; Neuhofer et al., 2014; Yung &

Khoo-Lattimore, 2017). This is particularly valuable when testing services physically before purchase is difficult. The adoption of VR in tourism has grown with decreasing hardware costs and standalone devices like Oculus GO or HTC Vive Focus. Yet, market expansion for VR devices has been slower than expected, posing challenges for understanding user interactions and developing innovative experiences (Flavián et al., 2019). VR headsets provide rich sensory and immersive experiences that increase user engagement. This is especially significant during the pre-purchase phase when tourists explore and select destinations (Marasco et al., 2018). Most research focuses on adoption, decision-making, and industry benefits (Barnes, 2016; Guttentag, 2010; Marasco et al., 2018; Tussyadiah et al., 2018). However, the concept of technological embodiment, how VR devices integrate with users' sensory and bodily functions, remains underexplored (Ihde, 1990; Tussyadiah et al., 2017). High levels of technological embodiment enhance immersion and sensory stimulation, influencing engagement and behavioral intentions toward a destination (Flavián et al., 2018).

VR helps tourism managers design optimal customer journeys, particularly before the actual experience (Lemon & Verhoef, 2016; Marasco et al., 2018; Tussyadiah et al., 2018). Understanding how technological embodiment affects user experience enables businesses to create compelling value propositions that leave lasting impressions. VR holds significant potential to transform consumer perceptions and behavior in tourism, supporting decision-making and influencing purchase intentions.

Given VR's growing impact on user experiences in digital platforms (Freina & Ott, 2015; Tussyadiah, 2017; Flavián et al., 2020), this study focuses specifically on the role of VR headsets. It examines how these devices may shape consumer perceptions, engagement, and relaxation within hospitality contexts.

2.3. Enhancing Engagement Through VR

Virtual Reality (VR) headsets play a central role in creating immersive tourism experiences by fostering active engagement with virtual environments. Through interactive interfaces, motion tracking, and dynamic 3D visuals, VR allows users to explore destinations in ways that traditional media cannot. This deeper interactivity encourages cognitive and behavioral involvement (Slater & Wilbur, 1997; Flavián et al., 2019).

Engagement in VR is driven by the responsiveness of the virtual environment. Users are not passive observers; they navigate, manipulate, and interact with digital elements. Such active involvement strengthens attention, focus, and participation (Cheong, 1995). It also promotes exploration and information-seeking behaviors, supporting decision-making processes, especially in tourism contexts where pre-experience evaluation of destinations is critical (Guttentag, 2010; Neuhofer et al., 2014).

VR further facilitates social and collaborative engagement. Shared virtual experiences allow users to interact with others within the environment, fostering social presence and cooperation (Epley et al., 2007; Jacobson et al., 2020; Rauschnabel & Ro, 2016). Humanized interactions, such as guided tours or group explorations, create opportunities for meaningful participation that extend beyond individual experiences (Söderlund & Jobs, 2016).

In tourism and experiential settings, VR redefines user engagement. By offering interactive and participatory platforms, VR encourages cognitive investment, sustained attention, and exploration. These elements collectively enhance overall engagement with both content and environment (Flavián et al., 2019).

Overall, VR headsets increase user engagement by enabling interactive exploration, active participation, and social interaction, fundamentally reshaping how individuals experience and interact with virtual tourism environments.

2.4. Enhancing Relaxation Through Virtual Reality

Relaxation has increasingly become a central goal in sectors where emotional experiences are crucial, such as tourism, wellness, and immersive entertainment environments. It is commonly defined as a pleasant, low-arousal emotional state, opposite to tension, stress, or anxiety, encompassing related feelings of calmness and serenity (Russell & Barrett, 1999; Watson & Tellegen, 1985). Physiologically, relaxation manifests as reduced autonomic nervous system activation, while cognitively, it reflects a mind freed from worries and intrusive thoughts. Beyond its emotional dimension, relaxation is associated with reduced stress, inner peace, and a sense of well-being (Benson, 2007; Lichstein, 1988), and has been shown to enhance customer satisfaction and even willingness to pay for products and services, particularly in tourism and immersive settings (Alexandris & Palialia, 1999; Huang & Hsu, 2010).

In tourism and wellness contexts, immersive technologies, particularly Virtual Reality (VR), play a pivotal role in promoting relaxation. VR experiences leverage multisensory stimulation to create a sense of presence that transports users away from real-world stressors, fostering a calming and emotionally restorative environment (Slater & Wilbur, 1997). Two factor, perceived enjoyment and sensory stimulation, emerge as key drivers of relaxation in immersive environments. Perceived enjoyment, defined as the intrinsic pleasure derived from an experience, has been shown to alleviate anxiety and enhance positive emotional states across multiple contexts, from therapeutic interventions to tourism activities. Sensory stimulation enriches these experiences by engaging multiple senses simultaneously, including visual, auditory, tactile, and olfactory inputs, creating immersive, memorable environments conducive to deep relaxation.

The interaction between perceived enjoyment and sensory stimulation in VR is particularly effective in inducing relaxation. For instance, immersive tourism experiences like "starry-sky simulations" provide soothing multisensory escapes that enhance travelers' emotional states while delivering memorable experiences (Bjelajac et al., 2021). Similarly, in healthcare and therapeutic settings, VR environments reduce stress and pain, improve mood, and enhance psychological resilience (Slater & Wilbur, 1997; Chirico, 2016; Dascal et al., 2017). Pediatric studies, for example, show that VR sessions for hospitalized children can reduce depressive symptoms and anxiety while increasing motivation and self-esteem .

By strategically combining multisensory stimulation and enjoyable immersive content, VR provides a powerful mechanism for enhancing relaxation. These experiences not only reduce stress but also contribute to emotional and cognitive well-being, highlighting the potential of VR as a tool for both leisure and therapeutic interventions. Consequently, designing VR environments that prioritize enjoyment and sensory engagement offers a promising pathway to optimize relaxation and emotional restoration in diverse contexts.

3. METHODOLOGY

This study adopts an exploratory qualitative approach to investigate how immersive virtual reality (VR) experiences in hospitality settings influence consumer perceptions of engagement, functional value, and well-being. The main objective is to explore how participants experience VR-enabled hotel tours, focusing on both the functional benefits of VR, such as exploration and decision support, and the psychological and emotional mechanisms, including relaxation and emotional restoration.

3.1. Study Context

The empirical investigation was conducted among hotel guests and frequent travelers in Tunisia between September and October 2025. This period was selected to capture insights from participants with recent exposure to both physical and virtual hospitality experiences, reflecting contemporary trends in immersive technologies and digital tourism. Participants were invited to engage with VR hotel tours using head-mounted displays (HMDs) (Figure **1**) and to reflect on their experiences during semi-structured interviews.

Figure 1. Immersive virtual travel experience: Exploring destinations through VR

3.2. Sample

The study sample consisted of 15 participants, aged between 22 and 45 years, representing a range of travel experience, familiarity with technology, and demographic characteristics. Participants were recruited voluntarily through social media and hospitality networks, and informed consent was obtained prior to the interviews. All participants were assured of anonymity, confidentiality, and their right to withdraw at any time without consequences.

The sample aimed to capture a diversity of perceptions regarding VR experiences, functional engagement, and immersive well-being outcomes. Data saturation, defined as the point at which no new themes emerged, was reached after the 13th interview, and two additional interviews were conducted to confirm saturation. This sample size aligns with recommendations for qualitative exploratory research.

3.3. Data Collection

Interviews were conducted face-to-face, lasting approximately 25–40 minutes each. With participants' consent, sessions were audio-recorded for transcription and analysis. The semi-structured interview guide covered four main themes derived from the study objectives:

- Knowledge and Familiarity with Immersive Technologies: Participants discussed their awareness and prior experience with VR, AR, and MR technologies, including perceptions of differences between traditional and immersive media.

- Functional Value and Engagement: Questions explored how VR facilitated exploration of hotel facilities and services, supported decision-making, and promoted active engagement. Participants reflected on cognitive and behavioral involvement, interactivity, and social or collaborative aspects of their VR experiences.
- Relaxation and Well-Being: Participants shared their emotional responses, including feelings of calmness, stress reduction, and psychological restoration during and after VR experiences. The focus was on understanding how immersive experiences contributed to sustained well-being rather than transient satisfaction.
- Individual Differences and Preferences: Participants provided insights into how personal characteristics (e.g., gender, technology readiness, travel experience) influenced their perceptions of VR, engagement levels, and emotional outcomes.

This thematic structure ensured that the interviews captured both the functional and experiential dimensions of VR in hospitality, allowing a comprehensive understanding of how immersive technologies shape consumer engagement, perceived value, and emotional well-being.

3.4. Data Analysis

All interviews were transcribed verbatim to preserve the nuances of participants' responses. A thematic content analysis was conducted manually, following Braun and Clarke's (2006) methodology, to identify patterns, themes, and sub-themes related to immersive VR experiences and consumer relaxation. Themes included participants' perceptions of VR realism, sensory stimulation, emotional engagement, relaxation outcomes, and the influence of individual differences. This approach allowed a deep understanding of the subjective experiences of participants and the factors shaping their well-being in immersive hospitality contexts.

4. STUDY RESULTS

4.1. Knowledge and Familiarity with Immersive Technologies

Participants shared diverse experiences and perceptions regarding immersive technologies, including virtual reality (VR), augmented reality (AR), and mixed reality (MR). Some participants were encountering these technologies for the first time, while others had prior exposure through gaming or virtual tours, although not specifically within hospitality contexts. Many participants noted the distinctiveness of immersive technologies compared to traditional media, emphasizing the sense of presence and interactivity offered by VR. One participant reflected, *"I had never tried VR before, but it allowed me to move through the hotel as if I were actually there."* Another stated, *"Unlike photos or videos online, I could choose where to go and look around, which made the experience feel much more realistic."* Similarly, a participant commented, *"It's fascinating to see the details of the room and the lobby; it really helps me imagine being there."* These responses illustrate a wide range of familiarity levels and perceptions, highlighting how participants engage cognitively and emotionally with immersive environments, without assuming prior expertise.

4.2. VR Hotel Tours: Functional Value and Engagement

Participants highlighted that VR hotel tours primarily provided functional benefits, supporting planning and informed decision-making. The immersive experience allowed users to explore room layouts, common areas, and amenities in detail, providing a clearer understanding of the property than static images or conventional online content. One participant stated, *"Navigating the rooms virtually helped me understand the layout before even arriving, it made planning my stay much easier."* Another explained, *"Seeing the hotel spaces in VR gave me confidence about what to expect and helped me decide which room I would prefer."*

Participants also emphasized that VR facilitated efficient evaluation of hotel offerings. Being able to examine facilities such as the gym, spa, or dining areas virtually allowed them to prioritize and compare options effectively: *"I could check the spa and gym before booking, which made my choice more straightforward and reduced uncertainty."*

Overall, the findings indicate that VR tours enhance the functional value of hotel experiences by improving spatial understanding, supporting informed choices, and streamlining pre-arrival planning.

4.3. Relaxation and Well-Being

Participants reported that VR hotel tours contributed to emotional restoration and relaxation during the experience. The immersive visual and auditory elements, such as calming room designs, ambient sounds, and scenic environments, created a sense of tranquility. One participant explained, *"Walking through the virtual spa and garden areas felt soothing, it was like a short mental retreat."* Another noted, *"Even though I was at home, the VR experience helped me unwind and feel refreshed."*

Several participants highlighted that VR allowed them to access relaxing experiences they might not have been able to engage with physically, due to time, travel constraints, or stress. As one participant mentioned, *"I couldn't visit the hotel in person, but exploring it in VR helped me relax and gave me a break from my daily routine."*

Overall, VR appears to provide a meaningful avenue for psychological restoration, enabling users to experience calmness and stress reduction through immersive interactions with hotel environments.

4.5. Influence of Individual Differences

Participants' experiences varied according to technology familiarity and prior exposure to VR. Those comfortable with VR devices reported smoother interactions and higher engagement: "*I play VR games, so exploring the hotel felt intuitive and engaging.*" Gender differences were observed subtly: female participants tended to focus on aesthetic details and ambiance, while male participants emphasized functional features such as layout and amenities. Overall, participants agreed that VR can complement physical travel and, in some cases, partially substitute for it in providing both informational and restorative benefits.

Table 1. Summary of key findings: Functional and emotional outcomes of VR in hospitality

Theme	Sub-theme	Verbatims	Occurrences
Travel Experiences and Expectations	Planning & control	*"Seeing the hotel online or through VR helps me understand the space and plan better, it makes me feel more in control." "Being able to preview the rooms and facilities lets me organize my schedule before arriving." "I can check amenities virtually and decide what I want to do during my stay."*	6
Travel Experiences and Expectations	Anticipation & confidence	*"Exploring the hotel virtually gave me confidence that my stay would be comfortable.". "VR made me feel less anxious about traveling because I knew what to expect." "I felt reassured seeing the layout and activities beforehand."*	4
VR Hotel Tours	Functional engagement	*"Being able to navigate rooms and common areas virtually gave me a real sense of the layout." "I could see every detail of the room, from furniture to lighting, which helped me make choices.". "VR made me understand the size and flow of spaces better than pictures or videos."*	9
VR Hotel Tours	Interactivity & exploration	*"I liked selecting different areas of the hotel to visit, it made me more involved in the experience." "Moving around virtually and choosing where to go felt very engaging.". "I enjoyed exploring every corner of the hotel at my own pace."*	7

continued on following page

Table 1. Continued

Theme	Sub-theme	Verbatims	Occurrences
VR Hotel Tours	Social collaboration	*"Exploring the hotel with friends virtually made the experience more dynamic and fun." "We discussed rooms and facilities in real time, which helped us make decisions together." "Sharing the VR experience added a social dimension I didn't expect."*	3
Relaxation and Well-Being	Emotional restoration	*"Even though I couldn't travel physically, the VR experience helped me feel refreshed and calm." "Walking through the spa and garden areas in VR felt like a mini-vacation." "I felt my stress melt away while navigating the hotel virtually." "VR made me forget daily worries for a short while."*	8
Relaxation and Well-Being	Immersive enjoyment	*"The visuals and sounds in VR were very realistic and enjoyable." "I could almost feel the ambiance of the hotel, it was immersive." "I genuinely enjoyed exploring spaces I haven't visited before; it felt playful and relaxing."*	5
Individual Differences	Technology familiarity	*"I play VR games, so exploring the hotel felt intuitive and engaging." "It was easy to use the headset because I've tried similar apps before." "Even with little prior experience, I quickly got the hang of it."*	6
Individual Differences	Gender & perception	*"I noticed layout and amenities more than decor, which my friend appreciated more." "I paid attention to functional details, while my sister focused on colors and decoration." "Men in my group tended to look at room size and facilities, women more at ambiance."*	5
Individual Differences	Prior travel experience	1. "Having visited similar hotels before, VR helped me compare and better understand what I could expect." "It reminded me of past stays and helped me imagine my next visit." "Prior knowledge made me more critical, but VR still added value."	4

5. SUMMARY: A PROPOSED MODEL OF INTERACTION BETWEEN FUNCTIONAL ENGAGEMENT AND RELAXATION THROUGH VR IN HOSPITALITY

Figure 2 presents an integrative model summarizing the relationships between consumers' perceptions of hotel experiences and VR-enabled immersive environments. At the core of the model are consumers' perceptions and cognitive-emotional responses, representing how users interpret and engage with VR hotel tours.

The model organizes the findings around four key dimensions:

- Travel Experiences and Expectations: capturing participants' prior hotel experiences, expectations for comfort, relaxation, and informed decision-making.
- Functional Engagement with VR Hotel Tours: reflecting active exploration, interactivity, navigation, and information-seeking behaviors that enable users to understand the hotel environment before physically visiting.
- Relaxation and Well-Being: illustrating the emotional and psychological outcomes of VR engagement, including reduced stress, enhanced calmness, and emotional restoration.
- Individual Differences: encompassing factors such as technology familiarity, prior VR experience, and gender, which influence how participants engage with VR and derive relaxation benefits.

The model highlights dynamic interactions among these dimensions: prior travel expectations drive active engagement with VR, which facilitates informed exploration and supports cognitive investment. This engagement, in turn, contributes to relaxation and well-being, while individual characteristics moderate the strength and nature of these effects.

Overall, the framework demonstrates that VR in hospitality settings provides functional value by enabling meaningful exploration and decision-making, which concurrently enhances emotional outcomes such as relaxation and psychological restoration. This model underscores VR's dual role in supporting both practical engagement and sustained well-being for hotel guests.

Figure 2. Summary: A proposed model of interaction between functional engagement and relaxation through VR in hospitality

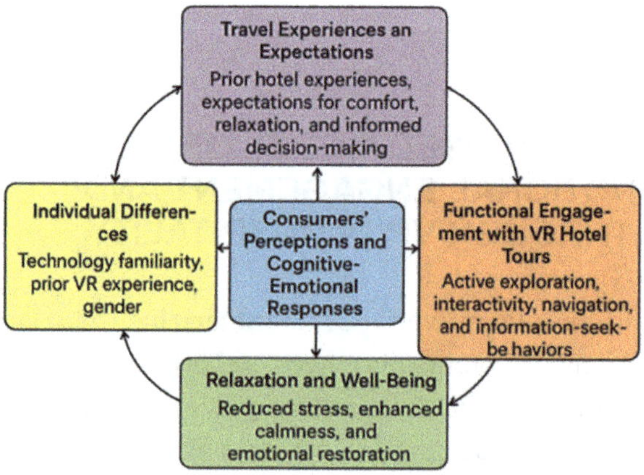

6. DISCUSSION

This study examines consumer perceptions and experiences related to the use of immersive Virtual Reality (VR) in the hospitality industry. The research focuses on the potential of VR technologies to enhance hotel experiences through functional engagement, emotional restoration, and informed decision-making.

The findings underscore the centrality of travel experiences characterized by relaxation, comfort, and a sense of control. Participants consistently emphasized that VR previews of hotels, ranging from room layouts to amenities and surrounding environments, facilitated cognitive engagement and reduced uncertainty. By enabling consumers to explore and evaluate facilities virtually before arrival, VR technologies supported informed decision-making and enhanced planning efficiency (AAnter, 2025; Abou-Shouk et al., 2024). This aligns with broader literature on experiential technologies, highlighting that functional clarity and interactivity can strengthen engagement and satisfaction (Barta et al., 2023; Arghashi & Yuksel, 2022).

Moreover, VR hotel tours were reported to significantly increase active engagement compared to traditional online content. Participants valued the ability to navigate rooms, interact with objects, and select areas to explore, noting that these interactive features encouraged focused attention and cognitive investment. The study also highlighted the social and collaborative potential of VR experiences, with shared virtual tours enhancing enjoyment and engagement. Minor challenges, such as initial discomfort with headsets, did not detract from the overall experience once users adapted, demonstrating the robustness of VR as a tool for immersive engagement (Araiza-Alba et al., 2021; Bretos et al., 2024).

Importantly, VR experiences were shown to contribute to emotional well-being and relaxation. Visual and auditory cues, such as serene room designs and ambient sounds, provided participants with a sense of calm and restorative experiences, even in the absence of physical travel (Cieślik, 2025; Bhardwaj & Kalro, 2024). These findings suggest that VR engagement in hospitality fulfills a dual role: it supports functional, decision-making processes while simultaneously offering affective benefits, enhancing the overall perception of the hotel experience.

Individual differences also shaped VR experiences. Familiarity with VR technology facilitated smoother interactions and higher engagement, while prior exposure influenced participants' comfort and confidence in navigating virtual environments. Subtle gender differences emerged: female participants tended to emphasize aesthetic and ambient elements, whereas male participants focused more on functional aspects such as layout and amenities. Overall, participants agreed that VR can complement physical travel and, in certain cases, partially substitute for it by providing both informational and restorative benefits (Abdo-Salloum & Al-Mousawi, 2025; Bilgihan & Ricci, 2024).

While VR demonstrates clear advantages in planning, engagement, and emotional restoration, it does not entirely replace physical travel experiences. Human interaction, on-site presence, and multisensory engagement remain irreplaceable components of the overall hospitality experience. Nonetheless, VR presents a promising avenue for enhancing pre-consumption visualization, cognitive engagement, and emotional satisfaction, suggesting that future hotel marketing and service delivery strategies could benefit from integrating immersive technologies alongside traditional experiences (Boccalini et al., 2025; Buhalis et al., 2023). Immersive VR experiences in the hospitality sector can enhance consumer engagement, decision-making, and well-being. Their effectiveness depends on striking a balance between interactivity, visual clarity, and sensory cues, while considering individual differences in technology familiarity and preferences. Future research and development should focus on optimizing VR design to maximize functional and emotional benefits, thereby supporting both informed decision-making and restorative experiences in hospitality contexts.

6.1. Theoretical Implications

The findings of this study contribute to the existing literature in several key ways.

This study advances the literature on immersive virtual reality (VR) in hospitality by providing a comprehensive understanding of how VR experiences influence guests' engagement, emotional responses, and psychological well-being. While prior research has predominantly emphasized functional and transactional outcomes such as purchase intention, satisfaction, or decision support (Flavián, Ibáñez-Sánchez, & Orús, 2019; Fan, Jiang, & Deng, 2022; Guttentag, 2010), the findings of this study highlight the affective and experiential dimensions of VR that contribute to guests' holistic experience. Guests emphasized that VR enabled them to visualize hotel spaces, navigate rooms, and interact with virtual environments in ways that enhanced their sense of control and involvement, echoing prior evidence that immersive environments can foster cognitive engagement and perceived autonomy (Dwivedi et al., 2023; Emerson et al., 2020).

Grounded in flow theory, this research demonstrates that immersive VR environments can induce deep engagement and intrinsic enjoyment, which in turn facilitate emotional restoration and relaxation (Csikszentmihalyi, 1990; Gaggioli et al., 2020). The multisensory richness of VR, including spatial interactivity, ambient sound, and visual realism, appears to promote a state of flow that is both engaging and restorative. This aligns with studies on mindfulness and experiential immersion, showing that environments encouraging focused attention and enjoyment can positively impact psychological well-being (Emerson et al., 2020; Flavián, Guinaliu, & Lu, 2020). In the context of hospitality, these findings suggest that VR does not merely support functional decision-making but also provides opportunities for meaningful, emotionally rewarding experiences that enhance overall guest satisfaction (Eshaghi, Afshardoost, & Bowden, 2023; Gretzel & Stankov, 2021).

The study also enriches theoretical perspectives on value creation in immersive experiences. VR contributes to multiple forms of value beyond the functional dimension: emotional value arises from enjoyment and positive affect, immersive value emerges from the psychological sense of presence in the hotel environment, and effort-reducing value stems from facilitating exploration without physical or cognitive strain (Flavián, Ibáñez-Sánchez, & Orús, 2021; Gleim et al., 2024; Kalender & Guzmán, 2025). This multidimensional view aligns with consumer well-being literature, highlighting that experiential technologies can enhance emotional, cognitive, and psychological outcomes simultaneously (Eshaghi, Afshardoost, & Bowden, 2023; Dwivedi et al., 2023).

The results regarding the influence of individual differences provide an important contribution to the literature on the use of virtual reality (VR) in hospitality contexts. By adopting an exploratory qualitative approach, this study highlights that immersive experiences cannot be considered uniform across all users. Familiarity with technology and prior exposure to VR directly influence interaction, engagement levels, and the smoothness of experiences, confirming that users' technical competencies modulate their appropriation of immersive environments. Furthermore, the observed gender differences underline that perceptual and cognitive preferences play a central role in how individuals interact with virtual environments (Epley, 2018; Epley et al., 2007; Gubler et al., 2025). Female participants tended to value aesthetic and ambiance aspects, while male participants prioritized functional features and spatial layout. These observations enrich the theoretical understanding of immersive experiences by showing that individual factors affect the perception of both functional and emotional value in VR. Thus, the study contributes to a more nuanced perspective on VR experiences in hospitality, emphasizing the need to consider individual characteristics when designing optimized immersive environments.

By integrating insights from flow theory and immersive technology research, this study contributes to a richer understanding of how VR can be strategically employed to enhance guest experience in hospitality. The findings support the notion that VR environments, when designed with attention to multisensory stimulation and enjoyable content, can create psychologically restorative experiences that extend beyond functional utility, promoting relaxation, engagement, and emotional flourishing (Hoffman & Novak, 2009; Hsiao, Wang, & Lin, 2024; Flavián, Ibáñez-Sánchez, & Orús, 2019). This perspective complements and extends prior theoretical work on immersive experiences, metaverse engagement, and digital well-being (Dwivedi et al., 2023; Kalender & Guzmán, 2025), positioning VR as a key tool for designing emotionally impactful hospitality services.

The study provides a coherent framework linking immersive VR experiences to psychological and emotional outcomes. By highlighting the interplay between sensory stimulation, engagement, and perceived enjoyment, it emphasizes the transformative potential of VR in hospitality contexts, offering both theoretical and practical insights for researchers and practitioners seeking to understand and leverage immersive technologies to enhance consumer well-being and holistic guest experiences (Flavián, Guinaliu, & Lu, 2020; Fan, Jiang, & Deng, 2022; Gaggioli et al., 2020; Eshaghi, Afshardoost, & Bowden, 2023).

6.2. Managerial Implications

This study provides several managerial implications, offering practical recommendations to enhance customer experience, engagement, and well-being in the hospitality sector through immersive virtual reality.

Firstly, the findings highlight that immersive VR can significantly enhance guests' cognitive engagement and decision-making. By enabling users to explore hotel layouts, amenities, and leisure spaces virtually before arrival, VR reduces uncertainty and fosters confidence in booking choices. Managers can leverage these interactive previews to guide visitors in comparing options, planning activities, and making informed decisions, thereby increasing overall satisfaction and reducing post-booking anxiety.

Secondly, VR offers opportunities to promote relaxation and emotional well-being. Incorporating calming visuals, ambient sounds, and virtual leisure environments, such as spa or garden areas, can provide restorative experiences for guests constrained by travel limitations, stress, or time pressures. By focusing on emotional and sensory aspects in VR content, managers can create positive associations with the hotel and strengthen guests' overall experience.

Thirdly, interactivity within VR environments drives engagement and attention. Allowing guests to navigate spaces, interact with objects, and choose areas to explore encourages active participation rather than passive observation. Shared or collaborative virtual experiences, such as exploring the hotel with friends or family, further enhance enjoyment and meaningful emotional involvement. Managers should therefore prioritize designing immersive experiences that maximize guest interaction and engagement.

Fourthly, individual differences such as technology familiarity, prior VR experience, and personal preferences shape the perception and effectiveness of VR experiences. Managers should ensure intuitive navigation and offer options catering to both functional exploration and aesthetic appreciation. Considering subtle variations, such as gender-related preferences for functional versus ambient features, can improve emotional satisfaction and perceived value, ultimately fostering loyalty and positive word-of-mouth.

Finally, VR provides valuable insights to inform strategic innovation and service design. Observing which virtual spaces attract attention, which interactions engage guests, and which elements promote relaxation can guide investments in physical spaces, service offerings, and experiential programming. Integrating VR across multiple touchpoints, from pre-arrival to in-hotel leisure, creates a seamless continuum between virtual and physical experiences, enhancing cognitive preparation, emotional engagement, and overall well-being. This dual role of VR, supporting both functional and emotional dimensions, enables managers to deliver guest-centered experiences that differentiate the brand, increase satisfaction, and promote long-term loyalty.

6.3. Limitations and Future Research Directions

This study provides valuable insights into consumers' perceptions and experiences with immersive virtual reality (VR) in hospitality settings. However, several limitations should be acknowledged, which also highlight opportunities for future research.

Firstly, the study focused on qualitative data collected directly from consumers who experienced immersive VR previews of hotel environments. This approach allowed for an in-depth exploration of their perceptions, emotions, and engagement. However, the findings are limited to the profiles of the participants and the specific VR experiences offered. Future research could extend the study to other customer segments or different types of hotels and hospitality services to examine whether similar themes emerge and to increase the generalizability of the results.

Secondly, the study primarily examined relaxation and emotional engagement as outcomes of immersive VR experiences. Although these aspects are central to well-being, future qualitative studies could explore additional dimensions, such as stress recovery, anticipation, emotional resilience, or cognitive engagement. Expanding the scope to consider multiple facets of consumer well-being would provide a more holistic understanding of the psychological impact of VR in hospitality.

Thirdly, the study did not extensively consider cultural or individual differences. Consumer responses to immersive VR may vary according to cultural background, prior exposure to digital technologies, or personal preferences. Future research could examine how these factors influence the adoption, perception, and effectiveness of VR experiences in hospitality, helping to tailor offerings to diverse guest segments.

Fourthly, this research highlighted the positive potential of VR but did not explore possible challenges or limitations associated with its adoption. Future studies could investigate issues such as technology-induced fatigue, accessibility barriers, or discomfort with immersive environments. Such investigations would help hospitality providers design VR applications that are inclusive, comfortable, and ethically responsible.

Finally, the study did not examine the long-term effects of repeated VR usage on consumer perceptions and well-being. While participants provided insights based on single VR experiences, it remains unclear how continuous or repeated engagement with immersive hotel previews influences satisfaction, emotional connection, or future booking intentions. Future research could explore longitudinal effects, tracking consumer responses over multiple VR interactions to better understand the lasting impact of immersive technologies in hospitality.

REFERENCES

AAnter, N. W. (2025). The Application of Artificial Intelligence (Virtual Reality and Augmented Reality) as a Training Tool in the Hospitality Industry. *The International Journal of Tourism and Hospitality Studies*, *8*(1), 191–214.

Abdo-Salloum, A. M., & Al-Mousawi, H. Y. (2025). Accounting students' technology readiness, perceptions, and digital competence toward artificial intelligence adoption in accounting curricula. *Journal of Accounting Education*, *70*, 100951.

Abou-Shouk, M., Zouair, N., Abdelhakim, A., Roshdy, H., & Abdel-Jalil, M. (2024). The effect of immersive technologies on tourist satisfaction and loyalty: The mediating role of customer engagement and customer perceived value. *International Journal of Contemporary Hospitality Management*, *36*(11), 3587–3606.

Akar, E. (2021). Customers' online purchase intentions and customer segmentation during the period of COVID-19 pandemic. *Journal of Internet Commerce*, *20*(3), 371–401.

Alexandris, K., & Palialia, E. (1999). Measuring customer satisfaction in fitness centres in Greece: An exploratory study. *Managing Leisure*, *4*(4), 218–228.

Anderson, L., Naughton, R. J., Close, G. L., Di Michele, R., Morgans, R., Drust, B., & Morton, J. P. (2017). Daily distribution of macronutrient intakes of professional soccer players from the English Premier League. *International Journal of Sport Nutrition and Exercise Metabolism*, *27*(6), 491–498. PMID: 28657805

Araiza-Alba, P., Keane, T., Chen, W. S., & Kaufman, J. (2021). Immersive virtual reality as a tool to learn problem-solving skills. *Computers & Education*, *164*, 104121.

Arghashi, V., & Yuksel, C. (2022). Interactivity, inspiration, and perceived usefulness! How retailers' AR-apps improve consumer engagement through flow. *Journal of Retailing and Consumer Services*, *64*(2), 102756. DOI: 10.1016/j.jretconser.2021.102756

Barnes, E. (2016). *The minority body: A theory of disability*. Oxford University Press.

Barta, S., Gurrea, R., & Flavián, C. (2023). How augmented reality increases engagement through its impact on risk and decision process. *Cyberpsychology, Behavior, and Social Networking*, *26*(3), 177–187. PMID: 36706429

Barta, S., Gurrea, R., & Flavián, C. (2025). Augmented reality experiences: Consumer-centered augmented reality framework and research agenda. *Psychology and Marketing*, *42*(2), 634–650.

Benson, P. (2007). Autonomy in language teaching and learning. *Language Teaching*, *40*(1), 21–40.

Bhardwaj, P., & Kalro, A. D. (2024). Consumer well-being: A systematic literature review and research agenda using TCCM framework. *International Journal of Consumer Studies*, *48*(1), e12991.

Bilgihan, A., & Ricci, P. (2024). The new era of hotel marketing: Integrating cutting-edge technologies with core marketing principles. *Journal of Hospitality and Tourism Technology*, *15*(1), 123–137.

Bjelajac, D., Đerčan, B., & Kovačić, S. (2021). Dark skies and dark screens as a precondition for astronomy tourism and general well-being. *Information Technology & Tourism*, *23*(1), 19–43.

Boccalini, S., Patrizi, M., Vernuccio, M., & Pastore, A. (2025). Enhancing eudaimonic well-being through brand experiences in the VR-based metaverse: Implications for brand-self connection and brand love. *Journal of Product and Brand Management*, *34*(6), 817–831.

Bretos, M. A., Ibáñez-Sánchez, S., & Orús, C. (2024). Applying virtual reality and augmented reality to the tourism experience: A comparative literature review. *Spanish Journal of Marketing - ESIC*, *28*(3), 287–309.

Buhalis, D., Leung, D., & Lin, M. (2023). Metaverse as a disruptive technology revolutionising tourism management and marketing. *Tourism Management*, *97*(1), 104724.

Buttussi, F., & Chittaro, L. (2023). Acquisition and retention of spatial knowledge through virtual reality experiences: Effects of VR setup and locomotion technique. *International Journal of Human-Computer Studies*, *177*, 103067.

Çakiroğlu, Ü., & Gökoğlu, S. (2019). A design model for using virtual reality in behavioral skills training. *Journal of Educational Computing Research*, *57*(7), 1723–1744.

Calvet, L., Bourdin, P., & Prados, F. (2019, November). Immersive technologies in higher education: Applications, challenges, and good practices. In *Proceedings of the 2019 3rd International Conference on Education and E-Learning* (pp. 95-99).

Chen, Y. M., Hsu, T. H., & Lu, Y. J. (2018). Impact of flow on mobile shopping intention. *Journal of Retailing and Consumer Services*, *41*, 281–287.

Cheong, R. (1995). The virtual threat to travel and tourism. *Tourism Management*, *16*(6), 417–422.

Chirico, F. (2016). Spiritual well-being in the 21st century: It's time to review the current WHO's health definition. *Journal of Health and Social Sciences*, *1*(1), 11–16.

Cho, M., Ko, E., & Jung, H. (2024). Virtual reality luxury fashion show: How imaginary space influences brand word of mouth. *International Journal of Advertising*, •••, 1–20.

Choi, D., & Kim, J. (2022). Why people continue to play online games: In search of critical design factors to increase customer loyalty to online contents. *Cyberpsychology & Behavior*, *7*(1), 11–24. PMID: 15006164

Cieślik, B. (2025). Mechanisms of Virtual Reality-Based Relaxation in Older Adults: A Scoping Review. *Journal of Clinical Medicine*, *14*(17), 6126. PMID: 40943883

Csikszentmihalyi, M. (1990). *Flow: The psychology of optimal experience*. Harper & Row.

Csikszentmihalyi, M. (1997). *Flow and the psychology of discovery and invention*. HarperPerennial.

Cucinella, S. L., de Winter, J. C., Grauwmeijer, E., Evers, M., & Marchal-Crespo, L. (2025). Towards personalized immersive virtual reality neurorehabilitation: A human-centered design. *Journal of Neuroengineering and Rehabilitation*, *22*(1), 7. PMID: 39833912

Dascal, J., Reid, M., IsHak, W. W., Spiegel, B., Recacho, J., Rosen, B., & Danovitch, I. (2017). Virtual reality and medical inpatients: A systematic review of randomized, controlled trials. *Innovations in Clinical Neuroscience*, *14*(1-2), 14. PMID: 28386517

Davis, F. D., Bagozzi, R. P., & Warshaw, P. R. (1989). Technology acceptance model. *Journal of Management Science*, *35*(8), 982–1003.

Dhalmahapatra, K., Maiti, J., & Krishna, O. B. (2021). Assessment of virtual reality-based safety training simulator for electric overhead crane operations. *Safety Science*, *139*, 105241.

Dwivedi, Y. K., Hughes, L., Wang, Y., Alalwan, A. A., Ahn, S. J., Balakrishnan, J., & Wirtz, J. (2023). Metaverse marketing: How the metaverse will shape the future of consumer research and practice. *Psychology and Marketing*, *40*(4), 750–776.

Emerson, L. M., De Diaz, N. N., Sherwood, A., Waters, A., & Farrell, L. (2020). Mindfulness interventions in schools: Integrity and feasibility of implementation. *International Journal of Behavioral Development*, *44*(1), 62–75. DOI: 10.1177/0165025419866906

Epley, N. (2018). A mind like mine: The exceptionally ordinary underpinnings of anthropomorphism. *Journal of the Association for Consumer Research, 3*(4), 591–598.

Epley, N., Adam, W., & John, T. (2007). On seeing human: A three-factor theory of anthropomorphism. *Psychological Review, 114*(4), 864–886. PMID: 17907867

Eshaghi, M. S., Afshardoost, M., & Bowden, J. L. H. (2023). Consumer well-being (CWB): Conceptualisation, contextualisation and a research agenda. *Service Industries Journal, 43*(9-10), 618–641.

Fan, X., Jiang, X., & Deng, N. (2022). Immersive technology: A meta-analysis of augmented/virtual reality applications and their impact on tourism experience. *Tourism Management, 91*(2), 104534.

Feng, Z., González, V. A., Ma, L., Al-Adhami, M., & Mourgues, C. (2018). Rapid 3D reconstruction of indoor environments to generate virtual reality serious games scenarios. *arXiv preprint* arXiv:1812.01706.

Flavián, C., Guinaliu, M., & Lu, Y. (2020). Mobile payments adoption–introducing mindfulness to better understand consumer behavior. *International Journal of Bank Marketing, 38*(7), 1575–1599.

Flavián, C., Ibáñez-Sánchez, S., & Orús, C. (2019). The impact of virtual, augmented and mixed reality technologies on the customer experience. *Journal of Business Research, 100*(2), 547–560.

Flavián, C., Ibáñez-Sánchez, S., & Orús, C. (2021). The influence of scent on virtual reality experiences: The role of aroma-content congruence. *Journal of Business Research, 123*(4), 289–301.

Freina, L., & Ott, M. (2015, April). A literature review on immersive virtual reality in education: state of the art and perspectives. In *The International Scientific Conference eLearning and Software for Education* (Vol. 1, No. 133, pp. 10-1007).

Gaggioli, A., Mazzoni, E., Benvenuti, M., Galimberti, C., Bova, A., Brivio, E., & Chirico, A. (2020). Networked flow in creative collaboration: A mixed method study. In *Creative Learning in Digital and Virtual Environments* (pp. 68–95). Routledge.

Gamberini, L., Bettelli, A., Benvegnù, G., Orso, V., Spagnolli, A., & Ferri, M. (2021). Designing "safer water." A virtual reality tool for the safety and the psychological well-being of citizens exposed to the risk of natural disasters. *Frontiers in Psychology, 12*, 674171. PMID: 34177732

Giessen, H. W. (2015). Media-based learning methodology: Stories, games, and emotions. In *International Handbook of E-Learning* (Vol. 2, pp. 43–54). Routledge.

Gleim, M., McCullough, H., Ferrell, O. C., & Gabler, C. (2024). Metaverse: Shifting the reality of services. *Journal of Services Marketing*, *38*(1), 13–27.

Gretzel, U., & Stankov, U. (2021). ICTs and wellbeing: Challenges and opportunities for tourism. *Information Technology & Tourism*, *23*, 1–4.

Gubler, D. A., Janelt, T., Roth, M., Schlegel, K., Guggisberg, J., & Troche, S. J. (2025). The DOES Scale: Measuring sensory processing sensitivity as a trait constellation. *Journal of Personality Assessment*, *107*(2), 205–220. PMID: 39321392

Guttentag, D. A. (2010). Virtual reality: Applications and implications for tourism. *Tourism Management*, *31*(5), 637–651.

Hoffman, D. L., & Novak, T. P. (2009). Flow online: Lessons learned and future prospects. *Journal of Interactive Marketing*, *23*(1), 23–34.

Hsiao, S. H., Wang, Y. Y., & Lin, T. L. (2024). The impact of low-immersion virtual reality on product sales: Insights from the real estate industry. *Decision Support Systems*, *178*, 114131.

Huang, J., & Hsu, C. H. (2010). The impact of customer-to-customer interaction on cruise experience and vacation satisfaction. *Journal of Travel Research*, *49*(1), 79–92.

Ihde, I. (1990). *The Indiana Series in the Philosophy of Technology*. Indiana University Press.

Isleyen, E., & Duzgun, H. S. (2019). Use of virtual reality in underground roof fall hazard assessment and risk mitigation. *International Journal of Mining Science and Technology*, *29*(4), 603–607.

Jacobson, J., Gruzd, A., & Hernández-García, Á. (2020). Social media marketing: Who is watching the watchers? *Journal of Retailing and Consumer Services*, *53*, 101774.

Kalender, Y., & Guzmán, F. (2025). What Drives Consumers to Engage in Immersive Technologies? A Consumer Metaverse Engagement Motivation Model. *Psychology and Marketing*, *42*(3), 921–950.

Kim, D., Im, H., Hyeon, J., & Jwa, J. (2021). Development of the rule-based smart tourism chatbot using Neo4J graph database. *International Journal of Internet. Broadcasting and Communication*, *13*(2), 179–186.

Lemon, K. N., & Verhoef, P. C. (2016). Understanding customer experience throughout the customer journey. *Journal of Marketing*, *80*(6), 69–96.

Lichstein, K. L. (1988). Sleep compression treatment of an insomnoid. *Behavior Therapy*, *19*(4), 625–632.

Loureiro, S. M. C., Bilro, R. G., & Angelino, F. J. D. A. (2021). Virtual reality and gamification in marketing higher education: A review and research agenda. *Spanish Journal of Marketing - ESIC*, *25*(2), 179–216.

Luan, C. C., & Phan, T. A. (2024). The effect of emotion type and similarity of experience on consumers' willingness to pay for cause-related products: Construal level perspective. *Journal of Consumer Behaviour*, *23*(2), 808–824.

Marasco, A., Buonincontri, P., Van Niekerk, M., Orlowski, M., & Okumus, F. (2018). Exploring the role of next-generation virtual technologies in destination marketing. *Journal of Destination Marketing & Management*, *9*, 138–148.

Martínez-Molés, V., Jung, T. H., Pérez-Cabañero, C., & Cervera-Taulet, A. (2022). Gathering pre-purchase information for a cruise vacation with virtual reality: The effects of media technology and gender. *International Journal of Contemporary Hospitality Management*, *34*(1), 407–429.

Matsas, E., & Vosniakos, G. C. (2017). Design of a virtual reality training system for human–robot collaboration in manufacturing tasks. [IJIDeM]. *International Journal on Interactive Design and Manufacturing*, *11*(2), 139–153.

Mora-Serrano, J., Muñoz-La Rivera, F., & Valero, I. (2021). Factors for the automation of the creation of virtual reality experiences to raise awareness of occupational hazards on construction sites. *Electronics (Basel)*, *10*(11), 1355.

Neuhofer, B., Buhalis, D., & Ladkin, A. (2014). A typology of technology-enhanced tourism experiences. *International Journal of Tourism Research*, *16*(4), 340–350.

Rauschnabel, P. A., & Ro, Y. K. (2016). Augmented reality smart glasses: An investigation of technology acceptance drivers. *International Journal of Technology Marketing*, *11*(2), 123–148.

Riches, S., Taylor, L., Jeyarajaguru, P., Veling, W., & Valmaggia, L. (2024). Virtual reality and immersive technologies to promote workplace wellbeing: A systematic review. *Journal of Mental Health (Abingdon, England)*, *33*(2), 253–273. PMID: 36919828

Rodriguez-Abad, C., Fernández-de-la-Iglesia, J. D. C., Martinez-Santos, A. E., & Rodriguez-Gonzalez, R. (2021). A systematic review of augmented reality in health sciences: A guide to decision-making in higher education. *International Journal of Environmental Research and Public Health*, *18*(8), 4262. PMID: 33920528

Russell, J. A., & Barrett, L. F. (1999). Core affect, prototypical emotional episodes, and other things called emotion: Dissecting the elephant. *Journal of Personality and Social Psychology*, *76*(5), 805. PMID: 10353204

Saghafian, M., Laumann, K., Akhtar, R. S., & Skogstad, M. R. (2020). The evaluation of virtual reality fire extinguisher training. *Frontiers in Psychology*, *11*, 593466. PMID: 33240182

Slater, M., & Wilbur, S. (1997). A framework for immersive virtual environments (FIVE): Speculations on the role of presence in virtual environments. *Presence (Cambridge, Mass.)*, *6*(6), 603–616.

Söderlund, G. B., & Jobs, E. N. (2016). Differences in speech recognition between children with attention deficits and typically developed children disappear when exposed to 65 dB of auditory noise. *Frontiers in Psychology*, *7*, 34. PMID: 26858679

Suntornteerasut, P., Darawong, C., & Wongvedvanij, R. (2024). The impact of travel experience on tourist satisfaction and intention to revisit towards wellness tourism in Thailand. *Journal of Business, Innovation and Sustainability (JBIS)*, *19*(4).

Sweetser, P., & Wyeth, P. (2005). GameFlow: A model for evaluating player enjoyment in games. [CIE]. *Computers in Entertainment*, *3*(3), 3–3.

Tussyadiah, I. P., Wang, D., Jung, T. H., & Tom Dieck, M. C. (2018). Virtual reality, presence, and attitude change: Empirical evidence from tourism. *Tourism Management*, *66*, 140–154.

Valmorisco, S., Raya, L., & Sanchez, A. (2024). Enabling personalized VR experiences: A framework for real-time adaptation and recommendations in VR environments. *Virtual Reality (Waltham Cross)*, *28*(3), 128.

Watson, D., & Tellegen, A. (1985). Toward a consensual structure of mood. *Psychological Bulletin*, *98*(2), 219. PMID: 3901060

Yung, R., & Khoo-Lattimore, C. (2019). New realities: A systematic literature review on virtual reality and augmented reality in tourism research. *Current Issues in Tourism*, *22*(17), 2056–2081.

Chapter 9
Using Artificial Neural Networks to Predict Visitor Satisfaction at Heritage and Pilgrimage Events

Aruditya Jasrotia
https://orcid.org/0000-0002-8274-5609
Amity University, Noida, India

Sourav Mangoch
https://orcid.org/0009-0008-0242-6386
Shri Mata Vaishno Devi University, Katra, India

ABSTRACT

The aim of this study is to investigate the factors that will facilitate visitor satisfaction at Bahu Fort during Bahu Mela. Bahu Fort is one of the essential locations in Jammu (India), and it is of enormous religious and spiritual importance. Data was collected from 253 pilgrims by structured questionnaire during three days Bahu Mela. Artificial Neural Networks (ANNs) was employed to develop a predictive model to identify the critical predictors of visitor satisfaction during the Mela. The model was trained on a comprehensive dataset encompassing various features related to pilgrim experiences, including demographic variables and non-demographic variables. The results of the study found that "Perceived barriers and expectations" is the most influential factor in determining visitor satisfaction, followed by "Environmental

DOI: 10.4018/979-8-3373-6450-6.ch009

and experiential quality of the destination" and "Tourists service quality and expectations." The study's findings contribute to improving Mela's overall facilities and costs. Implications of the study are also discussed.

1. INTRODUCTION

Religious tourism has received considerable importance in recent years because of its socio-cultural and economic contribution to destinations across the globe (Rautela et al., 2025; Singh & Rana, 2023). India, rich in religious heritage, has numerous pilgrimages and festivals attracting millions of pilgrims each year (Parker et al., 2024; Shinde, 2022). Such heritage and pilgrimage events are not only spiritual gatherings but also cultural and economic assets that strengthen local communities, preserve traditions, and promote sustainable tourism development. Among them, one such religious and cultural fest is the Bahu Mela, celebrated at Bahu Fort in Jammu, which attracts thousands of pilgrims annually ("Understanding Culture and Society in India," 2021). Dedicated to Goddess Kali (Bawe Wali Mata), the mela is an important heritage and pilgrimage event where visitors seek divine blessings, observe traditional rituals, and indulge in festive behavior (Jesenský et al., 2024). With the increased flow of tourists at such sites, achieving high levels of visitor satisfaction has become a crucial area of tourism management (Nian et al., 2023; Shinde, 2015). The properly managed experiences at heritage and pilgrimage events contribute not only to spiritual fulfillment but also to destination sustainability through repeat visitation, word-of-mouth promotion, and long-term engagement with cultural traditions (Hassan et al., 2022).

Visitor satisfaction at heritage and pilgrimage events is a multifaceted construct and is influenced by a wide range of factors, such as the quality of infrastructure, management of crowds (Verma et al., 2022), spiritual satisfaction (Ngatindriatun et al., 2024), accessibility (Srivastava et al., 2025), safety (Fernandes et al., 2018), hygiene (Yoon et al., 2009), and efficiency in service (Kanaujiya & Tiwari, 2025). A successful pilgrimage or heritage event experience relies on the effective integration of these diverse elements, as they play a pivotal role in shaping visitors' perceptions and overall satisfaction (Chen & Chen, 2025; Lee et al., 2020). However, measuring and predicting satisfaction is often challenging because these factors are interconnected and may influence one another in nonlinear ways (Gao et al., 2021). The conventional methods of assessing satisfaction have traditionally been survey-based and statistically analyzed, which, although valuable, are often limited in their ability to capture the complexity and interdependencies of multiple influencing variables. This creates the need for more sophisticated analytical tools that can identify hidden relationships, predict outcomes with higher precision, and provide actionable insights for planners and managers (Sharma et al., 2024).

Artificial Neural Networks (ANNs) have emerged as a powerful analytical tool in tourism research, particularly for understanding complex patterns in visitor behavior and satisfaction. Unlike traditional statistical models, ANNs can process nonlinear relationships between multiple variables—such as service quality, cultural authenticity, accessibility, crowd management, and emotional experience—to generate accurate predictive insights. In the context of heritage and pilgrimage events, where visitor satisfaction is influenced by both tangible (infrastructure, amenities) and intangible (spiritual fulfillment, cultural immersion) factors, ANNs provide a robust framework for capturing these intricate interdependencies. Their capacity for self-learning and adaptive pattern recognition allows tourism managers to move beyond descriptive analysis toward predictive intelligence. By training neural network models with data collected from visitor surveys, social media sentiment, and real-time event monitoring, destination planners can identify the key determinants that drive satisfaction and loyalty. Predictive outputs from ANNs can guide event organizers in optimizing crowd control, enhancing interpretive experiences, and aligning services with visitor expectations. For instance, the model can forecast potential dissatisfaction triggers—such as overcrowding or inadequate facilities—enabling timely interventions. Ultimately, integrating ANN-based predictive analytics into heritage and pilgrimage event management supports data-driven decision-making, leading to sustainable visitor experiences and improved destination competitiveness. AI applications raise several ethical and data governance issues that require careful attention. Ethically, AI can perpetuate bias and discrimination if trained on unfair data, compromise privacy through excessive data collection, and lack transparency in decision-making. Questions of accountability also arise when AI systems make mistakes, and automation can lead to job displacement. From a data governance perspective, challenges include ensuring data quality, clarifying ownership, protecting user privacy, and complying with data protection laws. Addressing these issues is essential to build trust, fairness, and responsible use of AI in society (Figure 1).

Figure 1. Conceptual model on ethical and data governance issues in AI applications

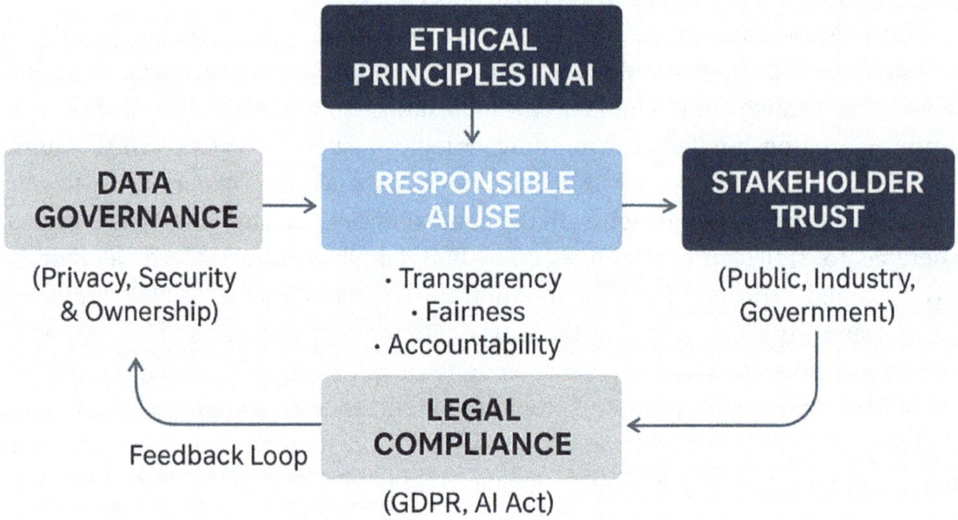

Over the last decade, machine learning (ML) (Salazar-Reyna et al., 2020), and artificial intelligence (AI) (Toto et al., 2025) have transformed data analysis across multiple disciplines, including tourism and hospitality (Doborjeh et al., 2021). Within this broader AI landscape, artificial neural networks (ANNs) have emerged as one of the most powerful and flexible predictive modeling techniques (Arar & Halicioglu, 2025). ANNs, inspired by the structure of biological neural networks, are extremely efficient in identifying implicit patterns, capturing nonlinear relationships, and forecasting outcomes with precision (Höpken et al., 2020; Bozkurt & Şeker, 2023). Unlike traditional regression-based methods, ANN models are capable of handling large, complex, and high-dimensional data sets where variables are interdependent and interactions are not straightforward (Chowdhury et al., 2023; Moges et al., 2022). This makes them particularly well-suited for studying visitor satisfaction at heritage and pilgrimage events, where emotional, cultural, spiritual, and logistical dimensions often overlap (Xiang et al., 2025).

By combining advanced computational approaches with tourism research, this study seeks to contribute to the current literature on the measurement and prediction of visitor satisfaction at heritage and pilgrimage events. It emphasizes how ANN-based models can provide deeper insights into the determinants of satisfaction and generate predictions that are more reliable than conventional techniques (Grewal et al., 2025). The findings of this study can serve as a valuable reference for tourism planners, destination managers, and local governments in designing better management strategies, improving infrastructure, and enhancing the spiritual as well as logistical aspects of pilgrimage events (Harun et al., 2024; Albahar et al., 2023). Furthermore, this research underscores the importance of bridging the gap between conventional tourism literature and AI-driven approaches, paving the way for more accurate, scalable, and actionable insights in the context of religious and heritage tourism (Pathak & Pallasena, 2025; Kumar et al., 2024). By employing ANN models, this study not only demonstrates the potential of AI in predicting visitor satisfaction but also sets an example for future research to adopt data-driven approaches in enhancing the tourist experience at heritage and pilgrimage events.

2. LITERATURE REVIEW AND THEORETICAL FRAMEWORK

India is known for its many colourful celebrations, some of which are honoured regionally while others are universally recognized (Sanyal & Sarkar, 2025; Jauhari & Munjal, 2015). Within this context, the sociocultural and religious tourism industries heavily rely on fairs and melas to attract visitors, with domestic tourism increasingly centered on pilgrimages (Rana & Singh, 2011; Vijayanand, 2012). The pilgrimage tourism thus occupies a unique space at the intersection of spirituality, culture, and the tourism industry (Smith, 1992; Fleischer, 2000). Religious tourism encompasses both pilgrimages driven by deep devotion and visits to sacred locations for sightseeing, adventure, or pleasure (Mangoch & Jain, 2022; Mu et al., 2007). Despite modern influences, tourism development through religiously connected events continues to gain momentum, supported by state-level advertising and marketing campaigns that position pilgrimages as vital to both cultural identity and economic growth.

The application of Artificial Neural Networks in tourism satisfaction studies bridges the gap between qualitative visitor experiences and quantitative analysis. Heritage and pilgrimage tourism often involve deeply emotional, spiritual, and cultural dimensions that are difficult to measure through conventional methods. ANNs, with their ability to handle diverse and unstructured data, such as text, audio, and images, enable researchers to integrate both emotional expressions and factual responses into a unified predictive model. This multidimensional approach helps in translating intangible sentiments—like spiritual fulfillment or cultural pride—into measurable variables that can inform tourism policy and management strategies.

In heritage and pilgrimage contexts, visitor satisfaction is not merely a product of service delivery but is intertwined with authenticity, symbolism, and the perceived sanctity of the experience. ANNs can process large datasets from diverse visitor profiles—domestic and international tourists, first-time and repeat visitors, or faith-based and cultural travelers—to detect subtle variations in satisfaction drivers. For instance, international visitors may prioritize interpretation and accessibility, while pilgrims may emphasize emotional and religious aspects. Neural networks can identify these distinct satisfaction clusters, allowing for more tailored event planning and heritage interpretation programs. Moreover, ANN-based models can assist in post-event evaluation by analyzing real-time feedback and comparing predicted satisfaction with actual visitor responses. This continuous learning mechanism helps event organizers refine their strategies over time, improving future events' quality and visitor engagement. When integrated with tools such as Geographic Information Systems (GIS) and Internet of Things (IoT) devices, ANNs can even predict satisfaction levels based on environmental factors like temperature, crowd density, or noise levels, offering a holistic and dynamic approach to managing visitor experiences. Finally, the adoption of ANN-driven predictive systems contributes to the sustainable development of heritage and pilgrimage destinations. By anticipating visitor needs and minimizing negative experiences, destinations can enhance cultural preservation, promote positive word-of-mouth, and strengthen local economies. In the long term, such data-driven insights foster a balance between visitor satisfaction and heritage conservation. The integration of Artificial Neural Networks thus represents not only a technological advancement but also a strategic shift toward intelligent and responsible tourism management.

2.1 Pilgrimage Tourism and Visitor Satisfaction

Pilgrimages represent a continuum between ancient treks and modern tourism experiences (Liutikas, 2025). The improved facilities at religious sites and evolving services have driven the expansion of pilgrimage tourism, transforming it into an organized industry that caters to diverse expectations and beliefs (Singh & Bhuyan, 2024; Ahmed, 1992). Visitor satisfaction, defined as an individual's subjective assessment of how well expectations align with actual experiences, is a critical outcome for religious tourism (Handriana et al., 2019). The prior studies indicate that factors such as demographics (Cahyadi et al., 2024), accessibility (Srivastava et al., 2025), service quality (Kanaujiya & Tiwari, 2025), and cultural engagement (Khan, 2024) strongly shape satisfaction levels at pilgrimage events (Tătăru anu et al., 2021).

Globally, similar findings emerge. In Spain, religious festivals enhance community pride and tourist loyalty when visitor experiences exceed expectations (Molina-Gómez et al., 2021; Oviedo-García et al., 2017). In Saudi Arabia, studies on Hajj highlight safety, crowd management, and service quality as decisive in shaping visitor satisfaction (Almuhrzi & Alsawafi, 2017). In East Asia, Buddhist pilgrimage sites show that spiritual authenticity and emotional engagement drive satisfaction more than physical infrastructure (Lopez et al., 2019). These perspectives suggest that while determinants of satisfaction vary by cultural context, they consistently involve a complex interaction between spiritual, logistical, and social dimensions.

2.2 Determinants of Satisfaction at Heritage and Pilgrimage Events

Pilgrimage and mela experiences are shaped by both tangible and intangible attributes (Tsaur et al., 2025). Tangible factors include infrastructure, hygiene, accessibility, pricing, and safety (Jauhari & Sanjeev, 2010; Painuly & Goutami, 2022), while intangible elements such as ritual authenticity, cultural symbolism, and spiritual fulfillment play equally critical roles (Rotherham, 2007; Terzidou et al., 2017). The sensory experiences such as sights, sounds, smells, and performances enhance engagement and strengthen visitors' emotional connection with events (Luo et al., 2025; Agapito et al., 2014). The marketing studies emphasize that family bonding and communal participation amplify satisfaction, as collective experiences carry higher emotional value (Pavicic et al., 2007).

Despite these insights, research on melas in India remains fragmented (Geetha & Chakravarti, 2024). The extant literature describes their cultural significance and economic contribution (Tribhuwan & Tribhuwan, 2003; Munjal, 2015), but fewer studies systematically examine the drivers of visitor satisfaction (Nguyen et al., 2022). The literature often highlights logistical challenges such as overcrowding, inadequate amenities, and travel distances (Jauhari & Sanjeev, 2010), but it lacks holistic models that integrate these diverse determinants into a predictive framework.

2.3 Theoretical Lens: Expectation-Confirmation Theory

The Expectation-Confirmation Theory (ECT) provides a strong foundation for conceptualizing satisfaction in pilgrimage and heritage tourism (Cao et al., 2024). According to ECT, satisfaction depends on the degree to which visitors' pre-visit expectations align with their post-visit experiences (Moufahim & Lichrou, 2018). Positive disconfirmation when experiences exceed expectations leads to higher satisfaction, whereas negative disconfirmation results in dissatisfaction (Shrestha & Shrestha, 2023; Atapattu et al., 2016). In pilgrimage settings, expectations may encompass ritual authenticity, crowd management, service efficiency, hospitality, and spiritual fulfilment (Damari & Mansfeld, 2014). Studies show that satisfied visitors are more likely to engage in repeat visitation, word-of-mouth promotion, and emotional loyalty (Wu et al., 2018). Albahar et al. (2023) confirm that managing expectations through superior service quality enhances satisfaction, strengthening long-term engagement with religious destinations. Thus, ECT underscores the importance of expectation management as a strategic tool for event organizers and destination managers.

2.4 Towards Advanced Predictive Approaches

Although ECT offers valuable insights, its application has largely relied on survey-based and regression-oriented methods. These conventional models struggle to capture the nonlinear and multidimensional interdependencies among the determinants of satisfaction (Abenoza et al., 2019). For instance, the interaction between crowd density, ritual authenticity, and perceived safety cannot be fully understood through linear models alone (Gayathri et al., 2017). This creates a methodological gap in the literature. The emerging research in tourism suggests that Artificial Neural Networks (ANNs) can address this limitation by modeling nonlinear relationships and identifying hidden patterns within complex datasets (Höpken et al., 2020; Bozkurt & Şeker, 2023). ANNs have been successfully applied in predicting hotel guest satisfaction (Chowdhury et al., 2023), tourism demand forecasting (Moges et al., 2022), and destination choice modeling (Doborjeh et al., 2021). Their ability to process large, high-dimensional datasets makes them particularly suitable for studying visitor satisfaction, which depends on diverse cultural, emotional, and logistical variables.

Below is a concise, citation-backed table 1 summarizing recent empirical studies that use artificial neural networks (ANNs) or deep-learning models to predict or analyze visitor satisfaction, perceptions, or related outcomes at heritage and pilgrimage events.

Table 1. Recent empirical studies on artificial neural networks (ANNs) to predict or analyze visitor satisfaction, perceptions

Study (author, year)	Context / Setting	ANN / ML method	Data & sample	Key findings	Major limitations
Alasmari et al., 2024 — "Sentiment analysis of pilgrims using CNN-LSTM"	Hajj pilgrims / pilgrimage perceptions	CNN + LSTM hybrid for text (sentiment) analysis	Social media / social posts and reviews; dataset described in paper (Pilgrim posts across Hajj 2021)	CNN-LSTM captures temporal and spatial patterns in text better than classical methods; useful proxy for pilgrim satisfaction and complaint detection.	Reliance on social media (selection bias); limited transparency of model explainability for managerial decisions.
Albahar et al., 2023 — "Exploring Hajj pilgrim satisfaction with hospitality services"	Hajj pilgrims / hospitality satisfaction	Deep learning model (feedforward / tailored DL architecture) combined with Expectation–Confirmation Theory	Hotel reviews and structured survey data collected around Hajj seasons	Deep model improved predictive accuracy for satisfaction over simpler regression models; confirms expectation–confirmation constructs are predictive when combined with DL features.	Model interpretability and policy implications are under-discussed; generalizability beyond sampled hotels uncertain.
Shambour, 2022 — "Analyzing perceptions of a global event using CNN-LSTM"	Hajj (global event) — perception/ sentiment analysis	CNN-LSTM on social text data	Tweets and online posts about Hajj 2021; labeled sentiment subsets	Hybrid deep nets found to outperform baseline NLP models for event-level perception analysis; useful for near-real-time monitoring of visitor sentiment.	Sentiment labels noisy; cultural/ language nuances affect accuracy (multi-lingual challenges).
Moral Cuadra et al., 2021 — "Tourists' profile estimation through ANN" (Peer-reviewed conference / article)	Cultural / heritage city tourists (peer-to-peer / cultural-tourism)	Multilayer Perceptron (MLP) ANN	Survey data on sociodemographics and motivations (city: cultural-tourism)	MLP effectively estimated tourist profiles and segments from survey inputs; supports targeted service design for heritage visitors.	Focus on profiling, not direct satisfaction prediction; small/ regionally limited sample may limit transferability.

continued on following page

Table 1. Continued

Study (author, year)	Context / Setting	ANN / ML method	Data & sample	Key findings	Major limitations
Castaño-Prieto et al., 2025 — "Profiling Intangible Cultural Heritage Visitors through ANN" (2025)	Intangible cultural heritage festival (Fiesta de los Patios, Córdoba)	ANN (profiling MLP / tailored network)	Questionnaire responses from festival visitors; inputs = motivations, preferences	ANN allowed creation of visitor "identikits" to inform product/ service design and satisfaction drivers in heritage events.	Recent study; replication across different heritage forms needed; model explainability for managers could be improved.
Doan, 2023 — "Back-propagation neural network for tourism prediction"	Tourist arrivals / demand forecasting (implication for resource planning at events)	Back-propagation ANN vs ARIMA	Time-series data of tourist arrivals to a site/region	ANN outperformed ARIMA in short-term forecasting—helpful for staffing and service provisioning at large heritage/pilgrimage events.	Forecasting arrivals is not the same as predicting satisfaction; linking demand forecasts to satisfaction outcomes requires additional behavioural data.

Source: Literature Review

3. RESEARCH METHODOLOGY

3.1. Questionnaire Development

A literature review was conducted to develop a structured questionnaire related to the satisfaction of visitors. It comprises 24 items adapted from previous studies. The researchers in this study primarily relied on quantitative methods to gather data from the respondents. This involves surveying the intended respondents using a survey questionnaire that contains questions regarding the destination's image, unique selling points, the quality of its tourism amenities, the weather and accessibility, and the motivations of visitors. Table 2 shows the demographic profile of the respondents. The demographic data for the study were collected using a comprehensive set of indicators, including respondents' age, gender, occupation, religion, educational qualifications, and monthly income. These variables were carefully selected to ensure a nuanced understanding of the participants' socio-economic and cultural backgrounds.

3.2. Data Collection

An offline questionnaire was distributed to gather responses from the respondents visiting the Bahu Mela at Bahu Fort. The respondents were required to have experience of a place or be those who frequently visit a place. The respondents were targeted during their visit to Bahu Mela. The survey was taken during a three-day Bahu Mela held at Bahu Fort using a convenience sampling technique. This sampling was chosen to ensure that the data collected were relevant and reflective of the experiences of respondents known to face unique experiences and opportunities (Singh & Bhuyan, 2025). By using this method, the study aimed to capture the perceptions on the interplay between visitors' satisfaction, motivation, and the overall facilities they use. A total of 300 questionnaires were distributed, and 279 were completed and returned. Out of these, 26 were rejected due to missing data, resulting in a final sample size of 253 responses. According to guidelines, the minimum sample size required for the present study is 240, based on the rule of having ten times the number of statements (Franke & Mueller, 1996).

3.3. Profile of the respondents

Table 2 shows the demographic profile of the respondents: 40.72% of visitors were below 30, 37.15% were between 31 and 50, and 22.13% were over 50. Regarding gender, 52.56% of visitors are male and 47.44% of visitors are female. Most visitors were students (30.83%), followed by employees (25.70%) and business-people (23.32%). In terms of religion, most of the visitors were Hindus (73.52%), followed by the visitors of other religions (09.09%). In terms of education, 47.83% held post-graduate degrees, 23.32% had graduate degrees, and 20.15% had higher secondary-level education. Regarding monthly income, the majority of the visitors have a monthly income between 25,001 and 50,000 (27.28%), followed by those below 10,000 (26.08%).

Table 2. Respondents profile (N = 253)

Demographic characteristics	Frequency	Percentage
Age		
Below 30	103	40.72
31 – 50	94	37.15
51 and above	56	22.13
Gender		

continued on following page

Table 2. Continued

Demographic characteristics	Frequency	Percentage
Male	133	52.56
Female	120	47.44
Occupation		
Employee	65	25.70
Business	59	23.32
Student	78	30.83
Others	51	20.15
Religion		
Hinduism	186	73.52
Muslim	11	04.34
Christian	14	05.54
Sikhism	19	07.51
Others	23	09.09
Education		
12th Standard	51	20.15
Graduation	59	23.32
Post Graduation	121	47.83
Others	22	08.70
Income (Monthly)		
Below 10,000	66	26.08
10.001 – 25,000	56	22.13
25,001 – 50,000	69	27.28
50,001 and above	62	24.51

Source: Author's own compilation

4. ANALYSIS AND RESULTS

4.1. Exploratory Factor Analysis

In the present study, exploratory factor analysis (EFA) was performed using SPSS to achieve two primary objectives. The first objective was to identify underlying latent factors that emerge from the internal correlations among the directly measured variables. These latent factors are not directly observable but are inferred through the relationships between observed indicators (Borgstede & Eggert, 2022;

Borsboom, 2008). The second objective was to ensure that the extracted factors maximize the explained variance while minimizing the number of factors to retain, thus achieving parsimony in the model. Furthermore, it was essential to maintain high levels of reliability for these extracted factors to ensure meaningful and consistent interpretation (Saeed et al., 2021). The Bartlett's Test of Sphericity was employed to assess the suitability of the data for factor analysis. A statistically significant Bartlett's test result ($p < 0.05$) indicates that the correlation matrix is not an identity matrix, justifying further analysis. Additionally, Kaiser-Meyer-Olkin (KMO) Measure of Sampling Adequacy was applied to determine whether the sample size was adequate for factor extraction (Nkansah, 2011). A KMO value above 0.50 is considered acceptable for conducting EFA (Khairani & Adnan, 2019). Table 3 shows a KMO value of 0.924 was obtained, which demonstrates the high adequacy of the sample data, confirming that the dataset is appropriate for factor analysis. The total variance explained table in the EFA output revealed that the initial set of 24 observed variables was reduced to four latent factors, capturing the underlying structure of the data. These four extracted factors represent higher-order factors with distinct conceptual meanings. Below is a Table 4 of the extracted factors and their corresponding item groupings: *Factor 1* - Overall Tourist Destination Quality (OTDQ) – This factor comprises 11 items and reflects the perceived quality and attractiveness of the destination, including infrastructure, amenities, and general satisfaction with the destination. *Factor 2* - Perceived Barriers and Expectations (PBE) – This factor includes 4 items and relates to travellers' anticipated obstacles, constraints, and their expectations from the destination. *Factor 3* - Tourist Service Quality and Expectations (TSQE) – This factor consists of 5 items, representing tourists' evaluations of service standards and the extent to which their expectations are met by service providers and Factor 4 - Environmental and Experiential Quality of Destination (EEQD) – This factor, composed of 4 items, captures the environmental appeal, sustainability, and experiential aspects of the destination, such as eco-friendliness and immersive experiences. The EFA results indicate that the four extracted components explain a significant portion of the total variance, thereby reducing the complexity of the dataset while retaining essential information relevant to the study's objectives. This reduction enhances the interpretability of the model and strengthens the empirical foundation for subsequent analysis.

Table 3. Factor analysis

Factors	Items	Factor loadings	Internal Reliability (Cronbach Alpha)
Overall tourist destination quality	Safety and security at destination.	0.717	0.943
	Quality & hygiene at tourist place, accommodation & eateries.	0.713	
	Completeness of roads and road signage to destinations.	0.710	
	Availability of leisure and recreational activities.	0.672	
	Availability and adequateness of transportation facilities.	0.670	
	Cleanliness & maintenance of public convenience facilities.	0.645	
	Availability of information centres.	0.638	
	Attractions (natural, man-made, artificial, purpose built, heritage, special events).	0.602	
	Hospitality and friendliness of local people.	0.536	
	Telecommunication facilities near tourist destinations.	0.526	
	A rich spiritual and cultural heritage.	0.516	
Perceived barriers and expectations	I have to put more effort to visit religious tourism.	0.753	0.840
	I consider travelling to religious tourism is expensive.	0.749	
	I have to spend more time to visit religious tourism.	0.737	
	My expectation towards reliability.	0.617	
Tourists service quality and expectations	Ancillary services (services used by tourists such as banks, post, newsagent, hospital, etc.).	0.762	0.888
	Amenities (accommodation and catering facilities, retailing, other tourist's services).	0.637	
	My overall expectation of quality is.	0.602	
	Activities and events (all activities available at the destinations and what tourists will do during the visits).	0.570	
	My expectation towards customization is.	0.520	

continued on following page

Table 3. Continued

Factors	Items	Factor loadings	Internal Reliability (Cronbach Alpha)
Environmental and experiential quality of destination	Pleasant weather and climate.	0.832	0.843
	Spiritual attractions are well kept and restored.	0.691	
	The destinations are unique and authentic.	0.602	
	The destinations are free from air and noise pollution.	0.586	

Source: IBM SPSS 23.0

Table 4. KMO and Bartlett's test

Kaiser-Meyer-Olkin Measure of Sampling Adequacy.	0.924	
Bartlett's Test of Sphericity	Approx. Chi-Square	2068.147
	df	276
	Sig.	0.000

Source: IBM SPSS 23.0

4.2. Artificial Neural Network (ANN) Analysis

Several vital factors justify the application of Artificial Neural Networks (ANN) in this study. First, ANN is well-suited for handling datasets with non-normal distributions and accommodating non-linear relationships between exogenous and endogenous variables (Mishra et al., 2023). Unlike traditional statistical models, ANN demonstrates robustness in the presence of noise, outliers, and small sample sizes (Dawar et al., 2024). Additionally, ANN can manage non-compensatory models, where the decline in one predictor variable does not necessitate compensation by an increase in another. This flexibility enhances the model's ability to capture complex interactions between variables (Guo et al., 2025). The ANN analysis was performed using the neural network module available in IBM SPSS (Sugiarto et al., 2025). A primary advantage of ANN is its capability to detect linear and non-linear patterns in data without assuming normality (Soltani & Lee, 2024; Teo et al., 2015). The network is trained using a feed-forward backpropagation (FFBP) algorithm, which processes inputs in a forward direction and propagates errors backward to adjust the network's weights iteratively (Taneja & Arora, 2018).

Figure 2. Artificial neural network diagram (hidden layer activation function: hyperbolic tangent; output layer activation function: identity)

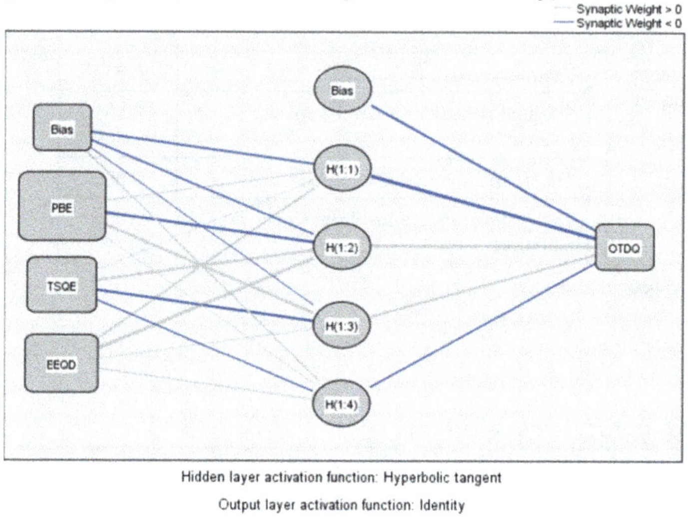

This study employed four factors from EFA results as an input neuron for the conduction of Artificial Neural Network (Figure 2). A multilayer perceptron's (MLPs) with sigmoid activation functions in the input and hidden layers, ensuring non-linear transformations and enhancing the network's learning capacity (Nwankpa et al., 2021). The model's learning process involved several iterations to minimize errors and refine the prediction accuracy progressively (Idrissi et al., 2018). In line with established methodologies (Leong et al., 2018), 90% of the dataset was allocated for training the model, while the remaining 10% was reserved for testing to assess the model's generalizability (Wang et al., 2023). To mitigate the risk of overfitting, a ten-fold cross-validation technique was implemented, which ensures that every data point has a chance to be part of both the training and testing sets, enhancing model reliability (Nissa et al., 2024). The model's performance was evaluated using the root mean square error (RMSE), a standard metric for predictive accuracy. The results in Table 5 indicate that the mean RMSE values for the training and testing phases were recorded at 0.665 and 0.594, respectively, suggesting high predictive precision among the visitors at Bahu Fort. These findings confirm that the ANN framework offers a robust and reliable tool for analysing complex, multi-dimensional datasets, ensuring accuracy and resilience against common data-related challenges (Ooi & Tan, 2016).

Table 5. RMSE values

Training			Testing			
N	SSE	RMSE	N	SSE	RMSE	Total samples
97	34.215	0.594	15	2.883	0.438	253
104	52.288	0.709	8	2.689	0.580	253
101	45.235	0.669	11	2.894	0.513	253
97	47.683	0.701	15	15.541	1.018	253
104	51.959	0.707	8	0.727	0.301	253
102	34.316	0.580	10	1.464	0.383	253
99	49.295	0.706	13	3.734	0.536	253
101	49.033	0.697	11	2.054	0.432	253
99	30.844	0.558	13	6.433	0.703	253
99	52.951	0.731	13	14.018	1.038	253
Mean	44.782	0.665	Mean	5.244	0.594	
Standard deviation	8.414	0.063	Standard deviation	5.262	0.254	

Note: SSE = Sum square of errors, RMSE = Root mean square of errors, N = sample size.
Source: IBM SPSS 23.0

The sensitivity analysis conducted in the artificial neural network (ANN) model evaluates the predictive power of individual input neurons, highlighting their relative importance in influencing the output (Belouz et al., 2021; Nourani & Fard, 2012). This analysis assesses how sensitive the model's performance is to changes in its input parameters. In the context of ANN, sensitivity refers to the degree to which variations in input parameters affect the entire network's behaviour and output predictions (Mishra et al., 2022). High sensitivity values indicate that small changes in input parameters can significantly alter the model's performance, underscoring their critical influence on system behaviour. Conversely, parameters with low sensitivity exert minimal impact on the model's overall performance, presenting a lower risk to prediction accuracy. The normalized importance of each input neuron was further calculated to provide a comparative measure of influence. This was achieved by dividing the absolute importance value of each neuron by the value of the most significant input parameter, followed by expressing the result as a percentage. The analysis revealed that "Perceived barriers and expectations" emerged as the most influential factor in determining visitor satisfaction, serving as a key driver of predictive accuracy. It was followed closely by "Environmental and experiential quality of the destination" which showed a normalized importance of 94% relative to the most significant factor. "Tourists service quality and expectations" ranked third in importance, demonstrating a normalized significance of 72%. These findings indicate that satisfaction among visitors is primarily shaped by psychological and experiential dimensions, with environmental quality and service expectations playing substantial but secondary roles (Rita et al., 2024). Table 6 presents the sensitivity analysis outcomes based on the first-order partial derivative method, which quantifies the marginal effect of each input parameter on the ANN model's output, ensuring a robust and systematic evaluation of the input-output relationship (Belouz et al., 2021). This detailed sensitivity analysis enhances the understanding of the ANN model's behaviour and aids in identifying the most critical factors requiring attention to optimize visitor satisfaction.

Table 6. Sensitivity analysis

Neural Network (NN)	PBE	TSQE	EEQD
NN (I)	0.406	0.284	0.310
NN (II)	0.253	0.316	0.431
NN (III)	0.440	0.284	0.275
NN (IV)	0.480	0.306	0.215
NN (V)	0.617	0.054	0.329
NN (VI)	0.389	0.334	0.278
NN (VII)	0.351	0.392	0.257
NN (VIII)	0.414	0.294	0.292
NN (IX)	0.407	0.352	0.241
NN (X)	0.006	0.091	0.903
Average importance	0.376	0.271	0.353
Normalized importance (%)	100	72	94

Note: PBE = Perceived barriers and expectations, TSQE = Tourists service quality and expectations, EEQD = Environmental and experiential quality of destination.

Source: IBM SPSS 23.0

5. DISCUSSION

Artificial Neural Networks (ANN) is a robust tool for predictive analytics, particularly in forecasting visitor satisfaction and identifying key determinants impacting their experience at Bahu Fort. Using ANN models, intricate patterns and relationships within the data were assessed to determine how factors identified through exploratory factor analysis (EFA) contribute to overall satisfaction. EFA facilitated the extraction of latent variables, providing a focused set of factors that feed into the ANN model for further analysis. By training the ANN on this structured dataset, we could uncover complex, non-linear associations and accurately predict satisfaction outcomes, thereby enhancing the model's reliability in identifying pivotal satisfaction drivers among visitors.

The complicated relationship between perceived barriers and expectations of visitor satisfaction defines the pilgrimage experience (Damanik & Yusuf, 2021). Logistics (like travel distance and costs), structural issues (like poor infrastructure and inadequate facilities), psychological concerns (like crowd anxiety or security), and cultural differences can make visitors uncomfortable and dissatisfied. High obstacles reduce enjoyment, especially if they conflict with the spiritual objective of the voyage. Visitors religious and cultural expectations about the facilities, atmosphere, and services they will experience also matter (Gapor et al., 2023; Olsen, 2013). According to disconfirmation theory, pilgrimage pleasure is attained when the experience meets or surpasses expectations, disappointed expectations might cause dissatisfaction. The expectations may also mitigate identifiable barriers. Visitors who accept crowded areas or basic amenities may be more satisfied than those who seek cleanliness or service (Song et al., 2020; Gupta & Basak, 2018). Visitors may mentally prepare or make alternate plans to mitigate the effect of expected hurdles on enjoyment. The consequences of practical pilgrimage site management arise from this interaction. Infrastructure and service improvements may address structural hurdles, while clear pre-travel information helps visitors prepare. By offering linguistic help may also reduce cultural barriers and improve visitors' comfort and happiness. Further study should explore how emotional support or community at these places mitigates obstacles and how visitors' happiness affects their probability of returning or promoting the site.

Visitor satisfaction at sacred destinations is significantly influenced by the character of the environment and the experience. A visitor's perception of the sanctity and comfort of the visit is directly influenced by the environmental quality, which encompasses pollution levels, maintenance of natural environment, and sanitation (Sinaga et al., 2025; Rech, 2022). The environment's purity and tranquillity frequently profoundly impact visit, as it is consistent with the spiritual objectives of their voyage. Conversely, experiential quality refers to the comprehensive experience determined by the destination's infrastructure, accessibility, hospitality, and safety levels (Karim et al., 2023; Kim, 2014). Visitors' satisfaction is significantly increased by the comfort, convenience, and alignment of the voyage and stay with their expectations, which is guaranteed by high experiential quality. Visitors are more likely to have a meaningful, memorable, and gratifying experience when environmental and experiential attributes are maintained. This results in higher satisfaction levels and an increased likelihood of recommending or revisiting the destination.

Visitor satisfaction in pilgrimage tourism is significantly influenced by the quality of service and the expectations of tourists, who must be satisfied with their spiritual and practical requirements (Tătăru anu et al., 2021; Islam, 2021). The visitors provide a seamless and satisfying experience through high-quality services, including spotless accommodations, reliable local transportation, safety measures, and knowledgeable guidance. Satisfaction is enhanced when these services meet the expectations of visitors, which may encourage return visits and promote positive word-of-mouth (Wang et al., 2017). Visitors' satisfaction is significantly influenced by their expectations, which are influenced by the spiritual and cultural significance of the site, prior experiences, and recommendations (Zhang et al., 2018). It is essential to meet or exceed these expectations, as discrepancies can result in dissatisfaction despite the quality of the service. As practical services, emotional and spiritual satisfaction is equally crucial to visitors, tranquil environment, cultural authenticity, and respectful treatment are critical. Consequently, the pilgrimage site's appeal to future tourists is enhanced, and its positive image is established when service quality meets or exceeds expectations, thereby maximizing satisfaction.

Artificial Intelligence (AI) predictions play a transformative role in shaping managerial decisions and enhancing visitor experiences, particularly within the tourism and hospitality sectors. By analyzing large volumes of real-time data—such as visitor behavior, preferences, and feedback—AI enables managers to make informed, data-driven decisions that improve operational efficiency and service personalization. Predictive analytics help forecast visitor demand, optimize resource allocation, and tailor marketing strategies to specific audience segments. For visitors, these insights translate into smoother, more engaging experiences, such as personalized recommendations, dynamic pricing, and responsive customer service. Ultimately, the integration of AI predictions into managerial decision-making fosters a proactive, adaptive management approach that not only enhances satisfaction and loyalty but also strengthens the organization's competitive advantage in a rapidly evolving digital landscape.

6. RESEARCH IMPLICATIONS

6.1. Theoretical Implications

This study advances theoretical understanding of tourist satisfaction by employing Artificial Neural Networks (ANNs) to uncover complex, non-linear relationships among the multiple factors that influence visitors' experiences. By incorporating both demographic and non-demographic variables, the study improves upon traditional satisfaction models that rely on linear assumptions, providing a more nuanced understanding of how perceived barriers, environmental quality, service expectations, and other interdependent factors shape overall visitor experiences. The findings reveal patterns that do not neatly fit into existing integrative models combining traditional tourism theories with data-driven approaches, highlighting a gap in current theoretical frameworks. This indicates a need for further research to explore how tourists' behaviors and satisfaction evolve in real-time. Most importantly, this paradigm shift not only extends existing theoretical constructs, such as Expectation Confirmation Theory, but also demonstrates the value of machine learning techniques in identifying hidden patterns and refining theories related to pilgrimage tourism. By bridging conventional tourism theories with AI-driven predictive models, this study contributes to the development of adaptive, dynamic frameworks for long-term heritage management, sustainable tourism, and enhanced visitor experience strategy.

6.2. Practical Implications

At the operational level, the ANN model provides actionable insights for policymakers and industry stakeholders by predicting visitor satisfaction from real-time, multidimensional data. For policymakers, these insights can guide evidence-based decisions to enhance infrastructure planning, crowd management, and service quality at heritage sites such as Bahu Fort. The targeted investments in areas such as sanitation, transportation, and security can reduce perceived barriers and ensure that regulations and operational practices align with visitor expectations. For industry stakeholders including event organizers, hospitality providers, and local businesses, the predictive model serves as a strategic tool for optimizing resource allocation, customizing services, and designing offerings for specific segments of visitors. By integrating real-time feedback mechanisms, such as mobile applications and sensor networks, the ANN-based approach enables adaptive management practices that iteratively improve the visitor experience. Additionally, these insights can establish benchmarking standards for cultural and religious events, helping destinations differentiate themselves, foster sustainable growth in pilgrimage tourism, and ensure that operational improvements reflect the evolving needs and preferences of tourists.

7. CONCLUSION AND FUTURE RESEARCH

The present study on visitor satisfaction at Bahu Mela, held at Bahu Fort in Jammu, identifies the critical factors influencing visitor experiences at this culturally and spiritually significant event. By examining multiple dimensions of the pilgrimage experience including event organization, accessibility, facilities, cultural immersion, and spiritual fulfilment, the study provides a comprehensive understanding of the determinants of visitor satisfaction. The findings reveal that effective administration, high-quality infrastructure, and opportunities for meaningful artistic and spiritual engagement are the primary drivers of high satisfaction levels. These insights not only help event organizers enhance operational efficiency but also foster stronger connections with visitors, encouraging repeat visitation and positive word-of-mouth promotion.

The use of Artificial Neural Networks (ANNs) in this study highlights the value of advanced computational approaches in capturing complex, non-linear interactions among satisfaction determinants. This shows the potential of integrating AI-driven predictive models with conventional tourism theory to improve both theoretical understanding and practical management of pilgrimage and heritage events. By aligning operational strategies with visitor expectations, stakeholders can promote sustainable growth while preserving the cultural and spiritual integrity of events such as Bahu Mela.

Future research can build on these findings in several ways. The studies could explore visitor satisfaction across multiple pilgrimage and heritage events to validate the generalizability of the ANN-based approach. The incorporation of real-time visitor feedback and longitudinal data could enhance predictive accuracy and inform adaptive management strategies. Additionally, future work could investigate the role of emerging technologies, such as mobile applications, sensor networks, and augmented reality, in shaping visitor experiences. The researchers may also examine cross-cultural comparisons to understand how demographic, social, and cultural factors influence satisfaction in different pilgrimage contexts. These directions can further strengthen the integration of AI-driven methods with tourism theory, contributing to both sustainable heritage management and enriched visitor experiences.

REFERENCES

Abenoza, R. F., Cats, O., & Susilo, Y. O. (2019). Determinants of traveler satisfaction: Evidence for non-linear and asymmetric effects. *Transportation Research Part F: Traffic Psychology and Behaviour*, *66*, 339–356. DOI: 10.1016/j.trf.2019.09.009

Agapito, D., Valle, P. O. D., & Mendes, J. (2014). The sensory dimension of tourist experiences: Capturing meaningful sensory-informed themes in Southwest Portugal. *Tourism Management*, *42*, 224–237. DOI: 10.1016/j.tourman.2013.11.011

Ahmed, Z. U. (1992). Islamic pilgrimage (Hajj) to Ka'aba in Makkah (Saudi Arabia): An important international tourism activity. *Journal of Tourism Studies*, *3*(1), 35–43. https://www.cabdirect.org/abstracts/19921898582.html

Alasmari, A., Farooqi, N., & Alotaibi, Y. (2024). Sentiment analysis of pilgrims using CNN-LSTM deep learning approach. *PeerJ. Computer Science*, *10*, e2584. DOI: 10.7717/peerj-cs.2584 PMID: 39896353

Albahar, M., Gazzawe, F., Thanoon, M., & Albahr, A. (2023). Exploring Hajj pilgrim satisfaction with hospitality services through expectation-confirmation theory and deep learning. *Heliyon*, *9*(11), e22192. DOI: 10.1016/j.heliyon.2023.e22192 PMID: 38034756

Albahar, M., Gazzawe, F., Thanoon, M., & Albahr, A. (2023). Exploring Hajj pilgrim satisfaction with hospitality services through expectation-confirmation theory and deep learning. *Heliyon*, *9*(11), e22192. DOI: 10.1016/j.heliyon.2023.e22192 PMID: 38034756

Arar, E., & Halicioglu, F. H. (2025). Understanding Artificial Neural Networks as a Transformative Approach to Construction Risk Management: A Systematic Literature review. *Buildings (Basel, Switzerland)*, *15*(18), 3346. DOI: 10.3390/buildings15183346

Atapattu, M., Sedera, D., Ravichandran, T., & Grover, V. (2016). Customers' View of Agility: The Expectation-Confirmation Theory Perspective. *Gyeong'yeong Jeongbohag Yeon'gu/Gyeong-yeong Jeongbohak Yeon-gu, 26*(1), 80–108. https://doi.org/DOI: 10.14329/apjis.2016.26.1.80

Belouz, K., Nourani, A., Zereg, S., & Bencheikh, A. (2021). Prediction of greenhouse tomato yield using artificial neural networks combined with sensitivity analysis. *Scientia Horticulturae*, *293*, 110666. DOI: 10.1016/j.scienta.2021.110666

Borgstede, M., & Eggert, F. (2022). Squaring the circle: From latent variables to theory-based measurement. *Theory & Psychology*, *33*(1), 118–137. DOI: 10.1177/09593543221127985

Borsboom, D. (2008). Latent variable Theory. *Measurement: Interdisciplinary Research and Perspectives*, *6*(1–2), 25–53. DOI: 10.1080/15366360802035497

Bozkurt, A., & Şeker, F. (2023). Harmonizing heritage and artificial neural networks: The role of Sustainable tourism in UNESCO World Heritage Sites. *Sustainability*, *15*(17), 13031. DOI: 10.3390/su151713031

Cahyadi, H. S., Sumardi, V., Rosadi, A., & Nurjamal, D. (2024). Exploring pilgrimage tourist typologies in Cikakak Tourism Village. *Journal of Tourism Sustainability*, *4*(1), 34–41. DOI: 10.35313/jtospolban.v4i1.117

Cao, C., Liu, H., & Wang, Z. (2024). The Influencing Factors of Tourist Loyalty in Camping Destinations Based on Expectation Confirmation Theory: The Mediating Role of Satisfaction and Well-Being. *Heliyon*. Advance online publication. DOI: 10.2139/ssrn.4873472

Castaño-Prieto, L., Solano-Sánchez, M. Á., Hidalgo-Fernández, A., & López-Guzmán, T. L. G. (2025). Profiling intangible cultural heritage visitors through multilayer perceptron's model. *Investigaciones Turísticas*, (29), 101–123. DOI: 10.14198/INTURI.27353

Chen, H., & Chen, M. (2025). Journey of the soul: Participants' event experience satisfaction, and psychological well-being during a Pilgrimage tourism event. *Event Management*. Advance online publication. DOI: 10.3727/152599525x174581767 67800

Damanik, J., & Yusuf, M. (2021). Effects of perceived value, expectation, visitor management, and visitor satisfaction on revisit intention to Borobudur Temple, Indonesia. *Journal of Heritage Tourism*, *17*(2), 174–189. DOI: 10.1080/1743873x.2021.1950164

Damari, C., & Mansfeld, Y. (2014). Reflections on pilgrims' identity, role and interplay with the pilgrimage environment. *Current Issues in Tourism*, *19*(3), 199–222. DOI: 10.1080/13683500.2014.957660

Dawar, I., Singal, M., Singh, V., Lamba, S., & Jain, S. (2024). Air quality prediction using Machine Learning Models: A Predictive study in the Himalayan city of Rishikesh. *SN Computer Science*, *5*(8). Advance online publication. DOI: 10.1007/s42979-024-03339-6

Doan, T.-N. (2023). A back-propagation neural network with delay and shift window for tourism demand forecasting. [IJCSE]. *International Journal on Computer Science and Engineering*.

Doborjeh, Z., Hemmington, N., Doborjeh, M., & Kasabov, N. (2021). Artificial intelligence: A systematic review of methods and applications in hospitality and tourism. *International Journal of Contemporary Hospitality Management, 34*(3), 1154–1176. DOI: 10.1108/ijchm-06-2021-0767

Fernandes, C., Silva, G., & Gómez-Ullate, M. (2018). Rethinking safety issues within the context of pilgrimage routes. In *CABI eBooks* (pp. 63–76). https://doi.org/DOI: 10.1079/9781786392282.0063

Fleischer, A. (2000). The tourist behind the pilgrim in the Holy Land. *International Journal of Hospitality Management, 19*(3), 311–326. DOI: 10.1016/s0278-4319(00)00026-8

Franke, G. R., & Mueller, R. O. (1996). Basic Principles of Structural Equation Modeling: An Introduction to LISREL and EQS. *JMR, Journal of Marketing Research, 33*(2), 255. DOI: 10.2307/3152154

Gao, K., Yang, Y., & Qu, X. (2021). Examining nonlinear and interaction effects of multiple determinants on airline travel satisfaction. *Transportation Research Part D, Transport and Environment, 97*, 102957. DOI: 10.1016/j.trd.2021.102957

Gapor, S. A., Chin, C. H., Ngian, E. T., Wong, W. P. M., Kiew, J. P., & Toh, T. L. (2023). Cultural events' service quality, satisfaction and loyalty: A case on an annual cultural diversity event in Borneo. *International Journal of Event and Festival Management, 15*(2), 191–212. DOI: 10.1108/ijefm-07-2023-0054

Gayathri, H., Aparna, P., & Verma, A. (2017). A review of studies on understanding crowd dynamics in the context of crowd safety in mass religious gatherings. *International Journal of Disaster Risk Reduction, 25*, 82–91. DOI: 10.1016/j.ijdrr.2017.07.017

Geetha, V., & Chakravarti, U. (2024). Understanding popular culture. In *Routledge eBooks* (pp. 139–155). https://doi.org/DOI: 10.4324/9781003482437-9

Grewal, D. K., Senthilkumaran, V., & K, H. P. (2025). Enhancing customer satisfaction through Artificial Neural networks (ANNS): principles, architectures, and practical applications. In *Emerald Publishing Limited eBooks* (pp. 103–119). https://doi.org/DOI: 10.1108/978-1-83549-418-920251007

Guo, J., Lin, J., & Luo, X. (2025). Enhancing organizational resilience through big data analytics capability: The mediating role of strategic flexibility. *Information Technology & People*, •••, 1–39. DOI: 10.1108/itp-06-2024-0786

Gupta, S., & Basak, B. (2018). Exploring pilgrim satisfaction on facilities for religious events: A case of Ratha Yatra at Puri. *Asia Pacific Journal of Tourism Research, 23*(8), 765–779. DOI: 10.1080/10941665.2018.1486864

Handriana, T., Yulianti, P., & Kurniawati, M. (2019). Exploration of pilgrimage tourism in Indonesia. *Journal of Islamic Marketing, 11*(3), 783–795. DOI: 10.1108/jima-10-2018-0188

Harun, A., Ahmad, N., Farradia, Y., & Hussein, Z. (2024). Analysing Umrah Attributes in relation to Tourist Travel behaviour: A Systematic literature review of religious destinations and future Perspectives. *Journal of Islamic Thought and Civilization, 14*(2), 72–105. DOI: 10.32350/jitc.142.06

Hassan, T., Carvache-Franco, M., Carvache-Franco, W., & Carvache-Franco, O. (2022). Segmentation of Religious tourism by Motivations: A study of the pilgrimage to the city of Mecca. *Sustainability, 14*(13), 7861. DOI: 10.3390/su14137861

Höpken, W., Eberle, T., Fuchs, M., & Lexhagen, M. (2020). Improving tourist arrival prediction: A big data and artificial neural network approach. *Journal of Travel Research, 60*(5), 998–1017. DOI: 10.1177/0047287520921244

Idrissi, T. E., Idri, A., & Bakkoury, Z. (2018). Systematic map and review of predictive techniques in diabetes self-management. *International Journal of Information Management, 46*, 263–277. DOI: 10.1016/j.ijinfomgt.2018.09.011

Islam, M. M. (2021). The Satisfaction of Bangladeshi Pilgrims: Service gaps in spiritual tourism based on gender and expenditure. *International Journal of Religious Tourism and Pilgrimage, 9*(1), 10. DOI: 10.21427/2hw0-cd28

Jauhari, V., & Munjal, S. (2015). Fairs and festivals in India: The cultural and economic potential. *Worldwide Hospitality and Tourism Themes, 7*(4), 324–330. DOI: 10.1108/whatt-03-2015-0012

Jauhari, V., & Sanjeev, G. M. (2010). Managing customer experience for spiritual and cultural tourism: An overview. *Worldwide Hospitality and Tourism Themes, 2*(5), 467–476. DOI: 10.1108/17554211011090094

Jesenský, M., Kornecká, E., Molokáč, M., & Tometzová, D. (2024). Development of Pilgrimage Tourism in Slovakia over the Past Decades: Examples of Selected Pilgrimage Sites. *Heritage, 7*(3), 1801–1821. DOI: 10.3390/heritage7030085

Kanaujiya, N. K., & Tiwari, N. V. (2025). A comprehensive analysis of the multi-faceted significance of the Kumbh mela in India: An emerging epicenter of global Hindu religious tourism. *World Journal of Advanced Research and Reviews*, *25*(2), 561–569. DOI: 10.30574/wjarr.2025.25.2.0339

Karim, R. A., Rabiul, M. K., & Arfat, S. M. (2023). Factors influencing tourists' behavioural intentions towards beach destinations: The mediating roles of destination experience and destination satisfaction. *Journal of Hospitality and Tourism Insights*, *7*(4), 2033–2054. DOI: 10.1108/jhti-04-2023-0276

Khairani, A. Z., & Adnan, R. (2019). Exploratory Factor Analysis (EFA) for Adversity Quotient (AQ) Instrument among Youth. *Journal of Critical Reviews*, *6*(6), 234–242. http://www.jcreview.com/?mno=302645174

Khan, N. A. (2024). Artificial intelligence, self-efficacy and engagement in religious tourism: Evidence from Arbaeen pilgrimage. *Journal of Hospitality and Tourism Insights*, *7*(3), 1660–1678. DOI: 10.1108/jhti-10-2023-0725

Kim, J. (2014). The antecedents of memorable tourism experiences: The development of a scale to measure the destination attributes associated with memorable experiences. *Tourism Management*, *44*, 34–45. DOI: 10.1016/j.tourman.2014.02.007

Kumar, V., Ashraf, A. R., & Nadeem, W. (2024). AI-powered marketing: What, where, and how? *International Journal of Information Management*, *77*, 102783. DOI: 10.1016/j.ijinfomgt.2024.102783

Lee, T. H., Jan, F., & Lin, Y. H. (2020). How Authentic Experience Affects Traditional Religious Tourism Development: Evidence from the Dajia Mazu Pilgrimage, Taiwan. *Journal of Travel Research*, *60*(5), 1140–1157. DOI: 10.1177/0047287520921240

Liutikas, D. (2025). Introduction to Sacred Landscape, Pilgrimage, and Ritual Practices. In *Creating the Sacred Landscape Pilgrimages and Ritual Practices* (pp. 1–20). https://doi.org/DOI: 10.1007/978-3-031-86232-8_1

Luo, D., Doucé, L., & Nys, K. (2025). Immersive art exhibitions: Sensory intensity effects on visitor satisfaction via visitor attention and visitor experience. *Visitor Studies*, •••, 1–22. DOI: 10.1080/10645578.2025.2510838

Mangoch, S., & Jain, D. (2022). Factors Determining Tourists Motivation to Visit a Place for Adventure Tourism: A Systematic Review. *Academy of Marketing Studies Journal*, *26*(3).

Mishra, A. K., Bansal, R., Maurya, P. K., Kar, S. K., & Bakshi, P. K. (2022). Predicting the antecedents of consumers' intention toward purchase of mutual funds: A hybrid PLS-SEM-neural network approach. *International Journal of Consumer Studies*, *47*(2), 563–587. DOI: 10.1111/ijcs.12850

Mishra, N., Srivastava, P., Mahato, S., & Shivani, S. (2023). Use and acceptance of crypto currencies in India: An evaluation of block chain application in financial sector using PLS SEM and ANN approach. *International Journal of Quality & Reliability Management*. Advance online publication. DOI: 10.1108/ijqrm-03-2023-0093

Molina-Gómez, J., Mercadé-Melé, P., Almeida-García, F., & Ruiz-Berrón, R. (2021). New perspectives on satisfaction and loyalty in festival tourism: The function of tangible and intangible attributes. *PLoS One*, *16*(2), e0246562. DOI: 10.1371/journal.pone.0246562 PMID: 33626049

Moral-Cuadra, S., Solano-Sánchez, M. Á., López-Guzmán, T., & Menor-Campos, A. (2021). Peer-to-Peer Tourism: Tourists' profile estimation through artificial neural networks. *Journal of Theoretical and Applied Electronic Commerce Research*, *16*(4), 1120–1135. DOI: 10.3390/jtaer16040063

Moufahim, M., & Lichrou, M. (2018). Pilgrimage, consumption and rituals: Spiritual authenticity in a Shia Muslim pilgrimage. *Tourism Management*, *70*, 322–332. DOI: 10.1016/j.tourman.2018.08.023

Mu, Z. M. Z., & Li, H. L. H. JianHong, W. J. W., Ji, L. J. L., YanGeng, J. Y. J., & XiTing, L. X. L. (2007). Religious tourism and cultural pilgrimage: a Chinese perspective. In *CABI eBooks* (pp. 98–112). https://doi.org/DOI: 10.1079/9781845932251.0098

Munjal, P. G. (2015). The potential of a participatory approach in sustaining the fairs and festivals of small towns. *Worldwide Hospitality and Tourism Themes*, *7*(4), 347–366. DOI: 10.1108/whatt-03-2015-0008

Ngatindriatun, N., Alfarizi, M., & Widiastuti, T. (2024). Impact of Sharia hospital service standards and religiosity commitment on patient satisfaction and loyalty: Insights from certified Sharia hospital in Indonesia. *Journal of Islamic Accounting and Business Research*. Advance online publication. DOI: 10.1108/jiabr-12-2022-0344

Nguyen, H. T., Le, A. T. T., Phan, A. C., & Hoang, T. D. L. (2022). A multi-perspective approach of international tourist satisfaction in tourism service: From big data perspective. *Journal of Asia Business Studies*, *17*(4), 850–872. DOI: 10.1108/jabs-03-2022-0090

Nian, S., Chen, M., Zhang, X., Li, D., & Ren, J. (2023). How outstanding universal value attractiveness and tourism crowding affect visitors' satisfaction? *Behavioral Sciences (Basel, Switzerland)*, *13*(2), 112. DOI: 10.3390/bs13020112 PMID: 36829341

Nissa, N., Jamwal, S., & Neshat, M. (2024). A technical comparative heart disease prediction framework using boosting ensemble techniques. *Computation (Basel, Switzerland)*, *12*(1), 15. DOI: 10.3390/computation12010015

Nkansah, B. K. (2011). On the Kaiser-Meyer-Olkin's measure of sampling adequacy. *Math. Theory Model*, *8*, 52–76.

Nourani, V., & Fard, M. S. (2012). Sensitivity analysis of the artificial neural network outputs in simulation of the evaporation process at different climatologic regimes. *Advances in Engineering Software*, *47*(1), 127–146. DOI: 10.1016/j.advengsoft.2011.12.014

Nwankpa, C. E., Ijomah, W., Gachagan, A., & Marshall, S. (2021). Activation functions: comparison of trends in practice and research for deep learning. *arXiv (Cornell University)*. https://arxiv.org/pdf/1811.03378.pdf

Olsen, D. H. (2013). A Scalar Comparison of Motivations and Expectations of Experience within the Religious Tourism Market. *International Journal of Religious Tourism and Pilgrimage*, *1*(1), 5. DOI: 10.21427/d7zq51

Ooi, K., & Tan, G. W. (2016). Mobile technology acceptance model: An investigation using mobile users to explore smartphone credit card. *Expert Systems with Applications*, *59*, 33–46. DOI: 10.1016/j.eswa.2016.04.015

Painuly, P., & Goutami, K. L. (2022). Pilgrim Satisfaction towards the Basic Amenities with Reference to Badrinath: An Empirical Study. *Specialusis Ugdymas*, *1*(43), 7477–7490.

Parker, S., Steffen, R., Rashid, H., Cabada, M. M., Memish, Z. A., Gautret, P., Sokhna, C., Sharma, A., Shlim, D. R., Leshem, E., Dwyer, D. E., Lami, F., Chatterjee, S., Shafi, S., Zumla, A., & Mahomed, O. (2024). Sacred journeys and pilgrimages: Health risks associated with travels for religious purposes. *Journal of Travel Medicine*, *31*(8). Advance online publication. DOI: 10.1093/jtm/taae122 PMID: 39216102

Pathak, S., & Pallasena, R. K. (2025). Mapping the evolution of generative AI: Insights from bibliometric research. *Journal of Decision Systems*, •••, 1–30. DOI: 10.1080/12460125.2024.2438612

Pavicic, J., Alfirevic, N., & Batarelo, V. J. (2007). The management and marketing of religious sites, pilgrimage and religious events: challenges for Roman Catholic pilgrimages in Croatia. In *CABI eBooks* (pp. 48–63). https://doi.org/DOI: 10.1079/9781845932251.0048

Rana, P. S., & Singh, R. P. (2011). Perceptions and images of tourists and pilgrims in Banaras. *Holy Places and Pilgrimages: Essays on India. Planet Earth & Cultural Understanding Series. Pub*, *8*, 165–206.

Rautela, S., Sharma, A., & Panackal, N. (2025). Exploring the sacred-unravelling the growth and development of religious tourism in Islamic culture: A bibliometric analysis. *Cogent Business & Management*, *12*(1). Advance online publication. DOI: 10.1080/23311975.2025.2482020

Rech, G. (2022). Religious tourist attractions and ecological concerns in the Italian Dolomites: The case of the trekking of the Thinking Christ. *Sustainability*, *14*(24), 16331. DOI: 10.3390/su142416331

Rita, P., Tiago, M. T. B., & Sousa, N. (2024). Empirical Insights into Co-Creation, Satisfaction, and Willingness to Pay in Sustainable Tourism. *Journal of Tourism and Services*, *15*(29), 133–152. DOI: 10.29036/jots.v15i29.804

Rotherham, I. D. (2007). Sustaining tourism infrastructures for religious tourists and pilgrims within the UK. In *CABI eBooks* (pp. 64–77). https://doi.org/DOI: 10.1079/9781845932251.0064

Saeed, B., Tasmin, R., Mahmood, A., & Hafeez, A. (2021). Development of a multi-item Operational Excellence scale: Exploratory and confirmatory factor analysis. *The TQM Journal*. Advance online publication. DOI: 10.1108/tqm-10-2020-0227

Salazar-Reyna, R., Gonzalez-Aleu, F., Granda-Gutierrez, E. M., Diaz-Ramirez, J., Garza-Reyes, J. A., & Kumar, A. (2020). A systematic literature review of data science, data analytics and machine learning applied to healthcare engineering systems. *Management Decision*, *60*(2), 300–319. DOI: 10.1108/md-01-2020-0035

Sanyal, A., & Sarkar, A. (2025). Resilience and Sustainability Practices with Local Communities in Singalila National Park (SNP), India: Exploring Traditional Food, Festivals and Culture in a Globalized World. In *People and Mountain Environments Interconnectedness for Sustainable Development in the Himalayas* (pp. 1–51). https://doi.org/DOI: 10.1007/978-3-031-83553-7_14

Shambour, M. K. (2022). Analyzing perceptions of a global event using CNN-LSTM deep learning approach: The case of Hajj 1442 (2021). *PeerJ. Computer Science*. PMID: 36262123

Sharma, M., Kumar, P., & Gundewar, S. (2024). Leveraging AI and machine learning for predictive analytics in business intelligence. In *Advances in business information systems and analytics book series* (pp. 29–50). https://doi.org/DOI: 10.4018/979-8-3693-8844-0.ch002

Shinde, K. A. (2015). Religious tourism and religious tolerance: Insights from pilgrimage sites in India. *Tourism Review*, *70*(3), 179–196. DOI: 10.1108/tr-10-2013-0056

Shinde, K. A. (2022). How effective is a Buddhist pilgrimage circuit as a product and strategy for heritage tourism in India? *Heritage*, *5*(4), 3846–3863. DOI: 10.3390/heritage5040198

Shrestha, Y. M., & Shrestha, R. (2023). Analysis of Differences between Expected and Perceived Satisfaction Score of Pilgrims: A Case of Chhinnamasta Temple of Nepal. *Nepalese Journal of Hospitality and Tourism Management*, *4*(1), 21–34. DOI: 10.3126/njhtm.v4i1.53312

Sinaga, F., Kanca, I. N., & Suarja, I. K. (2025). Tanah Lot temple: Navigating the tension between tourism development and cultural preservation. *Journal of Commerce Management and Tourism Studies*, *4*(1), 155–170. DOI: 10.58881/jcmts.v4i1.328

Singh, R. P. B., & Rana, P. S. (2023). Hindu pilgrimages (India) and religious functionaries. In *Perspectives on Asian tourism* (pp. 163–178). https://doi.org/DOI: 10.1007/978-981-19-9677-1_10

Singh, V., & Bhuyan, A. (2024). *Four decades of research on religious tourism: Prevalent themes and future research area.* https://www.ajol.info/index.php/rhm/article/view/296818

Singh, V., & Bhuyan, A. (2025). How tourist motivations shape perceptions of service quality at pilgrimage sites. *International Journal of Tourism Policy*, *15*(3), 235–251. DOI: 10.1504/ijtp.2025.147440

Smith, V. L. (1992). Pilgrimage and tourism: the quest in guest. *Annals of Tourism Research.* https://ixtheo.de/Record/1100836292

Soltani, A., & Lee, C. L. (2024). The non-linear dynamics of South Australian regional housing markets: A machine learning approach. *Applied Geography (Sevenoaks, England)*, *166*, 103248. DOI: 10.1016/j.apgeog.2024.103248

Song, H., Park, C., & Kim, M. (2020). Tourism Destination Management Strategy for Young Children: Willingness to pay for Child-Friendly tourism facilities and services at a heritage site. *International Journal of Environmental Research and Public Health*, *17*(19), 7100. DOI: 10.3390/ijerph17197100 PMID: 32998261

Srivastava, R., Kumar, S., Sidhant, P. C., Kumari, P., Singh, D. K., & Dundappa, J. (2025). Evaluating healthcare services at MahaKumbh 2025, India: A mixed-methods study of visitor perceptions and public health strategies. *Bioinformation, 21*(04), 789–792. DOI: 10.6026/973206300210789 PMID: 40636196

Sugiarto, H. D., Prayogo, D., & Anastasia, N. (2025). Developing machine learning algorithms for predicting house prices in Surabaya using IBM SPSS Modeler. In *Lecture notes in civil engineering* (pp. 779–787). https://doi.org/DOI: 10.1007/978-981-96-5654-7_71

Taneja, A., & Arora, A. (2018). Modeling user preferences using neural networks and tensor factorization model. *International Journal of Information Management, 45*, 132–148. DOI: 10.1016/j.ijinfomgt.2018.10.010

Tătăru anu, M., Butnaru, G. I., Ni ă, V., Neculăesei, A., & Ciortescu, E. (2021). The Influence of Interpretation through Guiding Tour, Quality of Reception and Relics' Worship on the Satisfaction of Pilgrims Attending the Iasi Feast. *Sustainability, 13*(12), 6905. DOI: 10.3390/su13126905

Teo, A., Tan, G. W., Ooi, K., Hew, T., & Yew, K. (2015). The effects of convenience and speed in m-payment. *Industrial Management & Data Systems, 115*(2), 311–331. DOI: 10.1108/imds-08-2014-0231

Terzidou, M., Scarles, C., & Saunders, M. N. (2017). Religiousness as tourist performances: A case study of Greek Orthodox pilgrimage. *Annals of Tourism Research, 66*, 116–129. DOI: 10.1016/j.annals.2017.06.009

Toto, G. A., Grilli, L., Traetta, L., Villani, R., Petito, A., & Serviddio, G. (2025). Convergence of disciplines: A systematic review of multidisciplinary development approaches in artificial intelligence. *Frontiers in Digital Health, 7*. Advance online publication. DOI: 10.3389/fdgth.2025.1400338 PMID: 40881734

Tribhuwan, R. D., & Tribhuwan, P. K. (2003). *An Introduction to Tribal Fairs and Festivals: Theoretical Consideration*. Fairs and Festivals of Indian Tribes.

Tsaur, S., Yen, C., & Yan, C. (2025). Effects of destination sacredness on tourists' spiritual well-being and destination commitment: Mediation effect of spiritual experiences. *Current Issues in Tourism*, •••, 1–19. DOI: 10.1080/13683500.2025.2513670

Understanding culture and society in India. (2021). In *Springer eBooks*. https://doi.org/DOI: 10.1007/978-981-16-1598-6

Verma, A., Gayathri, H. S., Karthika, P. S., Choubey, N., & Khandelwal, T. (2022). Crowd management guidelines for mass religious gatherings. In *Springer transactions in civil and environmental engineering* (pp. 151–165). https://doi.org/DOI: 10.1007/978-981-16-9636-7_8

Vijayanand, S. (2012). Origin and evolution of pilgrimage tourism management. *South Asian Journal of Marketing & Management Research*, *2*(4), 151–170.

Wang, T., Tran, P. T. K., & Tran, V. T. (2017). Destination perceived quality, tourist satisfaction and word-of-mouth. *Tourism Review*, *72*(4), 392–410. DOI: 10.1108/tr-06-2017-0103

Wang, X., Daryapour, M., Shahrabadi, A., Pirasteh, S., & Razavirad, F. (2023). Artificial neural networks in predicting of the gas molecular diffusion coefficient. *Process Safety and Environmental Protection*, *200*, 407–418. DOI: 10.1016/j.cherd.2023.10.035

Wu, H., Chang, Y., & Wu, T. (2018). Pilgrimage: What drives pilgrim experiential supportive intentions? *Journal of Hospitality and Tourism Management*, *38*, 66–81. DOI: 10.1016/j.jhtm.2018.11.001

Xiang, C., Rosni, N. B., & Ghafar, N. A. (2025). A Landscape Narrative Model for Visitor Satisfaction Prediction in the living Preservation of Urban Historic Parks: A Machine-Learning Approach. *Sustainability*, *17*(12), 5545. DOI: 10.3390/su17125545

Yoon, Y., Lee, J., & Lee, C. (2009). Measuring festival quality and value affecting visitors' satisfaction and loyalty using a structural approach. *International Journal of Hospitality Management*, *29*(2), 335–342. DOI: 10.1016/j.ijhm.2009.10.002

Zhang, H., Cho, T., Wang, H., & Ge, Q. (2018). The influence of Cross-Cultural awareness and tourist experience on authenticity, tourist satisfaction and acculturation in world cultural heritage sites of Korea. *Sustainability*, *10*(4), 927. DOI: 10.3390/su10040927

Chapter 10
Monetary Shocks in the Age of AI: How QE and QT Shape Investor Engagement on Digital Platforms in Europe

Donia Aloui
https://orcid.org/0000-0002-3422-5334
Tunis Business School, University of Tunis, Tunisia

ABSTRACT

This study examines how European Central Bank (ECB) monetary policy shocks, including quantitative easing (QE) and quantitative tightening (QT), influence AI-linked equity markets. Using a Time-Varying Parameter VAR (TVP-VAR) model on monthly data from 2018 to 2025, we analyze the responses of two technology-focused exchange-traded funds (ETFs): NasdaqAI and BOTZ. The findings reveal that market reactions vary across time and sectors. NasdaqAI responds negatively to QT, consistent with its long-duration valuation structure, while BOTZ shows positive responses linked to its exposure to industrial technology and automation. In periods of policy normalization, both indices react positively. These results highlight the changing nature of monetary transmission in innovation-intensive markets, shaped by investor sentiment and digital trading behavior.

1. INTRODUCTION

During the previous decade, the global financial system has experienced deep structural changes driven by two significant factors: the speeding up of technological

DOI: 10.4018/979-8-3373-6450-6.ch010

progress and the development of monetary policy frameworks. Artificial intelligence (AI), which was a marginal concept in economic modeling, has emerged as a central technology driver in the areas of productivity, capital accumulation, labor markets, and firm value (Brynjolfsson and McAfee, 2017; Cockburn et al., 2019). Meanwhile, central banks in developed countries have extended their policy agendas from traditional interest rate changes to comprehensive asset purchase programs, forward guidance policies, and, more recently, balance sheet normalization policies (Gagnon et al., 2011; Altavilla et al., 2015). These two trends are intricately linked: on one hand, AI is revolutionizing the infrastructure and tempo of financial markets, while on the other hand, monetary policy choices are increasingly impacting the price, volatility, and sentiment of AI-related assets.

Equities associated with AI and automation, such as thematic exchange-traded funds (ETFs) and sectoral indices, have come to represent a new breed of financial instruments. These assets are normally associated with high growth potential, long-duration earnings profiles, and high sensitivity to discount rate changes (Kogan et al., 2017). As instruments whose values are contingent on future cash flow projections and innovation cycles, they are particularly sensitive to changes in liquidity conditions and macro-financial variables. Even small changes in interest rate expectations or ECB policy communication can have a disproportionately large impact on the pricing of these technology-linked portfolios. The question of how such policy communications affect AI-focused equities has, therefore, become increasingly pertinent.

Concurrent with these monetary and technological developments, the informational architecture of financial markets has also undergone changes. The growth of online trading sites, algorithmic trading systems, and community-driven platforms such as Reddit, eToro, and X (previously Twitter) has led to an augmentation of the role of sentiment, narrative construction, and behavioral feedback effects in price determination (Barber et al., 2021; Brogaard et al., 2022). These online platforms have accentuated the effects of central bank announcements, influencing retail investors in real-time. Consequently, the transmission of monetary policy has become a function of both traditional macro-financial links and online-driven changes in investor attention, herding, and psychological anchoring.

Within the euro area, all these developments take place in a highly complex macroeconomic environment. After the global financial crisis and the subsequent sovereign debt turmoil, the ECB progressively shifted toward unconventional monetary policies. Negative interest rates, targeted long-term refinancing operations, and large-scale asset purchase programs became the new policy toolkit, designed to fight persistent low inflation, financial fragmentation, and dysfunctions in credit markets (Draghi, 2015).

These instruments affect financial markets through several interconnected channels: the cost of capital, bank lending conditions, portfolio rebalancing, and investor risk-taking behavior (Bernanke and Gertler, 1995; Andrade et al., 2016). In expansionary phases, when yields on safe assets are compressed, these mechanisms tend to push investors toward riskier, high-growth and innovation-driven sectors, such as artificial intelligence.

By contrast, policy normalization and quantitative tightening (QT) can generate the opposite dynamics. QT raises long-term interest rates, increases equity risk premia, and drains liquidity from financial markets. For long-duration and speculative assets, including AI and robotics stocks, such shifts can trigger sharp and sometimes abrupt market corrections. These effects are often amplified by behavioral forces, as narrative-driven sectors display strong non-linear reactions to macroeconomic uncertainty and central bank communication (Shiller, 2017).

While economic theory clearly suggests that innovation-intensive industries are particularly exposed to monetary shocks, empirical evidence on this relationship remains surprisingly limited.

The existing literature has primarily examined the aggregate effects of unconventional monetary policy on sovereign bond yields, systemic risk, and broad equity market indices (Rostagno et al., 2019; Boeckx et al., 2017). By contrast, far fewer studies have investigated the sector-specific implications of such policies for innovation-intensive financial assets. Research on the AI sector has largely remained confined to microeconomic dimensions, such as technology adoption, productivity gains, or firm-level performance, without explicitly linking these developments to shifts in the macroeconomic and monetary policy environment (Brynjolfsson et al., 2021).

Although recent work on digital investor sentiment highlights the amplifying role of social media and platform-based communication in shaping market dynamics (Cookson and Niessner, 2020), our understanding of how these behavioral forces interact with the monetary transmission mechanism in AI-linked equity markets remains limited.

This gap is particularly salient in the European context. The European Union is currently rolling out the world's first comprehensive regulatory framework for artificial intelligence, a development that is expected to shape expectations regarding innovation, compliance costs, and long-term investment prospects. At the same time, the ECB is moving from an extended phase of emergency monetary accommodation toward a gradual normalization of policy. Together, these structural and policy shifts are reshaping investor expectations and asset allocation decisions, especially in technology sectors where valuation depends critically on long-term growth narratives and regulatory clarity.

This paper contributes to filling this gap by examining how ECB monetary policy shocks, specifically quantitative easing (QE) and quantitative tightening (QT), affect the pricing of AI-related stock indices and investor sentiment. We employ a Time-Varying Parameter Vector Autoregression (TVP-VAR) model with stochastic volatility to capture evolving interdependencies, nonlinear responses, and structural breaks over the 2018–2025 period. This framework allows us to identify how the sensitivity of AI-linked assets to monetary policy shocks changes across distinct macro-financial regimes.

The contribution of this study is threefold. First, it provides new empirical evidence on the differential impact of unconventional monetary policy on AI-focused financial assets, a dimension that has remained largely unexplored in the macro-financial literature. Second, it proposes an integrated framework linking monetary policy, sectoral equity responses, and digital sentiment dynamics, offering a more comprehensive view of monetary transmission in the digital age. Third, it demonstrates the relevance of time-varying econometric models for analyzing high-volatility, narrative-driven sectors where standard assumptions of linearity and stationarity are unlikely to hold.

In doing so, the study advances our understanding of the interaction between central bank policy, technological investment, and investor behavior, and sheds light on how monetary authorities may manage sectoral spillovers in financial markets increasingly shaped by innovation narratives and behavioral amplification.

The remainder of the paper is organized as follows. Section 2.1 reviews the literature on monetary policy, technological transformation, and investor behavior, with a particular focus on the ECB and unconventional policy tools. Section 2.4 discusses AI as a structural economic force and outlines the key characteristics of AI-driven financial assets. Section 2.5 examines the role of digital platforms, narratives, and investor sentiment as amplifiers of monetary transmission. Section 3 presents the empirical methodology based on a TVP-VAR model with stochastic volatility, while Section 4 describes the data. Section 5 reports the empirical results on time-varying sectoral responses to monetary shocks, and Section 7 concludes with policy implications.

2. LITERATURE REVIEW

2.1. Monetary Policy, Technological Transformation, and Investor Behavior

The interaction between monetary policy, technological innovation, and investor behavior has become a central theme in modern macro-finance. Since the global financial crisis of 2008, the euro area has faced a prolonged environment of low inflation, subdued growth, and recurrent episodes of financial fragmentation. In response, the European Central Bank (ECB) progressively expanded its policy toolkit far beyond conventional interest rate adjustments. Large-scale asset purchase programmes, targeted refinancing operations, forward guidance, and negative policy rates became core instruments of monetary stabilization.

According to the IMF's *World Economic Outlook* (2025) and recent ECB communication studies, these unconventional tools have reshaped the monetary transmission mechanism by placing greater weight on expectations management, portfolio rebalancing, and risk-taking incentives, alongside the traditional cost-of-capital channel.

At the same time, the rapid rise of artificial intelligence has fundamentally transformed the structure and behavior of financial markets. Recent evidence from Aldasoro et al. (2024) at the Bank for International Settlements shows that AI is now embedded across the entire investment cycle, from price discovery and risk modeling to liquidity provision and portfolio construction. Beyond its impact on firm productivity and innovation dynamics, AI has also given rise to a distinct class of financial assets whose valuation is tightly linked to technological potential and long-term growth narratives.

AI-themed equities are typically characterized by long duration, elevated valuation multiples, and strong exposure to speculative sentiment. These features make them particularly sensitive to macro-financial conditions such as interest rates, liquidity provision, and central bank communication.

The convergence of unconventional monetary policy and AI-driven financial innovation has thus created a new transmission environment in which policy signals interact with markets increasingly shaped by technological expectations and behavioral dynamics. Traditional macroeconomic frameworks describe monetary policy as operating through well-established channels involving interest rates, credit markets, exchange rates, and aggregate asset prices. By contrast, technology-centered markets tend to react more strongly to shifts in expectations, speculative positioning, and narratives about future innovation. As emphasized by Pforr, Pape, and Petry (2025), the performance of AI-related assets depends not only on discount-rate fundamentals but also on investor beliefs about technological breakthroughs and regulatory trajectories.

Investor behavior itself has also undergone a structural transformation. The widespread adoption of digital trading platforms, social media, and real-time financial commentary has reshaped how information is processed and how markets respond to policy signals. Studies by Hassan et al. (2025) and Ileana and Marian (2024) show that digital ecosystems now play a central role in shaping investor reactions, particularly in sectors characterized by high uncertainty and informational asymmetry. Retail investors have become more influential and frequently respond to monetary announcements through sentiment, attention dynamics, and narrative interpretation rather than purely rational expectations.

These feedback mechanisms are especially visible in AI-linked markets, where volatility can be amplified by algorithmic trading and online coordination. As a result, the interaction between monetary shocks and investor sentiment complicates the transmission process in ways that are not fully captured by standard macro-financial models.

Despite the growing importance of these structural and behavioral forces, empirical evidence on the transmission of ECB monetary policy to AI-related financial assets remains scarce. While a large literature documents the effects of quantitative easing and tightening on aggregate equity indices, credit spreads, and sovereign bond yields, much less is known about how these policies affect innovation-intensive sectors such as AI. Similarly, research on technological finance has focused on AI adoption, automation, and algorithmic trading, but has rarely linked these developments to macroeconomic policy dynamics. Work on digital sentiment and retail investor behavior has documented rapid market reactions to policy announcements, yet without a sector-specific focus on emerging technology assets.

The European context further reinforces the relevance of this research agenda. As the European Union advances toward comprehensive regulatory frameworks for artificial intelligence and digital markets, investor expectations regarding future regulation increasingly influence asset valuations. At the same time, the euro area's bank-centered financial structure and institutional heterogeneity suggest that monetary shocks are likely to affect sectors differently depending on their exposure to credit conditions, innovation risk, and forward-looking valuation.

Against this backdrop, this study examines how ECB monetary policy shocks, in the form of quantitative easing and quantitative tightening, influence AI-related stock indices and investor sentiment. To capture evolving relationships over time and account for regime shifts and volatility dynamics, the analysis employs a Time-Varying Parameter Vector Autoregression (TVP-VAR) model with stochastic volatility. This framework is particularly well suited to environments in which financial responses depend on macroeconomic conditions, investor behavior, and policy credibility.

The findings contribute to the literature in several ways. First, they provide new evidence on the monetary policy sensitivity of AI-linked financial assets, an increasingly important yet underexplored segment of capital markets. Second, the analysis integrates digital sentiment indicators to illuminate how online investor behavior mediates the impact of policy announcements. Third, by relying on a flexible econometric framework, the study shows how time-varying interactions and nonlinear dynamics can uncover transmission patterns that remain hidden in conventional fixed-parameter models.

Overall, the paper contributes to a deeper understanding of how monetary policy operates in technologically advanced and behaviorally complex financial environments. It offers insights for central banks seeking to anticipate the sectoral spillovers of their actions and for investors navigating markets shaped simultaneously by innovation narratives and policy uncertainty.

2.2 ECB Monetary Policy and the Macroeconomic Transmission Mechanism

The monetary transmission mechanism refers to the process through which central bank decisions influence financial conditions, macroeconomic variables, and, ultimately, real economic activity. Traditional macroeconomic frameworks, including the IS–LM model, New Keynesian dynamic stochastic general equilibrium (DSGE) models, and the literature on credit frictions, identify a set of core channels through which monetary policy affects aggregate demand and asset prices.

The most established of these is the interest rate channel. This channel operates through the cost of borrowing. When policy rates are reduced, short-term market interest rates decline, encouraging credit expansion, private investment, and household consumption. Conversely, monetary tightening raises borrowing costs and restrains demand. However, following the global financial crisis of 2008, the effectiveness of this channel weakened in the euro area as policy rates approached the effective lower bound, limiting the ECB's ability to stimulate the economy through conventional rate cuts.

Another classical pathway is the exchange rate channel, which operates through international capital flows and currency valuation. Monetary easing typically leads to a depreciation of the domestic currency, stimulating net exports and supporting inflation. This channel is particularly relevant for the euro area given its deep integration into global trade networks and its strong exposure to external demand.

The credit channel, developed within the financial accelerator framework, emphasizes the role of banks in amplifying monetary impulses. Monetary easing improves bank balance sheets and raises collateral values, thereby expanding lending capacity. Monetary tightening has the opposite effect, constraining credit supply and reinforcing downturns. The bank-lending variant of this channel is especially important in the euro area, where member states display significant heterogeneity in banking structures, financial regulation, and credit intermediation.

A more forward-looking dimension of monetary transmission is captured by the expectations channel. In this framework, central bank actions and communication shape market participants' beliefs about the future path of interest rates, inflation, and economic activity. Through forward guidance and strategic signaling, monetary authorities influence long-term yields and risk premia, thereby affecting investment and consumption decisions. This channel is particularly relevant for long-duration assets such as AI-related equities, whose valuation depends heavily on long-term technological and revenue expectations.

As conventional channels weakened after the financial and sovereign debt crises, central banks increasingly turned to non-standard policy instruments. These tools introduced additional transmission pathways that now play a central role in shaping financial conditions.

One of the most important of these is the portfolio rebalancing channel. Under quantitative easing (QE), central banks purchase large quantities of long-term securities, reducing the supply of safe assets in the market and compressing term premia. Investors are therefore incentivized to rebalance their portfolios toward riskier assets, including equities and long-duration growth sectors. This mechanism has been particularly supportive of innovation-driven sectors such as AI, where valuations are closely tied to expectations of future technological breakthroughs.

Closely related is the risk-taking channel. Prolonged periods of low interest rates and subdued volatility encourage investors to increase their exposure to riskier assets in search of yield. The signaling channel further reinforces this effect by conveying the central bank's commitment to maintaining accommodative conditions over an extended horizon. In contrast, quantitative tightening (QT), through balance sheet reduction or the cessation of reinvestments, is interpreted as a signal of policy normalization, raising long-term interest rates and curbing investor risk appetite.

Another relevant pathway is the market liquidity channel. Central bank interventions in bond markets improve trading conditions, enhance market depth, and reduce bid–ask spreads, thereby facilitating asset reallocation and supporting valuations. When these interventions are reversed during QT, liquidity conditions may deteriorate, amplifying volatility and increasing market fragility.

In the euro area, the configuration and effectiveness of these channels are shaped by unique institutional features. Structural differences across member states in banking systems, fiscal capacity, and capital market development influence how monetary policy is transmitted across the union. These asymmetries strengthen the case for flexible and broad-based policy instruments, particularly in periods of crisis or economic divergence.

2.3 The ECB's Evolving Role

The European Central Bank has progressively assumed a more complex and multifaceted role in the post-crisis policy landscape. Unlike central banks operating within unified fiscal and regulatory systems, the ECB conducts a single monetary policy across a highly heterogeneous monetary union, composed of member states with different economic structures, financial systems, and institutional frameworks.

This structural diversity shapes the nature of monetary transmission in the euro area and reinforces the need for non-standard policy instruments to preserve policy effectiveness.

Recent research highlights the ECB's increasingly strategic position within the broader architecture of European economic governance. Beyond its core mandate of price stability, the ECB now operates in an environment where monetary policy interacts with major European policy initiatives, including digital regulation and technological sovereignty. As emphasized by Passador (2024), the ECB's policy stance increasingly overlaps with regulatory developments such as the EU Artificial Intelligence Act, which establishes the first comprehensive legal framework for AI governance worldwide. While the ECB is not directly involved in regulatory design, its policies shape the financial ecosystem in which AI firms evolve. Investor perceptions of innovation risk, access to capital, and long-term competitiveness depend not only on monetary conditions, but also on the coherence between central bank policy and the European regulatory agenda.

The ECB's unconventional policy programmes, notably the Asset Purchase Programme (APP) and the Pandemic Emergency Purchase Programme (PEPP), have played a decisive role in stabilizing euro area financial markets. These interventions contributed to reducing sovereign bond spreads, restoring credit market functioning, and supporting investor confidence during periods of acute uncertainty. By compressing yields on long-term safe assets, they encouraged portfolio reallocation toward sectors associated with higher expected returns and strong innovation potential. In this environment, AI-related equities benefited from lower discount rates, abundant liquidity, and a favorable risk-taking climate, generating upward valuation pressures.

Quantitative easing also contributed to a reduction in macroeconomic uncertainty. Stable financing conditions and compressed risk premia supported long-horizon investment strategies, particularly in sectors where revenues are projected far into the future. By contrast, the transition toward quantitative tightening is associated with a reversal of these dynamics. The withdrawal of central bank support raises long-term interest rates, tightens financial conditions, and reshapes investor expectations. As a result, duration-sensitive and growth-oriented sectors tend to experience valuation corrections and higher volatility. This pattern is consistent with recent IMF evidence (2025), which links QT announcements to tighter financial conditions and market adjustments in speculative and innovation-driven equity segments.

ECB communication has also become a central pillar of monetary policy transmission. In an environment where policy rates remain constrained by the effective lower bound, forward guidance and strategic signaling have emerged as powerful policy tools. Press conferences, policy statements, and official speeches are closely monitored by financial markets, often through algorithmic and sentiment-extraction technologies. In AI-linked markets, where investor behavior is highly expectation-driven, these communications can trigger rapid repricing and shifts in trading behavior.

Finally, the European Union's broader digital and industrial strategies further reinforce the interdependence between monetary policy and sector-specific investment dynamics. Policies aimed at strengthening technological autonomy and digital sovereignty shape how investors evaluate the strategic importance of sectors such as artificial intelligence. ECB policy is therefore increasingly interpreted not only through a macro-stabilization lens, but also in terms of its implications for capital allocation toward emerging technologies. This dual perspective, combining financial and industrial policy considerations, plays a key role in shaping investor sentiment and risk-taking behavior in technology markets.

Overall, the ECB has evolved into a central institution not only for monetary stabilization, but also for the broader configuration of financial and technological development in the euro area. Its policy actions interact with multiple transmission channels that extend well beyond traditional interest rate mechanisms. These interactions are particularly pronounced in AI-focused financial markets, where valuation is driven by expectations, regulatory context, and liquidity conditions. Understanding this evolving role is therefore essential for assessing how monetary shocks propagate through innovation-intensive sectors in a rapidly transforming economic environment.

2.4 Impact of Quantitative Tightening and Policy Normalization

The transition from quantitative easing to quantitative tightening represents one of the most consequential phases of the modern monetary policy cycle. This shift carries profound implications for financial markets, long-duration earnings expectations, and sensitivity to macroeconomic risk. Whereas quantitative easing injects liquidity, compresses term premia, and encourages risk-taking behavior, quantitative tightening reverses these dynamics by shrinking the central bank's balance sheet and withdrawing systemic liquidity. As a result, asset valuations adjust, yield curves reprice, and portfolio allocation strategies are re-optimized. Innovation-driven sectors such as artificial intelligence, biotechnology, and clean technology are particularly exposed to these forces because of both the structure of their valuation models and the behavioral profile of their investor base.

One of the main channels through which quantitative tightening affects high-growth sectors operates through the term structure of interest rates. As central banks reduce their holdings of long-duration securities, the supply of government bonds in secondary markets increases, placing upward pressure on long-term yields. Under both expectations theory and affine term-structure frameworks, higher long-term yields translate into higher discount rates applied to future cash flows. For sectors such as AI, where a large share of firm value is derived from earnings expected far in the future, even small changes in discount factors can have a disproportionate impact on current valuations.

This sensitivity is well illustrated by standard valuation models for growth equities, including the Gordon growth model and multi-stage discounted cash flow frameworks. A modest increase in long-term interest rates can generate a substantial decline in the net present value of distant cash flows. Consequently, announcements related to balance sheet normalization frequently trigger immediate price corrections in AI-related equities, even in the absence of any deterioration in near-term fundamentals. This pattern highlights how expectations about future monetary policy dominate current cash flow realizations in the pricing of innovation-intensive assets.

Quantitative tightening also reverses the portfolio rebalancing effects that prevailed under quantitative easing. When central bank asset purchases compress yields on safe securities, investors are encouraged to search for yield by reallocating capital toward riskier and higher-growth sectors. Under QT, this mechanism operates in reverse. As interest rates rise and returns on safe assets become more attractive, institutional investors rebalance their portfolios back toward government bonds and investment-grade credit. This shift exerts downward pressure on sectors that previously benefited from yield compression. AI equities are therefore particularly vulnerable to capital outflows.

Recent empirical work by Sapir, Kirkegaard, and Zettelmeyer (2025) further shows that portfolio adjustments during QT episodes are not only sizable but increasingly algorithm-driven. Quantitative strategies that track policy communication and macroeconomic indicators are programmed to reduce exposure to high-duration equities once tightening signals are detected. Thematic exchange-traded funds and machine-learning–based trading systems can therefore react in a highly synchronized manner, amplifying sell-off dynamics across AI-related asset baskets. In this environment, even incremental QT announcements may generate disproportionate portfolio shifts and elevated market volatility.

Beyond valuation effects, quantitative tightening also operates through a powerful liquidity channel by withdrawing reserves from the financial system. Theoretical models of liquidity constraints, notably those developed by Holmström and Tirole, emphasize that a reduction in systemic liquidity tightens financing conditions, constrains leverage, and raises borrowing costs. These frictions are particularly binding for AI firms, many of which remain in early growth phases and operate without stable or positive earnings. When access to external financing becomes more restricted, firms may be forced to delay product development, scale back research investment, or slow their expansion strategies. These constraints reinforce investor concerns about long-term viability and increase perceived innovation risk.

Market microstructure dynamics further amplify the impact of tightening on AI-related equities. As liquidity declines, bid–ask spreads widen and market depth deteriorates. Emerging technology sectors, which are typically characterized by lower capitalization and thinner trading volumes, exhibit heightened sensitivity to order-flow imbalances. As QT progresses, reductions in dealer balance sheets and lower trading activity increase the price impact of even moderately sized trades. In this environment, AI equities become more vulnerable to abrupt price adjustments in response to macroeconomic news, policy signals, or temporary imbalances in the order book.

Investor psychology also plays a central role in shaping the transmission of QT to innovation-driven markets. Behavioral finance research shows that monetary tightening is often interpreted through a prism of rising risk aversion, herding behavior, and deteriorating sentiment. Markets that are strongly driven by narratives, such as those surrounding artificial intelligence and disruptive technologies, tend to be especially exposed to shifts in collective investor mood. Evidence from Marian (2024) and Hassan et al. (2025) indicates that sentiment indicators extracted from digital platforms decline sharply following QT-related communications. These negative sentiment shocks can accelerate market exits and reinforce downward price momentum, particularly in environments already marked by elevated macroeconomic uncertainty.

Quantitative tightening typically unfolds in periods when inflation risks, geopolitical tensions, or cyclical slowdowns are already contributing to heightened market fragility. In such contexts, the interaction between rising discount rates and falling sentiment generates nonlinear responses. Market reactions tend to be asymmetric, with losses during tightening phases exceeding the gains observed during preceding easing cycles. For high-duration assets, this asymmetry is magnified, as valuation effects and behavioral amplification mechanisms reinforce one another in driving prices lower.

In sum, quantitative tightening introduces a complex set of challenges for innovation-driven financial markets. It reshapes the yield curve, triggers institutional portfolio reallocation, reduces systemic liquidity, and undermines investor confidence. These effects are particularly pronounced for AI-related equities due to their structural dependence on future earnings, reliance on external capital, and exposure to powerful behavioral feedback loops. A clear understanding of these dynamics is therefore essential for assessing how monetary normalization influences the pricing and volatility of technological assets in the post-QE era.

2.5 AI as a Structural Economic Force

Artificial intelligence has moved far beyond its origins as a narrow technological subfield. It has become a structural force that is reshaping productivity, industrial organization, global value chains, and financial markets. In the spirit of the literature on general-purpose technologies, AI exhibits the defining features of past transformative innovations such as electricity, computing, and the internet: it is pervasive, continuously improving, and highly complementary with a broad range of other technologies. As AI diffuses across sectors, it transforms business models, disrupts traditional production processes, and redefines the long-term determinants of firm valuation and investor behavior.

From a macroeconomic perspective, AI is increasingly viewed as a core engine of productivity growth. Reports from the OECD and the IMF emphasize that AI adoption enhances economic efficiency through automation, improved forecasting, and more sophisticated decision-making. These mechanisms reduce operational costs, expand production capacity, and allow for more dynamic resource allocation. Labor markets are also being reshaped through task reallocation, skill-biased technological change, and new complementarities between human expertise and algorithmic systems. Firms that integrate AI into logistics, customer analytics, and manufacturing tend to exhibit stronger productivity gains, higher innovation capacity, and improved competitive positioning. These structural advantages lie at the heart of the growing investor focus on AI-linked companies.

Within financial markets, AI plays a dual role. It is both a major investment theme and a technological infrastructure that is transforming the functioning of the financial system itself. As an investment class, AI has attracted substantial capital through thematic exchange-traded funds, venture capital, and public equity markets. AI-focused firms typically trade at elevated valuation multiples, reflecting expectations of scalable business models, disruptive potential, and rapid revenue growth. As emphasized by Pforr, Pape, and Petry, these expectations are reinforced by powerful narratives of technological transformation, which amplify investor enthusiasm and generate price dynamics driven jointly by fundamentals and sentiment.

At the same time, AI is reshaping how financial markets operate. AI-based tools are now embedded in risk management, trading execution, asset allocation, and market surveillance. As documented by Aldasoro et al., these systems enhance forecast accuracy, automate trading strategies, and optimize portfolio decisions using high-dimensional data. They process macroeconomic indicators, financial news, social media sentiment, and real-time order flows to react almost instantaneously to changing market conditions. This integration of AI into market infrastructure alters how information is absorbed, how shocks propagate, and how volatility is transmitted across asset classes.

The use of AI in trading and risk systems carries important macro-financial implications. It accelerates price discovery by compressing the time between information arrival and market reaction. It improves market efficiency but can also increase short-term volatility around major announcements, including monetary policy decisions. Moreover, it strengthens cross-asset spillovers, as AI-driven strategies rely on correlated signals and shared risk assessments. Sentiment extraction from digital platforms further reinforces these dynamics by linking online discourse to capital flows into sectors perceived as innovative or strategically important.

The structural relevance of AI is further reinforced by its central role in shaping modern technological ecosystems. Firms at the frontier of AI development form the backbone of digital industrial strategies and are deeply embedded in global supply chains. Their growth trajectories are sensitive to regulatory frameworks, capital availability, and macroeconomic conditions. In the European context, the emerging regulatory architecture surrounding AI introduces an additional layer of complexity by embedding policy-related risks and compliance costs into valuation models.

From a financial perspective, AI-related assets display the defining features of long-duration equities. Their valuations are largely driven by expectations of future earnings, which makes them highly sensitive to changes in discount rates and liquidity conditions. When interest rates rise, the present value of distant cash flows declines more sharply for these firms than for companies with near-term earnings concentration. As shown by Sapir, Kirkegaard, and Zettelmeyer, growth sectors such as AI respond strongly to monetary tightening not because of deteriorating fundamentals, but because of the structural sensitivity of their valuation frameworks to financial conditions.

Retail investor participation further amplifies these dynamics. Digital trading platforms, fintech applications, and social media communities have democratized access to AI-themed indices and speculative technology stocks. These platforms generate feedback loops through narrative-driven behavior, as retail traders respond to perceived breakthroughs, regulatory announcements, and public discourse on innovation. Shifts in collective attention, combined with algorithmic trading systems, intensify price movements both during periods of optimism and episodes of heightened uncertainty.

In this environment, AI-linked assets occupy a unique position at the intersection of technological innovation, macroeconomic policy, and behavioral finance. Their valuations reflect firm-level innovation cycles, but also broader forces such as liquidity conditions, monetary policy expectations, and investor sentiment. This combination makes AI-related equities especially sensitive to central bank policy signals, particularly during phases of quantitative easing and tightening. As monetary regimes evolve, the dual role of AI makes it a powerful lens through which to study time-varying and nonlinear policy transmission effects.

Understanding AI as a structural economic force is therefore essential for analyzing how financial markets respond to monetary shocks. AI-related indices provide a natural empirical setting for observing how unconventional monetary policies interact with innovation narratives, digital behavior, and valuation models driven by expectations and sentiment. In the context of ECB policy, these assets offer a window into how sector-specific dynamics respond to the broader macro-financial environment and reflect the evolving nature of monetary transmission in a digitally transformed economy.

2.6 Characteristics of AI-Driven Financial Assets

AI-driven financial assets have a profile that is very different from traditional assets. Their behavior is shaped by the technological nature of AI, its long-term economic potential, and the powerful narratives that surround its development. Together, these elements create specific patterns of valuation, sensitivity to macroeconomic conditions, and strong reactions to monetary policy.

A first key feature of AI-related assets is their strong link to long-term growth expectations. Companies operating in AI, cloud computing, data infrastructure, and advanced chip manufacturing are increasingly seen as the backbone of the future digital economy. Investors expect these firms to dominate tomorrow's productivity landscape and generate strong revenue growth over long horizons. In financial terms, this means that AI stocks have high duration. Just like long-term bonds or early-stage tech firms, most of their value comes from earnings expected far in the future.

As a result, AI assets are extremely sensitive to changes in interest rates and long-term yields, which are directly influenced by monetary policy. Even small increases in long-term rates during quantitative tightening can lead to sharp price declines, because the present value of future profits falls quickly.

AI assets also trade at high valuation multiples compared to the rest of the market. This premium reflects investor belief in the scalability, network effects, and disruptive power of AI business models. Breakthrough expectations and technological spillovers justify high forward price-to-earnings or price-to-sales ratios. But this upside comes with downside risk. When expectations change corrections can be fast and severe. This valuation asymmetry is typical of innovation-driven assets and explains the high volatility observed in AI markets.

Another defining feature is their strong dependence on market narratives. Unlike traditional industries whose value is based on stable cash flows or physical capital, AI firms are partly priced on beliefs about digital transformation, future dominance, and technological disruption. Investor sentiment therefore plays a major role in short-term price movements. Periods of easy monetary policy often coincide with optimism about innovation, pushing capital toward AI sectors. AI stocks can surge even when fundamentals do not change, simply because investor beliefs shift.

AI markets are also shaped by the growing role of algorithmic trading and data-driven investment strategies. These assets tend to absorb information very quickly. Sentiment extraction, big-data analytics, and machine-learning trading models allow investors to react almost instantly to central bank announcements and macroeconomic news. While this improves efficiency, it also increases short-term volatility, especially around monetary policy decisions, when uncertainty about future interest rates and liquidity is high.

Regulation adds another layer of sensitivity. Unlike mature industries with stable legal frameworks, AI operates in an evolving regulatory environment. Issues related to ethics, data protection, algorithmic transparency, and systemic risk directly affect investor expectations. The European AI Act, for example, introduces new compliance costs and policy uncertainty that influence how investors value AI firms. During monetary easing, easy credit can offset these concerns. During tightening, regulatory costs appear more binding and weigh more heavily on valuations.

Together, these characteristics: high duration, valuation premia, narrative dependence, regulatory sensitivity, and algorithmic trading, make AI assets highly responsive to interest rates, liquidity conditions, and risk sentiment. Their reliance on future earnings exposes them to discount-rate movements, while their behavioral dimension amplifies reactions to policy signals.

Retail investors further strengthen these dynamics. AI-themed ETFs and technology stocks are highly visible on trading apps and social media. Many retail investors are attracted by the promise of technological disruption and follow innovation narratives, regulatory news, and breakthrough stories. These platforms encourage momentum trading and herding behavior, accelerating both rallies and sell-offs. Monetary policy announcements can therefore trigger strong sentiment shifts that spread rapidly through digital channels.

Empirical evidence shows that the relationship between monetary policy and AI assets is fundamentally expectations-driven. Quantitative easing supports AI valuations by lowering discount rates and boosting risk appetite. Policy normalization and QT do the opposite: they reduce liquidity, raise discount rates, and weaken the appeal of long-duration assets, triggering portfolio reallocation. This creates clear cycles in AI pricing, with rallies under accommodative regimes and corrections during tightening phases.

In sum, AI-driven financial assets have a unique structural and behavioral profile. Their high growth expectations, sensitivity to interest rates, exposure to narratives, and regulatory dependence place them at the crossroads of technology, macroeconomics, and finance. They offer an ideal setting to study how monetary policy affects innovation-intensive markets and how modern transmission mechanisms evolve in a world shaped by digital transformation and investor behavior.

2.7. Digital Platforms as Sentiment Amplifiers

The digitalization of trading has deeply transformed the informational structure of financial markets. It has changed not only how information is produced and distributed, but also how it is interpreted and acted upon. In the past, market narratives were largely shaped by institutional analysts, financial news agencies, and official macroeconomic reporting. Today, financial markets increasingly react to decentralized and user-generated content coming from social media platforms and online trading communities.

Platforms such as eToro, Reddit finance forums, X.com, and investor networks on Discord now host continuous real-time discussions on investment strategies, monetary policy interpretation, and market sentiment. These platforms allow retail investors to actively participate in shaping market narratives a role that was traditionally reserved for institutional players.

This transformation has significantly amplified the importance of sentiment and behavioral dynamics in asset pricing. Digital platforms accelerate information diffusion, encourage opinion convergence, and create powerful feedback loops that are often disconnected from firm-level fundamentals. When a central bank announcement is released, it is immediately interpreted by thousands of users whose reactions are rapidly shared, reposted, and amplified. Unlike traditional financial media, which offers curated and structured analysis, digital discourse is fast, emotional, heterogeneous, and highly reactive. As a result, investor expectations are formed and reshaped in real time.

In this environment, sentiment is no longer just a reflection of market beliefs, it becomes an active force driving trading behavior and price dynamics. This is particularly visible in innovation-driven sectors such as AI. Retail investors, who are highly active in thematic and speculative markets, are especially sensitive to narratives about technological disruption and future policy regimes.

A dovish message from the ECB, for example, can quickly generate optimism on digital platforms about the growth prospects of AI firms, triggering inflows into AI-themed ETFs and technology stocks. By contrast, signals of quantitative tightening often spark concerns about rising discount rates and valuation risk. These fears spread rapidly across platforms and can lead to coordinated selling, amplified by viral content, algorithmic trading, and crowd behavior.

Recent empirical evidence from Hassan et al. (2025) confirms this structural shift. Using machine-learning models and high-frequency textual analysis, the authors show that sentiment extracted from user-generated digital content increasingly anticipates market movements following policy announcements. Their results point to a transformation in monetary transmission, where decentralized and behaviorally charged sentiment now acts as a transmission channel in its own right.

The interaction between digital sentiment and algorithmic trading further strengthens these effects. Many trading algorithms continuously monitor platforms such as X.com and Reddit using natural language processing tools. They translate qualitative language into quantitative trading signals by tracking tone, message volume, and keyword intensity. This allows markets to reposition almost instantly after major policy news. In highly reactive sectors such as AI, where expectations are already unstable, the integration of social sentiment into trading systems intensifies price movements and post-announcement volatility.

This process introduces strong nonlinearities into monetary transmission. Behavioral finance shows that investors react more strongly to negative news than to positive surprises. As a result, tightening signals tend to generate sharper and more abrupt market reactions than accommodative announcements. Digital platforms reinforce this asymmetry. Negative sentiment spreads faster, attracts more attention, and dominates discourse more persistently. This can lead to self-reinforcing sell-offs, price overshooting, and temporary liquidity imbalances that deviate from standard equilibrium models.

More broadly, digital platforms have expanded the influence of monetary policy beyond traditional macro-financial channels. Market outcomes are now shaped by collective sentiment, crowd behavior, and algorithmic interpretation of decentralized discourse. This transformation is especially important for AI-related assets, whose valuations depend heavily on expectations, investor psychology, and perceived policy trajectories.

As digital participation continues to grow and algorithmic processing becomes more sophisticated, monetary transmission will increasingly depend on how policy signals are interpreted, shared, and acted upon within these digital ecosystems.

2.8 AI Narratives and Retail Investor Confidence

Narratives around artificial intelligence have become a central driver of retail investor psychology. These narratives go far beyond simple reactions to news. They shape how investors interpret macroeconomic signals, technological progress, and the future prospects of AI firms. As shown by Iona cu (2024) and Marian (2024), discussions about AI breakthroughs, whether related to generative models, semiconductor innovation, or the strategies of leading technology companies play a key role in forming expectations about future profitability and global technological leadership.

Retail investors engage with these narratives mainly through digital platforms that filter, reframe, and amplify their meaning. Central bank signals, including those coming from the European Central Bank, are therefore processed through an already active discussion space. When a policy announcement points to economic uncertainty or tighter financial conditions, it is often interpreted as a threat to the funding environment of high-growth sectors such as AI. In response, many retail investors reduce exposure to long-duration technology stocks, move toward more liquid assets, or adopt a more defensive portfolio stance.

By contrast, an accommodative policy message that emphasizes liquidity support and financial stability tends to restore confidence in the growth potential and scalability of AI firms. These moments are often followed by renewed interest in thematic AI ETFs and concentrated positions in companies linked to machine learning, robotics, and automation. Retail behavior reflects not only rational reactions to interest rates, but also emotional and narrative-based interpretations of the economic climate.

Even during supportive monetary phases, however, optimism toward AI remains fragile. As noted by Olbert (2025), uncertainty surrounding regulation, especially related to the European Union's AI Act, continues to weigh on investor confidence. Concerns also persist about the sustainability of innovation cycles and the intensity of global competition in AI industries. These risks become particularly important when the ECB signals a tightening cycle. In such phases, investors tend to view policy normalization as a potential constraint on the financing capacity and research intensity of firms operating at the technological frontier.

This interaction between macro-financial conditions and AI narratives creates a feedback loop in which confidence is shaped jointly by economic signals and beliefs about technological progress. Investor reactions are therefore driven not only by objective indicators such as interest rates or earnings, but also by expectations about future innovation and the policy environment that enables or restricts it. This dual dependency sets AI-related equities apart from traditional asset classes and helps explain their heightened sensitivity to central bank communication.

2.9 Sentiment as a Transmission Channel

Investor sentiment has become a distinct and increasingly powerful transmission channel of monetary policy. Unlike traditional channels that operate through interest rates, credit conditions, or asset price adjustments, the sentiment channel works through changes in expectations and emotional reactions to economic signals. These reactions depend on how investors interpret central bank actions and how these interpretations spread across digital communication networks.

Today, digital trading platforms and social media play a central role in shaping investor sentiment. After an ECB announcement, financial narratives immediately circulate across communities on Reddit, X.com, and online brokerage forums. These interpretations often emerge before institutional research or formal analysis is published. They influence investor behavior in real time, contributing to rapid opinion formation and market-wide reactions that reflect prevailing mood rather than changes in economic fundamentals.

In sectors such as artificial intelligence, which rely heavily on long-term innovation stories and future earnings expectations, sentiment plays a particularly important role. AI-linked assets display strong expectation sensitivity, meaning their valuations respond sharply to perceived changes in the macroeconomic environment. A small shift in the tone of ECB communication can therefore alter investor beliefs about the growth potential of AI business models and trigger large price movements.

Algorithmic trading systems further amplify the role of sentiment. Many of these systems monitor social media and online forums using natural language processing tools. They detect changes in tone, uncertainty, and confidence, and convert them into trading signals. When sentiment turns negative after a tightening signal, algorithms may automatically trigger sell orders, reinforcing downward market pressure. This creates a feedback loop in which retail sentiment and automated trading reinforce each other, accelerating market reactions.

Recognizing sentiment as a core element of monetary transmission is therefore essential. Financial market reactions to central bank decisions are now shaped as much by narrative interpretation as by quantitative effects. In innovation-driven sectors such as AI, where valuations depend on expectations about future growth, sentiment acts not only as an amplifier of policy signals but also as an independent driver of asset prices. Understanding how central banks influence sentiment, through communication and perceived economic risk, is now central to any modern analysis of monetary transmission.

3 EMPIRICAL METHODOLOGY

3.1 A Time-Varying Parameter VAR Approach

AI-driven financial markets are shaped by powerful narratives, strong sensitivity to investor sentiment, long-horizon valuation logic, and the widespread use of algorithmic trading. These features make them very different from traditional financial markets and directly challenge the assumptions of standard econometric models used to study monetary policy transmission.

In particular, conventional VAR models rely on stable relationships, linear interactions, and stationarity over time. However, in markets driven by rapid technological change, shifting policy regimes, and evolving investor behavior, these assumptions are increasingly unrealistic. In AI markets, the impact of monetary policy is not constant: it varies with market sentiment, macroeconomic conditions, and the phase of the policy cycle.

To address these limitations, we adopt a Time-Varying Parameter VAR (TVP-VAR) model with stochastic volatility. By allowing both coefficients and error variances to evolve over time, the TVP-VAR framework captures changing sensitivities of financial variables to monetary policy shocks. This flexibility is crucial when analyzing AI-related assets, whose response to quantitative easing and tightening is likely to fluctuate depending on investor mood, market uncertainty, and liquidity conditions. As shown by Primiceri (2005), TVP-VAR models are well suited for periods of elevated uncertainty, when both the magnitude and the direction of shocks may change over time.

The TVP-VAR framework is also well adapted to detecting asymmetries in market reactions to monetary policy. Tightening phases often trigger stronger and more abrupt price responses than accommodative regimes, especially for long-duration assets such as AI equities. By tracing the evolution of impulse responses over time, the model allows us to identify these asymmetries and examine how they vary across different phases of the monetary policy cycle.

Finally, the model can incorporate sentiment indicators, making it possible to capture both fundamental and behavioral channels of monetary transmission. This integrated approach provides a more realistic representation of how monetary policy operates in innovation-driven and behaviorally complex financial markets.

3.2 Model Specification

The empirical model can be written as:
The model is presented as follows:

$$Y_t = c_t + b_{1,t} Y_{t-1} + \ldots + b_{p,t} Y_{t-p} + u_t \; t = 1, \ldots., T \tag{1}$$

In this specification,, Y_t denotes a vector containing three endogenous variables, The term p denotes the lag order of the VAR., the term c_t stands for an $n \times 1$ vector of constants. $b_{p,t}$ corresponds to $n \times n$ coefficient matrix. Finally, u_t is an $n \times 1$ vector of structural shocks, assumed to follow a multivariate normal distribution with a time-varying covariance.

This formulation allows both the intercepts and autoregressive coefficients to evolve over time, thereby capturing potential shifts in the underlying economic relationships. The inclusion of stochastic volatility further enables the model to account for heteroskedasticity in structural shocks, which appears during periods of economic turbulence or policy uncertainty.

4. DATA DESCRIPTION

This study utilizes a monthly panel dataset covering the period from January 2018 to October 2025. The primary financial variables include price indices for two exchange-traded funds (ETFs) representing technology subsectors: the Nasdaq AI Index, which captures the performance of high-growth firms engaged in artificial intelligence and machine learning, and the BOTZ ETF, which tracks companies involved in robotics, industrial automation, and related manufacturing technologies. To measure monetary policy dynamics, we incorporate the European Central Bank (ECB) effective interest rate, transformed into first differences to capture unanticipated monetary shocks. This variable is used as the policy innovation in the structural VAR framework and allows us to examine the transmission of unexpected changes in the policy stance. The use of first differences rather than levels is consistent with standard practice in monetary transmission literature, especially when focusing on short-term impulse responses to policy surprises.

All price series are converted into logarithmic monthly returns to ensure stationarity and comparability across assets. The dataset is aligned temporally to maintain synchronization among all series and minimize missing observations. The final balanced panel consists of 94 monthly observations for each variable.

5. RESULTS

5.1 Time-Varying Sectoral Responses to Monetary Policy Shocks

Figure 1 and Figure 2 illustrate the time-varying impulse responses of the NasdaqAI and BOTZ indices following a one-standard-deviation shock to the interest rate. The contrasting behaviors across these two periods highlight the regime-dependent nature of monetary policy transmission in AI-linked financial markets.

During March 2020, at the height of the COVID-19 outbreak, both indices exhibit very limited and short-lived reactions to the interest rate shock. NasdaqAI records a small temporary increase, while BOTZ displays a similarly modest and brief positive adjustment before both series quickly converge back to zero.

Figure 1.

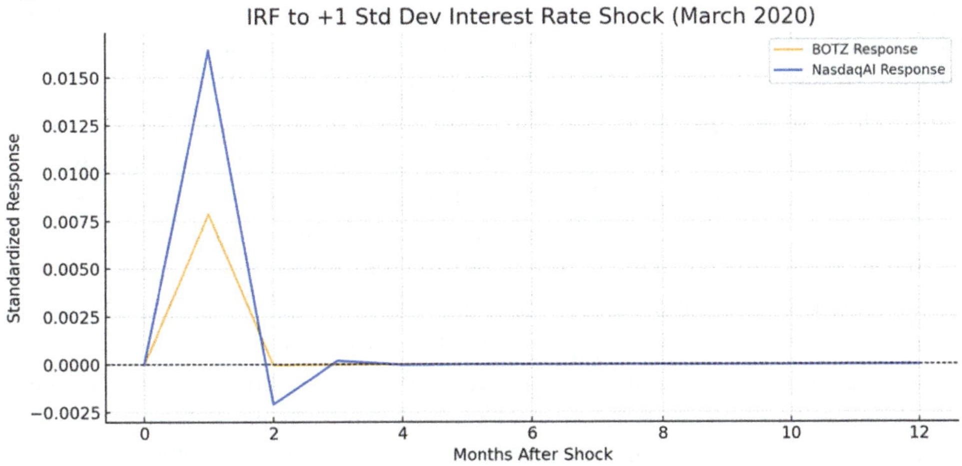

This muted pattern reflects the exceptional uncertainty and the dominance of non-monetary forces during the early pandemic period. Financial markets were primarily driven by health-related disruptions, emergency liquidity injections, and large-scale stabilization programmes. As a result, monetary policy signals carried little informational content for investors, and the standard transmission mechanisms were effectively overshadowed. The weak responses observed across both indices are therefore consistent with a regime in which exogenous shocks overwhelmingly shaped asset price dynamics and overshadowed the discount-rate channel.

Figure 2.

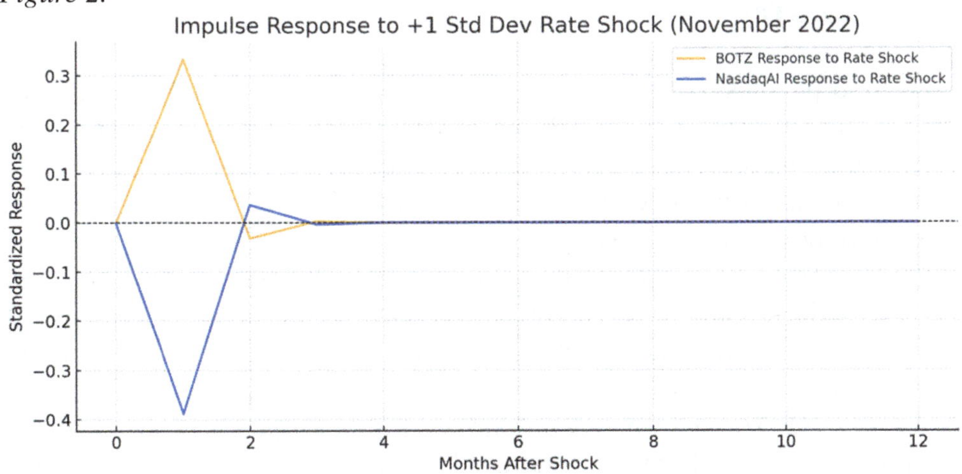

In Figure 2, a contrasting dynamic emerges in November 2022, when the European economy faced an aggressive tightening cycle. The NasdaqAI index displays a strong and persistent negative response to the interest rate shock. This pattern is fully consistent with the long-duration characteristics of AI-driven firms, whose valuations depend heavily on discounted future cash flows. The rise in interest rates during this period magnified discount-rate effects, reduced risk appetite, and triggered a revaluation of speculative and growth-oriented technology firms.

BOTZ, however, reacts positively and with greater persistence. Although seemingly counterintuitive, this behavior aligns with the index's sector composition, which includes robotics, automation, industrial equipment, and semiconductor-related firms. These segments were increasingly perceived as structurally resilient in a context of elevated inflation and tight labor markets, where automation and productivity-enhancing technologies were in high demand. Investors appear to have interpreted the tightening not as a recessionary signal but as a response to underlying economic strength, leading to a rotation toward industrial technology assets less sensitive to discount-rate movements.

Taken together, Figures 1 and 2 emphasize that the transmission of monetary policy shocks to AI-related equities is highly state-dependent. During crisis periods, shocks are absorbed with minimal impact, whereas in tightening regimes, sectoral characteristics become decisive: speculative AI firms exhibit pronounced sensitivity to higher rates, while industrial automation firms may benefit from the perceived resilience of real-economy technological demand. These results confirm the presence of structural asymmetries across AI-linked sectors and highlight the usefulness of time-varying models in capturing the evolving nature of monetary transmission.

6 FORECASTING

Figure 3 presents the three-month-ahead forecasts for NasdaqAI and BOTZ, expressed in standardized values and compared to their recent historical trajectories. The forecasts reveal a clear and consistent upward trend for both indices, indicating that the medium-term outlook for AI-related equities remains favorable under the current macroeconomic environment.

The historical segment of the figure (months −3 to −1) shows limited variation, with both indices exhibiting low and relatively stable standardized values. This flat pre-forecast pattern reflects the subdued market dynamics observed immediately before the projection window. Once the forecast horizon begins (months 1 to 3), both NasdaqAI and BOTZ shift sharply upward, suggesting a significant strengthening in expected market performance. NasdaqAI displays a robust acceleration, while

BOTZ projects an even steeper rise, indicating a marginally stronger anticipated momentum for the robotics and automation sector.

The synchronized growth of the two indices is consistent with the broader normalization of financial conditions and the easing of policy uncertainty documented earlier in the analysis. As monetary conditions stabilize and investor sentiment improves, AI-linked and automation-focused assets appear poised to benefit from renewed risk appetite, improved earnings expectations, and stronger capital flows into technology-driven sectors.

Overall, the forecast points to a near-term environment in which both speculative AI firms and industrial automation companies are expected to record substantial gains. This convergence reinforces the broader conclusion that, once macroeconomic volatility subsides, technology-linked financial markets tend to realign and experience coordinated upward adjustments.

Figure 3.

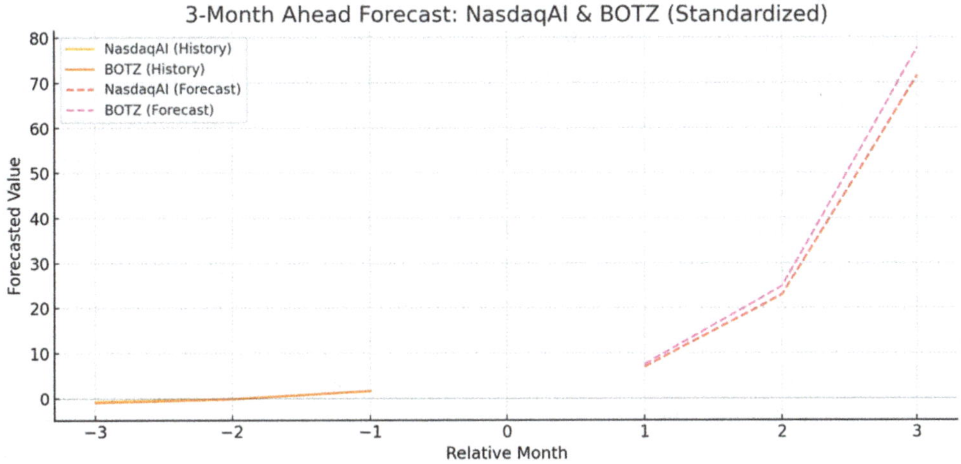

7. CONCLUSION

This study examines how monetary policy shocks particularly those associated with quantitative easing (QE) and quantitative tightening (QT), transmit into AI-related equity markets in the euro area. By adopting a TVP- VAR framework and by focusing on two structurally different technology indices, the analysis reveals pronounced sectoral asymmetries and evolving sensitivities to changes in the ECB's policy stance. The results show that monetary shocks do not diffuse uniformly across technology-linked assets. Instead, their impact depends on sector-specific fundamentals, prevailing macro-financial regimes, and shifts in investor expectations. Three main insights emerge from the empirical findings.First, during periods of extreme systemic stress, the onset of the COVID-19 crisis in March 2020, impulse responses indicate that monetary policy shocks were largely absorbed with minimal market impact. In this phase, monetary signals lost informational relevance as investors focused on pandemic uncertainty and emergency stabilization measures. As a result, both AI and automation-related equities displayed muted and short-lived reactions, consistent with a regime dominated by exogenous shocks.

Second, the tightening cycle of late 2022 generated a clear divergence in sectoral responses. NasdaqAI exhibited a strong and persistent negative reaction, reflecting the high duration and valuation sensitivity of speculative, growth-oriented AI firms. By contrast, BOTZ showed a positive and relatively sustained response to the same policy shock, suggesting that investors viewed industrial automation firms as more resilient in an environment of elevated inflation, labor shortages, and rising productivity needs. This contrast highlights the heterogeneous nature of the broader technology sector and underlines the importance of distinguishing between narrative-driven innovation assets and real-economy technology exposures.

Third, the normalization phase of 2024 was marked by a synchronized positive reaction across both indices, pointing to a regime shift in which monetary tightening was reinterpreted as a signal of macroeconomic stabilization rather than financial stress. This interpretation is reinforced by the three-month-ahead forecasts, which indicate strong and aligned growth trajectories for both NasdaqAI and BOTZ. Together, these results suggest a re-convergence of sectoral dynamics as uncertainty declines and investor expectations become more anchored.

The contribution of this study lies in its integration of macroeconomic policy analysis, asset pricing theory, and behavioral dynamics within a time-varying econometric framework. By documenting heterogeneous and nonlinear responses of AI-linked assets to monetary shocks, the analysis highlights the central role of narrative expectations, regulatory context, and digital sentiment in shaping the transmission mechanism. Unlike static models, the time-varying specification captures the evolving nature of these interactions and allows us to distinguish between temporary disruptions and more persistent structural shifts in investor behavior.

From a policy perspective, the results highlight the increasingly complex environment in which monetary authorities now operate. In financial markets shaped by rapid technological change and strong narrative dynamics, conventional interest-rate adjustments no longer transmit uniformly across sectors. Innovation-linked assets, such as AI-related equities, display nonlinear and time-varying responses that can generate asymmetric or unintended market effects during both easing and tightening cycles.

For central banks such as the ECB, this reinforces the central role of communication, forward guidance, and policy transparency. Market reactions are driven not only by the mechanical impact of policy instruments on financial conditions, but also by how policy decisions are framed, interpreted, and disseminated through digital information channels. In innovation-driven sectors, investor expectations are highly sensitive to perceived policy credibility, regulatory alignment, and long-term macroeconomic narratives. As a result, policy signals can influence asset prices through both financial and behavioral channels.

As artificial intelligence and automation continue to expand their footprint in economic activity, the interaction between monetary policy and technological investment will become increasingly important. Monetary authorities will need to account for sectoral heterogeneity, narrative-driven volatility, and the growing role of digital sentiment in shaping market dynamics. This implies that effective policy transmission now requires not only appropriate instrument design, but also strategic communication that anticipates how signals propagate through modern, digitally connected financial markets.

Overall, this study assess how monetary policy operates in a structurally evolving financial system. By emphasizing the importance of time variation, sector-specific sensitivities, and behavioral amplification mechanisms, it provides both analytical insight and practical guidance for policymakers and investors navigating the frontier between innovation finance and macroeconomic stabilization.

ACKNOWLEDGMENT

The author gratefully acknowledges the use of AI-based tools in the preparation of this manuscript.

REFERENCES

Aldasoro, I., Gambacorta, L., Korinek, A., Shreeti, V., & Stein, M. (2024). Intelligent financial system: How ai is transforming finance. Working Paper 1193, Bank for Interna- tional Settlements, Basel.

Altavilla, C., Carboni, G., & Motto, R. (2015). Asset purchase programmes and financial markets: Lessons from the euro area. Working Paper Series 1864, European Central Bank, Frankfurt.

Andrade, P., Breckenfelder, J., De Fiore, F., Karadi, P., & Tristani, O. (2016). The ecb's asset purchase programme: An early assessment. Working Paper Series 1956, European Central Bank, Frankfurt.

Barber, B. M., Morse, A., & Yasuda, A. (2021). Impact investing. *Journal of Financial Economics*, *139*(1), 162–185.

Bernanke, B. S., & Gertler, M. (1995). Inside the black box: The credit channel of monetary policy transmission. *The Journal of Economic Perspectives*, *9*(4), 27–48.

Boeckx, J., Dossche, M., & Peersman, G. (2017). Effectiveness and transmission of the ecb's balance sheet policies. *International Journal of Central Banking*, *13*(1), 297–333.

Brogaard, J., Nguyen, T. H., Putnins, T. J., & Wu, E. (2022). What moves stock prices? The roles of news, noise, and information. *Review of Financial Studies*, *35*(9), 4341–4386.

Brynjolfsson, E., & McAfee, A. (2017). *Machine, Platform, Crowd: Harnessing Our Digital Future*. W. W. Norton & Company.

Brynjolfsson, E., Rock, D., & Syverson, C. (2021). The productivity j-curve: How intan- gibles complement general purpose technologies. *American Economic Journal. Macroeconomics*, *13*(1), 333–372.

Cockburn, I. M., Henderson, R., & Stern, S. (2019). The impact of artificial intelligence on innovation: An exploratory analysis. In Agrawal, A., Gans, J., & Goldfarb, A. (Eds.), *The Economics of Artificial Intelligence: An Agenda* (pp. 115–148). University of Chicago Press.

Cookson, J. A., & Niessner, M. (2020). Why don't we agree? evidence from a social network of investors. *The Journal of Finance*, *75*(1), 173–228.

Draghi, M. (2015). Monetary policy: Past, present and future. Speech at the Frankfurt European Banking Congress. Frankfurt am Main.

Gagnon, J., Raskin, M., Remache, J., & Sack, B. (2011). *Large-scale asset purchases by the federal reserve: Did they work? Economic Policy Review 17(1)*. Federal Reserve Bank of New York.

Hassan, T. A., Hollander, S., & Kalyani, A. (2025). Text as data in economic analysis. *The Journal of Economic Perspectives*, *39*(3).

ILEANA, M., & MARIAN, C. V. (2024). Unlocking new horizons with Virtual Reality and Digital Learning to facilitate career transitions in IT and science. *On Virtual Learning*, 81.

Kogan, L., Papanikolaou, D., Seru, A., & Stoffman, N. (2017). Technological innovation, resource allocation, and growth. *The Quarterly Journal of Economics*, *132*(2), 665–712.

Passador, M. L. (2024). *Ai act and the ecb: Steering financial supervision in the eu*. Columbia Journal of European Law.

Primiceri, G. E. (2005). Time varying structural vector autoregressions and monetary policy. *The Review of Economic Studies*, *72*(3), 821–852.

Rostagno, M., Altavilla, C., Carboni, G., Lemke, W., Motto, R., Saint Guilhem, A., & Yiangou, G. (2019). A tale of two decades: The ecb's monetary policy at 20. Working Paper Series 2346, European Central Bank, Frankfurt.

Shiller, R. J. (2017). Narrative economics. *The American Economic Review*, *107*(4), 967–1004.

Conclusion

This book has explored how human-centered interactive technologies reshape consumer engagement across a wide range of digital and experiential contexts. It demonstrates that technologies such as artificial intelligence, immersive media, personalization systems, and data-driven platforms are no longer passive enablers of interaction, but active forces that shape consumers' perceptions, emotions, and behaviors throughout the customer journey. Across the chapters, engagement emerges as a multidimensional construct influenced not only by technological performance, but also by design choices that reflect human values and contextual sensitivity. Elements such as responsiveness, perceived agency, immersion, personalization intensity, and co-creation opportunities are shown to significantly affect trust, presence, flow, satisfaction, retention, and advocacy. These findings reinforce the idea that meaningful engagement cannot be engineered through technology alone; it must be cultivated through human-centered design principles.

The book also highlights the strategic relevance of engagement by linking individual-level consumer experiences to organizational and market-level outcomes. Empirical contributions illustrate how engagement mediates the relationship between interactive technologies and key performance indicators, including conversion, loyalty, innovation capacity, and competitive advantage. In doing so, the volume positions engagement as both a psychological response and a strategic resource in AI-driven environments.

From a managerial perspective, the chapters provide actionable insights for designing and managing interactive systems that enhance engagement while respecting ethical boundaries. Issues of privacy, transparency, trust, and responsible personalization emerge as critical conditions for sustaining engagement over time. For scholars and students, the book opens avenues for future research, particularly regarding longitudinal engagement dynamics, cross-contextual comparisons, and the evolving role of immersive and intelligent technologies. *Impacts of Human-Centered Interactive Technologies on Consumer Engagement* affirms that engagement lies at the heart of successful digital interaction. As technologies continue to evolve, the challenge for organizations is not merely to innovate, but to do so in ways that foster meaningful, trust-based, and sustainable relationships with consumers.

Compilation of References

AAnter, N. W. (2025). The Application of Artificial Intelligence (Virtual Reality and Augmented Reality) as a Training Tool in the Hospitality Industry. *The International Journal of Tourism and Hospitality Studies*, *8*(1), 191–214.

Abdo-Salloum, A. M., & Al-Mousawi, H. Y. (2025). Accounting students' technology readiness, perceptions, and digital competence toward artificial intelligence adoption in accounting curricula. *Journal of Accounting Education*, *70*, 100951.

Abenoza, R. F., Cats, O., & Susilo, Y. O. (2019). Determinants of traveler satisfaction: Evidence for non-linear and asymmetric effects. *Transportation Research Part F: Traffic Psychology and Behaviour*, *66*, 339–356. DOI: 10.1016/j.trf.2019.09.009

Abid, M. F., Shamim, A., Khan, Z., & Khan, I. (2022). Value creation or value destruction: Conceptualizing the experiential nature of value-in-use. *Journal of Consumer Behaviour*, *21*(3), 583–601.

Abou-Shouk, M., Zouair, N., Abdelhakim, A., Roshdy, H., & Abdel-Jalil, M. (2024). The effect of immersive technologies on tourist satisfaction and loyalty: The mediating role of customer engagement and customer perceived value. *International Journal of Contemporary Hospitality Management*, *36*(11), 3587–3606.

Acemoglu, D., & Restrepo, P. (2018). Artificial intelligence, automation, and work. In *The economics of artificial intelligence: An agenda* (pp. 197–236). University of Chicago Press.

Acquisti, A., Brandimarte, L., & Loewenstein, G. (2015). Privacy and human behavior in the age of information. *Science*, *347*(6221), 509–514. PMID: 25635091

Adam, M., Wessel, M., & Benlian, A. (2021). AI-based chatbots in customer service and their effects on user compliance. *Electronic Markets*, *31*(2), 427–445.

Adekunle, B. I., Chukwuma-Eke, E. C., Balogun, E. D., & Ogunsola, K. O. (2023). Improving customer retention through machine learning : A predictive approach to churn prevention and engagement strategies. *International Journal of Scientific Research in Computer Science. Engineering and Information Technology*, *9*(4), 507–523.

Agapito, D., Valle, P. O. D., & Mendes, J. (2014). The sensory dimension of tourist experiences: Capturing meaningful sensory-informed themes in Southwest Portugal. *Tourism Management*, *42*, 224–237. DOI: 10.1016/j.tourman.2013.11.011

Aguirre, E., Roggeveen, A. L., Grewal, D., & Wetzels, M. (2016). The personalization-privacy paradox : Implications for new media. *Journal of Consumer Marketing*, *33*(2), 98–110.

Ahmad, A., Alshurideh, M., Al Kurdi, B., Aburayya, A., & Hamadneh, S. (2021). Digital transformation metrics: A conceptual view. *Journal of Management Information and Decision Sciences*, *24*(7), 1–18. https://www.abacademies.org/articles/digital-transformation-metrics--a--conceptual--view-11806.html

Ahmed, Z. U. (1992). Islamic pilgrimage (Hajj) to Ka'aba in Makkah (Saudi Arabia): An important international tourism activity. *Journal of Tourism Studies*, *3*(1), 35–43. https://www.cabdirect.org/abstracts/19921898582.html

Aishwarya, K. M., Hemanth, K., & Ashwini, P. J. (2025). Predictive Analytics for Social Media Engagement. *International Journal of Advanced Research in Computer and Communication Engineering*, *14*(8), 155–162. DOI: 10.17148/IJARCCE.2025.14816

Ajzen, I. (1991). The theory of planned behavior. *Organizational Behavior and Human Decision Processes*, *50*(2), 179–211.

Akar, E. (2021). Customers' online purchase intentions and customer segmentation during the period of COVID-19 pandemic. *Journal of Internet Commerce*, *20*(3), 371–401.

Aktaş, M., & Durmaz, Y. (2025). The Mediating Role of Customer Satisfaction in the Effect of Artificial Intelligence-Enabled Chatbots on Online Shopping Experience and Repurchase Intention. *REFLEKTİF Sosyal Bilimler Dergisi*, *6*(3), 969–990.

Al Khaldy, I. A. (2024). Impact of digital marketing techniques in increasing effectiveness of conversion rate optimization (CRO) among telecommunication organizations in Jordan. *International Research Journal of Economics and Management Studies*, *3*(2), 251–259. DOI: 10.56472/25835238/IRJEMS-V3I2P131

Alasmari, A., Farooqi, N., & Alotaibi, Y. (2024). Sentiment analysis of pilgrims using CNN-LSTM deep learning approach. *PeerJ. Computer Science*, *10*, e2584. DOI: 10.7717/peerj-cs.2584 PMID: 39896353

Albahar, M., Gazzawe, F., Thanoon, M., & Albahr, A. (2023). Exploring Hajj pilgrim satisfaction with hospitality services through expectation-confirmation theory and deep learning. *Heliyon*, *9*(11), e22192. DOI: 10.1016/j.heliyon.2023.e22192 PMID: 38034756

Aldasoro, I., Gambacorta, L., Korinek, A., Shreeti, V., & Stein, M. (2024). Intelligent financial system: How ai is transforming finance. Working Paper 1193, Bank for Interna- tional Settlements, Basel.

Aldunate, Á., Maldonado, S., Vairetti, C., & Armelini, G. (2022). Understanding customer satisfaction via deep learning and natural language processing. *Expert Systems with Applications*, *209*, 118309.

Alexandris, K., & Palialia, E. (1999). Measuring customer satisfaction in fitness centres in Greece: An exploratory study. *Managing Leisure*, *4*(4), 218–228.

Alfiyahsari, R., Taurina, R. A., & Priyanka, G. (2023). The effectiveness of using digital marketing communication strategies and their conversion effects (Case study on DatascripMall.ID). [JoSS]. *Journal of Social Sciences*, *2*, 507–522. DOI: 10.57185/joss.v2i6.96

Allal-Chérif, O., Puertas, R., & Carracedo, P. (2024). Intelligent influencer marketing : How AI-powered virtual influencers outperform human influencers. *Technological Forecasting and Social Change*, *200*, 123113. DOI: 10.1016/j.techfore.2023.123113

Allen, B. J., Chandrasekaran, D., & Basuroy, S. (2018). Design crowdsourcing: The impact on new product performance of sourcing design solutions from the "Crowd". *Journal of Marketing*, *82*(2), 106–123.

Allen, C. T., Machleit, K. A., & Kleine, S. S. (1992). A comparison of attitudes and emotions as predictors of behavior at diverse levels of behavioral experience. *The Journal of Consumer Research*, *18*(4), 493–504.

Allen, C. T., Machleit, K. A., & Marine, S. S. (1988). On assessing the emotionality of advertising via Izard's differential emotions scale. *Advances in Consumer Research. Association for Consumer Research (U. S.)*, *15*(1), 226–231.

Altavilla, C., Carboni, G., & Motto, R. (2015). Asset purchase programmes and financial markets: Lessons from the euro area. Working Paper Series 1864, European Central Bank, Frankfurt.

Alves, T., Natálio, J., Henriques-Calado, J., & Gama, S. (2020). Incorporating personality in user interface design : A review. *Personality and Individual Differences, 155*, 109709. DOI: 10.1016/j.paid.2019.109709

Ami, R. (2021). AI in Automated Content Moderation on Social Media. *International Journal of Artificial Intelligence and Machine Learning, 4*(3). https://itaimle.com/index.php/ijaiml/article/download/249/26

Ammar, O., Chrysochou, P., & Trabelsi Trigui, I. (2017, May). Consumer Perceptions And Response Toward Co-Designed Packaging. In *22nd International Conference on Corporate and Marketing Communications*, Zaragoza, Spain, May 4-5

Anderson, L., Naughton, R. J., Close, G. L., Di Michele, R., Morgans, R., Drust, B., & Morton, J. P. (2017). Daily distribution of macronutrient intakes of professional soccer players from the English Premier League. *International Journal of Sport Nutrition and Exercise Metabolism, 27*(6), 491–498. PMID: 28657805

Andrade, P., Breckenfelder, J., De Fiore, F., Karadi, P., & Tristani, O. (2016). The ecb's asset purchase programme: An early assessment. Working Paper Series 1956, European Central Bank, Frankfurt.

Anitha, M. V. (2024). *Enhancing customer experience through digital transformation: Strategies and impact*. Today's Multidisciplinary Research Perspectives.

Araiza-Alba, P., Keane, T., Chen, W. S., & Kaufman, J. (2021). Immersive virtual reality as a tool to learn problem-solving skills. *Computers & Education, 164*, 104121.

Arar, E., & Halicioglu, F. H. (2025). Understanding Artificial Neural Networks as a Transformative Approach to Construction Risk Management: A Systematic Literature review. *Buildings (Basel, Switzerland), 15*(18), 3346. DOI: 10.3390/buildings15183346

Araujo, T. (2018). Living up to the chatbot hype: The influence of anthropomorphic design cues and communicative agency framing on conversational agent and company perceptions. *Computers in Human Behavior, 85*, 183–189.

Arghashi, V., & Yuksel, C. (2022). Interactivity, inspiration, and perceived usefulness! How retailers' AR-apps improve consumer engagement through flow. *Journal of Retailing and Consumer Services, 64*(2), 102756. DOI: 10.1016/j.jretconser.2021.102756

Armutcu, B., Tan, A., Ho, S. P. S., Chow, M. Y. C., & Gleason, K. C. (2024). The effect of bank artificial intelligence on consumer purchase intentions. *Kybernetes, 54*(10), 5529–5553. DOI: 10.1108/K-01-2024-0145

Arrieta, A. B., Díaz-Rodríguez, N., Del Ser, J., Bennetot, A., Tabik, S., Barbado, A., García, S., Gil-López, S., Molina, D., & Benjamins, R. (2020). Explainable Artificial Intelligence (XAI) : Concepts, taxonomies, opportunities and challenges toward responsible AI. *Information Fusion*, *58*, 82–115.

Ashley, C., & Tuten, T. (2015). Creative strategies in social media marketing: An exploratory study of branded social content and consumer engagement. *Psychology and Marketing*, *32*(1), 15–27.

Asli, I., & Bensassi, H. N. (2025). Intelligence Artificielle et Stratégies de Marketing Personnalisé : Une Revue Systématique de la Littérature. *Revue Française d'Economie et de Gestion*, *6*(7). Advance online publication. DOI: 10.5281/zenodo.16374934

Atakan, S. S., Bagozzi, R. P., & Yoon, C. (2014). Consumer Participation in the Design and Realization Stages of Production: How Self production Shapes Consumer Evaluations and Relationships to Products. *International Journal of Research in Marketing*, *31*(4), 395–408.

Atapattu, M., Sedera, D., Ravichandran, T., & Grover, V. (2016). Customers' View of Agility: The Expectation-Confirmation Theory Perspective. *Gyeong'yeong Jeongbohag Yeon'gu/Gyeong-yeong Jeongbohak Yeon-gu, 26*(1), 80–108. https://doi.org/DOI: 10.14329/apjis.2016.26.1.80

Attruia, F. (2021). L'autorité des jeunes influenceurs du Web dans le genre de l'«unboxing»: un cas d'étude français/italien. *Argumentation et Analyse du Discours, 26*.

BAE, K. P., & Park, H. (2025). Optimizing Personalized Marketing Strategies with NLP and Machine Learning on Customer Review Data. *Cuestiones de Fisioterapia*, *54*(1), 151–159.

Bag, S., Srivastava, G., Al Bashir, M. M., Kumari, S., Giannakis, M., & Chowdhury, A. H. (2022). Journey of customers in this digital era: Understanding the role of artificial intelligence technologies in user engagement and conversion. *Benchmarking*, *29*(7), 2074–2098. DOI: 10.1108/BIJ-07-2021-0415

Bailie, R. A., & Urbina, N. (2013). *Content strategy: Connecting the dots between business, brand, and benefits*. XML Press.

Ball, M. (2022). *The metaverse: And how it will revolutionize everything*. Liveright Publishing.

Baltes, L. P. (2015). Content marketing-the fundamental tool of digital marketing. *Bulletin of the Transilvania University of Brasov. Series V, Economic Sciences*, •••, 111–118. https://www.scirp.org/reference/referencespapers?referenceid=4034107

Bandura, A. (1963). Social reinforcement and behavior change—Symposium, 1962: 1. Behavior theory and identificatory learning. *The American Journal of Orthopsychiatry*, *33*(4), 591. PMID: 13966305

Bandura, A. (1989). Human agency in social cognitive theory. *The American Psychologist*, *44*(9), 1175. PMID: 2782727

Bansal, G., Chamola, V., Hussain, A., Guizani, M., & Niyato, D. (2024). Transforming conversations with AI—A comprehensive study of ChatGPT. *Cognitive Computation*, •••, 1–24.

Barber, B. M., Morse, A., & Yasuda, A. (2021). Impact investing. *Journal of Financial Economics*, *139*(1), 162–185.

Bargh, J. A., Chen, M., & Burrows, L. (1996). Automaticity of social behavior: Direct effects of trait construct and stereotype activation on action. *Journal of Personality and Social Psychology*, *71*(2), 230. PMID: 8765481

Barnes, E. (2016). *The minority body: A theory of disability*. Oxford University Press.

Barta, S., Gurrea, R., & Flavián, C. (2023). How augmented reality increases engagement through its impact on risk and decision process. *Cyberpsychology, Behavior, and Social Networking*, *26*(3), 177–187. PMID: 36706429

Barta, S., Gurrea, R., & Flavián, C. (2025). Augmented reality experiences: Consumer-centered augmented reality framework and research agenda. *Psychology and Marketing*, *42*(2), 634–650.

Bartels, M., Drummond, P., & Carrigan, M. (2023). The persuasive influence of branded content on children's purchase intentions. *Journal of Business Ethics*, •••, 1–17.

Bauman, S., & Tatum, T. (2009). Web sites for young children: Gateway to online social networking?. *Professional School Counseling, 13*(1), 2156759X0901300102.

Bazi, S., Filieri, R., & Gorton, M. (2023). Social media content aesthetic quality and customer engagement: The mediating role of entertainment and impacts on brand love and loyalty. *Journal of Business Research, 160*, 113778. DOI: 10.1016/j.jbusres.2023.113778

Beenders, C. (2023). *How to Approach the Development Process of a Lead Scoring Model* [Bachelor's thesis, Oulu University of Applied Sciences]. https://www.theseus.fi/handle/10024/812465

Belch, M. A., Krentler, K. A., & Willis-Flurry, L. A. (2005). Teen internet mavens: Influence in family decision making. *Journal of Business Research*, *58*(5), 569–575.

Belouz, K., Nourani, A., Zereg, S., & Bencheikh, A. (2021). Prediction of greenhouse tomato yield using artificial neural networks combined with sensitivity analysis. *Scientia Horticulturae*, *293*, 110666. DOI: 10.1016/j.scienta.2021.110666

Ben Youssef, A., & Dahmani, M. (2023). Examining the drivers of e-commerce adoption by Moroccan firms: A multi-model analysis. *Information (Basel)*, *14*(7), 1–19. DOI: 10.3390/info14070378

Benbouja, A., & Cavalli, P. (2010). Les 15-17 ans internautes et le comportement de consommation des parents: Le cas des Français et des Italiens. *9Th International Marketing Trends Conference*, Venice, January.

Bénédict, T. M. (2022). Usage des réseaux sociaux Facebook et WhatsApp et leur impact sur l'éducation des jeunes en ville de Butembo.

Benson, P. (2007). Autonomy in language teaching and learning. *Language Teaching*, *40*(1), 21–40.

Berey, L. A., & Pollay, R. W. (1968). The influencing role of the child in family decision making. *JMR, Journal of Marketing Research*, *5*, 70–72.

Bernanke, B. S., & Gertler, M. (1995). Inside the black box: The credit channel of monetary policy transmission. *The Journal of Economic Perspectives*, *9*(4), 27–48.

Bhambri, P., & Rani, S. (2024). Issues Related to Chatbots. In Design and Development of Emerging Chatbot Technology (pp. 130-147). IGI Global.

Bhardwaj, P., & Kalro, A. D. (2024). Consumer well-being: A systematic literature review and research agenda using TCCM framework. *International Journal of Consumer Studies*, *48*(1), e12991.

Bhaskaran, V. (2024). Designing for trust: The crucial role in digital user experiences. *Journal of User Experience*, *19*(2), 53–59. https://uxpajournal.org/wcontent/uploads/sites/7/2024/02/JUX_Bhaskaran_Feb-2024.pdf

Bhatnagr, P. (2025). Virtual influencers on Instagram : A text mining study of consumer sentiments in China. *Journal of Modelling in Management*. Advance online publication. DOI: 10.1108/JM2-01-2025-0024

Bhattacharya, C., Parasar, A., Sudhakar, P. K., Kumar, S., & Bakshi, S., & Shinde, Sonal. B. (2025). AI-Powered Predictive Models Transforming the Future of Digital Marketing and Customer Engagement. *Journal of Informatics Education and Research*, *5*(1). Advance online publication. DOI: 10.52783/jier.v5i1.2015

Bhattacherjee, A. (2001). Understanding information systems continuance: An expectation-confirmation model. *Management Information Systems Quarterly*, •••, 351–370.

Bilal, M., Zhang, Y., Cai, S., Akram, U., & Halibas, A. (2024). Artificial intelligence is the magic wand making customer-centric a reality! An investigation into the relationship between consumer purchase intention and consumer engagement through affective attachment. *Journal of Retailing and Consumer Services*, *77*, 103674.

Bilgihan, A., & Ricci, P. (2024). The new era of hotel marketing: Integrating cutting-edge technologies with core marketing principles. *Journal of Hospitality and Tourism Technology*, *15*(1), 123–137.

Bilro, R. G., & Loureiro, S. M. C. (2020). A consumer engagement systematic review: Synthesis and research agenda. *Spanish Journal of Marketing - ESIC*, *24*(3), 283–307.

Bingley, W. J., Curtis, C., Lockey, S., Bialkowski, A., Gillespie, N., Haslam, S. A., Ko, R. K., Steffens, N., Wiles, J., & Worthy, P. (2023). Where is the human in human-centered AI? Insights from developer priorities and user experiences. *Computers in Human Behavior*, *141*, 107617.

Biocca, F. (1997). The cyborg's dilemma: Progressive embodiment in virtual environments. *Journal of Computer-Mediated Communication*, *3*(2).

Biocca, F., Harms, C., & Burgoon, J. K. (2003). Toward a more robust theory and measure of social presence: Review and suggested criteria. *Presence (Cambridge, Mass.)*, *12*(5), 456–480.

Bjelajac, D., Đerčan, B., & Kovačić, S. (2021). Dark skies and dark screens as a precondition for astronomy tourism and general well-being. *Information Technology & Tourism*, *23*(1), 19–43.

Black, J. J. (2024). *Predictors of Online Purchase Conversions Using Clickstream Data and Sentiment Analysis* [PhD Thesis, University of South Alabama]. https://search.proquest.com/openview/7d2a048972585e4ff973097e0f66ea0e/1?pq-origsite=gscholar&cbl=18750&diss=y

Blut, M., Wang, C., Wünderlich, N. V., & Brock, C. (2021). Understanding anthropomorphism in service provision: A meta-analysis of physical robots, chatbots, and other AI. *Journal of the Academy of Marketing Science*, *49*(4), 632–658.

Boccalini, S., Patrizi, M., Vernuccio, M., & Pastore, A. (2025). Enhancing eudaimonic well-being through brand experiences in the VR-based metaverse: Implications for brand-self connection and brand love. *Journal of Product and Brand Management, 34*(6), 817–831.

Boeckx, J., Dossche, M., & Peersman, G. (2017). Effectiveness and transmission of the ecb's balance sheet policies. *International Journal of Central Banking, 13*(1), 297–333.

Boistel, P. (2014). Réputation : Un concept à définir. *Communication et organisation. Revue scientifique francophone en Communication organisationnelle, 46*, Article 46. DOI: 10.4000/communicationorganisation.4796

Boistel, P., & Laroutis, D. (2019). E-réputation et réputation : Similitudes et différences. Une analyse comparative conceptuelle. *RIMHE : Revue Interdisciplinaire Management. Homme & Entreprise, 368*(3), 104–120. DOI: 10.3917/rimhe.036.0104

Bonhomme, M. (2014). *Pragmatique des figures du discours*. Honoré Champion.

Bonnéry, S., & Pasquali, P. (2023). Le "métier d'enfant" 50 ans après: Penser l'éducation et la socialisation avec Jean-Claude Chamboredon. *Revue Française de Pédagogie*, •••, 5–15.

Booz, Allen, & Hamilton (1982), New Products Management for the 1980s.

Borgstede, M., & Eggert, F. (2022). Squaring the circle: From latent variables to theory-based measurement. *Theory & Psychology, 33*(1), 118–137. DOI: 10.1177/09593543221127985

Borsboom, D. (2008). Latent variable Theory. *Measurement: Interdisciplinary Research and Perspectives, 6*(1–2), 25–53. DOI: 10.1080/15366360802035497

Bouaddi, M., Sanaa, M., & Siham, K. (2024). The effect of using social media by brands on customer engagement: Content quality, personalization, and constant presence as key factors. In Proceedings of the International Conference on Information Technology, Multimedia, Architecture, Design, and E-Business (Vol. 3, pp. 533-545).

Bowden, J. L.-H. (2009). The process of customer engagement: A conceptual framework. *Journal of Marketing Theory and Practice, 17*(1), 63–74. DOI: 10.2753/MTP1069-6679170105

Bowman, D., Minehart, D., & Rabin, M. (1999). Loss aversion in a consumption–savings model. *Journal of Economic Behavior & Organization, 38*(2), 155–178.

Bozkurt, A., & Şeker, F. (2023). Harmonizing heritage and artificial neural networks: The role of Sustainable tourism in UNESCO World Heritage Sites. *Sustainability, 15*(17), 13031. DOI: 10.3390/su151713031

Brée, J. (1993). *Les enfants, la consommation et le marketing* (1ère éd.). Paris, Presses Universitaires de France.

Brée, J. (2021). *Kids Marketing* (3e éd.). Éditions EMS.

Brée, J. (1990). Les enfants et la consommation: Un tour d'horizon des recherches. *Revue et Applications en Marketing, 1/90*, 43–69.

Brée, J., & Pantin-Sohier, G. (2023). Chapitre 1. De l'importance de comprendre le consommateur. *Les Topos, 5*, 9–40.

Brem, A., Giones, F., & Werle, M. (2021). The AI digital revolution in innovation: A conceptual framework of artificial intelligence technologies for the management of innovation. *IEEE Transactions on Engineering Management, 70*(2), 770–776.

Bretos, M. A., Ibáñez-Sánchez, S., & Orús, C. (2024). Applying virtual reality and augmented reality to the tourism experience: A comparative literature review. *Spanish Journal of Marketing - ESIC, 28*(3), 287–309.

Brodie, R. J., Hollebeek, L. D., Jurić, B., & Ilić, A. (2011). Customer engagement: Conceptual domain, fundamental propositions, and implications for research. *Journal of Service Research, 14*(3), 252–271.

Brogaard, J., Nguyen, T. H., Putnins, T. J., & Wu, E. (2022). What moves stock prices? The roles of news, noise, and information. *Review of Financial Studies, 35*(9), 4341–4386.

Brusilovski, P., Kobsa, A., & Nejdl, W. (2007). *The adaptive web : Methods and strategies of web personalization* (Vol. 4321). Springer Science & Business Media.

Brynjolfsson, E., & McAfee, A. (2017). *Machine, Platform, Crowd: Harnessing Our Digital Future*. W. W. Norton & Company.

Brynjolfsson, E., & Mcafee, A. N. D. R. E. W. (2017). Artificial intelligence, for real. *Harvard Business Review, 1*, 1–31.

Brynjolfsson, E., Rock, D., & Syverson, C. (2021). The productivity j-curve: How intan- gibles complement general purpose technologies. *American Economic Journal. Macroeconomics, 13*(1), 333–372.

Bud, I. (2022). La rhétorique publicitaire. *Annales Universitatis Apulensis. Series Philologica, 23*(1), 369–376.

Bughin, J., Hazan, E., & Sree Ramaswamy, P. DC, W., & Chu, M. (2017). Artificial intelligence the next digital frontier.

Buhalis, D., Leung, D., & Lin, M. (2023). Metaverse as a disruptive technology revolutionising tourism management and marketing. *Tourism Management*, *97*(1), 104724.

Buijzen, M., Cleeren, M., & Valkenburg, P. M. (2023). Understanding children's online advertising literacy: A framework and review of the literature. *Journal of Communication*, *73*(1), 74–98.

Burke, R. (2002). Hybrid Recommender Systems : Survey and Experiments. *User Modeling and User-Adapted Interaction*, *12*(4), 331–370. DOI: 10.1023/A:1021240730564

Burns, T., & Stalker, G. M. (1961). The management of innovation. London. *Tavistock Publishing. Cited in Hurley, RF and Hult, GTM (1998). Innovation, Market Orientation, and Organisational Learning: An Integration and Empirical Examination. Journal of Marketing*, *62*(4), 42–54.

Butt, A. H., Ahmad, H., & Shafique, M. N. (2021). AI-Powered "Voice Recognition Avatar": A New Way to Play Games. [IJGCMS]. *International Journal of Gaming and Computer-Mediated Simulations*, *13*(3), 1–17.

Buttussi, F., & Chittaro, L. (2023). Acquisition and retention of spatial knowledge through virtual reality experiences: Effects of VR setup and locomotion technique. *International Journal of Human-Computer Studies*, *177*, 103067.

Bu, Y., Parkinson, J., & Thaichon, P. (2022). Influencer marketing : Homophily, customer value co-creation behaviour and purchase intention. *Journal of Retailing and Consumer Services*, *66*, 102904. DOI: 10.1016/j.jretconser.2021.102904

Cahyadi, H. S., Sumardi, V., Rosadi, A., & Nurjamal, D. (2024). Exploring pilgrimage tourist typologies in Cikakak Tourism Village. *Journal of Tourism Sustainability*, *4*(1), 34–41. DOI: 10.35313/jtospolban.v4i1.117

Çakiroğlu, Ü., & Gökoğlu, S. (2019). A design model for using virtual reality in behavioral skills training. *Journal of Educational Computing Research*, *57*(7), 1723–1744.

Calder, B. J., Malthouse, E. C., & Schaedel, U. (2009). An experimental study of the relationship between online engagement and advertising effectiveness. *Journal of Interactive Marketing*, *23*(4), 321–331.

Calvet, L., Bourdin, P., & Prados, F. (2019, November). Immersive technologies in higher education: Applications, challenges, and good practices. In *Proceedings of the 2019 3rd International Conference on Education and E-Learning* (pp. 95-99).

Cao, C., Liu, H., & Wang, Z. (2024). The Influencing Factors of Tourist Loyalty in Camping Destinations Based on Expectation Confirmation Theory: The Mediating Role of Satisfaction and Well-Being. *Heliyon*. Advance online publication. DOI: 10.2139/ssrn.4873472

Cao, D., Meadows, M., Wong, D., & Xia, S. (2021). Understanding consumers' social media engagement behaviour: An examination of the moderation effect of social media context. *Journal of Business Research, 122*, 835–846. DOI: 10.1016/j.jbusres.2020.06.025

Carlson, D. R. J. C. L. (2001). Sélection Internationale. *Recherche et Applications en Marketing, 16*(1), 87.

Carter, D. (2018). How real is the impact of artificial intelligence? The business information survey 2018. *Business Information Review, 35*(3), 99–115.

Casaca, J., & Miguel, L. P. (2024). The influence of personalization on consumer satisfaction: Trends and challenges. In *Data-driven marketing for strategic success* (pp. 256–292). IGI Global., DOI: 10.4018/979-8-3693-3455-3.ch010

Castaño-Prieto, L., Solano-Sánchez, M. Á., Hidalgo-Fernández, A., & López-Guzmán, T. L. G. (2025). Profiling intangible cultural heritage visitors through multilayer perceptron's model. *Investigaciones Turísticas*, (29), 101–123. DOI: 10.14198/INTURI.27353

Cen, Z., & Zhao, Y. (2024). Enhancing user engagement through adaptive interfaces : A study on real-time personalization in web applications. *Journal of Economic Theory and Business Management, 1*(6), 1–7.

Chabry, L., Gillet-Goinard, F., & Jourdan, R. (2020). Outil 46. Le client ambassadeur. In *La Boîte à Outils* (p. 192). Dunod. https://shs.cairn.info/article/DUNOD_CHABR_2020_01_0126

Chaiken, S., & Trope, Y. (Eds.). (1999). *Dual-process theories in social psychology*. Guilford Press.

Chakraborty, U., Roy, S., & Kumar, S. (2023). *Rise of Generative AI and ChatGPT: Understand how Generative AI and ChatGPT are transforming and reshaping the business world (English Edition)*. BPB Publications.

Charry, K., & Pecheux, C. (2008). Enfance, alimentation et publicité: quels rôles pour le marketing?. *Reflets et perspectives de la vie économique*, (2), 9-17.

Chaudhry, S., & Dhawan, S. (2020). AI-Based Recommendation System for Social Networking. In Pant, M., Sharma, T. K., Verma, O. P., Singla, R., & Sikander, A. (Eds.), *Soft Computing : Theories and Applications* (Vol. 1053, pp. 617–629). Springer Singapore., DOI: 10.1007/978-981-15-0751-9_58

Chen, H., & Chen, M. (2025). Journey of the soul: Participants' event experience satisfaction, and psychological well-being during a Pilgrimage tourism event. *Event Management*. Advance online publication. DOI: 10.3727/152599525x174581767 67800

Chen, J., Zhou, W., & Frankwick, G. L. (2023). Firm AI Adoption Intensity and Marketing Performance. *Journal of Computer Information Systems*, •••, 1–18.

Chen, Y. M., Hsu, T. H., & Lu, Y. J. (2018). Impact of flow on mobile shopping intention. *Journal of Retailing and Consumer Services*, *41*, 281–287.

Cheong, R. (1995). The virtual threat to travel and tourism. *Tourism Management*, *16*(6), 417–422.

Chirico, F. (2016). Spiritual well-being in the 21st century: It's time to review the current WHO's health definition. *Journal of Health and Social Sciences*, *1*(1), 11–16.

Cho, I., Wang, D., Takahashi, R., & Saito, H. (2022). *A Personalized Dialogue Generator with Implicit User Persona Detection* (arXiv:2204.07372). arXiv. /arXiv.2204.07372DOI: 10.48550

Choi, D., & Kim, J. (2022). Why people continue to play online games: In search of critical design factors to increase customer loyalty to online contents. *Cyberpsychology & Behavior*, *7*(1), 11–24. PMID: 15006164

Cho, M., Ko, E., & Jung, H. (2024). Virtual reality luxury fashion show: How imaginary space influences brand word of mouth. *International Journal of Advertising*, •••, 1–20.

Chouk, I., & Guiot, D. (2014). *Publicité intrusive sur Internet: une étude exploratoire des profils de résistance. In 13ème journée de recherche sur le e-marketing/ marketing digital.*

Chowdary, K. M. T., Vallepu, M., Purushotham, A. N. S., & Kumari, N. (2024). Personalized Marketing and Recommendation Systems. In *Predictive Analytics and Generative AI for Data-Driven Marketing Strategies* (1re éd., p. 82-89). Chapman and Hall/CRC. https://www.taylorfrancis.com/chapters/edit/10.1201/9781003472544-7/personalized-marketing-recommendation-systems-mani-teja-chowdary-maniteja-vallepu-naga-sai-purushotham-neelam-kumari

Chowdhary, K. R. (2020). Natural Language Processing. In K. R. Chowdhary, *Fundamentals of Artificial Intelligence* (p. 603-649). Springer India. DOI: 10.1007/978-81-322-3972-7_19

Choy, J. E. (2024). AI unveiled: a comparative analysis of code accuracy and reliability across various chatbot platforms.

Christensen, B. T., Ball, L. J., & Halskov, K. (2017). *Analysing design thinking: Studies of cross-cultural co-creation*. CRC Press.

Chrysochou, P., Tiganis, A., Trigui, I. T., & Grunert, K. G. (2021). A Cross-Cultural Study on Consumer Preferences for Olive Oil. *Food Quality and Preference*, •••, 104460.

Chung, K., & Park, R. C. (2019). Chatbot-based heathcare service with a knowledge base for cloud computing. *Cluster Computing*, *22*, 1925–1937.

Chung, K., Thaichon, P., & Quach, S. (2022). Types of artificial intelligence (AI) in marketing management. In *Artificial intelligence for marketing management* (pp. 29–40). Routledge.

Cieślik, B. (2025). Mechanisms of Virtual Reality-Based Relaxation in Older Adults: A Scoping Review. *Journal of Clinical Medicine*, *14*(17), 6126. PMID: 40943883

Claeyssen, Y., Deydier, A., & Riquet, Y. (2011). *Le Marketing client multicanal. Prospection, fidélisation et reconquête du client*. Dunod., DOI: 10.3917/dunod.claey.2011.01

Claffey, E., & Brady, M. (2014). A model of consumer engagement in a virtual customer environment. *Journal of Customer Behaviour*, *13*(4), 325–346.

Clark, D. (2016). Content strategy: An integrative literature review. *IEEE Transactions on Professional Communication*, *59*(1), 7–23. DOI: 10.1109/TPC.2016.2537080

Cockburn, I. M., Henderson, R., & Stern, S. (2019). The impact of artificial intelligence on innovation: An exploratory analysis. In Agrawal, A., Gans, J., & Goldfarb, A. (Eds.), *The Economics of Artificial Intelligence: An Agenda* (pp. 115–148). University of Chicago Press.

Cohen, J. (2013). Statistical power analysis for the behavioral sciences. routledge.

Cookson, J. A., & Niessner, M. (2020). Why don't we agree? evidence from a social network of investors. *The Journal of Finance*, *75*(1), 173–228.

Cottin, J. (2022). Les symboles bibliques dans la publicité: développement, contextes, conflits. *Communiquer. Revue de communication sociale et publique, 34*, 21-32.

Coughlan, P., & Duff, P. A. (1994). Same task, different activities: Analysis of SLA task from an Activity Theory perspective. *Vygotskian approaches to second language research*, 173-193.

Csikszentmihalyi, M. (1990). *Flow: The psychology of optimal experience.* Harper & Row.

Csikszentmihalyi, M. (1997). *Flow and the psychology of discovery and invention.* HarperPerennial.

Cucinella, S. L., de Winter, J. C., Grauwmeijer, E., Evers, M., & Marchal-Crespo, L. (2025). Towards personalized immersive virtual reality neurorehabilitation: A human-centered design. *Journal of Neuroengineering and Rehabilitation*, *22*(1), 7. PMID: 39833912

Cuevas-Molano, E., Matosas-López, L., & Bernal-Bravo, C. (2021). Factors increasing consumer engagement of branded content in Instagram. *IEEE Access : Practical Innovations, Open Solutions*, *9*, 143531–143548. DOI: 10.1109/ACCESS.2021.3121186

Cui, T., Ye, H., & Teo, H. H. (2011). Value co-creation with customers through design toolkits: The importance of preference fit and *psychological* ownership. In the 9th European Conference on Information Systems, ECIS

Cummings, J. J., & Bailenson, J. N. (2016). How immersive is enough? A meta-analysis of the effect of immersive technology on user presence. *Media Psychology*, *19*(2), 272–309.

Damanik, J., & Yusuf, M. (2021). Effects of perceived value, expectation, visitor management, and visitor satisfaction on revisit intention to Borobudur Temple, Indonesia. *Journal of Heritage Tourism*, *17*(2), 174–189. DOI: 10.1080/1743873x.2021.1950164

Damari, C., & Mansfeld, Y. (2014). Reflections on pilgrims' identity, role and interplay with the pilgrimage environment. *Current Issues in Tourism*, *19*(3), 199–222. DOI: 10.1080/13683500.2014.957660

Darvidou, K. (2024). Content marketing strategy and development. *Technium Business and Management*, *10*, 55–67. DOI: 10.47577/business.v10i.11902

Dascal, J., Reid, M., IsHak, W. W., Spiegel, B., Recacho, J., Rosen, B., & Danovitch, I. (2017). Virtual reality and medical inpatients: A systematic review of randomized, controlled trials. *Innovations in Clinical Neuroscience*, *14*(1-2), 14. PMID: 28386517

Davenport, T., Guha, A., Grewal, D., & Bressgott, T. (2020). How artificial intelligence will change the future of marketing. *Journal of the Academy of Marketing Science*, *48*, 24–42.

Davis, A., Tuckey, M., Gwilt, I., & Wallace, N. (2023). Understanding co-design practice as a process of "welldoing". *International Journal of Art & Design Education*, *42*(2), 278–293.

Davis, F. D., Bagozzi, R. P., & Warshaw, P. R. (1989). Technology acceptance model. *Journal of Management Science*, *35*(8), 982–1003.

Dawar, I., Singal, M., Singh, V., Lamba, S., & Jain, S. (2024). Air quality prediction using Machine Learning Models: A Predictive study in the Himalayan city of Rishikesh. *SN Computer Science*, *5*(8). Advance online publication. DOI: 10.1007/s42979-024-03339-6

De Andrade, I. M., & Tumelero, C. (2022). Increasing customer service efficiency through artificial intelligence chatbot. *Revista de Gestão*, *29*(3), 238–251.

De Bruyn, A., Viswanathan, V., Beh, Y. S., Brock, J. K. U., & Von Wangenheim, F. (2020). Artificial intelligence and marketing: Pitfalls and opportunities. *Journal of Interactive Marketing*, *51*(1), 91–105.

De Pelsmacker, P., Geuens, M., & Bergh, J. (2013). Humor in advertising: A framework for understanding its effectiveness. *Journal of Marketing*, *77*(2), 3–20.

De Veirman, M., De Jans, S., Van den Abeele, E., & Hudders, L. (2020). Unravelling the power of social media influencers: a qualitative study on teenage influencers as commercial content creators on social media. In *The regulation of social media influencers* (pp. 126–166). Edward Elgar Publishing.

Deci, E. L., & Ryan, R. M. (1985). The general causality orientations scale: Self-determination in personality. *Journal of Research in Personality*, *19*(2), 109–134.

Denga, E. M., Vajjhala, N. R., & Rakshit, S. (2022). The role of digital marketing in achieving sustainable competitive advantage. In Digital transformation and internationalization strategies in organizations (pp. 44-60). https://doi.org/DOI: 10.4018/978-1-7998-8169-8.ch003

Deng, L., & Yuan, K. H. (2023). Which method is more powerful in testing the relationship of theoretical constructs? A meta comparison of structural equation modeling and path analysis with weighted composites. *Behavior Research Methods*, *55*(4), 1460–1479. DOI: 10.3758/s13428-022-01838-z PMID: 35653013

Derbaix, C., Gregory, P., Lavoisier, L. M., Lehu, J. M., Pecheux, C., Poncin, I., ... & Vanhamme, J. (2004). La Théorie de l'irrationalité retreinte, fondement de la communication persuasive.

DeSanctis, G., & Poole, M. S. (1994). Capturing the Complexity in Advanced Technology Use : Adaptive Structuration Theory. *Organization Science*, *5*(2), 121–147. DOI: 10.1287/orsc.5.2.121

Desmond, M., Muller, M., Ashktorab, Z., Dugan, C., Duesterwald, E., Brimijoin, K., & Pan, Q. (2021, April). Increasing the speed and accuracy of data labeling through an ai assisted interface. In *Proceedings of the 26th International Conference on Intelligent User Interfaces* (pp. 392-401).

Dessart, L., Veloutsou, C., & Morgan-Thomas, A. (2015). Consumer engagement in online brand communities: A social media perspective. *Journal of Product and Brand Management*, *24*(1), 28–42. DOI: 10.1108/JPBM-06-2014-0635

Deutsch, M., & Gerard, H. B. (1955). A study of normative and informational social influences upon individual judgment. *Journal of Abnormal and Social Psychology*, *51*(3), 629. PMID: 13286010

DeVellis, R. F. (2017). *Scale development: Theory and applications* (4th ed.). Sage.

Dhalmahapatra, K., Maiti, J., & Krishna, O. B. (2021). Assessment of virtual reality-based safety training simulator for electric overhead crane operations. *Safety Science*, *139*, 105241.

Dhiman, R., & Bhati, N. S. (2025). When AI meets influencers : Role of AI-powered instagram influencers driving consumers' purchase intentions: An integration of SMIV & SOR framework. *Journal of Open Innovation*, *11*(3), 100591. DOI: 10.1016/j.joitmc.2025.100591

Di Fatta, D., Patton, D., & Viglia, G. (2018). The determinants of conversion rates in SME e-commerce websites. *Journal of Retailing and Consumer Services*, *41*, 161–168. DOI: 10.1016/j.jretconser.2017.12.008

Dietrich, F. (2025). AI-based removal of hate speech from digital social networks : Chances and risks for freedom of expression. *AI and Ethics*, *5*(3), 2943–2953. DOI: 10.1007/s43681-024-00610-7

Dinev, T., & Hart, P. (2006). An extended privacy calculus model for e-commerce transactions. *Information Systems Research, 17*(1), 61–80.

Dingre, S. (2024). An approach to optimize conversion rate using behavioral economics. *Journal of Marketing Studies, 7*(1), 8–14. DOI: 10.47941/jms.1680

Doan, T.-N. (2023). A back-propagation neural network with delay and shift window for tourism demand forecasting. [IJCSE]. *International Journal on Computer Science and Engineering.*

Doborjeh, Z., Hemmington, N., Doborjeh, M., & Kasabov, N. (2021). Artificial intelligence: A systematic review of methods and applications in hospitality and tourism. *International Journal of Contemporary Hospitality Management, 34*(3), 1154–1176. DOI: 10.1108/ijchm-06-2021-0767

Dongbo, M., Miniaoui, S., Fen, L., Althubiti, S. A., & Alsenani, T. R. (2023). Intelligent chatbot interaction system capable for sentimental analysis using hybrid machine learning algorithms. *Information Processing & Management, 60*(5), 103440.

Draghi, M. (2015). Monetary policy: Past, present and future. Speech at the Frankfurt European Banking Congress. Frankfurt am Main.

Drus, Z., & Khalid, H. (2019). Sentiment analysis in social media and its application : Systematic literature review. *Procedia Computer Science, 161*, 707–714.

Du Plessis, C. (2017). The role of content marketing in social media content communities. *South African Journal of Information Management, 19*(1), 1–7. DOI: 10.4102/sajim.v19i1.866

Ducret, G. (2016). Outil 37. La prospection commerciale. In *La Boîte à outils de la TPE* (Dunod, p. 114-115). Dunod. https://shs.cairn.info/article/DUNOD_DUCRE_2016_01_0114

Durand-Mégret, B., Ezan, P., & Vanheems, R. (2012). Quand le cross-canal devient familial… Un nouveau pouvoir d'influence des adolescents au sein de la famille. *In Acte de conférence Etienne Thil.*

Dwivedi, Y. K., Hughes, L., Wang, Y., Alalwan, A. A., Ahn, S. J., Balakrishnan, J., & Wirtz, J. (2023). Metaverse marketing: How the metaverse will shape the future of consumer research and practice. *Psychology and Marketing, 40*(4), 750–776.

Dwivedi, Y. K., Ismagilova, E., Hughes, D. L., Carlson, J., Filieri, R., Jacobson, J., Jain, V., Karjaluoto, H., Kefi, H., Krishen, A. S., Kumar, V., Rahman, M. M., Raman, R., Rauschnabel, P. A., Rowley, J., Salo, J., Tran, G. A., & Wang, Y. (2021). Setting the future of digital and social media marketing research: Perspectives and research propositions. *International Journal of Information Management*, •••, 1–37. DOI: 10.1016/j.ijinfomgt.2020.102168

Efendioğlu, İ. H. (2024). Digital consumer behavior: A systematic literature review. *Prizren Social Science Journal*, *8*(1), 67–80. DOI: 10.32936/pssj.v8i1.479

Eggert, A., Ulaga, W., Frow, P., & Payne, A. (2018). Conceptualizing and communicating value in business markets: From value in exchange to value in use. *Industrial Marketing Management*, *69*, 80–90.

Eisend, M. (2021). Humor in advertising: A meta-analysis. *Journal of the Academy of Marketing Science*, *49*, 649–669.

El Koufi, N., & Belangour, A., & sadiq, M. (2024). Toward a decision-making system based on artificial intelligence for precision marketing : A case study of Morocco. *Journal of Open Innovation*, *10*(1), 100250. DOI: 10.1016/j.joitmc.2024.100250

Elhazziti, M. A., Ferraz, D., Elazzouzi, E., Mastere, M., & Gomes, J. S. (2023). Digital transformation in Morocco: Challenges and perspectives. *Journal of US-China Public Administration*, *20*(2), 83–97. DOI: 10.17265/1548-6591/2023.02.001

El-Merabet, O., Kinani, S., El-Merabet, Z., & El-Merabet, O. (2025). Enhancing eWOM Intention Through Social Media-based Brand Communities in the Higher Education Sector : The Mediating Effect of Brand Attachment. *Micro & Macro Marketing*, *2/2025*. Advance online publication. DOI: 10.1431/114094

Elmira, S. (2025). *The experience economy within the framework of virtual worlds*. Skolkovo School of Management. https://papers.ssrn.com/sol3/papers.cfm?abstract_id=5228674

Emerson, L. M., De Diaz, N. N., Sherwood, A., Waters, A., & Farrell, L. (2020). Mindfulness interventions in schools: Integrity and feasibility of implementation. *International Journal of Behavioral Development*, *44*(1), 62–75. DOI: 10.1177/0165025419866906

Emon, M. M. H., & Khan, T. (2024). A systematic literature review on sustainability integration and marketing intelligence in the era of artificial intelligence. *Review of Business and Economics Studies*, *12*(4), 6–28.

Epley, N. (2018). A mind like mine: The exceptionally ordinary underpinnings of anthropomorphism. *Journal of the Association for Consumer Research*, *3*(4), 591–598.

Epley, N., Adam, W., & John, T. (2007). On seeing human: A three-factor theory of anthropomorphism. *Psychological Review, 114*(4), 864–886. PMID: 17907867

Eshaghi, M. S., Afshardoost, M., & Bowden, J. L. H. (2023). Consumer well-being (CWB): Conceptualisation, contextualisation and a research agenda. *Service Industries Journal, 43*(9-10), 618–641.

Eslami, S. P., Ghasemaghaei, M., & Hassanein, K. (2022). Understanding consumer engagement in social media: The role of product lifecycle. *Decision Support Systems, 162*, 113707. DOI: 10.1016/j.dss.2021.113707

Evania, S., Listiana, E., Rosnani, T., & Fahruna, Y. (2023). The effect of influencer marketing and content marketing on customer engagement and purchase decisions on followers. Asian Journal of Economics. *Business and Accounting, 23*(2), 12–20. DOI: 10.9734/ajeba/2023/v23i2917

Fanni, S. C., Febi, M., Aghakhanyan, G., & Neri, E. (2023). Natural Language Processing. In Klontzas, M. E., Fanni, S. C., & Neri, E. (Eds.), *Introduction to Artificial Intelligence* (pp. 87–99). Springer International Publishing., DOI: 10.1007/978-3-031-25928-9_5

Fan, X., Jiang, X., & Deng, N. (2022). Immersive technology: A meta-analysis of augmented/virtual reality applications and their impact on tourism experience. *Tourism Management, 91*(2), 104534.

Favour, A., Kunle, A., Oladele, S., & Timileyin, J. (2025). *The Role of Natural Language Processing (NLP) in Enhancing Customer Experience in Fintech : Applications in Chatbots and Virtual Assistants*. https://www.researchgate.net/profile/Sunday-Oladele-2/publication/390454097_The_Role_of_Natural_Language_Processing_NLP_in_Enhancing_Customer_Experience_in_Fintech_Applications_in_Chatbots_and_Virtual_Assistants/links/67ee55069b1c6c4877726d7d/The-Role-of-Natural-Language-Processing-NLP-in-Enhancing-Customer-Experience-in-Fintech-Applications-in-Chatbots-and-Virtual-Assistants.pdf

Feng, Z., González, V. A., Ma, L., Al-Adhami, M., & Mourgues, C. (2018). Rapid 3D reconstruction of indoor environments to generate virtual reality serious games scenarios. *arXiv preprint* arXiv:1812.01706.

Feng, Y., Guo, Z., & Chiang, W. Y. K. (2009). Optimal digital content distribution strategy in the presence of the consumer-to-consumer channel. *Journal of Management Information Systems, 25*(4), 241–270.

Fernandes, C., Silva, G., & Gómez-Ullate, M. (2018). Rethinking safety issues within the context of pilgrimage routes. In *CABI eBooks* (pp. 63–76). https://doi.org/DOI: 10.1079/9781786392282.0063

Fernández, D. L., & Oliver, M. (2025). Methodology, strategies, and factors for business innovation in large companies. *International Journal of Innovation Studies*, *9*(2), 91–115. DOI: 10.1016/j.ijis.2025.02.002

Ferrera, A., Mezzotero, G., & Ursino, D. (2025). A linguistics-based approach to refining automatic intent detection in conversational agent design. *Information Sciences*, *689*, 121493.

Festinger, L. (1957). Social comparison theory. *Selective Exposure Theory*, *16*(401), 3.

Fishbein, M., Ajzen, I., & Belief, A. (1975). *Intention and Behavior: An introduction to theory and research.*

Fjelland, R. (2020). Why general artificial intelligence will not be realized. *Humanities & Social Sciences Communications*, *7*(1), 1–9.

Flavián, C., Guinaliu, M., & Lu, Y. (2020). Mobile payments adoption–introducing mindfulness to better understand consumer behavior. *International Journal of Bank Marketing*, *38*(7), 1575–1599.

Flavián, C., Ibáñez-Sánchez, S., & Orús, C. (2019). The impact of virtual, augmented and mixed reality technologies on the customer experience. *Journal of Business Research*, *100*(2), 547–560.

Flavián, C., Ibáñez-Sánchez, S., & Orús, C. (2021). The influence of scent on virtual reality experiences: The role of aroma-content congruence. *Journal of Business Research*, *123*(4), 289–301.

Fleischer, A. (2000). The tourist behind the pilgrim in the Holy Land. *International Journal of Hospitality Management*, *19*(3), 311–326. DOI: 10.1016/s0278-4319(00)00026-8

Fointiat, V., & Barbier, L. (2015). Persuasion et Influence: changer les attitudes, changer les comportements. Regards de la psychologie sociale. *Journal d'interaction personne-système, 4*(1), 1-18.

Fotheringham, D., & Wiles, M. A. (2022). The effect of implementing chatbot customer service on stock returns: An event study analysis. *Journal of the Academy of Marketing Science*, •••, 1–21.

Fox, J., Arena, D., & Bailenson, J. N. (2014). Virtual reality: A survival guide for the social scientist. *Journal of Media Psychology*, *26*(2), 65–75.

Frangieh, B., & Akiki, J. (2023). L'accompagnant scolaire des élèves à besoins éducatifs particuliers en situation d'intermétiers. *La nouvelle revue-Éducation et société inclusives, 95*(3), 43-56.

Franke, G. R., & Mueller, R. O. (1996). Basic Principles of Structural Equation Modeling: An Introduction to LISREL and EQS. *JMR, Journal of Marketing Research, 33*(2), 255. DOI: 10.2307/3152154

Franke, N., & Piller, F. (2004). Value creation by toolkits for user innovation and design: The case of the watch market. *Journal of Product Innovation Management, 21*(6), 401–415.

Freina, L., & Ott, M. (2015, April). A literature review on immersive virtual reality in education: state of the art and perspectives. In *The International Scientific Conference eLearning and Software for Education* (Vol. 1, No. 133, pp. 10-1007).

Fuchs, C., & Schreier, M. (2011). Customer empowerment in new product development. *Journal of Product Innovation Management, 28*(1), 17–32.

Füller, J., Hutter, K., & Faullant, R. (2011). Why co-creation experience matters? Creative experience and its impact on the quantity and quality of creative contributions. *R & D Management, 41*(3), 259–273.

Gaggioli, A., Mazzoni, E., Benvenuti, M., Galimberti, C., Bova, A., Brivio, E., & Chirico, A. (2020). Networked flow in creative collaboration: A mixed method study. In *Creative Learning in Digital and Virtual Environments* (pp. 68–95). Routledge.

Gagnon, J., Raskin, M., Remache, J., & Sack, B. (2011). *Large-scale asset purchases by the federal reserve: Did they work? Economic Policy Review 17(1).* Federal Reserve Bank of New York.

Galante, F., Garetto, M., & Leonardi, E. (2024). Competition of Influencers : A Model for Maximizing Online Social Impact. *ACM Web Science Conference*, 343-353. DOI: 10.1145/3614419.3644031

Gallopel, K., Rieunier, S., Debenedetti, S., Dion, D., & Le Gall-Ely, M. (2006). Impact des avertissements sanitaires dans la lutte contre le tabagisme: synthèse théorique ET résultats D'UNE étude qualitative. *Revue française du marketing*, (206).

Gamberini, L., Bettelli, A., Benvegnù, G., Orso, V., Spagnolli, A., & Ferri, M. (2021). Designing "safer water." A virtual reality tool for the safety and the psychological well-being of citizens exposed to the risk of natural disasters. *Frontiers in Psychology, 12*, 674171. PMID: 34177732

Gao, K., Yang, Y., & Qu, X. (2021). Examining nonlinear and interaction effects of multiple determinants on airline travel satisfaction. *Transportation Research Part D, Transport and Environment*, *97*, 102957. DOI: 10.1016/j.trd.2021.102957

Gapor, S. A., Chin, C. H., Ngian, E. T., Wong, W. P. M., Kiew, J. P., & Toh, T. L. (2023). Cultural events' service quality, satisfaction and loyalty: A case on an annual cultural diversity event in Borneo. *International Journal of Event and Festival Management*, *15*(2), 191–212. DOI: 10.1108/ijefm-07-2023-0054

Garg, V., Bohara, S., & Srivastav, A. (2025). AI-driven sustainability marketing transforming consumers' perception toward eco-friendly brands. *Discover Sustainability*, *6*(1), 984. DOI: 10.1007/s43621-025-01934-y

Gayathri, H., Aparna, P., & Verma, A. (2017). A review of studies on understanding crowd dynamics in the context of crowd safety in mass religious gatherings. *International Journal of Disaster Risk Reduction*, *25*, 82–91. DOI: 10.1016/j.ijdrr.2017.07.017

Geetha, V., & Chakravarti, U. (2024). Understanding popular culture. In *Routledge eBooks* (pp. 139–155). https://doi.org/DOI: 10.4324/9781003482437-9

Gefen, D. (2000). E-commerce: The role of familiarity and trust. *Omega*, *28*(6), 725–737.

Geiser, C., Litson, K., Bishop, J., Keller, B. T., Burns, G. L., Servera, M., & Shiffman, S. (2015). Analyzing person, situation and person× situation interaction effects: Latent state-trait models for the combination of random and fixed situations. *Psychological Methods*, *20*(2), 165. PMID: 25528499

George, O. O., Dosumu, R. E., & Makata, C. O. (2023). Integrating multi-channel brand communication: A conceptual model for achieving sustained consumer engagement and loyalty. *International Journal of Management and Organizational Research*, *2*(1), 254–260. DOI: 10.54660/IJMOR.2023.2.1.254-260

Ghanad, A. (2023). An overview of quantitative research methods. *International Journal of Multidisciplinary Research and Analysis*, *6*(8). Advance online publication. DOI: 10.47191/ijmra/v6-i8-52

Ghatge, S. K., & Parasar, A. (2023). Application of Artificial Intelligence (AI), Internet of Things (IoT), and Big Data in Healthcare, Finance, and Transportation. *PriMera Scientific Medicine and Public Health*, *2*, 27–36.

Ghosh, P. (2022). Reliability as a moderator in the relationship between the general attitude toward advertising and purchase intention. *South Asian Journal of Management*, *29*(2), 97–116.

Ghosh, S., & Dubey, S. (2025). The field of usability and user experience (UX) design. In *Navigating usability and user experience in a multi-platform world* (pp. 117–154). IGI Global.

Ghouse, S. M., Durrah, O., & Chaudhary, M. (2025). Children as consumers: Influence strategies and decision-making roles in Arab households. *Journal of Islamic Marketing*.

Giessen, H. W. (2015). Media-based learning methodology: Stories, games, and emotions. In *International Handbook of E-Learning* (Vol. 2, pp. 43–54). Routledge.

Gleim, M., McCullough, H., Ferrell, O. C., & Gabler, C. (2024). Metaverse: Shifting the reality of services. *Journal of Services Marketing*, *38*(1), 13–27.

Gnewuch, U., Morana, S., Adam, M., & Maedche, A. (2018). Faster is not always better: understanding the effect of dynamic response delays in human-chatbot interaction.

Godener, V. (1999). L'efficacité du stress en publicité (Doctoral dissertation, Paris 1).

Gonzalez-Aguirre, J. A., Osorio-Oliveros, R., Rodríguez-Hernández, K. L., Lizárraga-Iturralde, J., Morales Menendez, R., Ramirez-Mendoza, R. A., & Lozoya-Santos, J. D. J. (2021). Service robots: Trends and technology. *Applied Sciences (Basel, Switzerland)*, *11*(22), 10702.

Gretzel, U., & Stankov, U. (2021). ICTs and wellbeing: Challenges and opportunities for tourism. *Information Technology & Tourism*, *23*, 1–4.

Grewal, D. K., Senthilkumaran, V., & K, H. P. (2025). Enhancing customer satisfaction through Artificial Neural networks (ANNS): principles, architectures, and practical applications. In *Emerald Publishing Limited eBooks* (pp. 103–119). https://doi.org/DOI: 10.1108/978-1-83549-418-920251007

Griffin, M. A., Parker, S. K., & Neal, A. (2008). Is behavioral engagement a distinct and useful construct? *Industrial and Organizational Psychology: Perspectives on Science and Practice*, *1*(1), 48–51.

Grudin, J., & Jacques, R. (2019, May). Chatbots, humbots, and the quest for artificial general intelligence. In *Proceedings of the 2019 CHI conference on human factors in computing systems* (pp. 1-11).

Gubler, D. A., Janelt, T., Roth, M., Schlegel, K., Guggisberg, J., & Troche, S. J. (2025). The DOES Scale: Measuring sensory processing sensitivity as a trait constellation. *Journal of Personality Assessment*, *107*(2), 205–220. PMID: 39321392

Gudigantala, N., Bicen, P., & Eom, M. T. (2016). An examination of antecedents of conversion rates of e-commerce retailers. *Management Research Review, 39*(1), 82–114. DOI: 10.1108/MRR-05-2014-0112

Guenther, P., Guenther, M., Ringle, C. M., Zaefarian, G., & Cartwright, S. (2023). Improving PLS-SEM use for business marketing research. *Industrial Marketing Management, 111*, 127–142. DOI: 10.1016/j.indmarman.2023.03.010

Guitouni, M. (2000). Au cœur de l'identité. *L'intelligence émotionnelle.*

Gujar, V. (2024). New age marketing : AI personalization strategies in digital world. *International Advanced Research Journal in Science, Engineering and Technology, 11*(3). https://www.researchgate.net/profile/Vivek-Gujar/publication/379512526_New_Age_Marketing_AI_Personalization_Strategies_In_Digital_World/links/660d0c2d390c214cfd310d61/New-Age-Marketing-AI-Personalization-Strategies-In-Digital-World.pdf

Guo, J., Lin, J., & Luo, X. (2025). Enhancing organizational resilience through big data analytics capability: The mediating role of strategic flexibility. *Information Technology & People*, •••, 1–39. DOI: 10.1108/itp-06-2024-0786

Gupta, S., & Basak, B. (2018). Exploring pilgrim satisfaction on facilities for religious events: A case of Ratha Yatra at Puri. *Asia Pacific Journal of Tourism Research, 23*(8), 765–779. DOI: 10.1080/10941665.2018.1486864

Guttentag, D. A. (2010). Virtual reality: Applications and implications for tourism. *Tourism Management, 31*(5), 637–651.

Habib, A., & Jha, A. N. (2025). A critical review of "Digital marketing strategies - Through websites, digital funnels, social media and digital tools.". *EPH-International Journal of Business & Management Science, 11*(1). Advance online publication. DOI: 10.53555/eijbms.v11i1.203

Hair, J. F., Hult, G. T. M., Ringle, C. M., & Sarstedt, M. (2017). *A primer on partial least squares structural equation modeling (PLS-SEM)* (2nd ed.). Sage Publications.

Hair, J. F.Jr, Hult, G. T. M., Ringle, C. M., Sarstedt, M., Danks, N. P., & Ray, S. (2021). *Partial least squares structural equation modeling (PLS-SEM) using R: A workbook.* Springer Nature.

Haji, I., & Bouziane, A. (2021). Le marketing d'influence au Maroc, entre perception et professionnalisme des acteurs. *Alternatives Managériales Economiques, 3*(2), 23-42. DOI: 10.48374/IMIST.PRSM/ame-v3i2.27506

Hajtaieb El Aoud, N. (2003). La contribution de l'adolescent dans la prise de décision d'achat de la famille: un essai de modélisation. *Université Pierre Mendès-France, Grenoble, Thèse de doctorat en sciences de gestion.*

Haleem, A., Javaid, M., Qadri, M. A., Singh, R. P., & Suman, R. (2022). Artificial intelligence (AI) applications for marketing: A literature-based study. *International Journal of Intelligent Networks, 3*, 119–132.

Ha, M.-T. (2022). Data collection using online questionnaires in marketing. In *Doing research online* (pp. 1–12). SAGE Publications., DOI: 10.4135/9781529603569

Hamari, J., Shernoff, D. J., Rowe, E., Coller, B., Asbell-Clarke, J., & Edwards, T. (2016). Challenging games help students learn: An empirical study on engagement, flow and immersion in game-based learning. *Computers in Human Behavior, 54*, 170–179.

Hamdi-Kidar, L., Keinz, P., Le Nagard, E., & Vernette, E. (2019). Comparing lead users to emergent-nature consumers as sources of innovation at early stages of new product development. *Journal of Product Innovation Management, 36*(5), 616–631.

Handriana, T., Yulianti, P., & Kurniawati, M. (2019). Exploration of pilgrimage tourism in Indonesia. *Journal of Islamic Marketing, 11*(3), 783–795. DOI: 10.1108/jima-10-2018-0188

Harrigan, P., Evers, U., Miles, M. P., & Daly, T. M. (2017). Customer engagement and the relationship between involvement, engagement, self-brand connection and brand usage intent. *Journal of Business Research, 88*, 388–396. DOI: 10.1016/j.jbusres.2017.11.046

Harun, A., Ahmad, N., Farradia, Y., & Hussein, Z. (2024). Analysing Umrah Attributes in relation to Tourist Travel behaviour: A Systematic literature review of religious destinations and future Perspectives. *Journal of Islamic Thought and Civilization, 14*(2), 72–105. DOI: 10.32350/jitc.142.06

Hassan, T. A., Hollander, S., & Kalyani, A. (2025). Text as data in economic analysis. *The Journal of Economic Perspectives, 39*(3).

Hassan, T., Carvache-Franco, M., Carvache-Franco, W., & Carvache-Franco, O. (2022). Segmentation of Religious tourism by Motivations: A study of the pilgrimage to the city of Mecca. *Sustainability, 14*(13), 7861. DOI: 10.3390/su14137861

Hatchuel, A., & Weil, B. (2003). A new approach of innovative Design: an introduction to CK theory. *In the 14th International Conference on Engineering Design*, Stockholm.

Hayes, A. F. (2018). Partial, conditional, and moderated moderated mediation: Quantification, inference, and interpretation. *Communication Monographs*, *85*(1), 4–40.

Helme-guizon, A., & Magnoni, F. (2019). Consumer brand engagement and its social side on brand-hosted social media: How do they contribute to brand loyalty? *Journal of Marketing Management*, *35*, 1–26. DOI: 10.1080/0267257X.2019.1599990

Hendrayanti, S., & Nurauliya, V. (2021). Building competitive advantage through innovation, creativity, product quality. *BASKARA: Journal of Business and Entrepreneurship*, *4*(1), 85–94.

Herter, M. M., Shuqair, S., Pinto, D. C., Mattila, A. S., & Zandonai Pontin, P. (2023). Does crowdsourcing necessarily lead to brand engagement? The role of crowdsourcing cues and relationship norms on customer-brand relationships. *Journal of Product and Brand Management*, *32*(7), 988–1004.

Hewapathirana, I. U., & Perera, N. (2024). Navigating the age of AI influence : A systematic literature review of trust, engagement, efficacy and ethical concerns of virtual influencers in social media. *Journal of Infrastructure. Policy and Development*, *8*(8), 1–46. DOI: 10.24294/jipd.v8i8.6352

Hill, J., Ford, W. R., & Farreras, I. G. (2015). Real conversations with artificial intelligence: A comparison between human–human online conversations and human–chatbot conversations. *Computers in Human Behavior*, *49*, 245–250.

Hnylyakevych, I. Z., & Zinkova, S. V. (2024). Role of conversion rate optimisation (CRO) in marketing. *Market Economy Modern Management Theory and Practice*, *23*(1(56)), 36–53. DOI: 10.18524/2413-9998.2024.1(56).309063

Hoffman, B., & Nadelson, L. (2010). Motivational engagement and video gaming: A mixed methods study. *Educational Technology Research and Development*, *58*(3), 245–270.

Hoffman, D. L., & Novak, T. P. (2009). Flow online: Lessons learned and future prospects. *Journal of Interactive Marketing*, *23*(1), 23–34.

Hollebeek, L. (2011). Exploring customer brand engagement: Definition and themes. *Journal of Strategic Marketing*, *19*(7), 555–573.

Hollebeek, L. D., & Macky, K. (2019). Digital content marketing's role in fostering consumer engagement, trust, and value: Framework, fundamental propositions, and implications. *Journal of Interactive Marketing*, *45*, 27–41. DOI: 10.1016/j.intmar.2018.07.003

Homburg, C., Jozić, D., & Kuehnl, C. (2017). Customer experience management: Toward implementing an evolving marketing concept. *Journal of the Academy of Marketing Science*, *45*(3), 377–401.

Höpken, W., Eberle, T., Fuchs, M., & Lexhagen, M. (2020). Improving tourist arrival prediction: A big data and artificial neural network approach. *Journal of Travel Research*, *60*(5), 998–1017. DOI: 10.1177/0047287520921244

Hovland, C. I., Janis, I. L., & Kelley, H. H. (1953). Communication and persuasion.

Hristov, I. (2024). Web design for small businesses: Enhancing user experience [Bachelor's thesis, Haaga-Helia University of Applied Sciences]. Retrieved from https://www.theseus.fi/handle/10024/869156

Hsiao, K. L., & Chen, C. C. (2022). What drives continuance intention to use a food-ordering chatbot? An examination of trust and satisfaction. *Library Hi Tech*, *40*(4), 929–946.

Hsiao, S. H., Wang, Y. Y., & Lin, T. L. (2024). The impact of low-immersion virtual reality on product sales: Insights from the real estate industry. *Decision Support Systems*, *178*, 114131.

Hsieh, S. H., & Chang, A. (2016). The psychological mechanism of brand co-creation engagement. *Journal of Interactive Marketing*, *33*(1), 13–26.

Hsu, C. L., & Lin, J. C. C. (2023). Understanding the user satisfaction and loyalty of customer service chatbots. *Journal of Retailing and Consumer Services*, *71*, 103211.

Hsu, P.-F., Lu, Y.-H., Chen, S.-C., & Kuo, P. P.-Y. (2024). Creating and validating predictive personas for target marketing. *International Journal of Human-Computer Studies*, *181*, 103147. DOI: 10.1016/j.ijhcs.2023.103147

Huang, J., & Hsu, C. H. (2010). The impact of customer-to-customer interaction on cruise experience and vacation satisfaction. *Journal of Travel Research*, *49*(1), 79–92.

Huang, M. H., & Rust, R. T. (2021). A strategic framework for artificial intelligence in marketing. *Journal of the Academy of Marketing Science*, *49*(1), 30–50.

Huang, N., Sun, T., Chen, P., & Golden, J. M. (2019). Word-of-mouth system implementation and customer conversion: A randomized field experiment. *Information Systems Research*, *30*(3), 805–818. DOI: 10.1287/isre.2018.0832

Huang, Q., Zhang, Y., Ko, T., Liu, X., Wu, B., Wang, W., & Tang, H. (2023). Personalized dialogue generation with persona-adaptive attention. *Proceedings of the AAAI Conference on Artificial Intelligence*, *37*(11), 12916–12923. https://ojs.aaai.org/index.php/AAAI/article/view/26518

Huang, T. L., & Liao, S. (2017). Creating e-shopping multisensory flow experience through augmented-reality interactive technology. *Internet Research*, *27*(3), 449–475.

Hubermont, A., & Masset, J. (2023). Est-ce possible que Twitch devienne l'un des médias les plus influents d'ici 2035, comparable voire surpassant la télévision traditionnelle?

Huma, S., Ahmed, W., Ikram, M., & Najmi, A. (2025). Influence of mobile application service quality and convenience on young customer retention. *Spanish Journal of Marketing - ESIC*, *29*(4), 402–424. DOI: 10.1108/SJME-11-2023-0310

Hurley, Z. (2024). Understanding Social Media Marketing Managers' Intermediary Role : A Middle Eastern Case Study. *The Sage Handbook of Promotional Culture and Society*, 151.

Hussain, S., Ameri Sianaki, O., & Ababneh, N. (2019). A survey on conversational agents/chatbots classification and design techniques. In Web, Artificial Intelligence and Network Applications: Proceedings of the Workshops of the 33rd International Conference on Advanced Information Networking and Applications (WAINA-2019) 33 (pp. 946-956). Springer International Publishing.

Hu, Y., Xiao, Y., Hua, Y., Fan, Y., & Li, F. (2024). The More Realism, the Better? How Does the Realism of AI Customer Service Agents Influence Customer Satisfaction and Repeat Purchase Intention in Service Recovery. *Behavioral Sciences (Basel, Switzerland)*, *14*(12), 1182. DOI: 10.3390/bs14121182 PMID: 39767323

Iansiti, M., & Lakhani, K. R. (2020). *Competing in the age of AI: Strategy and leadership when algorithms and networks run the world*. Harvard Business Press.

Idrissi, T. E., Idri, A., & Bakkoury, Z. (2018). Systematic map and review of predictive techniques in diabetes self-management. *International Journal of Information Management*, *46*, 263–277. DOI: 10.1016/j.ijinfomgt.2018.09.011

Ihde, I. (1990). *The Indiana Series in the Philosophy of Technology*. Indiana University Press.

ILEANA, M., & MARIAN, C. V. (2024). Unlocking new horizons with Virtual Reality and Digital Learning to facilitate career transitions in IT and science. *On Virtual Learning*, 81.

Imai, K., Keele, L., & Tingley, D. (2010). A general approach to causal mediation analysis. *Psychological Methods*, *15*(4), 309. PMID: 20954780

International Society for Presence Research. (2002). *The concept of presence: Explication statement*. ISPR.

IPSOS. (2023). *World Mental Health Day 2023 : A Global Advisor Survey* (p. 15). IPSOS. https://www.ipsos.com/sites/default/files/ct/news/documents/2023-10/Ipsos-World_Mental_Health_Day_Survey_2023.pdf

Isibor, N. J., Attipoe, V., Oyeyipo, I., Ayodeji, D. C., Mayienga, B. A., Alonge, E., & Onwuzulike, O. C. (2025). Analyzing successful content marketing strategies that enhance online engagement and sales for digital brands. *International Journal of Advanced Multidisciplinary Research and Studies*, *5*(2), 842–851. DOI: 10.62225/2583049X.2025.5.2.3906

Islam, M. M. (2021). The Satisfaction of Bangladeshi Pilgrims: Service gaps in spiritual tourism based on gender and expenditure. *International Journal of Religious Tourism and Pilgrimage*, *9*(1), 10. DOI: 10.21427/2hw0-cd28

Isleyen, E., & Duzgun, H. S. (2019). Use of virtual reality in underground roof fall hazard assessment and risk mitigation. *International Journal of Mining Science and Technology*, *29*(4), 603–607.

Ismail, W. S., Ghareeb, M. M., & Youssry, H. (2024). Enhancing customer experience through sentiment analysis and natural language processing in e-commerce. *Journal of Wireless Mobile Networks, Ubiquitous Computing and Dependable Applications*, *15*(3), 60–72.

Izadi, S., & Forouzanfar, M. (2024). Error Correction and Adaptation in Conversational AI: A Review of Techniques and Applications in Chatbots. *AI*, *5*(2), 803–841.

Izard, C. E. (1977). Differential emotions theory. In *Human emotions* (pp. 43–66). Springer US.

Jacobson, J., Gruzd, A., & Hernández-García, Á. (2020). Social media marketing: Who is watching the watchers? *Journal of Retailing and Consumer Services*, *53*, 101774.

Janis, I. L. (1967). Effects of fear arousal on attitude change: Recent developments in theory and experimental research. *Advances in Experimental Social Psychology*, *3*, 166–224.

Jarek, K., & Mazurek, G. (2019). Marketing and artificial intelligence. Central European Business Review, 8(2).

Jauhari, V., & Munjal, S. (2015). Fairs and festivals in India: The cultural and economic potential. *Worldwide Hospitality and Tourism Themes*, *7*(4), 324–330. DOI: 10.1108/whatt-03-2015-0012

Jauhari, V., & Sanjeev, G. M. (2010). Managing customer experience for spiritual and cultural tourism: An overview. *Worldwide Hospitality and Tourism Themes*, *2*(5), 467–476. DOI: 10.1108/17554211011090094

Jbene, M., Chehri, A., Saadane, R., Tigani, S., & Jeon, G. (2025). Intent detection for task-oriented conversational agents : A comparative study of recurrent neural networks and transformer models. *Expert Systems: International Journal of Knowledge Engineering and Neural Networks*, *42*(2), e13712. DOI: 10.1111/exsy.13712

Jeong, Y., Kim, H., & King, K. W. (2021). The interplay of game involvement and in-game advertising effects: A comprehensive review. *Journal of Advertising*, *50*(1), 51–66.

Jesenský, M., Kornecká, E., Molokáč, M., & Tometzová, D. (2024). Development of Pilgrimage Tourism in Slovakia over the Past Decades: Examples of Selected Pilgrimage Sites. *Heritage*, *7*(3), 1801–1821. DOI: 10.3390/heritage7030085

Jeswani, R. (2023). The role and importance of social media marketing in brand building. *Irish Interdisciplinary Journal of Science & Research*, *7*(4), 1–9. DOI: 10.46759/IIJSR.2023.7401

Johansson, A. (2016). *Clustering user-behavior in a collaborative online social network : A case study on quantitative user-behavior classification* [Master's Thesis, KTH ROYAL INSTITUTE OF TECHNOLOGY]. https://www.diva-portal.org/smash/record.jsf?pid=diva2:945762

Joshi, R., Patel, N., Iyer, M., & Iyer, S. (2021). Leveraging reinforcement learning and natural language processing for AI-driven hyper-personalized marketing strategies. *International Journal of AI ML Innovations*, *10*(1). http://ijoaimli.com/index.php/v1/article/view/19

Joule, R. V., & Beauvois, J. L. (1989). Une théorie psychosociale: La théorie de l'engagement. Perspectives commerciales. [French Edition]. *Recherche et Applications en Marketing*, *4*(1), 79–90.

Joule, R. V., & Beauvois, J. L. (2002). *Petit traité de manipulation à l'usage des honnêtes gens*. Presses Universitaires de Grenoble.

Jussila, I., Tarkiainen, A., Sarstedt, M., & Hair, J. F. (2015). Individual psychological ownership: Concepts, evidence, and implications for research in marketing. *Journal of Marketing Theory and Practice*, *23*(2), 121–139.

Kahneman, D., & Tversky, A. (1979). Prospect theory: An analysis of decisions under risk. *Econometrica*, *47*(2), 263–291.

Kahn, W. A. (1990). Psychological conditions of personal engagement and disengagement at work. *Academy of Management Journal, 33*(4), 692–724.

Kalender, Y., & Guzmán, F. (2025). What Drives Consumers to Engage in Immersive Technologies? A Consumer Metaverse Engagement Motivation Model. *Psychology and Marketing*, *42*(3), 921–950.

Kalusivalingam, A. K., Sharma, A., Patel, N., & Singh, V. (2020). Enhancing Customer Service Automation with Natural Language Processing and Reinforcement Learning Algorithms. *International Journal of Artificial Intelligence and Machine Learning*, *1*(2).

Kamboj, S., Sarmah, B., Gupta, S., & Dwivedi, Y. (2018). Examining branding co-creation in brand communities on social media: Applying the paradigm of Stimulus-Organism-Response. *International Journal of Information Management*, *39*, 169–185.

Kanaujiya, N. K., & Tiwari, N. V. (2025). A comprehensive analysis of the multifaceted significance of the Kumbh mela in India: An emerging epicenter of global Hindu religious tourism. *World Journal of Advanced Research and Reviews*, *25*(2), 561–569. DOI: 10.30574/wjarr.2025.25.2.0339

Karim, R. A., Rabiul, M. K., & Arfat, S. M. (2023). Factors influencing tourists' behavioural intentions towards beach destinations: The mediating roles of destination experience and destination satisfaction. *Journal of Hospitality and Tourism Insights*, *7*(4), 2033–2054. DOI: 10.1108/jhti-04-2023-0276

Karthikeyan, G., & Aruna, P. (2025). User experience optimization in immersive technologies: Techniques, challenges, and opportunities. In *2025 International Conference on Intelligent Computing and Control Systems (ICICCS)* (pp. 908-917). IEEE.

Katz, E., Blumler, J. G., & Gurevitch, M. (1973). Uses and gratifications research. *Public Opinion Quarterly*, *37*(4), 509–523.

Kaur, P. (2024). Enhancing Customer Service Efficiency: Automating Responses to Customer Queries using Natural Language Processing and Radial Basis Function Neural Network (RBFNN). *Nanotechnology Perceptions*, •••, 797–818.

Kerbrat-Orecchioni, C. (2015). Dialogue théâtral et interactions médiatiques: Le fonctionnement du «trope communicationnel». *Littérature, linguistique et didactique du français: Les travaux Pratiques d'André Petitjean, 125*.

Khairani, A. Z., & Adnan, R. (2019). Exploratory Factor Analysis (EFA) for Adversity Quotient (AQ) Instrument among Youth. *Journal of Critical Reviews*, *6*(6), 234–242. http://www.jcreview.com/?mno=302645174

Khan, I. A., Hollebeek, L. D., Fatma, M., Islam, J. U., & Rahman, Z. (2020). Brand engagement and experience in online services. *Journal of Services Marketing*, •••, 1–34. DOI: 10.1108/JSM-03-2019-0106

Khan, N. A. (2024). Artificial intelligence, self-efficacy and engagement in religious tourism: Evidence from Arbaeen pilgrimage. *Journal of Hospitality and Tourism Insights*, *7*(3), 1660–1678. DOI: 10.1108/jhti-10-2023-0725

Khennouche, F., Elmir, Y., Himeur, Y., Djebari, N., & Amira, A. (2024). Revolutionizing generative pre-traineds: Insights and challenges in deploying ChatGPT and generative chatbots for FAQs. *Expert Systems with Applications*, *246*, 123224.

Kiesler, C. A. (1971). *The psychology of commitments: Experiments linking behavior to belief.* Academic Press.

Kim, D., Im, H., Hyeon, J., & Jwa, J. (2021). Development of the rule-based smart tourism chatbot using Neo4J graph database. *International Journal of Internet. Broadcasting and Communication*, *13*(2), 179–186.

Kim, H., & Han, S. (2025). Triggering the Personalization Backfire Effect: The Moderating Role of Situational Privacy Concern. *Behavioral Sciences (Basel, Switzerland)*, *15*(10), 1323. PMID: 41153114

Kim, J. (2014). The antecedents of memorable tourism experiences: The development of a scale to measure the destination attributes associated with memorable experiences. *Tourism Management*, *44*, 34–45. DOI: 10.1016/j.tourman.2014.02.007

Kim, J., & Lennon, S. J. (2013). Effects of reputation and website quality on online consumers' emotion, perceived risk and purchase intention: Based on the stimulus-organism-response model. *Journal of Research in Interactive Marketing*, *7*(1), 33–56.

Kim, M. J., & Hall, C. M. (2021). Do perceived risk and intervention affect crowdfunder behavior for the sustainable development goals? A model of goal-directed behavior. *Journal of Cleaner Production*, *311*, 127614.

Kim, M. J., Lee, C. K., & Jung, T. (2020). Exploring consumer behavior in virtual reality tourism using an extended stimulus-organism-response model. *Journal of Travel Research*, *59*(1), 69–89.

Klaus, P., & Zaichkowsky, J. (2020). AI voice bots: A services marketing research agenda. *Journal of Services Marketing*, *34*(3), 389–398.

Klimmt, C., & Vorderer, P. (2003). Media psychology "is not yet there": Introducing theories of media entertainment to the presence debate. *Presence (Cambridge, Mass.)*, *12*(4), 346–359.

Kock, N., & Hadaya, P. (2018). Minimum sample size estimation in PLS-SEM: The inverse square root and gamma-exponential methods. *Information Systems Journal, 28*(1), 227–261.

Kogan, L., Papanikolaou, D., Seru, A., & Stoffman, N. (2017). Technological innovation, resource allocation, and growth. *The Quarterly Journal of Economics, 132*(2), 665–712.

Koivisto, T. (2024). *The Use of AI in B2B Sales And Prospecting* [Bachelor's Thesis, Aalto University School of Business]. https://aaltodoc.aalto.fi/items/f22d33cb-2daa-41a4-b4be-7c945ea1842e

Komiak, S. Y., & Benbasat, I. (2006). The effects of personalization and familiarity on trust and adoption of recommendation agents. *Management Information Systems Quarterly*, •••, 941–960.

Koulouri, T., Macredie, R. D., & Olakitan, D. (2022). Chatbots to Support Young Adults' Mental Health: An Exploratory Study of Acceptability. [TiiS]. *ACM Transactions on Interactive Intelligent Systems, 12*(2), 1–39.

Kozinets, R. V., & Gretzel, U. (2021). Commentary: Artificial intelligence: The marketer's dilemma. *Journal of Marketing, 85*(1), 156–159.

Kumar, V., Ashraf, A. R., & Nadeem, W. (2024). AI-powered marketing : What, where, and how? *International Journal of Information Management, 77*, 102783. DOI: 10.1016/j.ijinfomgt.2024.102783

Kumar, V., & Pansari, A. (2016). Competitive Advantage through Engagement. *JMR, Journal of Marketing Research, 53*(4), 497–514. DOI: 10.1509/jmr.15.0044

Kumo, W. (2023). Leveraging consumer behavior research for effective marketing strategies. *Advances in Business & Industrial Marketing Research, 1*(3), 117–129. DOI: 10.60079/abim.v1i3.196

Laamouri, L. K., & Gharbi, J. E. (2008). L'impact de l'imagerie mentale générée par un site Web marchand sur la valeur perçue et l'intention de comportement. *7éme congrès sur les tendances Marketing*.

Lachmann, H., Schneider, T., & Wagner, L. (2024). AI Revolution : Evolving Skills in Marketing Agency Jobs. *Special Issue Innovative Brand Management, IV*, 53–74.

Lad, K. S., & Nayak, A. (2024). Impact of Emotional Response of Youth on Pester Power Advertising. Library of Progress-Library Science, *Information Technology & Computer*, 44(3).

Lamm, K. W., Borron, A., Holt, J., & Lamm, A. (2019). Communication channel preferences: A descriptive audience segmentation evaluation. *Journal of Applied Communications, 103*(3). Advance online publication. DOI: 10.4148/1051-0834.2238

Lamrhari, S., El Ghazi, H., Oubrich, M., & El Faker, A. (2022). A social CRM analytic framework for improving customer retention, acquisition, and conversion. *Technological Forecasting and Social Change*, *174*, 1–19. DOI: 10.1016/j.techfore.2021.121275

Laroche, M., Kiani, I., Economakis, N., & Richard, M.-O. (2014). Effects of multichannel marketing on consumers' online search behavior: The power of multiple points of connection. *Journal of Advertising Research*, *53*, 431–443. DOI: 10.2501/JAR-53-4-431-443

Lavoisier-Mérieux, L. M. (2002). De l'efficacité des stratégies de communication publicitaires menaçantes: une étude de la relation entre émotions négatives et persuasion dans le domaine de la lutte contre l'insécurité routière. *Actes du, 2*.

Lawal, K. (2025). Advertising Targeted at Children: Effects on Materialism and Brand Loyalty Formation.

Lawrence, P. R., & Lorsch, J. W. (1967). *Organization and environment : Managing differentiation and integration* (1re éd.). Harvard University Press. https://cir.nii.ac.jp/crid/1970867909784112773

Lawson, R. (2002). Consumer knowledge structures: Background issues and introduction. *Psychology and Marketing*, *19*(6), 447–455.

Leahy, W., & Sweller, J. (2011). Cognitive load theory, modality of presentation and the transient information effect. *Applied Cognitive Psychology*, *25*(6), 943–951.

Leblanc, C., & Roux, A. (2025). AI and Social Media : An Integrative Literature Review. *Communication Management*. https://hal.science/hal-05041614

Lee, Q. (2022). Value-sensitive Evaluation of Hybrid Human-AI Chatbots in Customer Services.

Lee, B. C., & Johar, G. V. (2025). The effect of personalized content in media entertainment on engagement with the domain. *The Journal of Consumer Research*. Advance online publication. DOI: 10.1093/jcr/ucaf018

Lee, T. H., Jan, F., & Lin, Y. H. (2020). How Authentic Experience Affects Traditional Religious Tourism Development: Evidence from the Dajia Mazu Pilgrimage, Taiwan. *Journal of Travel Research*, *60*(5), 1140–1157. DOI: 10.1177/0047287520921240

Lefébure, R., & Venturi, G. (2011). *Gestion de la relation client (2e* (Eyrolles, E., Ed.).

Lei, C., Hossain, M. S., & Wong, E. (2023). Determinants of repurchase intentions of hospitality services delivered by artificially intelligent (AI) service robots. *Sustainability, 15*(6), 4914.

Lemon, K. N., & Verhoef, P. C. (2016). Understanding customer experience throughout the customer journey. *Journal of Marketing, 80*(6), 69–96.

Leocádio, D., Guedes, L., Oliveira, J., Reis, J., & Melão, N. (2024). Customer service with AI-powered human-robot collaboration (HRC): A literature review. *Procedia Computer Science, 232*, 1222–1232.

Leont'ev, A. (1974). The problem of activity in psychology. *Social Psychology, 13*(2), 4–33.

Lichstein, K. L. (1988). Sleep compression treatment of an insomnoid. *Behavior Therapy, 19*(4), 625–632.

Lichy, J., McLeay, F., Burdfield, C., & Matthias, O. (2023). Understanding pre-teen consumers' social media engagement. *International Journal of Consumer Studies, 47*(1), 202–215.

Li, H., Daugherty, T., & Biocca, F. (2002). Impact of 3D advertising on product knowledge, brand attitude, and purchase intention: The mediating role of presence. *Journal of Advertising, 31*(3), 43–57.

Lim, Y. (2023). Emotional exaggeration and consumer resistance in digital advertising. *International Journal of Advertising, 42*(5).

Linden, G., Smith, B., & York, J. (2003). Amazon. com recommendations : Item-to-item collaborative filtering. *IEEE Internet Computing, 7*(1), 76–80.

Liu, H., Chu, H., Huang, Q., & Chen, X. (2016). Enhancing the flow experience of consumers in China through interpersonal interaction in social commerce. *Computers in Human Behavior, 58*, 306–314.

Liu-Thompkins, Y., Okazaki, S., & Li, H. (2022). Artificial empathy in marketing interactions: Bridging the human-AI gap in affective and social customer experience. *Journal of the Academy of Marketing Science, 50*(6), 1198–1218.

Liutikas, D. (2025). Introduction to Sacred Landscape, Pilgrimage, and Ritual Practices. In *Creating the Sacred Landscape Pilgrimages and Ritual Practices* (pp. 1–20). https://doi.org/DOI: 10.1007/978-3-031-86232-8_1

Liu, X. (2024). Research on the strategy of content innovation and audience experience improvement in media programs in the digital age. *Media and Communication Research, 5*(4), 104–111. DOI: 10.23977/mediacr.2024.050414

Liu, Y., Tan, H., Cao, G., & Xu, Y. (2024). Enhancing user engagement through adaptive UI/UX design: A study on personalized mobile app interfaces. *Computer Science & IT Research Journal*, *5*, 1942–1962. DOI: 10.51594/csitrj.v5i8.1457

Li, Y., & Sun, M. (2025). The impact of perceived interactivity on purchase intention in interactive video: A CAB-based chain mediation model of empathy, immersion, and arousal. *Frontiers in Communication*, *10*, 1615509.

Lombard, M., & Ditton, T. (1997). At the heart of it all: The concept of presence. *Journal of Computer-Mediated Communication*, *3*(2).

Lombardot, É. (2007). La nudité en publicité: Quelle influence sur l'attention portée à l'annonce et la fonction mémorielle de la marque? [French Edition]. *Recherche et Applications en Marketing*, *22*(4), 23–41.

Longoni, C., Bonezzi, A., & Morewedge, C. K. (2019). Resistance to medical artificial intelligence. *The Journal of Consumer Research*, *46*(4), 629–650.

Lopes, A. R., & Casais, B. (2022). Digital content marketing: Conceptual review and recommendations for practitioners. *Academy of Strategic Management Journal*, *21*(2), 1–17. https://www.scirp.org/reference/referencespapers?referenceid=3710429

Lopes, J. M., Gomes, S., & Rodrigues, I. (2024). Playing the gamification and co-creation game: A bibliometric literature review. *Management Review Quarterly*, *74*(1), 353–376.

López-Mas, L., Claret, A., Bermúdez, A., Llauger, M., & Guerrero, L. (2022). Co-creation with consumers for packaging design validated through implicit and explicit methods: Exploratory effect of visual and textual attributes. *Foods*, *11*(9), 1183. PMID: 35563908

Loureiro, S. M. C., Bilro, R. G., & Angelino, F. J. D. A. (2021). Virtual reality and gamification in marketing higher education: A review and research agenda. *Spanish Journal of Marketing - ESIC*, *25*(2), 179–216.

Lourenço, C. E., Hair, J. F.Jr, Zambaldi, F., & Canniatti Ponchio, M. (2022). Consumer brand engagement concept and measurement: Toward a refined approach. *Journal of Retailing and Consumer Services*, *68*. Advance online publication. DOI: 10.1016/j.jretconser.2022.103053

Luan, C. C., & Phan, T. A. (2024). The effect of emotion type and similarity of experience on consumers' willingness to pay for cause-related products: Construal level perspective. *Journal of Consumer Behaviour*, *23*(2), 808–824.

Luo, D., Doucé, L., & Nys, K. (2025). Immersive art exhibitions: Sensory intensity effects on visitor satisfaction via visitor attention and visitor experience. *Visitor Studies*, •••, 1–22. DOI: 10.1080/10645578.2025.2510838

Luo, X., Tong, S., Fang, Z., & Qu, Z. (2019). Frontiers: Machines vs. humans: The impact of artificial intelligence chatbot disclosure on customer purchases. *Marketing Science*, *38*(6), 937–947.

Lussak, A., Ramadhan, R., & Darmawan, I. (2024). Personalized digital marketing perspectives and practices in education industry. *Multidisciplinary Science Journal*, *6*(12), 1–7. DOI: 10.31893/multiscience.2024268

Luther, L., Tiberius, V., & Brem, A. (2020). User experience (UX) in business, management, and psychology: A bibliometric mapping of the current state of research. *Multimodal Technologies and Interaction*, *4*(2), 1–18. DOI: 10.3390/mti4020018

Makransky, G., & Petersen, G. B. (2021). The cognitive and emotional impact of immersive virtual field trips in education: An investigation of presence and flow. *Computers & Education*, *167*, 104160.

Malhotra, N. K., Kim, S. S., & Agarwal, J. (2004). Internet users' information privacy concerns (IUIPC): The construct, the scale, and a causal model. *Information Systems Research*, *15*(4), 336–355.

Mangoch, S., & Jain, D. (2022). Factors Determining Tourists Motivation to Visit a Place for Adventure Tourism: A Systematic Review. *Academy of Marketing Studies Journal*, *26*(3).

Marasco, A., Buonincontri, P., Van Niekerk, M., Orlowski, M., & Okumus, F. (2018). Exploring the role of next-generation virtual technologies in destination marketing. *Journal of Destination Marketing & Management*, *9*, 138–148.

Mariani, M. M., Perez-Vega, R., & Wirtz, J. (2022). AI in marketing, consumer research and psychology: A systematic literature review and research agenda. *Psychology and Marketing*, *39*(4), 755–776.

Martijn, G., Van Hooijdonk, C., Kunneman, F., & Hoeken, H. (2024). Reconfiguring the Customer Service Domain: Perspectives of Managers, Conversational Designers, and Human Agents on Human–Chatbot Collaboration. International Journal of Innovation and Technology Management, 2450028.

Martinez, B., & Seock, Y. K. (2017). Crowdsourcing the design process: The influence of consumer characteristics on participation and behavioral intentions. *Journal of Marketing Management and Consumer Behavior*, *2*(1).

Martínez, C., & Olsson, T. (2019). Making sense of YouTubers: How Swedish children construct and negotiate the YouTuber Misslisibell as a girl celebrity. *Journal of Children and Media*, *13*(1), 36–52.

Martínez-López, F. J., Aguilar-Illescas, R., Molinillo, S., Anaya-Sánchez, R., Coca-Stefaniak, J. A., & Esteban-Millat, I. (2021). The role of online brand community engagement on the consumer-brand relationship. *Sustainability*, *13*(7), 1–17. DOI: 10.3390/su13073679

Martinez, M. G. (2015). Solver engagement in knowledge sharing in crowdsourcing communities: Exploring the link to creativity. *Research Policy*, *44*(8), 1419–1430.

Martínez-Molés, V., Jung, T. H., Pérez-Cabañero, C., & Cervera-Taulet, A. (2022). Gathering pre-purchase information for a cruise vacation with virtual reality: The effects of media technology and gender. *International Journal of Contemporary Hospitality Management*, *34*(1), 407–429.

Mathew, S. M., Nayak, S., & Rao, V. (2025). Determinants of online apparel mass customization: A decade in review. *Journal of Fashion Marketing and Management*, *29*(1), 113–136.

Matsas, E., & Vosniakos, G. C. (2017). Design of a virtual reality training system for human–robot collaboration in manufacturing tasks. [IJIDeM]. *International Journal on Interactive Design and Manufacturing*, *11*(2), 139–153.

McCarthy, J., Minsky, M. L., Rochester, N., & Shannon, C. E. (2006). A proposal for the dartmouth summer research project on artificial intelligence, august 31, 1955. *AI Magazine*, *27*(4), 12–12.

McDowell, W. C., Wilson, R. C., & Kile, C. O.Jr. (2016). An examination of retail website design and conversion rate. *Journal of Business Research*, *69*(11), 4837–4842. DOI: 10.1016/j.jbusres.2016.04.040

McGhee, P. E. (1979). The role of laughter and humor in growing up female. In *Becoming female: Perspectives on development* (pp. 183–206). Springer US.

McKnight, D. H., Choudhury, V., & Kacmar, C. (2002). Developing and validating trust measures for e-commerce: An integrative typology. *Information Systems Research*, *13*(3), 334–359.

McQuarrie, E. F., & Mick, D. G. (1996). Figures of rhetoric in advertising language. *The Journal of Consumer Research*, *22*(4), 424–438.

McTear, M. (2022). *Conversational ai: Dialogue systems, conversational agents, and chatbots*. Springer Nature.

Mdaary, S. (2024). Artificial Intelligence and organizational performance : A literature review. *American Scientific Journal, 3*(23), 726–726. DOI: 10.5281/zenodo.11160590

Mehrabian, A., & Russell, J. A. (1974). *An approach to environmental psychology*. MIT Press.

Mehrabi, N., Morstatter, F., Saxena, N., Lerman, K., & Galstyan, A. (2022). A Survey on Bias and Fairness in Machine Learning. *ACM Computing Surveys, 54*(6), 1–35. DOI: 10.1145/3457607

Meineri, S., & Guéguen, N. (2014). Foot-in-the-door and action identification. Binding communication applied to environmental conservation. *European Review of Applied Psychology, 64*(1), 3–11.

Mertala, P. (2020). Young children's perceptions of ubiquitous computing and the Internet of Things. *British Journal of Educational Technology, 51*(1), 84–102.

Meyer, J. C. (2000). Humor as a double-edged sword: Four functions of humor in communication. *Communication Theory, 10*(3), 310–331.

Micheaux, A., & Bosio, B. (2019). Customer journey mapping as a new way to teach data-driven marketing as a service. *Journal of Marketing Education, 41*(2), 127–140.

Miikkulainen, R., Iscoe, N., Shagrin, A., Cordell, R., Nazari, S., Schoolland, C., . . . Lamba, G. (2017). Conversion rate optimization through evolutionary computation. In Proceedings of the Genetic and Evolutionary Computation Conference (pp. 1193-1199). GECCO '17. https://doi.org/DOI: 10.1145/3071178.3071312

Mirabi, V., Akbariyeh, H., & Tahmasebifard, H. (2015). A study of factors affecting on customers purchase intention. [JMEST]. *Journal of Multidisciplinary Engineering Science and Technology, 2*(1).

Mishra, A. K., Bansal, R., Maurya, P. K., Kar, S. K., & Bakshi, P. K. (2022). Predicting the antecedents of consumers' intention toward purchase of mutual funds: A hybrid PLS-SEM-neural network approach. *International Journal of Consumer Studies, 47*(2), 563–587. DOI: 10.1111/ijcs.12850

Mishra, N., Srivastava, P., Mahato, S., & Shivani, S. (2023). Use and acceptance of crypto currencies in India: An evaluation of block chain application in financial sector using PLS SEM and ANN approach. *International Journal of Quality & Reliability Management*. Advance online publication. DOI: 10.1108/ijqrm-03-2023-0093

Moati, P. (2011). *La nouvelle révolution commerciale*. Odile Jacob.

Mokkink, L. B., de Vet, H., Diemeer, S., & Eekhout, I. (2022). Sample size recommendations for studies on reliability and measurement error: An online application based on simulation studies. *Health Services and Outcomes Research Methodology*, *23*(24), 242–265. DOI: 10.1007/s10742-022-00293-9

Molina-Gómez, J., Mercadé-Melé, P., Almeida-García, F., & Ruiz-Berrón, R. (2021). New perspectives on satisfaction and loyalty in festival tourism: The function of tangible and intangible attributes. *PLoS One*, *16*(2), e0246562. DOI: 10.1371/journal.pone.0246562 PMID: 33626049

Montazer, F., & Ahmadi, M. (2024). Designing Adaptive Interfaces in the Metaverse : Reducing Cognitive Load for Enhanced User Experience. *International Journal of Advanced Human Computer Interaction*, *2*(2), 44–54.

Moral-Cuadra, S., Solano-Sánchez, M. Á., López-Guzmán, T., & Menor-Campos, A. (2021). Peer-to-Peer Tourism: Tourists' profile estimation through artificial neural networks. *Journal of Theoretical and Applied Electronic Commerce Research*, *16*(4), 1120–1135. DOI: 10.3390/jtaer16040063

Mora-Serrano, J., Muñoz-La Rivera, F., & Valero, I. (2021). Factors for the automation of the creation of virtual reality experiences to raise awareness of occupational hazards on construction sites. *Electronics (Basel)*, *10*(11), 1355.

Morreall, J. (1983). *Taking laughter seriously*. SUNY press.

Mou, A. J. (2024). Marketing capstone insights: Leveraging multi-channel strategies for maximum digital conversion and ROI. *Review of Applied Science and Technology*, *3*(04), 1–28. DOI: 10.63125/5w76qb87

Moufahim, M., & Lichrou, M. (2018). Pilgrimage, consumption and rituals: Spiritual authenticity in a Shia Muslim pilgrimage. *Tourism Management*, *70*, 322–332. DOI: 10.1016/j.tourman.2018.08.023

Mu, Z. M. Z., & Li, H. L. H. JianHong, W. J. W., Ji, L. J. L., YanGeng, J. Y. J., & XiTing, L. X. L. (2007). Religious tourism and cultural pilgrimage: a Chinese perspective. In *CABI eBooks* (pp. 98–112). https://doi.org/DOI: 10.1079/9781845932251.0098

Munjal, P. G. (2015). The potential of a participatory approach in sustaining the fairs and festivals of small towns. *Worldwide Hospitality and Tourism Themes*, *7*(4), 347–366. DOI: 10.1108/whatt-03-2015-0008

Murtarelli, G., Gregory, A., & Romenti, S. (2021). A conversation-based perspective for shaping ethical human–machine interactions: The particular challenge of chatbots. *Journal of Business Research*, *129*, 927–935.

Nabi, R. L., Myrick, J. G., & Kim, S. C. (2020). Feeling scared, happy, or both? The effects of mixed emotional appeals in advertising on attitudes and behavioral intentions. *Journal of Advertising*, *49*(4), 435–449.

Nadkarni, P. M., Ohno-Machado, L., & Chapman, W. W. (2011). Natural language processing : An introduction. *Journal of the American Medical Informatics Association : JAMIA*, *18*(5), 544–551. PMID: 21846786

Naeimi, M., & Family, Q. (2025). AI and Post-Purchase Behavior : Personalization, Behavioral Insights, and Ethical Challenges. *Behavioral Insights, and Ethical Challenges (September 07, 2025)*. https://papers.ssrn.com/sol3/papers.cfm?abstract_id=5460815

Naert, S., Puleston, J., Mayou, S., & Bardon, Y. (2025). *Personas in the age of AI : Promises and limitations* (IPSOS Views, p. 11). IPSOS. https://www.ipsos.com/sites/default/files/ct/news/documents/2025-07/ipsos-views-personas-in-the-age-of-AI.pdf

Nanayakkara, N. W. O. K. D. S. P. (2020). *Application of Artificial Intelligence in Marketing Mix : A Conceptual Review* (SSRN Scholarly Paper 3862936). Social Science Research Network. DOI: 10.2139/ssrn.3862936

Nardi, B. A. (1996). Activity theory and human-computer interaction. *Context and consciousness: Activity theory and human-computer interaction, 436*(1), 7-16.Chen, T., Dodds, S., Finsterwalder, J., Witell, L., Cheung, L., Falter, M., ... & McColl-Kennedy, J. R. (2021). Dynamics of wellbeing co-creation: a psychological ownership perspective. *Journal of Service Management*, *32*(3), 383–406.

Naumann, A., Hurtienne, J., Israel, J. H., Mohs, C., Kindsmüller, M. C., Meyer, H. A., & Husslein, S. (2007). Intuitive use of user interfaces: Defining a vague concept. In A. Holzinger (Ed.), Engineering psychology and cognitive ergonomics: 7th International Conference, EPCE 2007, Beijing, China, July 22-27, 2007, Proceedings (Lecture Notes in Computer Science, Vol. 4559, pp. 123-132). Springer. https://doi.org/DOI: 10.1007/978-3-540-73331-7_14

Nazir, S., Khadim, S., Ali Asadullah, M., & Syed, N. (2023). Exploring the influence of artificial intelligence technology on consumer repurchase intention : The mediation and moderation approach. *Technology in Society*, *72*, 102190. DOI: 10.1016/j.techsoc.2022.102190

Neuhofer, B., Buhalis, D., & Ladkin, A. (2014). A typology of technology-enhanced tourism experiences. *International Journal of Tourism Research*, *16*(4), 340–350.

Ngai, E. W., Lee, M. C., Luo, M., Chan, P. S., & Liang, T. (2021). An intelligent knowledge-based chatbot for customer service. *Electronic Commerce Research and Applications*, *50*, 101098.

Ngatindriatun, N., Alfarizi, M., & Widiastuti, T. (2024). Impact of Sharia hospital service standards and religiosity commitment on patient satisfaction and loyalty: Insights from certified Sharia hospital in Indonesia. *Journal of Islamic Accounting and Business Research*. Advance online publication. DOI: 10.1108/jiabr-12-2022-0344

Ng, S. C., Sweeney, J. C., & Plewa, C. (2020). Customer engagement: A systematic review and future research priorities. *Australasian Marketing Journal*, *28*(4), 235–252.

Nguyen, D.-N., Nguyen, V.-H., Trinh, T., Ho, T., & Le, H.-S. (2024). A personalized product recommendation model in e-commerce based on retrieval strategy. *Journal of Open Innovation*, *10*(2), 100303. DOI: 10.1016/j.joitmc.2024.100303

Nguyen, H. T., Le, A. T. T., Phan, A. C., & Hoang, T. D. L. (2022). A multi-perspective approach of international tourist satisfaction in tourism service: From big data perspective. *Journal of Asia Business Studies*, *17*(4), 850–872. DOI: 10.1108/jabs-03-2022-0090

Nian, S., Chen, M., Zhang, X., Li, D., & Ren, J. (2023). How outstanding universal value attractiveness and tourism crowding affect visitors' satisfaction? *Behavioral Sciences (Basel, Switzerland)*, *13*(2), 112. DOI: 10.3390/bs13020112 PMID: 36829341

Nicolescu, L., & Tudorache, M. T. (2022). Human-computer interaction in customer service: The experience with AI chatbots—a systematic literature review. *Electronics (Basel)*, *11*(10), 1579.

Nicolini, V. (2022). Fear vs humor appeals: A comparative study of children's responses to anti-smoking advertisements. *Asia Pacific Journal of Marketing and Logistics*, *34*(2), 166–184.

Nissa, N., Jamwal, S., & Neshat, M. (2024). A technical comparative heart disease prediction framework using boosting ensemble techniques. *Computation (Basel, Switzerland)*, *12*(1), 15. DOI: 10.3390/computation12010015

Nizamani, M. M., Zhang, H.-L., & Lai, Z. (2026). Human-centered AI : Advancing ethical, transparent, and context-aware systems for sustainable development. *Technology in Society*, *84*, 103121. DOI: 10.1016/j.techsoc.2025.103121

Nkansah, B. K. (2011). On the Kaiser-Meyer-Olkin's measure of sampling adequacy. *Math. Theory Model*, *8*, 52–76.

Nkomo, N., & Mupa, M. N. (2024). The Impact of Artificial Intelligence on Predictive Customer Behaviour Analytics in E-commerce : A Comparative Study of Traditional and AI-driven Models. *Iconic Research and Engineering Journals*, *8*(5), 432–451.

Norin, A., Ishfaq, H., Shaheen, W. A., & Abbas, Z. (2024). Advertising Effects on Young Minds: Probing into Environmental Awareness, Purchasing Patterns, and Attitudinal Shifts in Children. *Research Journal for Societal Issues*, *6*(1), 272–292.

Norvig, P., & Russell, S. J. (2010). Intelligenza artificiale. Un approccio moderno.

Nourani, V., & Fard, M. S. (2012). Sensitivity analysis of the artificial neural network outputs in simulation of the evaporation process at different climatologic regimes. *Advances in Engineering Software*, *47*(1), 127–146. DOI: 10.1016/j.advengsoft.2011.12.014

Novak, T. P., Hoffman, D. L., & Yung, Y. F. (2000). Measuring the customer experience in online environments: A structural modeling approach. *Marketing Science*, *19*(1), 22–42.

Nunnally, J. C., & Bernstein, I. H. (1994). *Psychometric theory* (3rd ed.). McGraw-Hill.

Nuruzzaman, M., & Hussain, O. K. (2018, October). A survey on chatbot implementation in customer service industry through deep neural networks. In 2018 IEEE 15th international conference on e-business engineering (ICEBE) (pp. 54-61). IEEE.

Nuseir, M., El-Refae, G., Aljumah, A., Alshurideh, M., Urabi, S., & Al Kurdi, B. (2023). Digital marketing strategies and the impact on customer experience. *Systematic Reviews.*

Nwabekee, S. U., Abdul-Azeez, O. Y., Agu, E. E., & Ijomah, T. (2024). Digital transformation in marketing strategies: The role of data analytics and CRM tools. International Journal of Finance. *Risk and Strategic Trends*, *3*(2), 56–72. DOI: 10.56355/ijfrst.2024.3.2.0047

Nwankpa, C. E., Ijomah, W., Gachagan, A., & Marshall, S. (2021). Activation functions: comparison of trends in practice and research for deep learning. *arXiv (Cornell University)*. https://arxiv.org/pdf/1811.03378.pdf

Okeleke, P. A., Ajiga, D., Folorunsho, S. O., & Ezeigweneme, C. (2024). Predictive analytics for market trends using AI : A study in consumer behavior. *International Journal of Engineering Research Updates*, *7*(1), 36–49.

Okonkwo, K. (2024). *Using Artificial Intelligence (AI) to Manage Buyer Persona in E-commerce based on Kotler & Keller's 2016 Model of Consumer Behaviour : Archival Research based on Secondary Data in form of Relevant Publications* [Bachelor's thesis]. Jamk University of Applied Sciences.

Okonkwo, C. (2024). Assessment of user experience (UX) design trends in mobile applications. *Journal of Technology and Systems*, *6*, 29–41. DOI: 10.47941/jts.2147

Oliver, R. L. (1977). Effect of expectation and disconfirmation on postexposure product evaluations : An alternative interpretation. *The Journal of Applied Psychology*, *62*(4), 480.

Oliver, R. L. (1980). A Cognitive Model of the Antecedents and Consequences of Satisfaction Decisions. *JMR, Journal of Marketing Research*, *17*(4), 460–469. DOI: 10.1177/002224378001700405

Ologunebi, J. O. (2023). Digital marketing strategies, plan and implementations: A case study of JumiaGroup and ASDA UK (MPRA Paper No. 118771) [Working paper]. MPRA. https://mpra.ub.uni-muenchen.de/118771/

Olsen, D. H. (2013). A Scalar Comparison of Motivations and Expectations of Experience within the Religious Tourism Market. *International Journal of Religious Tourism and Pilgrimage*, *1*(1), 5. DOI: 10.21427/d7zq51

Olujimi, P. A., & Ade-Ibijola, A. (2023). NLP techniques for automating responses to customer queries: A systematic review. *Discover Artificial Intelligence*, *3*(1), 20.

Ooi, K., & Tan, G. W. (2016). Mobile technology acceptance model: An investigation using mobile users to explore smartphone credit card. *Expert Systems with Applications*, *59*, 33–46. DOI: 10.1016/j.eswa.2016.04.015

Ooko, J. A., Aila, F. O., & Odondo, A. (2023). Relationship between customer satisfaction and brand loyalty. The International Journal of Business & Management, 11(9), Article BM2309-005. https://doi.org/DOI: 10.24940/theijbm/2023/v11/i9/BM2309-005

Orth, D. (2019). *Designing meaningful objects*. University of Technology Sydney.

Osemeike, G. E., Okpeke, P. P., & Ijomah, T. (2024). Strategic approaches for successful digital transformation in project management across industries. *International Journal of Frontiers in Engineering and Technology Research*, *7*(1), 1–11. DOI: 10.53294/ijfetr.2024.7.1.0037

Paine, A. L., Hashmi, S., Fink, E., Mitchell, P., & Howe, N. (2025). Humorous peer play and social understanding in childhood. *Communications Psychology*, *3*, 76. PMID: 40355511

Painuly, P., & Goutami, K. L. (2022). Pilgrim Satisfaction towards the Basic Amenities with Reference to Badrinath: An Empirical Study. *Specialusis Ugdymas*, *1*(43), 7477–7490.

Pal, A. (2024). Enhancing customer experience: Creating new touchpoints for experience-centric mobile services. Retrieved from https://helda.helsinki.fi/server/api/core/bitstreams/09e1fd78-f29d-40f0-87f3-47f56758b3b0/content

Pandian, A., Mohankumar, K. P., Padmini, S., Amaran, S., & Sreekumar, K. (2025). Enhancing Trust and Collaboration Using Explainability in Natural Language Processing for AI-Driven Healthcare. In A. Kumar, T. Ananth Kumar, P. Das, C. Sharma, & A. K. Dubey (Éds.), *Explainable Artificial Intelligence in the Healthcare Industry* (1re éd., p. 619-650). Wiley. DOI: 10.1002/9781394249312.ch26

Paramarta, V., & Aripin, Z. (2024, January). Optimizing Human-Ai Interaction: Artificial Empathy Strategies In Enhancing Affective And Social Customer Experiences. In Journal Of Jabar Economic Society Networking Forum (Vol. 1, No. 2, Pp. 46-62).

Parent, E. (2023). «Ça dépend»: Converser, publier et scroller sur les réseaux sociaux à l'adolescence.

Parker, S., Steffen, R., Rashid, H., Cabada, M. M., Memish, Z. A., Gautret, P., Sokhna, C., Sharma, A., Shlim, D. R., Leshem, E., Dwyer, D. E., Lami, F., Chatterjee, S., Shafi, S., Zumla, A., & Mahomed, O. (2024). Sacred journeys and pilgrimages: Health risks associated with travels for religious purposes. *Journal of Travel Medicine*, *31*(8). Advance online publication. DOI: 10.1093/jtm/taae122 PMID: 39216102

Parveen, N., Othman, R. O. M., Abbadi, D. M. A., Al-Lobani, E. M., Skhawat, H., Ali, M. S., & Mejdi, K. (2024). Digital marketing strategies in the age of social media: A comparative study of global brands. *Nanotechnology Perceptions*, *20*(S13), 212–242. DOI: 10.62441/nano-ntp.vi.2771

Pascucci, F., Savelli, E., & Gistri, G. (2023). How digital technologies reshape marketing: Evidence from a qualitative investigation. *Italian Journal of Marketing*, *2023*(1), 27–58. DOI: 10.1007/s43039-023-00063-6

Passador, M. L. (2024). *Ai act and the ecb: Steering financial supervision in the eu*. Columbia Journal of European Law.

Pastor-Escuredo, D., & Vinuesa, R. (2022). Towards an Ethical Framework in the Complex Digital Era. *AI*, *3*(4), 961–974. DOI: 10.3390/ai3040057

Pathak, S., & Pallasena, R. K. (2025). Mapping the evolution of generative AI: Insights from bibliometric research. *Journal of Decision Systems*, •••, 1–30. DOI: 10.1080/12460125.2024.2438612

Pavicic, J., Alfirevic, N., & Batarelo, V. J. (2007). The management and marketing of religious sites, pilgrimage and religious events: challenges for Roman Catholic pilgrimages in Croatia. In *CABI eBooks* (pp. 48–63). https://doi.org/DOI: 10.1079/9781845932251.0048

Pedrero-Esteban, L. M., & Barrios-Rubio, A. (2024). Digital communication in the age of immediacy. *Digital*, *4*(2), 302–315. DOI: 10.3390/digital4020015

Penga, X., & Li, L. (2024). Optimization strategies for enterprise brand communication from the perspective of digital marketing communication. *Proceedings of the 8th International Conference on Education Technology, Management and Humanities Science (ETMHS 2024)* (pp. 368-373). Francis Academic Press.

Pereira, R. S., Lieira, D. D., Silva, M. A. D., Pimenta, A. H., da Costa, J. B., Rosário, D., & Meneguette, R. I. (2020). RELIABLE: Resource allocation mechanism for 5G network using mobile edge computing. *Sensors (Basel)*, *20*(19), 5449. PMID: 32977383

Perloff, M. (2017). Eliot the Young Reviewer: The Formation of Aesthetic Judgment. *Literary Imagination*, *19*(2), 135–142.

Perumallaplli, R. (2014). Conversational AI for Customer Support : Automation in Large Enterprises. *SSRN*, *5228517*, •••. https://papers.ssrn.com/sol3/papers.cfm?abstract_id=5228517

Petty, R. E., & Cacioppo, J. T. (1986). Message elaboration versus peripheral cues. In *Communication and persuasion: Central and peripheral routes to attitude change* (pp. 141–172). Springer New York.

Pierce, J. L., Kostova, T., & Dirks, K. T. (2003). The state of psychological ownership: Integrating and extending a century of research. *Review of General Psychology*, *7*(1), 84–107.

Pietrini, R., Galdelli, A., Mancini, A., Frontoni, E., & Zingaretti, P. (2025). Machine Learning-Driven Marketing Personas for the Luxury Fashion Market. In A. Del Bue, C. Canton, J. Pont-Tuset, & T. Tommasi (Éds.), *Computer Vision – ECCV 2024 Workshops* (Vol. 15623, p. 402-416). Springer Nature Switzerland. DOI: 10.1007/978-3-031-91569-7_25

Piller, F., & Salvador, F (2016) Design toolkits, organizational capabilities, and firm performance. *Revolutionizing Innovation: Users, Communities, and Open Innovation*, 1.

Piris, Y., & Gay, A. C. (2021). Customer satisfaction and natural language processing. *Journal of Business Research, 124*, 264–271.

Prahalad, C. K., & Ramaswamy, V. (2004). Co-creation experiences: The next practice in value creation. *Journal of Interactive Marketing, 18*(3), 5–14.

Preston, C. (2005). *Thomas Browne and the writing of early modern science*. Cambridge University Press.

Primiceri, G. E. (2005). Time varying structural vector autoregressions and monetary policy. *The Review of Economic Studies, 72*(3), 821–852.

Prochaska, J. O., Fairhurst, S. K., Velicer, W. F., Velasquez, M. M., & Rossi, J. S. (1991). The process of smoking cessation: An analysis of precontemplation, contemplation, and preparation stages of change. *Journal of Consulting and Clinical Psychology, 59*(2), 295–304. PMID: 2030191

Prochaska, J. O., Rossi, J. S., & Wilcox, N. S. (1991). Change processes and psychotherapy outcome in integrative case research. *Journal of Psychotherapy Integration, 1*(2), 103.

Prochaska, J. O., Velicer, W. F., DiClemente, C. C., & Fava, J. (1988). Measuring processes of change: Applications to the cessation of smoking. *Journal of Consulting and Clinical Psychology, 56*(4), 520. PMID: 3198809

Prochaska, J. O., Velicer, W. F., Guadagnoli, E., Rossi, J. S., & DiClemente, C. C. (1991). Patterns of change: Dynamic typology applied to smoking cessation. *Multivariate Behavioral Research, 26*(1), 83–107. PMID: 26782613

Purnomo, Y. J. (2023). Digital marketing strategy to increase sales conversion on e-commerce platforms. [ADMAN]. *Journal of Contemporary Administration and Management, 1*(2), 54–62. DOI: 10.61100/adman.v1i2.23

Raeisi, S. (2017). The importance of customer engagement and service innovation in value co-creation. World Academy of Science, Engineering and Technology, International Journal of Social, Behavioral, Educational, Economic. *Business and Industrial Engineering, 11*(4). 775-780.Scholar.waset.org/1999.10/10006723

Rahman, W. N., Mutum, D. S., & Ghazali, E. M. (2022). Consumer engagement with visual content on Instagram: Impact of different features of posts by prominent brands. [IJESMA]. *International Journal of E-Services and Mobile Applications*, *14*(1), 1–21. DOI: 10.4018/IJESMA.295960

Rai, A. (2020). Explainable AI : From black box to glass box. *Journal of the Academy of Marketing Science*, *48*(1), 137–141. DOI: 10.1007/s11747-019-00710-5

Ramachandran, K. K. (2023). Evaluating ROI in digital marketing campaigns: Metrics, measurement, and insights. *International Journal of Management*, *14*(7), 190–204. https://iaeme.com/Home/issue/IJM?Volume=14&Issue=7

Ramaswamy, V., & Ozcan, K. (2018). What is co-creation? An interactional creation framework and its implications for value creation. *Journal of Business Research*, *84*, 196–205.

Rana, J., Jain, R., & Nehra, V. (2024). Utility and acceptability of AI-enabled chatbots on the online customer journey. *International Journal of Computing and Digital Systems*, *15*(1), 323–335.

Rana, P. S., & Singh, R. P. (2011). Perceptions and images of tourists and pilgrims in Banaras. *Holy Places and Pilgrimages: Essays on India. Planet Earth & Cultural Understanding Series. Pub*, *8*, 165–206.

Rane, N., Paramesha, M., Choudhary, S., & Rane, J. (2024). Artificial intelligence in sales and marketing : Enhancing customer satisfaction, experience and loyalty. *Experience and Loyalty (May 17, 2024)*. https://papers.ssrn.com/sol3/papers.cfm?abstract_id=4831903

Rani, A. (2022). The role of content marketing in the era of digitalization. *International Journal of Advanced Research*, *10*, 1355–1362. DOI: 10.21474/IJAR01/14349

Raschel, E. (2022). Peut-on rire de tout? Réflexions sur les « lois du genre » des expressions humoristiques. *Recueil Dalloz*, *27*, 1367.

Rauschnabel, P. A., & Ro, Y. K. (2016). Augmented reality smart glasses: An investigation of technology acceptance drivers. *International Journal of Technology Marketing*, *11*(2), 123–148.

Rautela, S., Sharma, A., & Panackal, N. (2025). Exploring the sacred-unravelling the growth and development of religious tourism in Islamic culture: A bibliometric analysis. *Cogent Business & Management*, *12*(1). Advance online publication. DOI: 10.1080/23311975.2025.2482020

Razkaoui, Y. (2022). Les rhétoriques de la publicité: Les figures de style. *Revue des Etudes Multidisciplinaires en Sciences Economiques et Sociales*, *7*(1).

Rech, G. (2022). Religious tourist attractions and ecological concerns in the Italian Dolomites: The case of the trekking of the Thinking Christ. *Sustainability*, *14*(24), 16331. DOI: 10.3390/su142416331

Rehman, A., Kumar, S., Salam, M. A., & Virmani, N. (2025). How does AI-powered virtual influencer's anthropomorphism impact trust and brand love? The moderating role of opinion leadership. *Technological Forecasting and Social Change*, *219*, 124198. DOI: 10.1016/j.techfore.2025.124198

Reis, J. (2024). Customer service through AI-Powered human-robot relationships: Where are we now? The case of Henn na cafe, Japan. *Technology in Society*, *77*, 102570.

Riches, S., Taylor, L., Jeyarajaguru, P., Veling, W., & Valmaggia, L. (2024). Virtual reality and immersive technologies to promote workplace wellbeing: A systematic review. *Journal of Mental Health (Abingdon, England)*, *33*(2), 253–273. PMID: 36919828

Rigaux-Bricmont, B. (1986). L'avenir de la recherche en matière de décision collective d'achat. *Recherche et Applications en Marketing*, *1*(2), 17–26.

Rihs, M.. (2024). Comparison of teleportation and walking in virtual reality: Effects on learning and presence. *Frontiers in Virtual Reality*, *4*, 1423911.

Rita, P., Tiago, M. T. B., & Sousa, N. (2024). Empirical Insights into Co-Creation, Satisfaction, and Willingness to Pay in Sustainable Tourism. *Journal of Tourism and Services*, *15*(29), 133–152. DOI: 10.29036/jots.v15i29.804

Ritterbusch, N., & Teichmann, K. (2023). Metaverse marketing: Conceptual foundations and research directions. *Journal of Business Research*, *160*, 113783.

Roba, G. B., & Maric, P. (2023). AI in Customer Relationship Management. In Kryvinska, N., Greguš, M., & Fedushko, S. (Eds.), *Developments in Information and Knowledge Management Systems for Business Applications* (Vol. 462, pp. 469–487). Springer Nature Switzerland., DOI: 10.1007/978-3-031-25695-0_21

Roblox Corporation. (2023). *Roblox advertising guide*. Roblox Documentation.

Rodriguez-Abad, C., Fernández-de-la-Iglesia, J. D. C., Martinez-Santos, A. E., & Rodriguez-Gonzalez, R. (2021). A systematic review of augmented reality in health sciences: A guide to decision-making in higher education. *International Journal of Environmental Research and Public Health*, *18*(8), 4262. PMID: 33920528

Rogers, R. W. (1975). A protection motivation theory of fear appeals and attitude change1. *The Journal of Psychology*, *91*(1), 93–114. PMID: 28136248

Rosch, E., & Mervis, C. B. (1975). Family resemblances: Studies in the internal structure of categories. *Cognitive Psychology*, *7*(4), 573–605.

Rostagno, M., Altavilla, C., Carboni, G., Lemke, W., Motto, R., Saint Guilhem, A., & Yiangou, G. (2019). A tale of two decades: The ecb's monetary policy at 20. Working Paper Series 2346, European Central Bank, Frankfurt.

Rotherham, I. D. (2007). Sustaining tourism infrastructures for religious tourists and pilgrims within the UK. In *CABI eBooks* (pp. 64–77). https://doi.org/DOI: 10.1079/9781845932251.0064

Rowi, A. S., Wahyudi, M. A., & Oswari, T. (2024). Role of digital marketing strategies in enhancing customer engagement and brand loyalty: A study of e-commerce platforms. *International Journal of Business Law and Education*, *5*(2), 2778–2788. DOI: 10.56442/ijble.v5i2

Ruan, Y., & Mezei, J. (2022). When do AI chatbots lead to higher customer satisfaction than human frontline employees in online shopping assistance? Considering product attribute type. *Journal of Retailing and Consumer Services*, *68*, 103059.

Rudy, R., Prabowo, H., Furinto, A., & Hamsal, M. (2021). The influence of digital technology, customer experience, and customer engagement on e-commerce customer loyalty. *Journal of Theoretical and Applied Information Technology*, *99*, 1149–1161.

Ruggieri, R., Savastano, M., Scalingi, A., Bala, D., & D'Ascenzo, F. (2018). The impact of digital platforms on business models: An empirical investigation on innovative start-ups. *Management & Marketing*, *13*(4), 1210–1225. DOI: 10.2478/mmcks-2018-0032

Russell, J. A., & Barrett, L. F. (1999). Core affect, prototypical emotional episodes, and other things called emotion: Dissecting the elephant. *Journal of Personality and Social Psychology*, *76*(5), 805. PMID: 10353204

Ryan, R. M., & Deci, E. L. (2000). Self-determination theory and the facilitation of intrinsic motivation. *The American Psychologist*, *55*(1), 68–78. PMID: 11392867

Saeed, B., Tasmin, R., Mahmood, A., & Hafeez, A. (2021). Development of a multi-item Operational Excellence scale: Exploratory and confirmatory factor analysis. *The TQM Journal*. Advance online publication. DOI: 10.1108/tqm-10-2020-0227

Saghafian, M., Laumann, K., Akhtar, R. S., & Skogstad, M. R. (2020). The evaluation of virtual reality fire extinguisher training. *Frontiers in Psychology*, *11*, 593466. PMID: 33240182

Sahut, J.-M., & Laroche, M. (2025). Using artificial intelligence (AI) to enhance customer experience and to develop strategic marketing : An integrative synthesis. *Computers in Human Behavior*, *170*, 108684. DOI: 10.1016/j.chb.2025.108684

Salazar-Reyna, R., Gonzalez-Aleu, F., Granda-Gutierrez, E. M., Diaz-Ramirez, J., Garza-Reyes, J. A., & Kumar, A. (2020). A systematic literature review of data science, data analytics and machine learning applied to healthcare engineering systems. *Management Decision*, *60*(2), 300–319. DOI: 10.1108/md-01-2020-0035

Salminen, J., Kandpal, C., Kamel, A. M., Jung, S. G., & Jansen, B. J. (2022). Creating and detecting fake reviews of online products. *Journal of Retailing and Consumer Services*, *64*, 102771.

Sanders, E. B. N., & Stappers, P. J. (2014). Probes, toolkits and prototypes: Three approaches to making in codesigning. *CoDesign*, *10*(1), 5–14.

Sandesara, M., Bodkhe, U., Tanwar, S., Alshehri, M. D., Sharma, R., Neagu, B.-C., Grigoras, G., & Raboaca, M. S. (2022). Design and experience of mobile applications: A pilot survey. *Mathematics*, *10*(14), 1–20. DOI: 10.3390/math10142380

Sands, S., Ferraro, C., Demsar, V., Cohen, J., & Gvirtz, A. (2024). Immersive advertising-A review and research agenda: Potential effects of and considerations for AR, VR, and MR advertisements. *Journal of Advertising Research*, *64*(3), 284–300. DOI: 10.2501/JAR-2024-018

Sang, V. M., Hương, N., & Giang, D. N. H. (2022). The role of social brand engagement on brand equity and purchase intention for fashion brands. *Cogent Business & Management*, *9*(1), 1–21. DOI: 10.1080/23311975.2022.2143308

Santoso, F., & Sudarmiatin, S. (2024). Analysis of the influence of multichannel marketing strategy in the 5.0 era: Integrating online and offline for optimal results. *Journal of Business Management and Economic Development*, *2*, 979–997. DOI: 10.59653/jbmed.v2i02.843

Santos, Z. R., Cheung, C. M. K., Coelho, P. S., & Rita, P. (2022). Consumer engagement in social media brand communities: A literature review. *International Journal of Information Management*, *63*. Advance online publication. DOI: 10.1016/j.ijinfomgt.2021.102457

Sanyal, A., & Sarkar, A. (2025). Resilience and Sustainability Practices with Local Communities in Singalila National Park (SNP), India: Exploring Traditional Food, Festivals and Culture in a Globalized World. In *People and Mountain Environments Interconnectedness for Sustainable Development in the Himalayas* (pp. 1–51). https://doi.org/DOI: 10.1007/978-3-031-83553-7_14

Sashi, C. M. (2021). Digital communication, value co-creation and customer engagement in business networks: A conceptual matrix and propositions. *European Journal of Marketing*, *55*(6), 1643–1663. DOI: 10.1108/EJM-01-2020-0023

Sassi-Chamsi, H. (2022). Les effets du ton d'un message persuasif en santé sur la motivation et l'intention de changer de comportement: Regards croisés de la Théorie de l'Auto-Détermination et de la Théorie des Niveaux de Représentation (Doctoral dissertation, Université Grenoble Alpes).

Saura, J. R., Palos-Sánchez, P., & Cerdá Suárez, L. M. (2017). Understanding the digital marketing environment with KPIs and web analytics. *Future Internet*, *9*(4), 1–13. DOI: 10.3390/fi9040076

Saxena, V., & Gautam, A. (2022). Can AI replace Human? A Study on Customer Perception and Attitude towards AI-Based Chatbot in Food Service.

Schanke, S., Burtch, G., & Ray, G. (2021). Estimating the impact of "humanizing" customer service chatbots. *Information Systems Research*, *32*(3), 736–751.

Scherer, K. R., Wranik, T., Sangsue, J., Tran, V., & Scherer, U. (2004). Emotions in everyday life: Probability of occurrence, risk factors, appraisal and reaction patterns. *Social Sciences Information. Information Sur les Sciences Sociales*, *43*(4), 499–570.

Schmitt, M., & de Jouvenel, M. (2022). *Le baromètre du numérique-édition 2022. Mondes virtuels–Perspectives et enjeux*, 112.

Schulz, T., Böhm, M., Gewald, H., & Krcmar, H. (2020). Smart mobility–an analysis of potential customers' preference structures. *Electronic Markets*, *31*(1), 105–124.

Shaheen, M. Y. (2021). Applications of Artificial Intelligence (AI) in healthcare: A review. ScienceOpen *Preprints*.

Shambour, M. K. (2022). Analyzing perceptions of a global event using CNN-LSTM deep learning approach: The case of Hajj 1442 (2021). *PeerJ. Computer Science*. PMID: 36262123

Sharma, M., Kumar, P., & Gundewar, S. (2024). Leveraging AI and machine learning for predictive analytics in business intelligence. In *Advances in business information systems and analytics book series* (pp. 29–50). https://doi.org/DOI: 10.4018/979-8-3693-8844-0.ch002

Sharma, V., Gupta, M., Jangir, K., Chopra, P., & Pathak, N. (2023). The Impact of Post-Use Consumer Satisfaction on Smart Wearables Repurchase Intention in the Context of AI-Based Healthcare Information. In *Enhancing Customer Engagement Through Location-Based Marketing* (pp. 77–101). IGI Global Scientific Publishing., DOI: 10.4018/978-1-6684-8177-6.ch007

Shen, L., & Dillard, J. P. (2021). Fear appeals and children: Understanding affective and cognitive responses to threatening messages. *Journal of Consumer Behaviour*, *20*(6), 1571–1583. DOI: 10.1002/cb.1987

Sherry, J. L. (2004). Flow and media enjoyment. *Communication Theory*, *14*(4), 328–347. DOI: 10.1111/j.1468-2885.2004.tb00318.x

Shiller, R. J. (2017). Narrative economics. *The American Economic Review*, *107*(4), 967–1004.

Shin, D. (2021). The effects of explainability and causability on perception, trust, and acceptance: Implications for explainable AI. *International Journal of Human-Computer Studies*, *146*, 102551.

Shinde, K. A. (2015). Religious tourism and religious tolerance: Insights from pilgrimage sites in India. *Tourism Review*, *70*(3), 179–196. DOI: 10.1108/tr-10-2013-0056

Shinde, K. A. (2022). How effective is a Buddhist pilgrimage circuit as a product and strategy for heritage tourism in India? *Heritage*, *5*(4), 3846–3863. DOI: 10.3390/heritage5040198

Shrestha, Y. M., & Shrestha, R. (2023). Analysis of Differences between Expected and Perceived Satisfaction Score of Pilgrims: A Case of Chhinnamasta Temple of Nepal. *Nepalese Journal of Hospitality and Tourism Management*, *4*(1), 21–34. DOI: 10.3126/njhtm.v4i1.53312

Sicilia, M., Ruiz, S., & Munuera, J. L. (2005). Effects of interactivity in a web site: The moderating effect of need for cognition. *Journal of Advertising*, *34*(3), 31–44. DOI: 10.1080/00913367.2005.10639202

Silayoi, P., & Speece, M. (2004). Packaging and purchase decisions: An exploratory study on the impact of involvement level and time pressure. *British Food Journal*.

Simms, C., & Trott, P. (2010). Packaging development: A conceptual framework for identifying new product opportunities. *Marketing Theory*, *10*(4), 397–415.

Sinaga, F., Kanca, I. N., & Suarja, I. K. (2025). Tanah Lot temple: Navigating the tension between tourism development and cultural preservation. *Journal of Commerce Management and Tourism Studies*, *4*(1), 155–170. DOI: 10.58881/jcmts.v4i1.328

Singh, B., & Kaunert, C. (2024). Future of Digital Marketing : Hyper-Personalized Customer Dynamic Experience with AI-Based Predictive Models. In *Revolutionizing the AI-Digital Landscape* (1re éd., p. 189-203). Productivity Press.

Singh, R. P. B., & Rana, P. S. (2023). Hindu pilgrimages (India) and religious functionaries. In *Perspectives on Asian tourism* (pp. 163–178). https://doi.org/DOI: 10.1007/978-981-19-9677-1_10

Singh, V., & Bhuyan, A. (2024). *Four decades of research on religious tourism: Prevalent themes and future research area*. https://www.ajol.info/index.php/rhm/article/view/296818

Singh, G., & Singh, J. (2023). Enhancing Customer Experience and Engagement on E-Commerce Platforms Through Ai-Integrated Chatbot Solutions. Available at *SSRN* 4483813.

Singh, P., & Singh, V. (2024). The power of AI : Enhancing customer loyalty through satisfaction and efficiency. *Cogent Business & Management*, *11*(1), 2326107. DOI: 10.1080/23311975.2024.2326107

Singh, V., & Bhuyan, A. (2025). How tourist motivations shape perceptions of service quality at pilgrimage sites. *International Journal of Tourism Policy*, *15*(3), 235–251. DOI: 10.1504/ijtp.2025.147440

Skadberg, Y. X., & Kimmel, J. R. (2004). Visitors' flow experience while browsing a Web site: Its measurement, contributing factors and consequences. *Computers in Human Behavior*, *20*(3), 403–422.

Slater, M. (2003). A note on presence terminology. *Presence Connect*, 3(3).

Slater, M., & Wilbur, S. (1997). A framework for immersive virtual environments (FIVE): Speculations on the role of presence in virtual environments. *Presence (Cambridge, Mass.)*, *6*(6), 603–616.

Smith, V. L. (1992). Pilgrimage and tourism: the quest in guest. *Annals of Tourism Research*. https://ixtheo.de/Record/1100836292

Smith, E. E. (2024). Building critical digital literacies for social media through educational development. *Journal of Contemporary Issues in Education*, *19*(2), 64–89.

Söderlund, G. B., & Jobs, E. N. (2016). Differences in speech recognition between children with attention deficits and typically developed children disappear when exposed to 65 dB of auditory noise. *Frontiers in Psychology*, *7*, 34. PMID: 26858679

Soltani, A., & Lee, C. L. (2024). The non-linear dynamics of South Australian regional housing markets: A machine learning approach. *Applied Geography (Sevenoaks, England)*, *166*, 103248. DOI: 10.1016/j.apgeog.2024.103248

Song, H., Park, C., & Kim, M. (2020). Tourism Destination Management Strategy for Young Children: Willingness to pay for Child-Friendly tourism facilities and services at a heritage site. *International Journal of Environmental Research and Public Health*, *17*(19), 7100. DOI: 10.3390/ijerph17197100 PMID: 32998261

Sonnentag, S. (2017). A task-level perspective on work engagement: A new approach that helps to differentiate the concepts of engagement and burnout. *Burnout Research*, *5*, 12–20.

Soulages, J. C. (2006). Les stratégies humoristiques dans le discours publicitaire. *Questions de Communication*, *10*, 103–118.

Spector, C. (2022). Rhétorique et pratique morale.

Spence, M. (1973). Job Market Signaling. *The Quarterly Journal of Economics*, *87*(3), 355–374. DOI: 10.2307/1882010

Srivastava, R., Kumar, S., Sidhant, P. C., Kumari, P., Singh, D. K., & Dundappa, J. (2025). Evaluating healthcare services at MahaKumbh 2025, India: A mixed-methods study of visitor perceptions and public health strategies. *Bioinformation*, *21*(04), 789–792. DOI: 10.6026/973206300210789 PMID: 40636196

Stein, C. M., Morris, N. J., & Nock, N. L. (2012). Structural equation modeling. In Hinrichs, A. R. (Ed.), *Methods in molecular biology* (Vol. 850, pp. 495–512). Humana Press., DOI: 10.1007/978-1-61779-555-8_27

Steyer, R., Schmitt, M., & Eid, M. (1999). Latent state–trait theory and research in personality and individual differences. *European Journal of Personality*, *13*(5), 389–408.

Stoilova, E. (2021). AI chatbots as a customer service and support tool. ROBONOMICS. *The Journal of the Automated Economy*, *2*, 21–21.

Stoner, J. L., Loken, B., & Stadler Blank, A. (2018). The name game: How naming products increases psychological ownership and subsequent consumer evaluations. *Journal of Consumer Psychology*, *28*(1), 130–137.

Strong, E. K.Jr. (1925). Theories of selling. *The Journal of Applied Psychology*, *9*(1), 75–98.

Sudirjo, F., Fajariana, D. E., Vandika, A. Y., & Sagena, U. (2024). The effect of digital transformation, user experience, and user interface on customer loyalty in technology startups in Bandung. *West Science Interdisciplinary Studies*, *2*(09), 1850–1856. DOI: 10.58812/wsis.v2i09.1305

Sugiarto, H. D., Prayogo, D., & Anastasia, N. (2025). Developing machine learning algorithms for predicting house prices in Surabaya using IBM SPSS Modeler. In *Lecture notes in civil engineering* (pp. 779–787). https://doi.org/DOI: 10.1007/978-981-96-5654-7_71

Suhaili, S. M., Salim, N., & Jambli, M. N. (2021). Service chatbots: A systematic review. *Expert Systems with Applications*, *184*, 115461.

Sundar, S. S., & Marathe, S. S. (2010). Personalization vs. customization: The importance of agency, privacy, and power. *Human Communication Research*, *36*(3), 298–322.

Suntornteerasut, P., Darawong, C., & Wongvedvanij, R. (2024). The impact of travel experience on tourist satisfaction and intention to revisit towards wellness tourism in Thailand. *Journal of Business, Innovation and Sustainability (JBIS)*, *19*(4).

Sun, W. (2025). Artificial Intelligence in Branding : The Influence of AI-Quality on Brand Perception and Consumer Loyalty. *International Journal of Advanced AI Applications*, *1*(8), 39–64.

Sweetser, P., & Wyeth, P. (2005). GameFlow: A model for evaluating player enjoyment in games. [CIE]. *Computers in Entertainment*, *3*(3), 3–3.

Sweller, J. (1988). Cognitive load during problem solving: Effects on learning. *Cognitive Science*, *12*(2), 257–285. DOI: 10.1207/s15516709cog1202_4

Tabaghdehi, S. A. H., & Foroudi, P. (2024). Introduction : Business Strategies and Ethical Challenges in the Digital Ecosystem. In *Business Strategies and Ethical Challenges in the Digital Ecosystem* (p. 1-4). Emerald Publishing Limited. https://www.emerald.com/insight/content/doi/10.1108/978-1-80455-069-420241001/full/html

Taherdoost, H., & Madanchian, M. (2023). Artificial intelligence and sentiment analysis: A review in competitive research. *Computers*, *12*(2), 37.

Tahiri, A. (2025). Marketing stratégique et intelligence artificielle : Vers un nouveau paradigme algorithmique. *Revue Française d'Economie et de Gestion*, *6*(9). https://www.revuefreg.fr/index.php/home/article/view/2341

Tam, K. Y., & Ho, S. Y. (2006). Understanding the impact of web personalization on user information processing and decision outcomes. *Management Information Systems Quarterly*, •••, 865–890.

Taneja, A. K., & Tripathi, C. (2020). AI-powered recommender systems : Personalization and bias. *Turkish Journal of Computer and Mathematics Education, 11*(1), 1090–1094.

Taneja, A., & Arora, A. (2018). Modeling user preferences using neural networks and tensor factorization model. *International Journal of Information Management, 45*, 132–148. DOI: 10.1016/j.ijinfomgt.2018.10.010

Tarnowska, K. A., & Ras, Z. W. (2019). Sentiment analysis of customer data. *Web Intelligence, 17*(4), 343–363. DOI: 10.3233/WEB-190423

Tarute, A., Nikou, S., & Gatautis, R. (2017). Mobile application driven consumer engagement. *Telematics and Informatics, 34*(4), 145–156.

Tătăru anu, M., Butnaru, G. I., Ni ă, V., Neculăesei, A., & Ciortescu, E. (2021). The Influence of Interpretation through Guiding Tour, Quality of Reception and Relics' Worship on the Satisfaction of Pilgrims Attending the Iasi Feast. *Sustainability, 13*(12), 6905. DOI: 10.3390/su13126905

Teepapal, T. (2025). AI-driven personalization : Unraveling consumer perceptions in social media engagement. *Computers in Human Behavior, 165*, 108549. DOI: 10.1016/j.chb.2024.108549

Teo, A., Tan, G. W., Ooi, K., Hew, T., & Yew, K. (2015). The effects of convenience and speed in m-payment. *Industrial Management & Data Systems, 115*(2), 311–331. DOI: 10.1108/imds-08-2014-0231

Terzidou, M., Scarles, C., & Saunders, M. N. (2017). Religiousness as tourist performances: A case study of Greek Orthodox pilgrimage. *Annals of Tourism Research, 66*, 116–129. DOI: 10.1016/j.annals.2017.06.009

Theraiyan, E. (2025). A Study on the Impact of Personalization in Increasing Customer Engagements. *International Journal for Research in Applied Science and Engineering Technology, 13*(4), 10–22214.

Tian, Y. (2020). Artificial intelligence image recognition method based on convolutional neural network algorithm. *IEEE Access : Practical Innovations, Open Solutions, 8*, 125731–125744.

Tkalčič, M., & Ferwerda, B. (2025). Adaptation and Personalization in Human-Centered AI. In Germanakos, P., Juhasz, M., Kongot, A., Marathe, D., & Sacharidis, D. (Eds.), *Human-Centered AI: An Illustrated Scientific Quest* (pp. 493–511). Springer Nature Switzerland., DOI: 10.1007/978-3-031-61375-3_7

Tobi, Y. (2023). *E-commerce and the digital economy in Morocco, a factor of social inclusivity and employment: Context, approach and limits (EuroMeSCo Paper No. 58)*. European Institute of the Mediterranean.

Tomar, G., Pandey, L., & Journals, C. (2024). Influence of personalized advertising on consumer engagement and conversion rates. https://doi.org/DOI: 10.13140/RG.2.2.30689.31844

Toto, G. A., Grilli, L., Traetta, L., Villani, R., Petito, A., & Serviddio, G. (2025). Convergence of disciplines: A systematic review of multidisciplinary development approaches in artificial intelligence. *Frontiers in Digital Health*, *7*. Advance online publication. DOI: 10.3389/fdgth.2025.1400338 PMID: 40881734

Tribhuwan, R. D., & Tribhuwan, P. K. (2003). *An Introduction to Tribal Fairs and Festivals: Theoretical Consideration*. Fairs and Festivals of Indian Tribes.

Tsakiris, M., Longo, M. R., & Haggard, P. (2007). Having a body versus moving your body: Neural signatures of agency and body-ownership. *Neuropsychologia*, *45*(13), 3010–3016. PMID: 20510255

Tsaur, S., Yen, C., & Yan, C. (2025). Effects of destination sacredness on tourists' spiritual well-being and destination commitment: Mediation effect of spiritual experiences. *Current Issues in Tourism*, •••, 1–19. DOI: 10.1080/13683500.2025.2513670

Tsimonis, G., & Dimitriadis, S. (2014). Brand strategies in social media. *Marketing Intelligence & Planning*, *32*(3), 328–344. DOI: 10.1108/MIP-04-2013-0056

Tulshan, A. S., & Dhage, S. N. (2019). Survey on virtual assistant: Google assistant, siri, cortana, alexa. In Advances in Signal Processing and Intelligent Recognition Systems: 4th International Symposium SIRS 2018, Bangalore, India, September 19–22, 2018, Revised Selected Papers 4 (pp. 190-201). Springer Singapore.

Turcotte, C. (2022). Les écrans chez les enfants d'âge préscolaire et leurs habiletés socioémotionnelles: Exploration de différents types d'utilisation des écrans et du rôle modérateur de la médiation parentale (Doctoral dissertation, Université Laval).

Tussyadiah, I. P., Wang, D., Jung, T. H., & Tom Dieck, M. C. (2018). Virtual reality, presence, and attitude change: Empirical evidence from tourism. *Tourism Management*, *66*, 140–154.

Umoren, P., Ukpe, A. P., & Akpolome, D. (2025). Digital communication in organizations: Trends, strengths, and weaknesses. *Direct Research Journal of Management and Strategic Studies*, *6*(1), 55–64. DOI: 10.26765/DRJMSS354001347

Understanding culture and society in India. (2021). In *Springer eBooks*. https://doi.org/DOI: 10.1007/978-981-16-1598-6

Usmonov, M. (2025). Crafting Connections : Generative AI's Impact on Post-Purchase Communication in E-Commerce. *Contemporary Issues of Communication*, *4*(1), 288–310.

Valkenburg, P. M., Beyens, I., Pouwels, J. L., van Driel, I. I., & Keijsers, L. (2022). Social media use and well-being in adolescents: A normative perspective. *Nature Communications*, *13*, 3311.

Vallacher, R. R., & Wegner, D. M. (2012). Action identification theory. *Handbook of theories of social psychology*, 1, 327-348.

Valmorisco, S., Raya, L., & Sanchez, A. (2024). Enabling personalized VR experiences: A framework for real-time adaptation and recommendations in VR environments. *Virtual Reality (Waltham Cross)*, *28*(3), 128.

Van Asperen, M., de Rooij, P., & Dijkmans, C. (2017). Engagement-based loyalty: The effects of social media engagement on customer loyalty in the travel industry. *International Journal of Hospitality & Tourism Administration*, *19*(3), 1–17. DOI: 10.1080/15256480.2017.1305313

Van den Broeck, E., Zarouali, B., & Poels, K. (2019). Chatbot advertising effectiveness: When does the message get through? *Computers in Human Behavior*, *98*, 150–157.

Van den Broek, E., Sergeeva, A., & Huysman, M. (2021). When the machine meets the expert : An ethnography of developing AI for hiring. *Management Information Systems Quarterly*, *45*(3), 1557–1580.

Van Doorn, J., Lemon, K. N., Mittal, V., Nass, S., Pick, D., Pirner, P., & Verhoef, P. C. (2010). Customer engagement behavior: Theoretical foundations and research directions. *Journal of Service Research*, *13*(3), 253–266.

Van Kerrebroeck, H., Brengman, M., & Willems, K. (2017). When brands come to life: Experimental study of the effectiveness of virtual reality advertising. *Journal of Interactive Marketing*, *40*, 1–13.

Vanheems, R. (2010). Quand le client multi-canal invite à réinventer le marketing du point de vente. *9ème Journées Normandes de Recherches sur la Consommation*, Session 5, 25 et 26 Mars, Rouen.

Vargo, S. L., Maglio, P. P., & Akaka, M. A. (2008). On value and value co-creation: A service systems and service logic perspective. *European Management Journal*, *26*(3), 145–152.

Varshneya, G., Das, G., & Khare, A. (2017). Experiential value: A review and future research directions. *Marketing Intelligence & Planning*, *35*(3), 339–357.

Vasalou, A., & Joinson, A. N. (2009). Me, myself and I: The role of interactional context on self-presentation through avatars. *Computers in Human Behavior*, *25*(2), 510–520.

Venkatesh, V., & Bala, H. (2008). Technology Acceptance Model 3 and a Research Agenda on Interventions. *Decision Sciences*, *39*(2), 273–315. DOI: 10.1111/j.1540-5915.2008.00192.x

Venkatesh, V., Morris, M. G., Davis, G. B., & Davis, F. D. (2003). User acceptance of information technology : Toward a unified view. *Management Information Systems Quarterly*, •••, 425–478.

Verma, A., Gayathri, H. S., Karthika, P. S., Choubey, N., & Khandelwal, T. (2022). Crowd management guidelines for mass religious gatherings. In *Springer transactions in civil and environmental engineering* (pp. 151–165). https://doi.org/DOI: 10.1007/978-981-16-9636-7_8

Vij, A., Vij, M., Farouk, M., & Kumar, P. (2024). Evaluating the Effectiveness of AI-Integrated Digital Marketing on Consumer Behavior, Brand Perception, and Sales Performance. *2024 2nd International Conference on Cyber Resilience (ICCR)*, 1-6. DOI: 10.1109/ICCR61006.2024.10533049

Vijayanand, S. (2012). Origin and evolution of pilgrimage tourism management. *South Asian Journal of Marketing & Management Research*, *2*(4), 151–170.

Vij, S., & Taneja, G. (2022). Digital marketing strategies: A comprehensive guide. In *Dynamics of management in a digital world* (pp. 1–22). Seema Sahitya Bhawan., DOI: 10.5281/zenodo.14483877

Vivek, S. D., Beatty, S. E., & Morgan, R. M. (2012). Customer engagement: Exploring customer relationships beyond purchase. *Journal of Marketing Theory and Practice*, *20*(2), 122–146.

Wahyudi, M., Oswari, T., & Purwoko, B. (2024). Role of digital marketing strategies in enhancing customer engagement and brand loyalty: A study of e-commerce platforms. *International Journal of Business, Law, and Education*, *5*, 2778–2788. DOI: 10.56442/ijble.v5i2.936

Wamba-Taguimdje, S. L., Fosso Wamba, S., Kala Kamdjoug, J. R., & Tchatchouang Wanko, C. E. (2020). Influence of artificial intelligence (AI) on firm performance: The business value of AI-based transformation projects. *Business Process Management Journal, 26*(7), 1893–1924.

Wang, D., Yang, Q., Abdul, A., & Lim, B. Y. (2019, May). Designing theory-driven user-centric explainable AI. In *Proceedings of the 2019 CHI conference on human factors in computing systems* (pp. 1-15).

Wang, G., Zhang, X., Tang, S., Wilson, C., Zheng, H., & Zhao, B. Y. (2017). Clickstream User Behavior Models. *ACM Transactions on the Web, 11*(4), 1–37. DOI: 10.1145/3068332

Wang, T., Tran, P. T. K., & Tran, V. T. (2017). Destination perceived quality, tourist satisfaction and word-of-mouth. *Tourism Review, 72*(4), 392–410. DOI: 10.1108/tr-06-2017-0103

Wang, X., Daryapour, M., Shahrabadi, A., Pirasteh, S., & Razavirad, F. (2023). Artificial neural networks in predicting of the gas molecular diffusion coefficient. *Process Safety and Environmental Protection, 200*, 407–418. DOI: 10.1016/j.cherd.2023.10.035

Wan, Y. (2023). Investigating the impact and effectiveness of digital marketing on brand awareness, sales and customer engagement. *Advances in Economics Management and Political Sciences, 51*(1), 146–152. DOI: 10.54254/2754-1169/51/20230651

Waqas, M., Hamzah, Z. L., & Mohd Salleh, N. A. (2021). Customer experience with branded content: A social media perspective. *Online Information Review, 45*(5), 964–982. DOI: 10.1108/OIR-10-2019-0333

Ward, S. (1974). Consumer socialization. *The Journal of Consumer Research, 1*, 1–14.

Watson, D., & Tellegen, A. (1985). Toward a consensual structure of mood. *Psychological Bulletin, 98*(2), 219. PMID: 3901060

Weinberger, M. G., & Gulas, C. S. (1992). The impact of humor in advertising: A review. *Journal of Advertising, 21*(4), 35–59.

Weitz, J., D'Angelica, M., Gonen, M., Klimstra, D., Coit, D. G., Brennan, M. F., & Karpeh, M. S. (2003). Interaction of splenectomy and perioperative blood transfusions on prognosis of patients with proximal gastric and gastroesophageal junction cancer. *Journal of Clinical Oncology, 21*(24), 4597–4603. PMID: 14673048

Wells, W. D., & Lo Sciuto, L. A. (1966). Direct observation of purchasing behavior. *JMR, Journal of Marketing Research, 3*, 227–283.

Wen, L., Lin, W., & Guo, M. (2022). Study on Optimization of Marketing Communication Strategies in the Era of Artificial Intelligence. *Mobile Information Systems, 2022*, 1–11. DOI: 10.1155/2022/1604184

Westbrook, R. A., & Oliver, R. L. (1991). The dimensionality of consumption emotion patterns and consumer satisfaction. *The Journal of Consumer Research, 18*(1), 84–91.

Wicaksono, A. T. S., & Sudarmiatin, S. (2025). Social Media Sentiment Analysis : Customer Perception of Digital Marketing. *Asian Journal of Applied Business and Management, 4*(2), 437–450.

Wiethof, C., & Bittner, E. A. (2022). Toward a hybrid intelligence system in customer service: collaborative learning of human and AI.

Wijethilak, H. P., Singh, S. K., & Dhand, S. (2025). AI for personalizing customer interactions : Improving engagement and satisfaction. In *AI, Corporate Social Responsibility, and Marketing in Modern Organizations* (p. 221-244). IGI Global Scientific Publishing. https://www.igi-global.com/chapter/ai-for-personalizing-customer-interactions/362263

Wild Ali, M. M., & Ortega-Gutierrez, J. (2025). Digital marketing: Strategies, challenges, and opportunities in the digital technology. *Global Journal of Economics and Business, 15*(1), 40–52. DOI: 10.31559/GJEB2025.15.1.3

Witkowski, A., & Wodecki, A. (2025). Where does AI play a major role in the new product development and product management process?. *Management Review Quarterly*, 1-38.

Witte, K. (1992). Putting the fear back into fear appeals: The extended parallel process model. *Communication Monographs, 59*(4), 329–349.

Wu, H., Chang, Y., & Wu, T. (2018). Pilgrimage: What drives pilgrim experiential supportive intentions? *Journal of Hospitality and Tourism Management, 38*, 66–81. DOI: 10.1016/j.jhtm.2018.11.001

Wu, X., Li, S., Guo, Y., & Fang, S. (2024). Human or AI robot? Who is fairer on the service organizational frontline. *Journal of Business Research, 181*, 114730.

Wu, Y. L., & Li, E. Y. (2018). Marketing mix, customer value, and customer loyalty in social commerce: A stimulus-organism-response perspective. *Internet Research, 28*(1), 74–104.

Xiang, C., Rosni, N. B., & Ghafar, N. A. (2025). A Landscape Narrative Model for Visitor Satisfaction Prediction in the living Preservation of Urban Historic Parks: A Machine-Learning Approach. *Sustainability, 17*(12), 5545. DOI: 10.3390/su17125545

Xie, X. (2023). The cognitive process of creative design: A perspective of divergent thinking. *Thinking Skills and Creativity, 48*, 101266.

Xu, Y., Shieh, C. H., van Esch, P., & Ling, I. L. (2020). AI customer service: Task complexity, problem-solving ability, and usage intention. *Australasian Marketing Journal, 28*(4), 189–199.

Xu, Z., Turel, O., & Yuan, Y. (2012). Online game addiction among adolescents: Motivation and prevention factors. *European Journal of Information Systems, 21*(3), 321–340.

Yang, S., Lin, S., Carlson, J., & Jr, W. (2016). Brand engagement on social media: Will firms' social media efforts influence search engine advertising effectiveness? *Journal of Marketing Management*, •••, 1–32. DOI: 10.1080/0267257X.2016.1143863

Yang, W. (2024). Research on the influence of brand interaction on social media platforms and consumers' purchasing decision-making process. *RSM, 7*, 622. Advance online publication. DOI: 10.61173/rsm7b622

Yoo, J. (2024). Can consumer engagement on social media affect brand extension success? The case of luxury fashion brands and restaurants. *Journal of Retailing and Consumer Services, 79*. Advance online publication. DOI: 10.1016/j.jretconser.2024.103885

Yoon, Y., Lee, J., & Lee, C. (2009). Measuring festival quality and value affecting visitors' satisfaction and loyalty using a structural approach. *International Journal of Hospitality Management, 29*(2), 335–342. DOI: 10.1016/j.ijhm.2009.10.002

Yuan, Z., Inoue, S., & Hoshino, J. (2023, June). Remote Customer Service Support System With Automatic Response AI And Human Switching. In 2023 Nicograph International (NicoInt) (pp. 88-88). IEEE.

Yu, J. (2025). AI-Generated Influencers. In *Encyclopedia of Artificial Intelligence in Marketing* (pp. 1–7). Springer., DOI: 10.1007/978-3-031-75316-9_18-1

Yu, J., Dickinger, A., So, K. K. F., & Egger, R. (2024). Artificial intelligence-generated virtual influencer : Examining the effects of emotional display on user engagement. *Journal of Retailing and Consumer Services, 76*, 103560. DOI: 10.1016/j.jretconser.2023.103560

Yuksel, M., Darmody, A., & Venkatraman, M. (2019). When consumers own their work: Psychological ownership and consumer citizenship on crowdsourcing platforms. *Journal of Consumer Behaviour, 18*(1), 3–11.

Yung, R., & Khoo-Lattimore, C. (2019). New realities: A systematic literature review on virtual reality and augmented reality in tourism research. *Current Issues in Tourism, 22*(17), 2056–2081.

Zahran, A. M., & Rolando, B. (2025). Understanding the Influence of Online Reviews on Brand Reputation in the Digital Age. *International Journal of Economics And Business Studies, 2*(1), 72–94. DOI: 10.1234/ijebs.v2i1.109

Zhang, J. (2022). Knowledge learning with crowdsourcing: A brief review and systematic perspective. *IEEE/CAA Journal of Automatica Sinica*, 9(5), 749-762.

Zhang, H., Cho, T., Wang, H., & Ge, Q. (2018). The influence of Cross-Cultural awareness and tourist experience on authenticity, tourist satisfaction and acculturation in world cultural heritage sites of Korea. *Sustainability, 10*(4), 927. DOI: 10.3390/su10040927

Zhang, Q., Lu, J., & Jin, Y. (2021). Artificial intelligence in recommender systems. *Complex & Intelligent Systems, 7*(1), 439–457.

Zhang, Y., & He, A.-Z. (2025). The impact of AI influencer endorsements on consumers' purchase intentions : The serial mediating roles of mind perception and brand trustworthiness. *Journal of Product and Brand Management, 34*(5), 754–765. DOI: 10.1108/JPBM-02-2024-4974

Zhang, Y., Wang, X., & Zhao, X. (2023). Supervising or assisting? The influence of virtual anchor driven by AI–human collaboration on customer engagement in live streaming e-commerce. *Electronic Commerce Research*, •••, 1–24.

Zheng, R., Li, Z., & Na, S. (2022). How customer engagement in live-streaming affects purchase intention and customer acquisition, E-tailer's perspective. *Journal of Retailing and Consumer Services, 68*, 103015. DOI: 10.1016/j.jretconser.2022.103015

Zhou, A., Men, L. R., & Tsai, W.-H. S. (2023). The power of AI-enabled chatbots as an organizational social listening tool. *Organizational listening for strategic communication*, 63-80.

Zidouri, C. (2023). La médiation pédagogique et le développement de la compétence interculturelle dans l'enseignement du FLE au secondaire algérien (Doctoral dissertation, Université IBN KHALDOUN-Tiaret).

Zulaikha, S., Mohamed, H., Kurniawati, M., Rusgianto, S., & Rusmita, S. A. (2025). Customer Predictive Analytics Using Artificial Intelligence. *The Singapore Economic Review*, *70*(04), 1009–1020. DOI: 10.1142/S0217590820480021

About the Contributors

Sihem Ben Saad is an Assistant Professor of Marketing at the Higher School of Sciences and Technology of Design in Tunisia. She earned her Ph.D. in Marketing from IHEC – Carthage Institute of Higher Commercial Studies. Dr. Ben Saad has broad expertise across multiple domains and teaches courses in marketing fundamentals, distribution management, digital marketing, branding and consumer behavior, as well as project management, entrepreneurship, and corporate culture. Her research has been published in prestigious journals, including the Journal of Consumer Behaviour, European Journal of Marketing, International Journal of Retail and Distribution Management, Marketing Intelligence and Planning, Journal of Marketing Management, International Journal of Contemporary Hospitality Management, and the Journal of Research in Marketing and Entrepreneurship, reflecting a significant scholarly impact in the field.

***

Donia Aloui is an Assistant Professor in Quantitative Methods at Tunis Business School, University of Tunis. She holds a dual PhD in Models, Methods and Algorithms (Université Grenoble Alpes, France) and in Finance (University of Tunis). Her research focuses on the transmission of unconventional monetary policies, green finance, energy markets, and advanced econometric modeling (TVP-VAR, BVAR, FAVAR). She has taught Mathematical Methods and has integrated Machine Learning into her Statistics and Data Analysis courses. Her work has been published in leading academic journals such as Resources Policy, Finance Research Letters, and the International Review of Financial Analysis.

Olfa Ammar is a PhD researcher in Marketing, affiliated with the Marketing Research Laboratory, at the University of Sfax. Her research interests include consumer behavior, new product development, value co-creation, crowdsourcing, and food marketing. She has participated in several international marketing conferences, published scholarly research, and taught a range of marketing courses at licence and MBA levels, serving as both a lecturer and teaching assistant at various higher education institutions. She currently holds a postdoctoral position within the PolyCIVIS project, where she works as the Communication Officer. In this role, she is responsible for the communication and dissemination of the project's education, policy, and teaching-related deliverables, as well as for stakeholder engagement across Euro-African contexts.

Özlem Arzu Azer is a Professor of Economics with extensive academic and professional experience. Prior to her academic career, she gained substantial experience in the banking sector, which has strongly informed her teaching and research. She has taught a wide range of courses, including Microeconomics, Macroeconomics, and Financial Decision Making, among others. Her academic and professional background enables her to effectively integrate economic theory with real-world financial practices.

Fakhri Bagirov, Ph.D., is an Assistant Professor of Marketing at Istanbul Atlas University. His research focuses on consumer behavior, digital and interactive marketing, and service and hospitality marketing, with particular interest in how emerging technologies influence consumer decision-making and customer experience. His work has been published in leading international journals, including the Journal of Interactive Marketing, the Journal of Hospitality Marketing & Management, and the Journal of Consumer Marketing, among others. Dr. Bagirov teaches undergraduate and graduate courses in marketing strategy, consumer behavior, and global marketing, and he actively engages in research that bridges academic theory with managerial practice.

Hajer Bellalouna is a Full Professor of Marketing at the Higher Institute of Commerce of Tunis, University of Manouba. She has extensive experience in teaching and research in marketing and has taught at several Tunisian higher education institutions. Her areas of expertise include services marketing, communication, sensory marketing, and research methodology in management sciences. She has authored and co-authored numerous scientific publications in recognized journals and conference proceedings and currently serves as Coordinator of the Research Master's Program in Marketing.

Zineb Benyahya is Assistant Professor at the Moroccan School of Engineering Sciences and PhD in Management Sciences from Hassan II University of Casablanca. Her research focuses on marketing, digital transformation in organizations, and entrepreneurship.

Mohamed Bouaddi is a researcher in Economics and Management at Moulay Ismail University of Meknes, Morocco. He is affiliated with the Faculty of Legal, Economic, and Social Sciences. His research interests broadly cover economics and management studies, with a particular focus on marketing, consumer behavior, and organizational practices in contemporary economic contexts.

Aruditya Jasrotia is working as an Assistant Professor in Amity Institute of Travel and Tourism, Amity University Uttar Pradesh. He completed his Ph.D. and M. Phil. from Central University of Jammu. He has published 40 Scopus indexed Publications, 2 Patents and more than 50 Publications in total including research papers and book chapters. His broad research areas of interest are: Smart Tourism, Tourism Marketing, Sustainable Tourism, Tourism Policy and Planning, Tourism Products and Services. He is also associated as a reviewer for various Scopus Indexed and ABDC listed international journals like International Journal of Tourism Cities, Journal of Hospitality, Leisure, Sport &Tourism Education, International Journal of Tourism Policy and Kybernets. He is also Associate Editor of ESTEEM Journal of Social Science and Humanities and International Journal of Hospitality & Tourism Management.

Adarsh Kumar is an Assistant Professor in the Department of Management at ITM, Gwalior, (M.P) India. He holds a Ph.D. in Management and has over eight years of experience in teaching, research, and academic administration. He currently serves as the Criteria Coordinator for NAAC and NBA, contributing to quality assurance, accreditation processes, and institutional development initiatives. Previously, he worked with the Ministry of Tourism, Government of India, where he was involved in project-based assignments related to tourism development and policy implementation. His academic and research interests include marketing management, consumer behavior, digital marketing, tourism marketing, and the application of emerging technologies in management education. Dr. Kumar has published research in peer-reviewed journals and contributed to edited volumes. His current research focuses on AI-driven personalization, consumer engagement, trust, and privacy in digital platforms. He is actively engaged in mentoring postgraduate students and integrating research with managerial practice.

Sourav Mangoch is a doctoral research scholar at School of Business, Shri Mata Vaishno Devi University, Katra, J&K, India. His current research interests include Adventure Tourism, Mountain Tourism, Travel Behaviour and Marketing Management. His article has been published in Asia Pacific Journal of Tourism Research. He may be contacted at Souravmangoch999@gmail.com.

Brahim Sabiri is Assistant Professor at the Moroccan School of Engineering Sciences and PhD in Economics from Hassan II University of Casablanca. His research focuses on individual and organizational behavior, behavioral and experimental approaches, as well as the use of new technologies in the service of management.

Afef Sahli holds a PhD in Marketing, a Research Master's degree in Marketing, and a Bachelor's degree in Hotel and Tourism Management. She is currently an Assistant Professor of Marketing with strong academic and research experience in digital marketing. Her research interests include consumer behavior, augmented reality, online shopping experience, influencer marketing, authenticity, intrusive advertising, artificial intelligence, and digital technologies. Dr. Sahli has published several peer-reviewed articles in indexed international journals and serves as a reviewer for various academic journals.

Asmahane Tahiri is Assistant Professor at the Moroccan School of Engineering Sciences and PhD in Management Sciences from Hassan II University of Casablanca. Her research focuses on digitalization and innovation in marketing, consumer behavior, and entrepreneurship.

Imen Touati Holds a PhD in Marketing from the Faculty of Economics and Management of Tunis. A marketing researcher and university lecturer, research interests include advertising resistance, persuasion knowledge, parental mediation, and consumer behavior in digital environments. Active involvement in academic service includes serving as treasurer and organizing committee member of the Tunisian Association of Marketing. Current research explores parenting practices and human agency in the age of artificial intelligence.

Zhang Ye is a Teaching Assistant and PhD Candidate at Koç University. Her research focuses on the role of artificial intelligence in marketing, with particular emphasis on how AI-driven technologies influence consumer behavior and marketing decision-making. Her work has been published in leading international journals, including the Journal of Interactive Marketing.

Index

F

H

I

M

O

P

Q

R

S

T

U

V

Y

www.ingramcontent.com/pod-product-compliance
Lightning Source LLC
LaVergne TN
LVHW080908300926
849162LV00003B/608